Candy Making

FOR

DUMMIES®

Candy Making

FOR

DUMMIES®

by David Jones

Wiley Publishing, Inc.

Candy Making For Dummies®

Published by
Wiley Publishing, Inc.
111 River St.
Hoboken, NJ 07030-5774
www.wiley.com

For general information on our other products and services, please contact our Customer Care Department within the U.S. at 877-762-2974, outside the U.S. at 317-572-3993, or fax 317-572-4002.

For technical support, please visit www.wiley.com/techsupport.

Wiley also publishes its books in a variety of electronic formats. Some content that appears in print may not be available in electronic books.

Library of Congress Control Number: 2005924626

ISBN-13: 978-0-7645-9734-3

ISBN-10: 0-7645-9734-5

Manufactured in the United States of America

10 9 8 7 6

1O/RV/RS/QX/IN

WILEY

About the Author

David Jones and his wife, Janet, left Atlanta for the Georgia mountains in June 1973 and, on impulse, took over a tiny candy shop in the Bavarian-style tourist village of Helen, Georgia, a couple of weeks later. David had no candy-making knowledge so, for the first three years, the couple simply bought candy and sold it to the tourists who visited the village. They named their little shop Hansel & Gretel Candy Store.

In 1976, the couple learned to make peanut brittle, which they made in their home because the shop was so small. Because of that one confection, the business grew to fill two large buildings in the Alpine village. The business, which encompasses more than 8,200 square feet, is now known as Hansel & Gretel Candy Kitchen to reflect the onsite production. David seemed to have a knack for making candy and learned to make many other delicious and eye-appealing confections, including fudges, caramels, creams, divinity, toffees, and all kinds of chocolates. And all these delicious confections were made so the public could watch.

Together David's shops attract more than 250,000 visitors per year, and David gives frequent chocolate tours and offers tips to visitors and callers who contact him for his expertise. David, Janet, and their staff are currently developing the Hansel & Gretel Institute, which will teach candy making and be a troubleshooting sounding board for candy makers.

Hansel & Gretel has been a member of Retail Confectioners International (RCI) since 1983, and David's association with that organization has influenced the growth of his company. RCI members share concepts and recipe ideas, and the association runs candy schools and candy classes for its members. David has attended the RCI Gus Pulakos Candy School and has taken a course in truffle making run by RCI. He previously served on RCI's board of directors and, in 2005, he once again was elected to the RCI board.

Helen, Georgia (`helenga.org`) is a Bavarian-style village that attracts more than 2 million visitors a year. David is a past president of the village's chamber of commerce, and he currently serves on the board of directors of the chamber.

Dedication

Dedicated to my late parents, Shuford and Katherine Jones, for always believing in me and being there when I needed help and understanding. They loved me; they loved my candy; and they would have loved this book.

Author's Acknowledgments

Thanks to my agent Jessica Faust of Bookends and to all the folks at Wiley Publishing for believing in a first-time author, especially Acquisitions Editor Stacy Kennedy for believing that a writer existed beyond the few phrases that she read. I have the greatest admiration for Georgette Beatty, my project editor, because she was able to keep me on task and always knew the right words to inspire me when I needed an "atta-boy." And thanks to Copy Editor Michelle Dzurny for correcting my Georgian grammar; to Recipe Tester Emily Nolan for checking all the recipes; and to General Reviewer and Nutritional Analyst Patty Santelli.

Thanks to Editor-in-Chief Michael Allured and Associate Editor Gail Schippman of *The Manufacturing Confectioner* magazine for recommending me as a possible author to get the ball rolling my way.

I appreciate my friends Gary Guittard and Gary Williams of Guittard Chocolate and Chuck Phelan of Peter's Chocolate for taking care of my chocolate needs (because we made countless recipes in our candy kitchen!).

I am especially grateful to John Roche, my production manager at Hansel & Gretel, and all my staff for their help in producing recipes that were smaller than our normal batches of candy and for doing so at odd times of the day or night. Thank you to my daughter Andrea, who taught me the necessary computer skills so vital to the writing of this book. Thanks to my daughter Diana for spending so much time in her teen years helping in the shop and for making decorating suggestions. And a special thanks to the person without whom I could never have created home-size recipes from large batches, Randy Hofberger, the Technical Manager for Nestle Chocolate and Confections Company. Randy was always there to answer my many questions and to correct my errors. I couldn't have written this book without him.

For all my friends — including my friends at Retail Confectioners International (RCI) — who accepted my excuses when I couldn't come out and play for six months — thank you for understanding.

And last but certainly not least, I want to thank my lovely wife, Janet, for tolerating the long days and nights I spent writing and for giving me her input when I needed an idea or an answer.

Publisher's Acknowledgments

We're proud of this book; please send us your comments through our Dummies online registration form located at www.dummies.com/register/.

Some of the people who helped bring this book to market include the following:

Acquisitions, Editorial, and Media Development

Project Editor: Georgette Beatty

Acquisitions Editor: Stacy Kennedy

Copy Editor: Michelle Dzurny

General Reviewer and Nutritional Analyst: Patty Santelli

Recipe Tester: Emily Nolan

Editorial Manager: Michelle Hacker

Editorial Assistants: Hanna Scott, Nadine Bell, Melissa S. Bennett

Cover Photo: © Ben Fink/FoodPix

Cartoons: Rich Tennant (www.the5thwave.com)

Photographer: David K. Lann

Composition Services

Project Coordinator: Shannon Schiller

Layout and Graphics: Andrea Dahl, Joyce Haughey, Barry Offringa, Lynsey Osborn

Special Art: Elizabeth Kurtzman

Proofreaders: Aptara, Leeann Harney, Jessica Kramer, Carl William Pierce

Indexer: Aptara

Publishing and Editorial for Consumer Dummies

Diane Graves Steele, Vice President and Publisher, Consumer Dummies

Joyce Pepple, Acquisitions Director, Consumer Dummies

Kristin A. Cocks, Product Development Director, Consumer Dummies

Michael Spring, Vice President and Publisher, Travel

Kelly Regan, Editorial Director, Travel

Publishing for Technology Dummies

Andy Cummings, Vice President and Publisher, Dummies Technology/General User

Composition Services

Gerry Fahey, Vice President of Production Services

Debbie Stailey, Director of Composition Services

Contents at a Glance

Recipes at a Glance

Table of Contents

Introduction

W hen my wife, Janet, and I started our candy business, we had no idea where to find answers to basic candy-making questions. We were in the candy business — buying candy and reselling it to our customers — for three years before we actually made any homemade candy. We gradually picked up recipes here and there, but we found no comprehensive source on how to make candy in small batches.

Over the years, we began to learn a few things about candy making and eventually operated a real candy kitchen where we made several products in public view. But we still wanted more variety in our homemade items. By asking questions, reading what little information I could find, and attending a couple of short candy schools, I eventually learned a great deal more, and my stores now manufacture what's probably the widest assortment of candies in Georgia.

Because I was unable to find any resources when I was a novice candy maker, I'm pleased to have the opportunity to write this book and give you the chance to make a vast array of very tasty candies in your home. Many of the recipes this book contains are scaled-down versions of, or variations of, my candy shops' best recipes. These candies are suitable to give as gifts or for your family to enjoy as special treats. The only way to enjoy this book (and the candies in it) is by getting into the kitchen and trying your hand at making some wonderful candy. Before I made my first batch all those years ago, I was terrified, but I found out I had nothing to fear. So have fun, and enjoy the candy making!

About This Book

This book is about basic candy making, and it includes virtually everything you need to know to produce fine candy at home. I tell you where to find utensils, ingredients, packaging materials, and any other essentials that you need to be a happy and prepared candy maker. And in the recipes I provide, I lay out every step you need to follow to produce remarkable results, even if you've never cooked before. I also explain the terms of the candy-making trade so you're down with the lingo.

Whatever the occasion, you'll find a suitable recipe in this book to satisfy your needs. If you're looking for something to make for the family, treats to keep around the house, or candies suitable for giving as a special gift, I offer you a variety of recipes to choose among; just follow the simple instructions, and enjoy the candy. With the knowledge of where to find what you need and the methods I describe in this book, you're well on your way to becoming a skilled candy maker!

One great feature about this book is that it's written in a modular format, meaning you don't have to read it from cover to cover (but I certainly don't mind if you do!). When skills in one chapter are helpful to completing recipes in another chapter, I tell you where to go for that information.

Conventions Used in This Book

By measuring carefully and accurately and by using the best and freshest ingredients — I learned long ago not to cut costs by using cheaper ingredients — you'll produce the best candies.

As you read the recipes in this book and as you begin to cook some candy, keep these few points in mind:

- Temperatures are expressed in Fahrenheit at sea level. See the Appendix for info on how to convert temperatures to Celsius.
- Room temperature is between 70 and 72 degrees.
- Sugar is granulated unless otherwise specified.
- Milk is whole milk.
- Butter is unsalted and is not margarine.
- Heavy cream is 40 percent butterfat.
- Whipping cream is 30 percent butterfat.
- Baking chocolate is unsweetened.
- Chocolate is real chocolate, not chocolate-flavored. Use premium chocolate or chocolate of the highest available quality, and make sure that the white chocolate you use contains cocoa butter.
- Dark chocolate is semi-sweet.

In addition, I use the following nonrecipe conventions to help you find your way around this book:

- ✔ *Italic* points out defined terms or emphasizes a word.
- ✔ **Boldface** text indicates keywords in bulleted lists and the action part of numbered steps.
- ✔ `Monofont` highlights Web addresses.

What You're Not to Read

Every once in a while, I go off on a tangent where I show off my technical knowledge, but you can skip this information, which I highlight with a Technical Stuff icon, because it's not critical to your understanding of candy making.

You can also skip reading the sidebars (the shaded boxes throughout the book) because, while they're interesting asides, they don't contain information that's essential to the candy-making process. If you skip the sidebars, I'll get over it.

Foolish Assumptions

When writing this book, I made a couple of assumptions about you:

- ✔ You've never made candy at home and would like to find out how.
- ✔ You have some candy-making experience but would like to gain more ideas and knowledge about it.

In my business, I have the opportunity to hire a lot of young people who are entering the job market for the first time. They're true novices in the business world. During the interview process, I tell them that on their first day on the job, they'll feel a little stupid; on the second day, they'll feel confused; and on the third day, they'll feel smart because they'll suddenly understand what they're doing. And I stress to these young people that they'll learn only by doing. Getting the most out of a book like this can be the same experience for you. If you've never made candy at home, you may feel a little stupid the first time you try (I know I did 29 years ago); you may feel a little confused for a while (I did, too); but then the processes begin to make sense. I promise that when you start using these recipes, you'll understand what I'm trying to tell you. When that light comes on, you'll suddenly feel so smart. And you'll become a great candy maker.

How This Book Is Organized

This book has six parts, each part pertaining to a different phase of preparation or candy making. Read on to find out what each part contains.

Part I: Welcome to Candyland

In this part, you find out what utensils you need to make the recipes in this book and where you can locate all those harder-to-find items. You also find out how to organize your kitchen. You don't have to set it up like a commercial candy kitchen, but you want to make the most of the space you have.

This part also covers the importance of using the best ingredients in order to achieve the best results. I cover a wide variety of basic but high-quality ingredients in this part and explain the differences in the types of chocolates, dairy products, and sugars you will use.

Part II: Concocting Creamy and Chewy Delights

This part offers recipes for a wide range of popular creamy and chewy candies, from fondants to caramels to fudge and a lot of delicious pieces in between. I also tell you how to make some wonderful divinity as well as fondues, meltaways, marshmallows, and more.

Part III: Getting a Little Nutty

Part III is an opportunity to make a variety of nutty confections, including toffee, brittles, pralines, and more. You'll also go nuts for fun and easy ways to sweeten your popcorn.

Part IV: Becoming a Chocolate Artist

In this part, you find out many ideas about what you can do with chocolate, including how to chop, melt, and temper it. Additionally, you find simple recipes for clusters, barks, and creams and find out the secrets of dipping and molding. Armed with the information in this part, you make truffles as beautiful as the ones sold in fancy chocolate shops.

Part V: Having Special Fun with Candy

You have the chance to make some seasonal candies in Part V, such as chocolate Easter eggs, Christmas specialties, and Valentine's Day candies. Also in this part, I give you quite a few ideas that the younger folks can use to whip up some sweet delights. The marshmallow treats, rice cereal bars, and other recipes in this part will keep them busy in the kitchen. After all, young folks need to start cooking somewhere, and this part is a good beginning. To wrap up, I give you plenty of tips and tricks for presenting your delicious candies as beautiful gifts.

Part VI: The Part of Tens

In the Part of Tens, you discover ten (or so) places where you can purchase the necessary utensils and ingredients. You also find ten (or so) candy companies to visit. I cover some basic problems that you may encounter and how to solve them, and I identify Web sites where you can find more recipes to test your skills.

Icons Used in This Book

You will see icons (the little symbols that identify specific information) throughout this book. The following symbols highlight information that's worthy of your attention.

This icon alerts you to a time-saving option or some other helpful bit of candy-making information.

This icon indicates information that you shouldn't forget as you make your sweet treats.

This icon highlights procedures that may be dangerous and tells you how to prevent something unwanted from occurring.

This icon points out interesting technical information about candy making, although this information isn't crucial to your understanding of candy making.

Where to Go from Here

If you're a complete beginner, consider how comfortable you feel in the kitchen, assess your skills, and take inventory of what you have at your disposal to begin making some candy. See Chapters 2, 3, and 4 for the scoop on prepping your kitchen, getting the right tools, and selecting great ingredients. Or try a simple recipe first — maybe one that involves a quick microwave preparation with a few ingredients, like a simple fudge (see Chapter 9). Then gradually move on to recipes that seem more difficult and you're on your way.

If you're more experienced, you may want to start with chocolates. Look at tempering methods in Chapter 14 first; it's a handy process to know. After you acquire some tempering skills, you're on your way to some real pleasures in candy making (like the truffles in Chapter 18).

I'm pretty corny, but I love making candy. I especially love to teach people how to make candy, and I'm most excited when I see one of my employees feel the joy of creating a new piece of candy. As you make your way through this book, I want you to feel that same joy.

Part I
Welcome to Candyland

The 5th Wave   By Rich Tennant

"...because I'm more comfortable using my own tools. Plus, the sander attachment is actually quite efficient."

In this part...

So you're ready to start making candy, eh? Hold on a minute! You don't want to start cooking without some basic preparation. In this part, I tell you how to equip and arrange your kitchen, give you a tour of the tools, and offer tips for selecting quality ingredients. This part answers any questions you have and alleviates your candy-making fears!

Chapter 1

Candy Making Made Easy (Because It Is)

. . . .

In This Chapter

▶ Gearing up to make candy

▶ Identifying some great confections

▶ Checking out special uses for your candy-making skills

Recipes in This Chapter

▶ Dream Dates

. . . .

*O*ne point I stress throughout this book is that candy making is pretty easy. After you learn a few basics and prepare yourself and your environment according to my simple guidelines, all you have to do is follow a few procedures. I hate to say this, but if I can make candy, you can make candy.

When I train new staff members in my candy shop, I observe that, at first, they're hesitant and overly careful about handling the product, as if it were very fragile. I assure them that they will not hurt the candy by being aggressive. I don't want them to be afraid of the candy, and you shouldn't be afraid, either. Most products you make are quite tolerant, and you can stir them hard, slap them, or just generally be rough with them. Don't be afraid to get your hands a little messy, and don't worry about making a bit of a mess. Have fun, because you're in charge.

To make a point, when someone observes that I have a spot of chocolate on my face, I dab even more on and ask, "Where, here?" Then I touch another spot with a big dab and ask, "Or was it here?" Before I finish, I have chocolate all over my face, but the new person is relaxed, confident that I am crazy and not worried about making a mess. I want you to have that feeling without my having to come to your house to make a fool of myself. And before I continue with the "newbie," I wash up. I do have a few rules.

In this chapter, I introduce you to my world: the world of candy making. I introduce you to the basics of preparation, tell you about a variety of sweet treats, and share tips for special candy situations. Through this book, I hope you'll acquire some of the affection for confection that I have. Candy has been very good to me, to paraphrase the old *Saturday Night Live* line, and I have made a career of pleasing folks with simple confections. Now you have the opportunity to bring a little joy to your family and loved ones as well as to yourself.

Putting together the candy-making puzzle

Since I was a teenager, one of my favorite pastimes has been working crossword puzzles. When I was in high school, I attempted to solve the daily crossword in the Atlanta newspaper; most days, I filled in only a few of the answers. The next day, I looked up the answers to see what I missed. I gradually learned patterns that puzzle makers used, and I learned that they repeated answers, occasionally rewording the clues. I eventually became an excellent crossword solver, and I am one of those weirdos who does the *New York Times* Sunday puzzle in ink. Although I may not finish the puzzle in 15 minutes, I seldom fail to complete the grid in 30 minutes to an hour.

The point — which I am coming to — is that if you look at the clues for a large puzzle, the maze of blocks can look impossible. If you read the answers in a completed grid, you see that, in most cases, the answers are really quite simple. You only sensed difficulty because of the clues.

Similarly, if you walk into a fine chocolate shop and look at some of the beautiful items on display, you may think that you could never make those items. However, the "clues," or the steps in the recipes, are really quite easy. You need only to acquire some knowledge and apply it to the steps as I specify. You will find that these simple clues lead to some very sophisticated results, chocolate and otherwise.

Getting Set to Make Candy

Your journey to becoming a candy-making expert begins with the simplest preparations. You must properly prepare yourself in terms of kitchen space, utensils, and ingredients. The better you prepare yourself for cooking, the easier your experience will be and the quicker you will become adept at making candy.

Now, I certainly don't expect you to reproduce a candy kitchen in your home. But I do believe that the closer you come to creating a cool, dry environment and the better equipped you are with basic candy tools, the better your results will be. Factor in using only quality ingredients, and you're in pretty good shape.

In this section, I discuss how to prepare your kitchen and tell you about the tools and ingredients you need for your candy.

Ensuring that you and your kitchen are ready

As you read through this book, you'll find numerous opportunities to make some great candies, and the hardest decision may be where to start. What should you do first? A good idea is to read several recipes that catch your eye and find something pretty simple. I've tried to make all the recipes in this book easy, but some are easier than others. Try one or two simple recipes and then select a recipe for a candy that you or someone in your family would really enjoy. Make that recipe. At that point you've gained confidence, and you're on your way.

I know you can't turn your home kitchen into a candy kitchen any more than you can turn it into a restaurant when you prepare dinner. Your objective, then, should be to create the best atmosphere possible to assure that your candies turn out great. You want a cool, dry environment to make a lot of candies, with an ideal room temperature of 70 to 72 degrees. Organize your ingredients; make sure that you have plenty of counter space; and check to see that your equipment is in working order, too.

See Chapter 2 for more ideas about how to prepare yourself and your kitchen before you begin making candies.

Considering a candy kitchen tour

If you've never visited a candy kitchen where the staff makes the candy in public view, you may want to do so before you make your first recipe so you can get some ideas about what you're trying to do. In my experience, actually seeing the candy being made has had a major influence on my understanding of what the results should look like.

When I suggest visiting a candy shop, I'm not talking about just a fudge shop; rather, look for a kitchen that produces a vast array of candies. (I mention a few candy kitchens that you can visit in Chapter 25.) Quality candy makers are found in most cities of any size and in a lot of smaller ones, like my little village. In a candy kitchen, you can see professionals making caramels, pralines, jellies, fudge, divinity, and a wide variety of chocolate items. Also, a visit to such a candy shop allows you to find some really creative packaging ideas for gifts you can make and give to loved ones. Even if the shop sells only candy that it purchased from others, you still see results that can give you direction.

When you see an actual working candy kitchen, make mental notes about the layout, the utensils the staff uses, and how the staff utilizes space. You may also ask general questions; the staff will usually provide you with good answers that should be quite helpful to you. Your questions shouldn't include queries about temperatures or specific ingredient measures because these elements fall into the proprietary area. At any rate, your visit should help you make basic preparations in your own kitchen.

Speaking the language of candy making

In the early years of my business — back when we made few candies ourselves — I found recipes in cookbooks and magazines, and I got some recipes from a few friends. Invariably, I would encounter a tool I didn't have and didn't know how to locate, or I would run into some candy term having to do with production that I simply didn't understand.

Candy makers often have their own language, and if you don't understand what the terms mean, you may be unable to make what actually is a very simple recipe. I avoid using candy-making jargon throughout this book, and if I use a jargony term, I explain what it means. So don't worry; the recipes in this book won't confuse you with candy-making speak.

Finding the proper tools

Aside from having the necessary ingredients, few things expedite production like having the right tools for the task at hand. For a full list of the equipment you need, check out Chapter 3. Most utensils you use in candy making are available in a grocery or discount store; kitchen stores and commercial equipment suppliers are two other options. You can also find many specialty items online (see Chapter 24 for a list of online suppliers).

Some of the handiest tools you can use include

- ✔ Measuring tools, such as measuring cups, measuring spoons, candy thermometers, and chocolate thermometers

- ✔ Pots and pans, including a double boiler, saucepans, baking pans, and cookie sheets

- ✔ Kitchen essentials, such as large knives, microwaveable bowls, spoons, whisks, and spatulas

- ✔ Small appliances, such as food processors and mixers

- ✔ Specialty tools, such as a marble slab, a piping bag, dipping tools, and chocolate molds

- ✔ Tools for cooling and storage, such as cooling racks and plastic containers

Using great ingredients

Most candy recipes use ingredients that you can find at your local grocery store. Among the most important types of ingredients are

- ✔ **Sugars and sweeteners:** These ingredients form the basis for virtually all candy recipes. You can use solid sweeteners, such as granulated sugar, confectioners' sugar, and brown sugar; you can also put liquid sweeteners, such as corn syrup and honey, to good use.

✔ **Dairy products:** "Cream" has many meanings in the world of candy making. The cream used to make fine candies may range from 10 percent butterfat (with the use of half-and-half) to more than 40 percent butterfat (with the use of heavy cream), and how a recipe turns out depends on what type of cream you use. Other useful dairy ingredients include butter, whole milk, condensed milk, and sweetened evaporated milk.

✔ **Nuts:** People can be very particular about the nuts they like in their candy. Some of the most popular nuts are peanuts, pecans, walnuts, and cashews. Nuts provide a wonderful crunch in candies, and they impart their own special, delicious flavors.

✔ **Chocolate:** You should appreciate the fine differences among the types of chocolates, in terms of the range from white to extra dark and in regard to quality. You can cut corners in quality, but I never recommend doing so; don't save a few pennies on a major ingredient if you want good results. The chocolate substitutions I offer as variations of recipes don't lower the quality of your candy; I offer those substitutions quite often so you can make varieties of a recipe with similar results.

When you gather the ingredients for a recipe, know that I had a reason for making those choices and that variations may produce different results than what the recipe intended.

Chapter 4 has everything you need to know about choosing and using the preceding ingredients. I also provide you with a list of less common (but still important) candy ingredients.

Putting your own twist on candy recipes

A number of years ago, I didn't know how to make a meltaway. Heck, I didn't even know what to call the piece; I simply knew how to describe it. I called four friends to get suggestions on how to make it, and I described the piece to them. Fortunately, they all knew what I was talking about and gave me satisfactory answers. However, each one also said that I might ask someone else, because that person made meltaways differently.

I discovered something that day: You can make the same basic candy many different ways because each person used a different process.

As you create candies from my recipes, you may find that you can do the same thing with modifications. If a recipe calls for corn syrup, for instance, try honey instead. Make a toffee or a brittle with a different nut than you usually use. Follow a basic truffle recipe, but substitute a spice or an unusual flavor that you've never tasted in candy. Go for it; by taking such actions, you become a true candy maker. You need to go beyond the exact recipes at some point. By doing so in my own kitchen, I create new pieces all the time.

Checking Out Delicious Types of Candies

I understand that you're capable of enjoying just so much of my text. Ultimately, you need to be exposed to some recipes, and you're not to be disappointed. You find about 100 recipes, and I group them by types of candies: creamy and chewy, nutty, and chocolaty.

Before you try any recipe, read through the available recipes and find one you're certain that you understand. Make that recipe first to get the feel of what you're doing, and move on from there. You should be able to prepare any candy in the book simply by following the directions I offer. If you feel like you need to ease into the more difficult recipes, you have that opportunity.

Fixing creamy and chewy treats

You encounter many excellent recipes in Part II, which features creamy and chewy concoctions.

In Chapter 5, I tell you how to prepare fondue. Fondue is a versatile treat that makes a nice interactive dessert; each family member gets to create his or her own special treat. Fondues are also great for romantic settings.

Chapter 6 includes directions for making fondant — a combination of sugar corn syrup, and water — that you can use to prepare other candies, such as mints. One nice thing about this fondant recipe is that you don't have to do any cooking to make it.

Another candy you make in Chapter 6 is the meltaway, which you can make in several flavors. The meltaway, a smooth piece that usually includes chocolate and some added fat (don't let that word scare you), is easy to make, and you should derive some pleasure from making something so good with so little effort.

Caramel is a major piece of the candy puzzle and, in Chapter 7, you find tasty caramel recipes that you can use in making other candies. You can make so many great candies using caramel, like caramel apples, caramel pecan clusters, and more.

One of the confections that my company could never be without is divinity, which I cover in Chapter 8. Although divinity is similar in appearance to marshmallow, this confection uses egg whites for aeration, which provides a very light, airy piece.

In Chapter 9, you find recipes for fudge. Fudge is one of those things that seems to bring a smile to folks' faces, so be prepared to create a few smiles as you make your own fudge. With the recipes in Chapter 9, you can make simple microwave fudge and progress to cooked fudges, which require a little more time. Cooked fudges involve actual cooking in a saucepan, which takes you a bit closer to being a real candy maker. You should enjoy the variety of flavors of fudge as well.

Chapter 10 provides you with easy recipes for good, light homemade marsh-mallows and fruit jellies. Marshmallows and jellies are cousins in the candy world because you make both with gelatin. You can master these candies using one flavor and, with only a couple of changes, you can make a variety of flavors. You even have the chance to make a very easy marzipan (for those of you who like that almond-based candy).

Noshing on nut-based candies

Sometimes you just have to get a little nutty, and you can fulfill that urge with a nice variety of the nutty confections in Part III.

One truly great candy that you commonly find in a candy shop is toffee, a buttery-rich, crunchy confection that's cooked to about 300 degrees. I show you how to make toffee as well as its cousin, the crunch, in Chapter 11. Crunches contain slightly less butter than toffees, but you still get a great buttery taste.

I also cover the praline in Chapter 11. This candy, which has Southern roots, is a delightful confection traditionally made with sugar, corn syrup, butter, and pecans. You should enjoy making this one; I know I do!

The first candy that my wife and I ever made was peanut brittle. In Chapter 12, you have your own chance to make some peanut brittle as well as a few other brittle variations. Brittles are cooked to a high temperature (around 300 degrees), so you're doing some serious cooking. But I think you'll enjoy the results.

If you consider popcorn to be a salty movie treat, I have a few surprises in store for you. In Chapter 13, I show you how to take basic popcorn and make a caramely, nutty treat. You also can add white chocolate to make a delight-fully sweet, melt-in-your-mouth confection that almost seems cool when you eat it. You won't think of popcorn as just a snack for movies anymore.

From pralines to toffee to pecan rolls, you should be able to find a nutty confec-tion to match your taste as well as your family's. Think of the smiles on your family members' faces when they taste the delicious pecan rolls you make for them. Imagine how they'll praise you for your peanut or pecan brittle. You will be so loved!

Meanwhile, I offer you an extremely simple nut-based recipe to get you started on your candy-making journey.

Dream Dates

This not-too-sweet treat — which includes roasted almonds, dates, confectioners' sugar, cocoa, and cinnamon — is good for so many occasions. You can offer it when a few friends come over and you don't want to tempt them with something too heavy or too sweet (not to mention that you can make this in just a few minutes).

Preparation time: *10 minutes*

Yield: *45 pieces*

1¾ cups pitted dates (about 45)

⅔ cup whole roasted, salted or unsalted almonds (about 90)

½ cup confectioners' sugar

1 teaspoon unsweetened cocoa

½ teaspoon cinnamon

1 Stuff each date with two of the almonds.

2 In a freezer bag, combine confectioners' sugar, cocoa, and cinnamon, and seal the bag. Shake the bag well to blend the ingredients and pour the contents onto a small plate.

3 Roll each date in the mixture to coat. You can store the dates overnight in a plastic container at room temperature.

Per serving: *Calories 36 (From Fat 10); Fat 1g (Saturated 0g); Cholesterol 0mg; Sodium 0mg; Carbohydrate 7g (Dietary Fiber 1g); Protein 1g.*

Entering the wide world of chocolate

My personal area of candy making, and that of many others, is the world of chocolate. Of all the candy that is made in my kitchens, nothing gives me the satisfaction that chocolate brings. In Part IV, I introduce you to the joy of chocolate and offer you the opportunity to put this information to work.

To coat and decorate many chocolate confections, you must temper the chocolate. *Tempering* is a controlled process of heating and cooling chocolate using movement to achieve the proper temperature and crystal structure so that your candy has a nice, glossy finish. It isn't rocket science, and you find that out in Chapter 14; you just need to know how to properly chop and melt chocolate in a double boiler or microwave. You can use one of several methods to temper: hand tempering, chunk tempering, or machine tempering. After you achieve the basic skills necessary, you're on your way to a lifetime of pleasure. I make the tempering process as easy as possible for you, but the only way to become proficient in handling chocolate is by getting your hands into the chocolate pot.

Chapter 15 is all about dipping treats into chocolate. You can dip treats by hand or using special dipping tools, and the variety of items you can dip is endless. The list includes fruits, pretzels, and much more.

Chapter 16 gives you the lowdown on barks and clusters. These two candies have the same ingredients (usually chocolate and nuts), but you shape them in different ways:

- Bark is poured into sheets and cut into bar-size pieces.
- Clusters are shaped into bite-size pieces about 1½ inches wide.

Chapter 17 covers creams, which are sugar-based centers. You find out how to make different cream centers and what to do with them when they're set: You dip them in your favorite chocolate, of course!

Chapter 18 is all about delectable truffles, which I put at the top of the list of the finest chocolate products available. The truffle, which is basically a rich center of chocolate and cream encased in a thin shell of chocolate, is simply one fine bite. Actually, most truffles are just that: one bite. I show you how to make, roll, and coat truffle centers. I also guide you on piping thin (but still rich) centers into chocolate shells.

Chapter 19 presents several fun methods on molding chocolates: solid molding, hollow molding, and shell molding. You can mold chocolates for so many different occasions, and you're pretty much limited only by your imagination; you can find a mold for just about anything you can think of.

Looking at Special Candy Considerations

Of course, you may be the type of person who plans to make every recipe in the book, sit down at a table, and eat every bit yourself — but I doubt it. Many folks like to make candy to give as gifts for friends, and many of these confections fit the bill nicely for a number of occasions. I show you some specific ideas for making holiday candies, which I hope will be an enjoyable process for you. Finally, you may want to make some special treats with the kids in your life, so I provide the opportunity for the younger set to go into the kitchen with recipes that are fun for them and for you.

Celebration time: Making festive holiday candies

As you consider what you can do to make a holiday occasion special, think about the lovely candies you make. For example, think about what treats you can make to put in an Easter basket. Give some thought to hand-crafting the beautiful chocolates commonly found in an expensive Valentine box. Think about the atmosphere the aroma of freshly made candy creates at Christmas time. With the recipes in this book, you're able to fill these needs yourself and create holiday magic (with the help of Chapter 20) for much less than you would spend in a store. Plus you can take pride in the fact that you made the candy yourself. You didn't simply give a gift or add to the festivities; you *earned* the accolades that came your way.

Look what I did today! Making kid-friendly candies

If you find yourself growing weary of dragging your kids to the store for their special treats, why not let them make their own goodies at home? Your kids can make simple treats with cereal, chips, cookies, and marshmallows using the recipes in Chapter 21. The list of ingredients your kids can use to make their own treats is long, and you may think of some that I haven't mentioned. One nice thing about making these candies is that you have no rules to follow. If you like it, go for it! Give the kids some candy-making guidelines, and turn them loose. (Save the harder tasks for yourself, of course.)

If you think you're proud of your creations, imagine how good the younger ones feel when they produce something worthy of your praise. And once you have them doing their own thing, you free up your own time!

Give a little bit (or a lot): Presenting candies with style

Once you have the ability to create some special candies, you probably will want to give some as gifts. Maybe giving gifts was your primary reason for making candy in the first place. At any rate, you find plenty of ideas in Chapter 22 for creating gifts with the treats you've made.

Before you select the container for any gift, picking the theme and size of your gift is essential. When you make those choices, you have various container options:

- ✔ Mugs, cups, and glasses
- ✔ Boxes and tins
- ✔ Baskets and trays
- ✔ Bags

Wrappings are also a consideration. You may want to wrap pieces in colorful foils or even seasonal foils. To do so, simply place each piece in its own paper cup, just as you see done in candy shops.

Of course, I've given you just a few ideas. The only limit to what you can do with your candy gifts is your imagination.

Chapter 2

Preparing Yourself (and Your Kitchen) for Candy Making

In This Chapter
▶ Choosing a candy to make
▶ Creating a candy kitchen in your own home

I don't expect you to make your kitchen over into a virtual commercial candy kitchen. Rather, you must find the best way to use your kitchen to produce a variety of candies while maintaining a feeling of normality. If you just do your best to create a cool environment with plenty of workspace, you certainly can make remarkably professional-looking confections in your kitchen.

For this book, I have a single goal: I want you to create and enjoy fine candies while feeling the joy of having made something wonderful. (Is that two goals?) So in this chapter, I start you off with tips on choosing recipes and setting up your kitchen successfully.

Selecting Your Confection

If you're a candy-making novice, you may want to make a simple recipe first and gradually move on to more difficult ones. By starting with a basic recipe and working your way up to more challenging ones, you're able to build your confidence. Just start slowly, and work your way through the procedures at a comfortable pace

For instance, if you want to make fudge, you find some very basic microwave recipes in Chapter 9 that require little time and few tools to produce. After you've gotten your feet wet, you can move on to the fudge recipes that require stirring a pot of hot candy on a stove for 30 minutes or so. You'll actually have to put some effort into this process but, fortunately, you'll be rewarded with some excellent results.

Before you dive into making a recipe, note whether it requires additional background information; sometimes you may need to refer to other chapters to complete a recipe. For example, if you want to make a candy coated with chocolate, you first need to know how to temper the chocolate coating, a procedure I cover in Chapter 14. But generally, you'll have no problem understanding the recipe and completing the simple tasks it requires. Your biggest problem may be deciding which delicious candy you want to make!

My last bit of advice before you begin cooking up a storm is to analyze carefully the ingredients and steps to make sure that you have everything you need as well as a clear mental picture of the procedure. Visualizing the entire process is a good way to successfully complete a recipe.

If you're still unsure which recipe to choose, I help you select treats for families, loved ones, and special occasions in the following sections. Don't worry about choosing the "wrong" recipe; one of the nice things about the recipes in this book is their adaptability to many different situations.

Preparing family treats

You probably have no aspirations about being a professional candy maker, but you probably wouldn't mind being able to make something that your family would enjoy eating. If making a few delicious treats to please your family is your goal, then you've come to the right place.

When deciding what recipe to tackle, think about what candy your family might like and check out the chapter in the book that covers it. You may want to try a simple recipe, when possible, and then move on to the more complicated formulas with more steps.

The list of candies that your family will enjoy is extensive and includes such a variety of themes that choosing one may be difficult. But the difficulty ends there, because all the recipes are fun and easy. For instance, in Chapter 21, I offer several chocolate-marshmallow recipes that the kids should enjoy. The younger folks may need some help tempering the chocolate, but they can take over when the chocolate is ready and whip up some wonderful marshmallow treats. The kids can also make some cereal clusters and some awesome rice cereal treats covered in chocolate. (Maybe if you're really nice, the kids will let you help.)

You can easily find recipes throughout the book within the abilities of the kids; for example, making their own chocolate lollipops should really delight them (see Chapter 19 for molding ideas). I suggest that you encourage them to try a batch of microwave fudge (which you can find in Chapter 9). You and the youngsters are also sure to enjoy making nutty caramel corn together, or some white chocolate popcorn (check out Chapter 13 for the scoop). Drizzling melted chocolate all over popcorn and mixing those two ingredients is about as easy as a treat gets.

One of the nice things about making candies for your family, especially as you start out, is that your family members tend to be understanding if you make a few mistakes. When you tell the kids that they have to eat some of your mistakes, they will likely be understanding and more than willing to be your guinea pigs.

Trying treats for lovers

When you make candy for a significant other, you more than likely want to make a really good impression, especially if you have future aspirations with that special someone. In this case, you probably don't want to test your ideas on your subject.

When making candy for that special someone, you want to create something that makes a statement on your behalf. For instance, you may want to try a "sexy" item, and one of the fondue recipes in Chapter 5 certainly fits that mood. Of all the recipes in this book, few have the impact that fondue has on a lover; you're dipping from the same small pot of chocolate, sharing the same treat in close proximity. Fondue can bring intimacy to a simple dessert. If you want to make a good impression with less effort, go for the fondue.

If you really want to make a special impression, go for the truffles in Chapter 18. Surely if you're able to place a beautiful box or tray of your homemade truffles in front of a loved one, you make a certain statement. The truffle is the epitome of chocolate decadence. If you can offer truffles to someone you care about, you look like someone special, and so does your chocolate.

Whatever you select as a worthy confection for your loved one, go to the trouble to create the mood with the appropriate setting. What that setting may be and the feeling you wish to convey to your loved one are up to you. You can plan ahead and make your confections earlier than the occasion for which they're intended or, with proper storage, you can create a nice assortment for the situation and still have leftovers for other uses. (You find out how to store the different candies in their respective chapters.)

Choosing treats for special occasions

A lot of your candy making will eventually involve making candy gifts for those special times when you want to add a personal touch. You can make that special statement in so many ways, using some of the easy-to-make confections in this book coupled with gift-presentation ideas from Chapter 22. Just be sure to consider the recipient and his or her tastes when you're selecting candies to whip up.

Chocolate lends itself to gift giving because you can easily shape and decorate it in so many ways. For example, you can find special molds and boxes at the suppliers listed in Chapter 24 and make chocolate roses for Mother's Day or a chocolate tie for Father's Day.

Certain aromas always seem to go with certain holidays; mint at Christmas is one example of a nice match (try some mint candies in Chapter 6). How about pumpkin at Thanksgiving? See Chapter 7 for a wonderful pumpkin caramel recipe that'll make your tongue beat your brains out. Chapter 20 is also full of holiday-specific treats that are sure to impress your family and friends.

For an elegant wedding favor, you can make a truffle assortment (see Chapter 18) packed in a small box and tied with a lovely ribbon. This presentation is quite popular nowadays.

Matching a gift with an occasion can be really easy, once you make a few candies. Use your imagination — I help with some of that — and you'll find yourself pleasing so many people with your newfound talents. Presenting a gift that you've made yourself gives you a nice feeling as well. The joy that your recipient feels matches your joy in having created something special.

Assessing the Kitchen and Planning Your Space

If you live in a house that contains a fully operational candy kitchen, you won't have a problem adjusting to whatever the recipe requires of you when the time comes to make the confections. For everyone else, you need to make some adjustments or at least do some careful planning.

In this section, I give you some tips for getting your kitchen organized, ensuring that your kitchen has the right conditions, determining that you have enough counter space, and figuring out how to best use some major appliances.

Getting organized

Before you embark on your latest candy-making endeavor, here are some helpful hints for organizing your kitchen:

✔ **Make sure that you have all the necessary ingredients.** You don't want to risk ruining your candy by having to run to the grocery store to get an ingredient. If you need to, keep a checklist of the items you need.

✔ **Check that you have all the necessary tools, and keep them handy.** Having to look for an essential tool is frustrating and wastes valuable time. If you assess the recipes in this book, you may note that you use some utensils — measuring spoons, measuring cups, certain size pans, spatulas, baking pans — more than others. You may want to have backups for many of these tools because you use them so often. (See Chapter 3 for more details on picking the right tools for making candies.)

✔ **Make sure that the equipment that you may need for candy making is in working order.** Keep a checklist handy, and always make good notes about the ingredients and utensils you used when you made a recipe and any other considerations that you may not have expected, such as needing an assistant on some tasks. Fix anything with which you were dissatisfied, and each experience should be more enjoyable.

Creating the proper atmosphere

Certain weather conditions can greatly affect the outcome of your candy recipes. For instance, higher humidity and excessive heat are two elements that can cause your chocolate recipes to turn out less than perfect. Chocolate requires a cool, dry setting for optimal results. Humidity and heat can cause your chocolate to develop spots from condensation or your chocolate may not set with a nice gloss. You're not going to wish to do anything involving tempering chocolate and chocolate dipping if the temperature in your kitchen is very warm with no hope of lowering.

If you were planning on making chocolates but the weather conditions are hot and humid, consider making nonchocolate candies, which can be made under warmer, damper conditions. Heat and humidity aren't bitter enemies of all candies — they just can have a dramatic effect on chocolate production.

Also, if you're in the midst of a rainy day, you may not want to make candy at all because some weather elements, such as 100 percent humidity and power outages in a thunderstorm, cause major problems with your best-laid plans. You haven't had fun making candy until you lose power in the middle of making a huge batch of candy. (Okay, maybe you don't need to experience that much fun.)

The best conditions for making candy are those of a nice, crisp fall day. I love a day when the humidity is low — you look at trees and notice individual leaves instead of shapes — and the temperature is about 70 degrees. I can make any candy I want on a day like that.

Although you may not have ideal candy-making conditions in your home kitchen, you can take these steps to create the best situation possible:

✔ Close windows and doors to minimize the area you need to control.

✔ Use air conditioning to create a stable work environment; aim for a room temperature between 70 and 72 degrees. Purchase a dehumidifier to remove excess water from the air; it's especially effective in a small, closed room. The humidity in my candy production areas is set between 40 and 42 percent.

✔ Purchase a small thermometer with a humidity gauge (you can find one at a discount store). This type of thermometer gives you an accurate reading of temperature and humidity.

I realize that you will experience elements that are out of your control, so my expectation is that you create the best environment you can. I want you to enjoy the trip (making the candy) as much as the destination (eating the candy). Believe me: A lot of excellent candy production takes place under less-than-perfect conditions.

Although candy makers routinely make allowances for weather, they base their decisions on experience and the number of batches that they produce. You may not be able to produce the best results with limited experience at home. Instead, choose your conditions wisely, and you will gradually acquire the skills and confidence to make candy under adverse conditions.

Sizing up your counter space

When you're busily attending to your candy, you don't want to feel cramped or short of space. Aside from making production difficult, you risk injuring yourself because many of the confections are quite hot. Additionally, not having enough space can be a bit disconcerting and may cause you to ruin something. For these reasons, prepare your workspace before you start any recipe.

Planning the amount of workspace you need is a good idea because you don't want to find out too late that you need more room. Typically, you need an area that's a minimum of 2 feet by 3 feet to 2 feet by 4 feet. Although the latter measurement is probably a bit more space than you normally need, overestimating is better than underestimating your space.

One way to increase the size of your workspace is to remove those nonessentials that end up on the kitchen counters. Because the kitchen is often the first place people come when they get home, they always seem to leave something behind. But making a batch of candy is a good excuse for getting those casually placed items out of the kitchen. Your family should be glad to help you: You're making candy for them!

Now that you have a clear workspace, you need to know where the utensils are in your kitchen. When making candy, be sure to keep your utensils on the countertop close to your workspace for easy access.

Another space issue you need to consider is where you will cool your candy. If you don't have a problem with the amount of counter space, you can leave the candy on the counter. However, because some batches require longer cooling times, you may want to clear the counter (if you haven't already).

If you're lacking in counter space, a baker's rack is a wonderful place to allow trays of candy to cool because it takes up less space and isn't in your way. You also can find a simple countertop rack to serve the same purpose.

Feeling at home with your range (and microwave)

I don't send you inside the oven; you're not doing any baking with *these* recipes. However, you need to know how to use the range and your microwave for lots of the recipes.

You cook plenty of candy on the range: caramels, fudges, divinity, and brittles, just to name a few. The stovetop is also quite useful when you use a double boiler to melt chocolate. You frequently use your range to heat a heavy saucepan over low or medium heat, which lessens the chances of burning and scorching small batches. If you do scorch a batch, you've ruined it, so be familiar with how your range works. The common phrases "ovens may vary" and "microwaves vary — these are simply guidelines" are in books for a very important reason. Some ranges have settings for low, medium, and high; some have numbers. Cooking times vary from stove to stove, too.

A microwave is another handy appliance for candy making; it's especially useful for some simple fudge recipes (among others) and for melting chocolate. A microwave, like a range, can heat something faster than you expect, so know how your microwave works. Usually a microwave between 900 and 1,000 watts is adequate for your needs.

Because every microwave and range is different, keep a notepad handy to make notes of any time variations you observe between a recipe and your microwave and range. Also take notes on required times for heating different substances in your microwave or on your stovetop to prevent errors in cooking.

Chilling out with your fridge

Depending on what recipe you're preparing, you may need some space in your refrigerator for cooling a batch. You usually don't need that space for more than a few minutes, but you need to plan for it well before the last minute.

Some pieces, especially chocolate molds (see Chapter 19), require some refrigerator time, and you may want to put some items in the refrigerator for cooling, if your kitchen is a little warm. I've found that a temperature between 36 and 38 degrees is good for a refrigerator. When making candy, keep in mind that the refrigerator is a vital tool sometimes, and set aside a little space for your candy.

While using the refrigerator to cool chocolates or for making molds is fine, don't leave chocolates in the refrigerator for extended periods of time (longer than an hour) because of potential condensation damage to the chocolate.

Chapter 3

Selecting the Right Tools

. . . .

In This Chapter

▶ Matching the tools to the job

▶ Locating and buying the tools you need

. . . .

*J*ust as you need the right gear to play a sport, you need the right utensils to make candy. If you've ever visited a candy shop where you can watch the staff make candy, you probably noticed the big copper kettles, long wooden paddles, marble tables, and big gas stoves. Those utensils are appropriate for candy making, though the size of the batches dictates the size of the equipment. When you're making candy at home, you don't need to produce huge batches of candy, but you'd like to make candy that's every bit as good as the candy you've seen made in a candy kitchen.

One of the secrets to making good candy is to have the proper equipment for what you're making and to know how to use it. In this chapter, I introduce you to the tools you need to make candy. Of course, you probably already have a lot of them in your kitchen, but I also provide a few guidelines on finding the pieces you don't have already.

Mastering Measuring Tools

When you start planning your candy making and considering your equipment needs, don't overlook the important everyday tools of the trade: measuring cups, measuring spoons, a reliable kitchen scale, and thermometers. In the following sections, I tell you everything you need to know about these tools.

Measuring cups

One tool that I find indispensable in the kitchen is a set of measuring cups. When you make candy, you need two different types of measuring cups: liquid measuring cups and dry measuring cups.

✔ **Liquid measuring cups:** The most common types of liquid measuring cups are glass or plastic, and either type is better than metal measuring cups because you can see through them when you measure liquids. Liquid measuring cups are marked with graduation lines to indicate cup measures, including ¼ cup, ⅓ cup, ½ cup, and 1 cup, with plenty of fractional measures in between. You can also find these cups in sizes larger than 1 cup.

The liquid cups differ from dry measuring cups in that the liquid cups have a pouring spout and room above the top measurement line. This extra room is important because you need to be able to pour liquids without spilling them.

✔ **Dry measuring cups:** When you use dry measuring cups, you measure an ingredient until it's level with the top of the cup, and spilling is no problem because dry measures don't slosh and spill like liquids do. Dry measuring cups usually come in four sizes: ¼ cup, ⅓ cup, ½ cup, and 1 cup. For measurements less than ¼ cup, you can use conversion charts that show you how tablespoons and teaspoons come into play (see the next section).

I prefer stainless steel dry measuring cups for their durability and ease of measuring.

Measuring spoons

Measuring spoons are such a basic item that you probably have at least one set in your kitchen. They're used for measuring liquid and dry ingredients. Most measuring spoons come in four graduated measurements: 1 tablespoon, 1 teaspoon, ½ teaspoon, and ¼ teaspoon. These sets are available in plastic or metal.

Occasionally, you can find sets that include graduations of ⅛ teaspoon and ¹⁄₁₆ teaspoon. You would do well to find a set like that for candy making because you make a lot of tiny measurements in candy recipes. If you don't have the smaller spoons, you can estimate pretty well: ⅛ of a teaspoon is a small fraction of ¼. For ¹⁄₁₆ teaspoon, you can use a dash, which is roughly the equivalent of a pinch. These measures involve just the slightest amount of an ingredient. A pinch is the amount of a dry ingredient that you can pinch between your fingertips; a dash is the equivalent of two to three drops of liquid.

Kitchen scales

Using a kitchen scale to measure a pound of this or a pound and a half of that (think measuring chocolate) is easier than using a conversion chart to figure out the weight. You can find a good kitchen scale at kitchen-supply stores or at discount stores without spending too much. You can buy a typical spring scale, which I recommend, for about $15; the price goes up as the scale gets fancier, but the less expensive one is fine for your needs. Electronic scales can cost $50 or more.

If you're weighing something in a container, a kitchen scale usually has the ability to deduct the container's weight. This mechanism is useful when you're measuring a bulky ingredient. You put the container on the scale, set the indicator to zero, and add the ingredient. Because you've deducted the container's weight (what is known as *tare*), the weight on the scale is for the ingredient only.

Thermometers

Thermometers are extremely important in the candy-making process because slight variances in temperature can make the difference between a successful batch of candy and one that's inedible. Two essential thermometers to have when you make candy are a candy thermometer and a chocolate thermometer.

If you visit a candy kitchen, you will see a variety of types of thermometers — some quite expensive and elaborate. Fancier thermometers give digital read-outs quickly and accurately. Some thermometers take readings by laser, but they don't penetrate beyond the surface of the candy, so they're less reliable for actual temperature readings. If you plan to make candy at home, a fairly inexpensive thermometer will do just fine; it just needs to give you accurate temperatures when you cook. However, if you plan on doing a lot of candy making, invest in quality thermometers because you want them to last through many, many uses.

In the following sections, I discuss the ins and outs of candy and chocolate thermometers.

Candy thermometers

Purchase a candy thermometer that clips to the side of a pot (see Figure 3-1) because you'll need to clip the thermometer on the pot during the cooking process to measure the temperature of your batch.

Figure 3-1:
You can attach a candy thermometer to a pot with a clip.

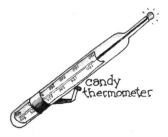

candy thermometer

When clipping the thermometer to your pot, make sure that the tip doesn't come into contact with the bottom of the pot because the thermometer will give you a false reading.

You can purchase basic or more sophisticated candy thermometers. Your decision depends on how often you plan to make candy. If you want to make candy a lot, you may consider investing a little more money in a better thermometer, as you would with any kitchen utensil you use a lot. I've seen prices from $12 for a simple thermometer to $35 for a digital thermometer.

To satisfy all your candy-making needs, look for a candy thermometer that measures a range from 100 degrees to 400 degrees; most thermometers have graduations of 5 degrees. Better candy thermometers have graduations of 2 degrees, which allow you to measure your batch's temperature more accurately. Some commercial thermometers have more detailed graduations within a specific range, perhaps from 160 degrees to 270 degrees, but these thermometers are designed for specific candies.

Chocolate thermometers

In its liquid state, chocolate exists in a range from 82 degrees to about 115 degrees, and this range is where you work all your candy-making magic. Your chocolate may occasionally reach 120 degrees, but watch out — you can easily scorch your chocolate then.

Because of the low temperature range of melted chocolate, chocolate thermometers are marked in 1-degree graduations from about 40 or 50 degrees to 130 degrees. (If your chocolate reaches 130 degrees, you have a problem.)

A simple chocolate thermometer costs between $12 and $15. Most chocolate thermometers are glass cylinders (see Figure 3-2), so when you're finished using your thermometer, clean it carefully with slightly warm water and store it where it won't get broken.

For a few dollars more, you can purchase a digital thermometer. This type of chocolate thermometer has a metal probe that you insert into a solution that gives an accurate reading for boiling cream and tempered chocolate. I like this style, but the glass thermometer should suffice for your chocolate needs.

Figure 3-2:
A chocolate thermometer is usually made of glass.

CHOCOLATE THERMOMETER

Picking Out Pots and Pans

Pots and pans are essential in the candy-making process. I cover the basics on these tools in the following sections.

Double boiler

You will find many uses for a double boiler, but one of the most common uses is for melting chocolate (which I cover in Chapter 14). Using a double boiler is a great way to melt your chocolate because you have no risk of scorching your chocolate. A double boiler melts chocolate slowly as you stir, so you control the melting process.

You can make your own double boiler by fitting a bowl snugly onto a bottom bowl. Just be sure that no steam or water vapor can escape from the bottom and get into the top pot.

If you purchase a double boiler set, you get a bottom that holds water and a top pan that fits snugly over the bottom pot (see Figure 3-3). In the top portion, you place whatever you're melting or heating. In the bottom pot, put enough water to fill the pot to just below the bottom of the top portion and heat it to approximately 140 degrees (use your candy thermometer to check the water's temperature). When you're using a double boiler to melt chocolate, remove the apparatus from the heat, and remove the top pan from the bottom. Dry the bottom of the top pan with a dry towel because you don't want water beads bubbling up into the top pan; water drops are the enemy of chocolate.

Figure 3-3:
A double boiler's top pan fits closely onto a bottom pan.

double boiler

The term "boiler" is misleading because it gives you the impression that you should be boiling water while you're using the apparatus. But when melting chocolate, do *not* boil water in your double boiler. First, you simply don't need to boil water to melt chocolate. Second, you don't want the moisture from the bottom pot to get into the chocolate in the top pot because beads of water can cause your chocolate to become thick and clumpy.

Saucepans

Surely you have a set of saucepans (or at least a saucepan) in your kitchen but, when you're making candy, you want to make sure that you're using *heavy saucepans,* or pans that are thick on the bottom. The sizes you need are 2-quart, 4-quart, and 5-quart. You may want to have a smaller 1-quart pan for some recipes, too.

Heavy saucepans tend to distribute heat better, which is important because it helps prevent scorching if you heat ingredients too quickly. Keep in mind that even though you're using heavy saucepans, you still need to use low or medium heat so you don't burn or scorch what you're cooking!

Copper pans are wonderful, if you have them, because copper distributes heat so well. Some people swear by cast-iron pots, and I like heavy aluminum pans, too.

Baking pans and liners

When making candy, you can choose among three types of baking pans: glass, heavy aluminum, and disposable aluminum. I like the latter two styles better than glass because I worry about breakage and flying glass shards. The heavy aluminum pans are washable and reusable, and the disposable type is pretty much what the name says, although you may get multiple uses out of a disposable pan if you use it carefully.

The recipes in this book mostly call for two sizes of baking pans: an 8 x 8-inch pan or a 9 x 13-inch pan. Both sizes are 2 inches deep. I recommend the use of baking pans in a number of recipes, especially fudge recipes (see Chapter 9).

You can brush the inside of a pan with butter or you can line the pan with paper to prevent your batch of candy from sticking. With liner paper, you can usually lift candy out of the pan by lifting the corners of the paper. This easy removal allows for easy cutting of a batch of candy like fudge or marshmallow.

If you're using liner paper in place of butter, I recommend using wax paper or parchment paper because regular liner paper is likely to tear easily after you fill the pan or when you remove the candy. Surely you'd prefer not to pick the little pieces of paper out of your candies!

Another liner option is nonwax paper, also known as a bakery tray liner (available from bakery suppliers). Candies that are small and cool — especially individually dipped pieces like chocolate creams or truffles — do quite well on nonwax paper compared with hotter candies like cooked fudges, caramels, and marshmallow; they release easily from these liners. If you don't have this paper handy, though, I recommend wax paper as an option.

Cookie sheets

I believe the cookie sheet may be the item I use in my home more than anything; this little tray (typically 13 x 18 inches) has countless uses. You can easily use cookie sheets in candy recipes that call for trays. Many times, cookie sheets are just the right size for cooling the batch of candy you're making, giving you instant mobility for moving your candy to a cool part of the kitchen. Smaller versions of cookie sheets may be flat with only one raised side, but I like sheets with four sides myself.

Checking Out Other Essential Tools

Among the tools of the candy-making trade are some utensils that sound rather unexciting but nonetheless play big roles in candy production. I cover the details in the following sections.

Large knives

Knives are useful for an obvious reason: cutting. In candy making, you need a large knife to chop your bars of chocolate into small pieces, which makes melting or tempering your chocolate easier (see Chapter 14). I like using a large double-handled knife for this purpose, but a large butcher knife also suffices. You can also use a smaller knife to cut prepared candies after they cool on those occasions when you don't want to use something bigger. You can cut fudge, for example, with a butter knife or a paring knife.

Microwaveable bowls

You prepare many of the recipes in this book using microwaveable bowls. Shop around to find a few sturdy, plastic microwaveable bowls because these bowls are a great tool for melting and tempering chocolate. You may place the bowl in the microwave for a few seconds, stir your batch, and continue using your chocolate. A 2-quart size is very handy for most tasks. Keeping your chocolate at the proper temperature is easier to do with a plastic bowl than with a glass bowl, which can retain heat longer and cause your chocolate to go out of temper.

Pastry brush

Although you won't make pastries with my recipes, a good pastry brush is an essential tool for washing down sugar crystals in a pan when batches of candy come to a boil (see Chapter 7 for details).

It's easier to use an angled brush for washing down sugar crystals, but straight brushes (like paintbrushes) are easier to find and work fine. I recommend using a brush with a longer handle (10 to 12 inches is ideal) to keep your distance from batches of hot candies.

Wooden and stainless steel spoons

In several recipes, I specify a wooden spoon for mixing candies. If you prefer, you can use a heavy metal spoon in place of a wooden spoon. I often use a stainless steel spoon with a black plastic handle, and these spoons last for years.

A good long spoon (14 inches or longer) keeps your hand farther from hot candy.

Whisks

Wire whisks are wonderful little tools for whipping and mixing some candies. Another common use for this tool is gently whisking cream and chocolate when you make a truffle center (see Chapter 18).

Whisks come in a variety of sizes, starting around 5 inches long and reaching lengths of 18 inches or longer with a handle grip. Try to find a whisk that's about 9 to 10 inches long; this size has a beater end that's about 2½ to 3 inches wide. A good whisk should cost less than $10.

Spatulas

When I use the term "spatula," I'm usually referring to one of two types of equipment essential to candy production: a hard rubber spatula and an offset stainless steel spatula.

Hard rubber spatulas

The hard rubber spatula is one of my favorite tools. When I'm making candy, I use it to fold or mix ingredients together and to scrape the contents out of a pot and into whatever form I'm pouring the batch.

These spatulas come in lengths from a few inches to about 16 inches long. You should keep several sizes on hand for different tasks. Some hard rubber spatulas have wooden handles, and some are entirely made of rubber (see Figure 3-4). I prefer solid rubber spatulas because wooden handles wear out with repeated washings.

Figure 3-4:
A sturdy, hard rubber spatula is essential in making candy.

I prefer using an all-rubber 12-inch to 16-inch spatula because of its versatility and strength. All-rubber spatulas aren't impossible to break, but they're pretty difficult to break.

Offset stainless steel spatulas

Offset stainless steel spatulas have many functions, such as tempering chocolate and spreading hot batches of candy. I especially like using an offset spatula to spread hot candies quickly. The *offset spatula* is so called because it has a bend in the shaft (see Figure 3-5). You may find this spatula more to your liking for spreading candies because the offset gives you more leverage.

Handy stainless steel spatulas come in various lengths, and I recommend having at least one that's 12 inches long or longer. Keeping several different sizes on hand is a good idea because you have different needs for different tasks.

Figure 3-5:
An offset spatula can help you spread candies more easily.

Strainer

You're likely to already have a large strainer, but you also want to have a small strainer for various tasks. For instance, when making truffles (see Chapter 18), you may need to strain cream when steeping it with a natural ingredient. Other uses for a strainer in candy making include sifting kernels out of popcorn (see Chapter 13) and sifting ingredients such as powdered sugar. You can use strainers made of either plastic or stainless steel with wire mesh.

Rolling pin

Another piece of equipment you may already have hanging out in your kitchen cabinets is a rolling pin. This tool is quite useful for a few candy recipes, such as making marzipan in Chapter 10. I like an aluminum rolling pin, but wood or marble are other options. Honestly, I've never seen a bad rolling pin.

Scrapers

One item I mention often in this book is a *scraper*, which is a metal triangular trowel-like tool. You use a scraper when making fondant, tempering chocolate, molding chocolate shells, or any of several other chocolate functions you encounter in Part IV of this book. When candy making, you want to have at least one fairly wide scraper and one narrower scraper on hand.

You can find excellent scrapers at a hardware store.

Small scoop

A good number of the pieces you make in this book — such as divinity, creams, and truffles — require a small scoop or a melon baller. Keep in mind the sizes of the pieces you will be making; for instance, you need a pretty small scoop (about 1 inch wide) for a typical truffle center, and baking scoops or melon ballers are good for creating this size.

Grater or zester

You occasionally need a fine grater when you make candy (such as when you grate toppings on truffles in Chapter 18). You may use one of several types of graters. You may use the smallest holes on a cheese grater to zest citrus, or you can use a slim zesting tool that's made for this purpose.

Powering Up with Small Appliances

Don't forget the importance of small appliances in candy making! The following sections give you the scoop.

Food processor

The food processor's primary role in candy making is chopping nuts to a fairly fine consistency. You don't have a food processor, you say? No matter: You can use a blender as a worthy substitute for the food processor. If you don't have either of these appliances, you may want to at least invest in a blender, which you can buy at a large discount store for about $20.

Kitchen mixer

For many of the candies in this book, you need a 4- or 5-quart stand mixer. This size provides the volume you need in a bowl for any recipe and has the power you need to mix a batch of candy. You certainly need a mixer of this size for making marshmallow and divinity (just to give you two examples), so make the investment, if you haven't already. The two attachments that I use most on a stand mixer are the whisk and the paddle, especially the latter.

You can use a hand mixer for small mixing jobs (like when making truffles in Chapter 18), but thicker candies like marshmallow will wear such a mixer out.

If possible, you may even want to get an extra bowl. An extra bowl isn't a necessity, but you may want to have a backup.

Chocolate tempering machine

In Chapter 14, I mention the possibility of using a chocolate tempering machine. Most chocolate shops have these machines, and some of these machines are quite large. But if you want a chocolate tempering machine to use at home, you can purchase a small countertop version. These machines share the principles of the big machines: They heat and cool chocolate, allowing you to quickly temper chocolate for use in a recipe, and the amount of chocolate tempered is enough for many of the recipes in the book.

If you plan to make a lot of chocolate, you may consider purchasing one of these machines. These smaller versions range in price from a few hundred dollars to a little more than $1,000 (the priciest are the cream of the crop). See Chapter 14 for more details on tempering machines.

Surveying Specialty Tools

The process of making candies calls for a few special tools, which I cover in the following sections.

Marble slab

You may have seen large marble tables in candy kitchens. You do not need a piece of marble quite that large; you want a smaller version that you can use at home from time to time. For instance, you can use a marble slab when you make fondant (see Chapter 6), or you may want to hand-temper your chocolate on a marble slab (see Chapter 14).

A slab that's 12 x 18 inches and about ¾ inches thick is ideal for tempering chocolate. Slabs are available at kitchen stores for between $12 and $15.

You can find a small piece of marble at a place that makes countertops for home kitchens. When these countertops are cut, the sink cutouts make great pieces for home candy makers. Just call around until you find a supplier who will sell you (or even give you) a small piece.

Piping bags

Piping is the method by which you fill a cone-shaped bag with a soft center mixture to squeeze it into the center of a preformed shell. When piping, you may use the following piping-bag options:

- **Disposable plastic bags:** These plastic bags are relatively cheap. I like to use a 12-inch plastic bag when I pipe truffles (see Chapter 18).

- **Parchment paper triangles:** You can form the paper triangles into cones for piping as well as for chocolate "writing." When you purchase a package of these triangles, it comes with instructions telling you how to fold the triangle into a cone.

- **Reusable cloth bags:** These bags come with an assortment of nozzles for making different patterns and are useful for larger molding. The different tips allow you to create different shapes.

Dipping utensils

You can dip bite-size candy pieces by hand using no utensils at all, but you may prefer to use tools designed for that task. You can purchase a set of dipping utensils (see Figure 3-6), which usually includes forks with two, three, and four prongs, and a spiral dipper for holding round pieces, among other shapes. A set of dipping utensils costs $12 to $15. To find out more about dipping techniques and tools, see Chapter 15.

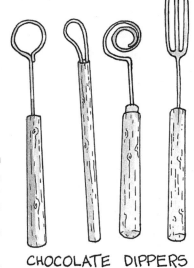

Figure 3-6:
Dipping utensils come in a variety of shapes.

CHOCOLATE DIPPERS

Molds

You can find plastic molds for chocolates in a variety of thicknesses, styles, and prices. So-called "hobby" molds are the cheapest and the flimsiest, but they're fine for limited use in chocolate molding. For more detail and for extended use, I recommend commercial molds, which are made of a heavier-gauge plastic and can be used repeatedly with proper care and storage.

You can purchase molds to make tiny chocolate pieces that weigh less than ½ ounce, but you can also find larger molds for producing 1-pound solid chocolate "sculptures." Check out Chapter 19 for the complete scoop on molds.

Wrapping Up with Cooling and Storage Tools

After you finish making your delicious candies, you need to protect them until it's time to enjoy them. I give you details on cooling and storage tools in the following sections.

Cooling racks

I'm a little spoiled because I have rooms full of cooling racks. I once had one rack, but now I have something like 25 racks for cooling and storing candy. For your purposes, a baker's rack is wonderful for cooling because it allows you to cool a lot of candy in a small space, but any cooling rack works.

Kitchen stores sell small racks that suit your needs perfectly. You can find stackable wire racks that are about 10 x 14 inches for cooling your confections. You can also purchase a metal rack that holds three 13 x 18 cookie sheets with room for your candy to cool. The former costs $12; the latter costs $25.

Wax paper, plastic wrap, foil, and paper cups

The following materials are useful for wrapping candies or for covering containers of candy.

- ✔ Wax paper is useful for cooling your candies, especially your chocolates, on. You can lay sheets on the counter to provide a simple space for this use, and wax paper is cheap and disposable. You can also use wax paper to separate layers of candy in storage containers. (Wax paper is also useful during the actual candy-making process; see "Baking pans and liners" earlier in this chapter.)

- ✔ Plastic kitchen wrap is wonderful for covering finished candies to protect them from the elements.

- ✔ Foil wraps, which range from 3½ inches square to 5 inches square, are useful for packaging individual candies.

- ✔ I recommend using #4 and #6 paper cups for wrapping your finished pieces and giving them a "professional" appearance. The #4 cups are about 1 inch wide at the base, and the #6 cups are ¼ inch wider.

Storage containers

Many candies require that you store them in an airtight container, and typical plastic containers fit that bill nicely. Such storage allows you to keep your candies for several weeks — if no one knows where you hid the containers! Have a variety of sizes of containers on hand, ranging from 6 x 6 inches to 10 x 12 inches, and at least one very large container for storing larger batches and bulky candies.

Finding What You Need with Ease

You probably already have many of the utensils you need in your kitchen; others you can easily find from several sources. You do not need to spend a fortune to arm yourself with the proper tools; just be resourceful and imaginative as you shop for what you need. I cover several shopping options in the following sections.

Aside from some of the typical commercial sources, keep hardware stores in mind for gadgets. Other great sources for supplying your needs are garage sales and yard sales. On any given weekend, you may find dozens of such outlets, and truly one man's trash is another man (or woman's) treasure, so don't discount these friendly gatherings as great places to fill your needs. These options are good places to find odds and ends, such as trays, baskets, and other items that you can use in gift presentation (see Chapter 22 for details on giving your candies as gifts).

Grocery and discount stores

You can find plenty of the items you need at a grocery store. Just walk down the aisle where they sell sugar, spices, and the like, and you will find a variety of kitchen utensils. Similarly, walk through the small-appliance section of a "Big Box" discount store, and you will find plenty of the items you need for candy making. These stores stock plenty of small cooking utensils, baking pans, spatulas, and more. Before you spend a lot of money somewhere else, check out these stores.

Kitchen stores

If you're in a mall anyway, take a look in one of the kitchen stores for harder-to-find candy-making supplies. These stores always have a wide selection of quality utensils, bowls, and small appliances. They're good places to find good storage containers, too. You pay more for these items at a kitchenware store than you do at a discount store, but you can usually count on better quality at one of these stores.

Commercial equipment suppliers

I like shopping for utensils in a commercial equipment store because I can find little items as well as huge pieces of equipment that I sometimes need. Some of the items I find there are hard rubber spatulas, large stainless steel spoons, scoops, spatulas, and so much more. Most cities have one or more of these stores so, if you can find one, you'll satisfy many of your candy-making needs, and the prices are usually lower than what you would pay at a kitchen store. You also find items that you don't usually find at a discount store.

The Internet

You can do a search on the Internet for any utensil you need. Simply use the item you seek as the keyword on a search engine such as Google or Yahoo!, and you instantly find a list of suppliers. You can scroll through the list of results until you find what you want, and you can shop by the price you want to spend. It's that easy! To get you started, I provide a list of suppliers that carry the utensils you need in Chapter 24.

Chapter 4

Picking Quality Ingredients

· ·

In This Chapter

▶ Sweetening your candies

▶ Checking out dairy products

▶ Cracking the right nuts

▶ Selecting good chocolates

▶ Discovering other essential ingredients

· ·

You produce the best candies by paying attention to the quality of all the ingredients. If you use some premium ingredients and cut corners in others, you won't be totally satisfied with your results.

In this chapter, I give you the lowdown on several groups of important candy ingredients: sweeteners, dairy products, nuts, and chocolate. I also provide you with a handy list of other ingredients that you may find useful as you begin to make candy.

You can find many of the ingredients used in making candies at your local grocery store. Don't worry about those harder-to-find ingredients, though; you can check out Chapter 24 for a list of online suppliers.

What a Sweetie: Types of Sugars and Sweeteners

A major portion and volume of candy consists of granulated sugar and its family of sweeteners, including brown sugar. Sugar not only gives candy its sweet taste, but it also gives it its *grain,* or crunchy texture, when that's desired.

Other sweeteners, including corn syrup, act as *stabilizers;* their use prevents the graining process from getting out of hand and results in a smoother texture.

Of course, you don't add all sugars to candy by the cupful or by the pound. Many products contain sugars that add to the overall sweetness and taste of the candy. For instance, milk contains *lactose,* or milk sugar, and fruits contain *fructose,* the sweetest of all sugars. So as you can see, you may be adding sugar in many forms without even knowing it. For this reason, make sure that your sugar measurements are level, not heaping, measures.

The following sections give you the scoop on different types of sweeteners, both solids and liquids, that you find in candy recipes.

Surveying solid sweeteners

Granulated sugar is by far the most common solid sugar used in candies, but you may come across several other types of sugar as you begin to make candy. Brown sugar, confectioners' sugar, fondant sugar, and invert sugar are other solid sweeteners that play roles in candy making.

Granulated sugar

Granulated sugar is the most common form of sugar that you use in candy recipes. It is the backbone of many candies and the primary sweetener for the majority of candies. This sugar is the kind you buy in 2-pound or 5-pound bags at the grocery store.

Brown sugar

I use brown sugar in a few recipes, such as fudge (see Chapter 9) and pralines (see Chapter 11). Brown sugar, which is granulated sugar with molasses added, comes in two forms: light and dark.

For recipes using brown sugar, I recommend dark brown sugar because I prefer the dark color that the darker sugar imparts. Feel free to use light brown instead; just know that the final product will be a little lighter in color.

When you use brown sugar, always firmly pack the measuring cup to attain the proper measure.

Confectioners' sugar

Some recipes — for example, fudge (see Chapter 9) — contain confectioners' sugar (also known as powdered sugar). Confectioners' sugar is granulated sugar that has been pulverized and has a small percentage (about 3 to 4 percent) of cornstarch. In the candy itself, confectioners' sugar dissolves much faster than granulated sugar, and this speed of dissolution makes confectioners' sugar a good choice for noncooked or microwaved candies.

Sometimes, I have you pour a little confectioners' sugar on your hands before you handle candy because it helps prevent stickiness. After dusting your hands with confectioners' sugar, you can more easily form your centers or whatever the task may be. To remove lumps, you should always sift confectioners' sugar before using.

I know that cornstarch isn't a sugar, but you can use it in place of confectioners' sugar for handling candies. For instance, I recommend using cornstarch when handling fruit jellies in Chapter 10; the cornstarch, which is virtually tasteless, acts as a drying agent in jellies.

Fondant sugar

Fondant sugar is a finely ground sugar, much like confectioners' sugar, but it doesn't contain cornstarch like confectioners' sugar does.

Fondant sugar looks a lot like confectioners' sugar when it comes out of the bag; it's quite powdery. You should sift fondant sugar with a flour sifter or simply shake it through a strainer because it is prone to forming lumps when stored.

You can produce many recipes using fondant sugar, and you don't have to do any (or much) cooking. I show you how to make creams in Chapter 17, and the method I use to make the centers is called a cold process, so called because you don't have to cook the center. You occasionally may heat the ingredients to about 160 degrees, but that hardly constitutes cooking.

Aside from being used in creams, fondant sugar is a component of cordial centers (see Chapter 15) and other candies.

Invert sugar

You may not be so familiar with *invert sugar,* which is a combination of the sugars glucose and fructose, but it's a staple in the candy industry. Sometimes folks use it as a substitute for other ingredients, such as corn syrup, because it helps control the graining process in a batch of candy. This substitution may result in slight variations in the final product, but the differences aren't detrimental to the overall result.

If you substitute invert sugar for corn syrup in a recipe, the result is a slightly darker candy. Invert sugar is also quite a bit sweeter than corn syrup.

Invert sugar occurs naturally in honey and fruits but, nowadays, manufacturers produce invert sugar artificially in massive quantities for use in candy making, among other uses. I like to use invert sugar in divinity, with wonderful results (see Chapter 8); the sugar, beaten with egg whites, produces a beautiful, fluffy white base for the divinity.

Looking at liquid sweeteners

Liquid sweeteners, particularly corn syrup, are essential to many candies. The following sections give you details on the most popular liquid sweeteners.

Corn syrup

Corn syrup is one of the most important ingredients you use in candy making. Aside from its sweetening properties, which are ample, corn syrup prevents sugar from graining and making a gritty batch of candy.

Recipes in any number of cookbooks call for light or dark corn syrup. The difference has to do with the source corn, which dictates the color of the syrup. I specify only light corn syrup in my recipes because I prefer the lighter result this syrup produces, and it's much more readily available. You may find corn syrup under several brand names in grocery stores.

If you're making caramel (see Chapter 7), you will note that the weight of the corn syrup is equal to or (more commonly) greater than the weight of the sugar in the recipe. An imbalance favoring corn syrup makes for a smoother, better-biting caramel, if that's the candy you're making. However, if the percentage of corn syrup in a batch is too high, the result is stickier caramel. This reason is one of the many that you want to weigh and measure your ingredients carefully.

Corn syrup is often one of the ingredients you use in making centers because it prevents bacterial growth. In this capacity, corn syrup serves the same purpose as invertase. (*Invertase* is a natural enzyme that controls bacterial growth; I mention it quite often as an ingredient in truffles. See Chapter 18.) However, your candies have a longer shelf life when you properly use invertase. (For more details on invertase, check out "Odds and Ends: Other Essential Candy Ingredients" later in this chapter.)

Honey

You can use honey in candies much the same way as invert sugar (which I cover earlier in this chapter). You can also use honey in place of corn syrup. Honey is a little sweeter than corn syrup and produces a little softer piece than you get with corn syrup. You can make substitutions on a one-for-one basis.

Udder Delights: Different Kinds of Dairy Products

Dairy products play a major role in candy making, and one of those roles is the amount of butterfat a specific dairy product brings to the recipe. Butterfat gives candy that delightful smooth texture that you so love in a piece of candy, and it also delivers its own rich, wonderful taste. You add butterfat to your candies by adding cream, which can mean different things to different people, so I specify in the recipes what I mean by "cream."

In the following sections, I cover the dairy products most often found in candies.

You can make substitutions for cream, but you have to make other adjustments to the recipe, too. For example, if you lower the butterfat content of your cream when making a truffle center, you have to increase the amount of chocolate you use. Without this adjustment, you make a much softer, thinner center, and you lose a bit of taste that the higher-fat cream has. Because dairy is key to the candy game, using the ingredient the recipe calls for is best. Doing so produces the best results.

Keep all dairy products refrigerated and use them by the expiration date for best results. Before dumping cream into a batch of candy, make sure it looks okay. Shaken cream has a smooth appearance; the cream shouldn't look lumpy or smell "cheesy." You really don't want to dump spoiled cream into your batch.

Butter

Ah, sweet butter is such a nice candy component. It imparts a certain . . . well, buttery flavor to the candies when you use it as an ingredient. Even if you're calorie conscious, you can't substitute anything for butter. Margarine is a nice nondairy product, but it's no butter. I don't suggest replacing butter with margarine in any recipe because butter is about 80 percent to 82 percent butterfat, and margarine can be all over the place, so determining its fat content may be difficult.

One more bit of advice: Using unsalted butter is preferable to salted butter because salt is often an ingredient anyway.

Heavy cream

In several recipes (the truffles in Chapter 18, especially), I specifically call for heavy cream. Heavy cream is at least 40 percent butterfat, and this high level of fat contributes greatly to the taste and texture of candies.

You may not always be able to find heavy cream in the dairy section of your grocery store but, if you ask, the store might order it for you. You may also ask a local bakery or candy maker to order you some. Heavy cream usually comes in half pints, pints, and quarts.

Whipping cream

Several recipes in this book require the use of whipping cream, which has a butterfat content of 30 percent. This ingredient is not the can of cream that you add to another dessert as a topping. (However, if you beat whipping cream, you can produce that topping.) In this book, you use whipping cream in fondue and caramel recipes (see Chapters 5 and 7).

You can usually find whipping cream in half-pint containers in the dairy section of your grocery store, but you can also find pints and quarts in some stores.

Half and half

Some fudge and praline recipes call for half and half, which has a lower butterfat cream, with a fat content of around 10.5 percent. If a recipe specifically calls for half and half, the confection needs specific levels of fat; however, if you substitute a cream for half and half, you change the overall texture and taste of the recipe. Half and half is available in half pints, pints, and quarts.

You can easily see and taste the difference between using a cup of heavy cream and a cup of half-and-half in a recipe because the approximately 30 percent difference in fat content has a dramatic effect on the outcome.

Whole milk

Whole milk is at the bottom of the butterfat scale. You use whole milk in some fudge recipes but, in most recipes that include milk, you find another source of fat, such as butter. Whole milk is about 4 percent fat and ranges down to skim milk (or fat-free milk), which contains no fat and doesn't really add much taste to candy.

Evaporated milk

One dairy product I use quite a bit is evaporated milk. You can find this item in caramel recipes (see Chapter 7), and I also use this milk in some creams for added richness (check out Chapter 17). But what exactly is evaporated milk? It's milk with about 60 percent of the water removed, which makes it quite thick, but it's a good ingredient for recipes in which you don't want added water. Sugar makes up between 10 and 12 percent of evaporated milk.

Sweetened condensed milk

Sweetened condensed milk is used less often than evaporated milk in candies; I see it more in baked goods. I do, however, include it in some fudge recipes (see Chapter 9). This milk is similar to evaporated milk, but before the water is removed, a lot of sugar is added. You're left with sticky, sweet milk that contains an excessively high percentage of sugar — as much as 65 percent of the volume of the can.

Not So Tough to Crack: Picking Nuts

Few ingredients have as much influence on people's candy preferences as the choice of nuts in the candy (at least, if you take chocolate out of the equation). Folks love chocolate, but nut preferences run all over the board and often depend on locale. Nowadays, most grocery stores carry large selections of shelled raw nuts, so you have the opportunity to pick your favorite nuts, so to speak, and put them in your confections.

Nuts commonly used in candy include

- **Peanuts:** Though the peanut is not really a nut (it's a legume in the bean and pea family), peanuts are big in the candy world and star in several categories of candies, including brittles (see Chapter 12), barks, and clusters (see Chapter 16). Peanut butter is part of lots of fudges (see Chapter 9), meltaways (see Chapter 6), and other wonderful candies.

- **Pecans:** Southerners tend to prefer candies with pecans, such as pralines (see Chapter 11), because of their ready availability in the South. The list of Southern candies featuring pecans is long and distinguished, including the ever-popular caramel pecan cluster (see Chapter 7). Chocolate pecan fudge is high on many folks' list as well.

- **Walnuts:** Walnuts are available in English and black walnut varieties. English walnuts are more commonly used and are less expensive than black walnuts. Some folks believe that black walnuts have a more bitter taste, and they can be the dickens to shell. Shelled English walnuts are available at the grocery in bags ranging in size from 4 ounces to 10 ounces. Black walnuts frequently come in small cans and are more expensive.

- **Almonds:** Almonds are a real favorite all over the country and are especially good in clusters and barks because of their flavor and the crunch they add to chocolate pieces. If I use almonds in a batch of fudge, I use sliced natural almonds because fudge with whole almonds is too difficult to cut; the almonds move around when the knife hits them and leave ugly gashes.

- ✔ **Cashews:** Most folks seem to love cashews in roasted nut assortments, but the little arched nuts fall down the list when combined with chocolate. I'm not sure what the reasons for this are but, if you like them with chocolate, you can add them to your candies! I show you how to make cashew brittle, and you can easily substitute cashews for other nuts in bark and clusters.

- ✔ **Macadamias:** Macadamias, which originated in Australia, were cultivated successfully in Hawaii in the late 1800s. Nowadays the hard-shelled nut is Hawaii's largest tree crop and is finding fans across the United States and elsewhere. You can cover these nuts in chocolate, mix them with chocolate to form bark, or add them to clusters.

- ✔ **Hazelnuts:** Hazelnuts have long been a favorite nut in Europe, where the hazelnut, or filbert, is the equivalent of the peanut in America. Many European candy makers make the centers of their candies, which they call "pralines," with a hazelnut paste. If a recipe calls for almonds or macadamias, you can substitute hazelnuts on an equal basis.

Selecting a favorite nut is one thing, but deciding whether to use raw nuts or roasted nuts is another. You also have to decide whether to use salted or unsalted nuts. Gee, I don't know how we candy makers do it some days.

When deciding whether to use raw or roasted nuts, go with your personal preference. I use raw pecans in my caramel pecan cluster candies in my stores, but I use roasted unsalted cashews and almonds. I also use roasted salted Spanish peanuts in clusters and bark, so I guess we all have our favorites.

If you buy shelled nuts in bags, leave them in the bag until you're ready to use them. They store well at room temperature, but you can also bag them in double freezer bags and freeze them for six months. When you're ready to use the nuts, remove them from the freezer and allow them to thaw in the bag overnight (or at least eight hours).

From Dark to Light: Checking Out Types of Chocolate

Although you can make many different candies with the recipes you find in this book, few results are more rewarding than candies made with good, rich chocolate. Frankly, many of the recipes in this book involve chocolate in some form, although the kind of chocolate you use in different recipes varies.

Exact definitions of the types of chocolate vary slightly due to variations in taste and production values worldwide. I based the following descriptions on the Food and Drug Administration's standards; these descriptions give you an understanding of the differences among chocolates.

To make the best chocolate candies, use premium chocolate, commonly called *couverture* in the chocolate trade. Couverture is considered the top of the line of fine chocolates because of its high cocoa butter content and extremely smooth texture. Chocolatiers commonly use this type of chocolate to mold better pieces and to coat such items as truffles.

To keep all types of chocolate fresh, store it in a closed plastic container in a cool, dark area (if possible). A good storage temperature is around 70 degrees. To find out more on the care and storage of chocolate, flip to Chapter 14.

Unsweetened baking chocolate

When you purchase unsweetened baking chocolate in a store, you're usually buying what those in the chocolate trade call chocolate liquor. This ingredient has nothing to do with alcohol. *Chocolate liquor,* the purest form of chocolate that you can buy, is made of cocoa butter and cocoa solids and contains no milk or sugar. Unsweetened chocolate is available in bars, chunks, or chips the size of quarters, requiring little work to prepare for melting. If you were to melt this chocolate and taste it, you would taste something very similar to what the Aztecs drank when Hernando Cortes made his discoveries of cacao beans in 1519. This chocolate has a bitter taste.

Unsweetened chocolate is an ingredient in a number of recipes, including fudge (see Chapter 9), chocolate butter creams (see Chapter 17), and chocolate caramels (see Chapter 7).

Cocoa powder

Cocoa powder, unsweetened as I use it, is pretty much ground pure chocolate. (Sweetened cocoa has sugar added, and I don't use that cocoa in any recipes.) Cocoa powder tastes the same as unsweetened chocolate: very bitter. Yet if you're a chocolate purist, you'll love adding it to a chocolate piece. For example, I roll a truffle dipped in dark chocolate in cocoa powder and shake off the excess. This combination creates a nice effect because the taste buds get the bitter taste just before the dark chocolate taste. At this point, the dark chocolate seems sweeter by comparison. (Hungry for a truffle now? Check out Chapter 18 for some great recipes.)

Dark chocolate

Dark chocolate falls into a few categories based on the content of chocolate liquor in the product. Because chocolate liquor is very bitter, the higher the chocolate liquor content, the more bitter the chocolate will be.

Chocolate on both sides of the Atlantic

Milk chocolate is the most popular chocolate consumed in the United States although, in recent years, more Americans have acquired a taste for dark chocolate. Nevertheless, the percentage of chocolates manufactured in the United States still leans heavily toward milk chocolate. On the other hand, Europeans usually prefer dark chocolate; the ratio of dark chocolate to milk chocolate consumption in Europe is nearly reversed from American tastes.

In fact, in some parts of the United States, European heritage may partially account for preferences for dark chocolate. Tastes vary in different parts of the United States, and areas that have had a large influx of European immigrants over the years tend to favor dark chocolate over milk chocolate.

To be considered a dark chocolate, the chocolate must contain at least 35 percent chocolate liquor, although many premium chocolates have an even higher percentage. Because dark chocolates also contain sugar, they fall into a category called "sweet chocolates," but that term can be misleading. The three types of dark chocolate are

- **Extra dark chocolate:** You can find extra dark chocolate with a chocolate liquor content exceeding 70 percent — talk about a bitter chocolate!

- **Bittersweet chocolate:** This chocolate has a high chocolate liquor content and a very dark color. Its chocolate liquor content is higher than 35 percent; a content of 55 percent chocolate liquor is fairly common. Bittersweet chocolate contains sugar, but the amount of sugar is lower than the amount of sugar in a semi-sweet chocolate.

- **Semi-sweet chocolate:** This chocolate falls at the bottom of the dark chocolate spectrum because of its high sugar content. Semi-sweet chocolate is quite good to eat, and I like using it to produce dark-chocolate molded candies, clusters, and other forms of chocolate for people who prefer something with a stronger taste than milk chocolate.

Milk chocolate

The most popular chocolate in the United States is milk chocolate. Milk chocolate must be at least 10 percent chocolate liquor, but sometimes the levels exceed semi-sweet minimums. Ingredients such as milk solids and sugar influence the variations in chocolate liquor levels, allowing for some milk chocolates to be darker and still be called mild chocolate.

The pros and cons of using chocolate-flavored coating

In the realm of items that resemble chocolate, you will find an item called chocolate-flavored coating, which candy makers commonly refer to as compound coating or summer coating. Although many manufacturers refer to this substance as chocolate, this product doesn't contain cocoa butter and isn't legally called chocolate. Chocolate-flavored coating isn't a bad product; it simply isn't chocolate, and chocolate-flavored coating doesn't taste like real chocolate. Anyone who enjoys real chocolate can tell the difference.

Compound coating is made primarily with cocoa powder, sugar, milk solids, and vegetable oils, including coconut oil or palm kernel oil. Often, when people taste a product made with vegetable oil, they think that paraffin has been added to it, but what they're experiencing is the mouthfeel that the oil has created. Vegetable oil tends to leave a strange aftertaste, whereas the cocoa butter in chocolate leaves a delightful taste of chocolate.

One of the pros to using compound coating is that it doesn't require tempering, so some folks like to use it for its ease of melting. Improperly tempered chocolate results in bloom or unsightly streaks in the chocolate, but bloom isn't usually a problem with compound coating. (I show you how to temper chocolate in Chapter 14, and you find that once you learn not to fear the process, tempering is worth the little bit of trouble.)

As you can see, chocolate-flavored coatings have their pros and their cons. But if you follow the steps in this book, you won't ever think of using a chocolate-flavored coating!

White chocolate

Folks often ask me what white chocolate is and if it is chocolate. Well, white chocolate is a name given to a product that is used extensively in the candy trade, but it's not a true chocolate. Although quality white chocolates contain a high percentage of cocoa butter, many are made with vegetable oils.

At any rate, white chocolate does not contain chocolate liquor, and the last seminar I attended that covered a discussion of white chocolate indicated that the FDA was still hesitant to allow the name to be used on product labels. Nonetheless, many of us in the trade refer to this product as white chocolate. I use that term frequently in this book.

Odds and Ends: Other Essential Candy Ingredients

Some ingredients come into play only occasionally, but they're very important when they're needed. You can find most of these items in your grocery store. For those harder-to-find ingredients, try checking out the suppliers in Chapter 24. Here are the items that you will occasionally need:

- **Baking soda:** You use baking soda when making brittles (see Chapter 12); this universal powder creates little air pockets for crispness.

- **Citric acid and fruit pectin:** You use these ingredients in fruit jellies (see Chapter 10). The citric acid provides tartness. The pectin has a similar effect to gelatin; it creates the rubbery effect in a jelly candy.

- **Flavored extracts and oils:** These items go beyond regular vanilla extract. Oils are excellent sources of flavoring in candies because they stand up to the heat of cooking; extracts, which are alcohol-based, can evaporate in heat. I use the oil flavorings in jellies and truffles (Chapter 18).

- **Food coloring:** I recommend mostly powdered food colorings in my recipes because I like the ease of measurement. I use these colorings in fruit jellies and for making some decorative toppings.

- **Invertase:** This enzyme is very helpful in maintaining the shelf life of a variety of pieces. You may call it a preservative; I call it a life-saver.

- **Popcorn salt:** This item is useful when making peanut butter meltaways (see Chapter 6) because it's finer than regular table salt, which is important for a smooth piece of candy. Salt in general appears in several different candies to act as a flavor enhancer.

- **Powdered egg white:** This ingredient is essential for making divinity (see Chapter 8), and it's much easier to use than fresh eggs.

- **Soy lecithin:** You use this item in toffee (see Chapter 11). Lecithin, in its role as an emulsifier, prevents fat from separating in a batch.

- **Unflavored gelatin:** This ingredient is important when you make jellies. It causes sugar to gel, forming a rubbery-textured confection.

Part II

Concocting Creamy and Chewy Delights

The 5th Wave   By Rich Tennant

4th OF JULY FAVORITE:
THE CHOCOLATE-COVERED CHERRY BOMB

In this part...

Got a taste for something creamy and chewy today? In this part, you get the chance to create some really popular and time-honored types of candies, including fondant, mints, meltaways, and caramels.

Before you know what's happening, you'll be making fluffy, white divinity as good as any Southern grandmother ever produced. (Okay, don't tell any Southern grandmothers I said that.) But seriously, in this part, you find recipes for making some incredible divinity; a wide variety of rich, creamy fudges; and some amazing marshmallows, jellies, and marzipan.

Chapter 5

Creating a Stir with Fondue

*Y*ou may think of fondue as more of a dessert than a candy. But chocolate fondue is, in essence, a variation of a truffle center, and truffles are just about the fanciest chocolates (see Chapter 18 for the lowdown on truffles). Using that loose definition, fondue seems like a pretty good candy.

Fondue is versatile: You can enjoy it as part of a romantic evening with the one you love or as part of a dinner with friends or family. Some fondue recipes are simple enough that even your children can prepare them — with a little guidance, that is (see Chapter 21 for more kid-friendly treats).

However you choose to enjoy your fondue, the difficult part is making the preparation look like work. Fondue is simple elegance, with the accent on simple. Okay, the accent is also on elegance.

Setting the Fondue Table

Before you invite your best friends for dinner or tell your mate that you have a big evening planned, you need to make several decisions, namely: What am I going to serve at this fondue function, and what equipment do I need? The answers to both those questions are quite simple, as I explain in the upcoming sections.

Choosing a fondue set

When purchasing a fondue set, consider how much you plan to use it. The determining factor for how much you spend should be how often you plan to make fondue. Remember that you can use fondue sets for making more than just desserts; you also can use them to prepare meals, so you aren't limited to only a few uses.

The price range for fondue equipment varies from pretty inexpensive to rather pricey. You can find a very decent stainless set for under $20 at a discount store or you can spend more than $100 at a department or specialty store for a fine copper set. You can find quite a variety of sets between those two price points as well.

Fondue sets (see Figure 5-1) come with a few basic components:

- ✔ **A pot:** The pot holds whatever you're heating.
- ✔ **A stand for the pot:** The pot stand includes a bottom or tray to hold the heating element.
- ✔ **A set of four to eight forks:** The forks are, of course, used to skewer whatever you choose to dip into the pot.

Figure 5-1:
A fondue set
includes a
pot with a
stand and a
set of forks.

You also need to purchase a heating element separately from the fondue set. To heat your fondue set, you can use a small, votive-size candle (commonly called a tea light) or *Sterno,* a fuel that comes in small cans and is available at most grocery stores. Either fuel is good for keeping fondue warm in the pot. Refer to the instructions that come with your fondue pot to determine which heating choice is best for you.

Before you start heating your fondue, set out small serving plates for yourself and your dining partners. Having a regular fork to disengage pieces from the fondue forks is also a good idea.

Getting your dipping treats ready

What you choose to dip into your concoction can run the gamut from bite-size pieces of pound cake to a wide variety of fruits. Strawberries are always a favorite, and don't discount seedless grapes and banana slices as good choices. What you choose to dip in your fondue is pretty much whatever you like and whatever will stay stuck on your fork as you dip. You're limited only by your taste buds!

When selecting items to dip — especially fruits — select pieces that are firm enough to stay on the fork. You want fruits to be ripe but not overripe.

Before you prepare any fondue recipe, make sure that you have everything you need. Nothing spoils a mood quite like discovering that you lack the fuel to heat your pot, except maybe determining that two days ago would have been the right time to use those berries in the refrigerator. If you already have the pot, forks, and fuel you need, make a list of the foods and ingredients you need to get. If necessary, make a quick trip to the store to get what you require.

If you're going to dip fruits that have been refrigerated, remove them from the refrigerator about one hour before you use them so they warm to room temperature and so you can blot away any condensation that forms. If you add this condensation to real chocolate, you run the risk of having the chocolate seize up and become clotted. Always blot items that may contain condensation.

When you use pieces of cake, cut the cake into bite-size pieces and allow them to sit on the counter for a couple of hours, giving the pieces time to firm up a little. Now you're ready to create eye-appealing platters of your fondue treats. I like to make a colorful arrangement of the fruits on one platter and place cake pieces and any other nonfruit pieces on another platter.

Preparing Fondue Smoothly

Before you get going on the following recipes, I want to share some winning tips that guarantee smooth-as-silk fondue.

Most of the recipes in this chapter involve chocolate. For some recipes, you want to melt the chocolate first and add the other ingredients later. If you're using blocks of chocolate, I recommend chopping the chocolate into small pieces (see Chapter 14 for more about chopping chocolate properly). If you're melting chocolate chips, those morsels are small enough already.

Don't confuse the terms *melting* and *tempering*. Tempering, which I explain in great detail in Chapter 14, is primarily for chocolate used as a coating or for molded pieces. Melting chocolate is fine when you're using it as a center or in a fondue, for example.

Melting is really quite simple: Place the chips or the chopped chocolate in a microwaveable bowl and melt the chocolate in the microwave. When you melt chocolate chips, the chips retain their shape even as they melt, so stop the microwave frequently and stir.

To melt chocolate in the microwave, follow these steps:

1. **Heat the chocolate in the microwave on high for about 45 seconds.** Then remove the bowl and stir the chocolate.

2. **Put the bowl back into the microwave for 45 seconds and then heat for 30 seconds at a time, stirring at each break until the chocolate is smooth when you stir it with a spatula.** The chocolate should feel warm to the touch. If you hold the container of chocolate in the palm of your hand and the bowl feels hot, the chocolate is too warm.

Here are some recommended microwave times on the high setting for chocolate, but remember that microwaves vary:

- 4 ounces of chopped milk chocolate: 1 minute and 15 seconds
- 8 ounces of chopped milk chocolate: 1 minute and 30 seconds
- 12 ounces of chopped milk chocolate: 2 minutes
- 16 ounces (or 1 pound) of chopped milk chocolate: 2 minutes and 15 seconds

Other recipes require you to heat cream or another liquid before you whisk in chopped chocolate. In these recipes, the chopped chocolate melts easily in the warm liquid. Heating cream to scalding is covered extensively in Chapter 18 in truffle production. Once you have blended the chocolate, cream, and any other ingredients called for in a fondue recipe, the mixture may be placed in the fondue pot with the fuel source ignited. You want to do this just before you are ready do serve the fondue because the heating elements have limited lives, and the fondue is not improved by simply sitting over heat.

A couple of options are common for heating cream or milk for recipes. When I am blending cream and chopped chocolate, I like to heat the cream or milk in a small saucepan to scalding. *Scalding* is the point at which the cream begins to bubble up but before a full boil. (As cream boils, it bubbles up rapidly and will overflow from the pan. You do not want to reach an active boil.) After the cream reaches scalding, wait about 1 minute; pour the cream into the chopped chocolate, and stir with a spatula to blend.

Fondue through the years

Fondue has been around for hundreds of years and maybe even longer, if you believe the ancient legends about herdsmen who used a similar process. The Swiss usually get credit for inventing fondue, which began with dipping cubes of cheese into heated wine.

Fondue as a dessert originated in 1964 at the New York restaurant Chalet Swiss when a chef by the name of Konrad Egli melted several Swiss chocolate bars and created chocolate fondue. He felt that the combination of chocolate, honey, and almonds in the bar would make a delicious dessert topping. He was right, and many variations on this original theme have been created since.

Fondue reached its peak in the early 1970s, with fondue restaurants and parties that were quite the rage. Fondue's popularity waned after a few years, but now the little meals and chocolate desserts are making a comeback in a big way.

Janet's Romantic Chocolate Sauce

Although my wife Janet has been involved in the candy business for more than 30 years, she doesn't eat a lot of candy. However, she enjoys an occasional bite of dark chocolate, and this fondue recipe is one she likes to prepare for friends. You may appreciate the romantic aspects of a good, rich dark chocolate fondue, which can set the mood, but this one also is good for any occasion that calls for fondue.

Yummy dippers for this fondue include strawberries, raspberries, tangerine slices, stemmed cherries, pound cake pieces, marshmallows, and crisp cookies.

Preparation time: *5 minutes*

Cooking time: *5 minutes*

Yield: *6 servings*

¾ cup evaporated milk

¾ cup light corn syrup

6 tablespoons butter

12 ounces semi-sweet chocolate chips or favorite dark chocolate, chopped

Dipping pieces as desired

1 Combine the milk, corn syrup, and butter in a medium saucepan. Bring the ingredients to a boil, occasionally stirring with a hard rubber spatula to blend.

2 Remove the mixture from the heat, whisk in the chocolate, and stir the mixture until it's smooth, which takes about 30 seconds to blend.

3 Place the mixture in a fondue pot and keep it warm with a fuel source.

Per serving (sauce only): Calories 528 (From Fat 273); Fat 30g (Saturated 19g); Cholesterol 41mg; Sodium 87mg; Carbohydrate 70g (Dietary Fiber 3g); Protein 5g.

Milk Chocolate Fondue

This recipe illustrates one of the key elements of so many candy recipes: making a *ganache,* or a chocolate-cream mixture. After you master the basics of this recipe, you can make substitutions to alter it as you like. Just remember to keep the measurements and proportions the same, and you should achieve similar results.

Great dippers for this fondue include strawberries, raspberries, marshmallows, crisp cookies, and stemmed cherries.

Preparation time: *10 minutes*

Cooking time: *3 to 5 minutes*

Yield: *6 to 8 servings*

½ cup heavy cream

12 ounces milk chocolate, chopped

Optional: 2 to 3 tablespoons brandy, Grand Marnier, or hazelnut liqueur (Instead of liqueur, you may use flavoring, such as a rum flavor)

Dippers as desired

1 In a medium saucepan, slowly heat the heavy cream to scalding (about 180 degrees on a candy thermometer), the stage at which the cream begins to bubble actively. Allow the cream to start bubbling heavily, but do not allow the cream to come to a full boil.

2 Remove the cream from the heat, and whisk in the chopped chocolate until the mixture is blended. This blending should take about 1 minute. You want to be sure that the mixture is smooth with no lumps.

3 Gently whisk in the liqueur until the mixture is smooth; about 15 seconds should be long enough to blend the flavor with the chocolate.

4 Place the mixture in a fondue pot, and keep it warm with a fuel source.

5 Select the first items to dip, and place them on the dipping forks for dipping.

Vary It! *You can substitute your favorite semi-sweet or darker chocolate for the milk chocolate. As you become accustomed to making these recipes, feel free to experiment with different flavoring agents. For instance, you may use 2 teaspoons of instant coffee crystals for a coffee fondue. Instead of using heavy cream (which may be harder to find), you can use whipping cream or half and half.*

Per serving (sauce only): Calories 261 (From Fat 158); Fat 18g (Saturated 9g); Cholesterol 20mg; Sodium 36mg; Carbohydrate 27g (Dietary Fiber 0g); Protein 3g.

Chocolate Cognac Fondue

If you want to add a little punch to your fondue, here's an idea that's sure to please your palate. You can liven up almost any fondue using this method, but don't get carried away: When you add liquid to fondue, you make the sauce thinner, and you surely don't want to lose the taste of the chocolate. Use alcohol in moderation as a flavoring agent.

Preparation time: *5 minutes*

Cooking time: *3 to 5 minutes*

Yield: *6 servings*

1 cup whipping cream	*¼ cup cognac*
4 ounces milk chocolate, chopped	*Dipping pieces as desired*
4 ounces dark chocolate, chopped	

1 In a small saucepan, heat the cream slowly to scalding (about 180 degrees on a candy thermometer). Allow the cream to start the heavy bubbling associated with early stages of boiling, but do not allow the cream to come to a full boil.

2 Remove from heat and whisk in chocolate until mixture is smooth.

3 Add the cognac and stir until the mixture is smooth; about 15 seconds should be enough to blend.

4 Place the mixture in a fondue pot and keep it warm with a fuel source.

Per serving (sauce only): Calories 342 (From Fat 248); Fat 28g (Saturated 16g); Cholesterol 54mg; Sodium 29mg; Carbohydrate 22g (Dietary Fiber 1g); Protein 4g.

Brandy Blizzard

Sometimes you just need a good white chocolate fondue, and this one should satisfy your craving nicely. This recipe is about as simple as a good treat can get!

Strawberries, raspberries, grapes, citrus fruit slices, or pound cake pieces make tasty dippers for this fondue.

Preparation time: *5 to 10 minutes*

Cooking time: *5 minutes*

Yield: *6 servings*

1 pound white chocolate, finely chopped	*2 tablespoons brandy*
1 cup whipping cream	*Dippers as desired*

1 Place the chopped white chocolate in a microwaveable bowl and melt it in the microwave on high, stopping to stir it with a hard rubber spatula every 30 seconds or so. Melting should take about 2 minutes and 15 seconds. Be careful not to overheat the chocolate — remember, melting chocolate retains its shape unless you stir it.

2 In a medium saucepan over low heat, heat the cream to scalding (about 180 degrees on a candy thermometer). At this stage, the cream starts the heavy bubbling associated with the early stages of boiling, but do not allow the cream to come to a full boil. Remove from heat.

3 Slowly pour the melted white chocolate into the cream, whisking to blend. Gently whisk the brandy into the mixture and place the mixture in a fondue pot, keeping it warm with a fuel source.

Per serving (sauce only): Calories 555 (From Fat 350); Fat 39g (Saturated 24g); Cholesterol 70mg; Sodium 83mg; Carbohydrate 46g (Dietary Fiber 0g); Protein 5g.

The following fondue recipe involves caramel, and you need to melt the caramel before you blend in the other ingredients. You can melt caramel in the microwave or over the stovetop.

- ✔ To melt caramel in the microwave, place the caramel in a microwaveable bowl and heat on high for about 30 to 45 seconds. You want to heat it to approximately 160 degrees on a candy thermometer. Remember, you're melting, not cooking, the caramel.

- ✔ To melt your caramel in a saucepan on top of the stove, place your caramel over low heat and stir fairly constantly because scorching caramels is quite easy to do. You want to heat the caramel to about 160 degrees on a candy thermometer, so check the temperature regularly because direct heat can quickly elevate the caramel's temperature.

After the caramel reaches 160 degrees, stir in your other ingredients. Keep the mixture on low heat while mixing and, when smooth, transfer to the fondue pot. If the mixture thickens, add 1 tablespoon of additional milk and stir it in to blend. Keep the fondue warm in the fondue pot by using the recommended fuels for heating purposes.

If you dip a rubber spatula into the caramel and lift it up, the caramel should fall in a smooth, steady flow back into the bowl. If the caramel is too cool, it will not flow. If the caramel is too hot, it will have a runny, thin flow, almost like water.

Creamy Caramel Fondue Sauce

For this recipe, you may use a commercial individually wrapped caramel or one of the bulk caramels available from the suppliers I identify in Chapter 24. You may even use one of the caramels made using the recipes in Chapter 7. The choice is up to you, but the following recipe is really simple in any case.

Creamy Caramel Fondue Sauce makes a great dip for slices of Granny Smith or other tart apples, marshmallows rolled in chopped almonds or pecans, and pieces of pound cake.

Preparation time: *8 minutes*

Cooking time: *3 to 5 minutes*

Yield: *4 servings*

1 pound caramel	*2 tablespoons butter*
4 tablespoons milk	*Dippers as desired*

1 Place the caramel in a microwaveable bowl to heat in the microwave or place it in a saucepan to heat over the stovetop. If using the microwave, heat the caramel on high until it reaches approximately 160 degrees on a candy thermometer (this temperature produces a good consistency). The melting time should take from 2 to 3 minutes; remember to stop every 45 seconds to stir the caramel. Ovens vary greatly, so check with a thermometer as you stop to stir during the melting. If you choose to heat the caramel over the stovetop, clip a thermometer to the side of the pan and cook the caramel until it reaches 160 degrees.

2 Stir in the milk and butter and mix with a hard rubber spatula until the mixture is consistent. Blending the milk and melting the butter should take about 30 seconds.

3 Place the mixture in a fondue pot and keep the sauce warm with a fuel source.

Per serving (sauce only): Calories 493 (From Fat 138); Fat 15g (Saturated 11g); Cholesterol 25mg; Sodium 286mg; Carbohydrate 88g (Dietary Fiber 1); Protein 6g.

Safely Storing the Leftovers

Okay, so sometimes you won't finish eating your entire pot of fondue, and you'll have some leftovers. Don't despair: You can safely refrigerate your fondue to enjoy another day.

After you finish your fondue and, assuming that you have some leftovers, you can save the remaining portion. Pour the unused fondue into a plastic storage container (complete with a tight-fitting lid) and store immediately in the refrigerator. If you think that the fondue is still too warm, let it cool for a few minutes.

When storing your leftover fondue, keep in mind that fondue usually contains milk products, so it has a limited storage time. Also, before you refrigerate fondue, check the sauce to make sure that no fruit or other dipping pieces have fallen off someone's fork. Although you can safely store the fondue for two days or so, you really don't want to take a chance on a piece of fresh fruit molding (because fruit can have a shorter shelf life than the fondue).

If you have a large volume of leftovers — clearly your friends aren't eating enough — you can pour the fondue into a plastic food container and freeze it. Then slip that into a freezer bag and seal tightly. You can store your fondue for up to six months.

Chapter 6

Focusing on Fondant, Mints, and Meltaways

*F*ondant, a mixture of sucrose (a form of sugar), corn syrup, and water, is a simple candy. It is a primary ingredient in the candy-making process, and several confections use fondant in their recipes.

In this chapter, I tell you how to make basic fondant and use it as an ingredient in mints and meltaways. *Meltaways* are a simple candy that you produce by adding fat to chocolate, which creates a very soft piece that you usually use as a center; then you coat the piece with chocolate. You also use fondant in making divinity, but I tell you about that in Chapter 8.

A Fondness for Fondant

When making candy, knowing how to make fondant is useful because you may need only a small amount for a recipe, and you can't just run to the grocery store and buy a pound of it. Sometimes you can purchase small amounts of commercially made fondant, but that task can prove difficult because this product is usually sold in pails. However, you can quite easily produce a small amount of fondant at home using one of the recipes in this section.

To produce most types of fondant, you cook sugar, corn syrup, and water and beat the cooled mixture into a creamy paste. You may find a fondant recipe that includes other ingredients, but the three primary ingredients are the ones listed here. In any case, follow the simple instructions in the recipe, and you've made a prime ingredient for a number of mouthwatering candies.

When making fondant, accurately measuring your ingredients is important because changing their ratios greatly affects the texture of the fondant. Adding too much sugar in relation to the syrup and water produces a harder, drier fondant that doesn't blend well when used in a recipe. Likewise, a fondant that's too thin doesn't provide enough density for the candy you're making to stand up.

When using confectioners' sugar in your fondant, watch out for lumps. You probably don't need to sift the sugar; just be careful as you pour or measure the sugar that you break up any lumps. If you leave the lumps in, they may not dissolve or break up during production, and you will have unmixed pockets of sugar in your fondant, which produces a different product that can affect the outcome of the recipe that you're preparing.

The fondant in recipes like mints (which I show you later in this chapter) and divinity (which you can find in Chapter 8) give the recipes the structure that allows the final candy to maintain its shape.

In this chapter, you can make fondant using two different methods:

- ✔ **Easy no-cook fondant:** This recipe is just as it sounds: You mix the ingredients without cooking to produce a very simple but useful fondant.

- ✔ **Basic fondant:** This recipe combines the three typical ingredients in a fondant: sugar, corn syrup, and water. After cooking the batch, you work the mass on a marble slab and use utensils and a little elbow grease to create a fondant. In this process, you work the fondant with a scraper until it reaches the right consistency, which takes only about 7 to 10 minutes to complete (see Figure 6-1).

If you're unable to get a marble slab, you can use a *silpat,* which is a versatile item made of silicone and fiberglass.

Figure 6-1:
Use a metal scraper to work your fondant on a slab until it becomes opaque.

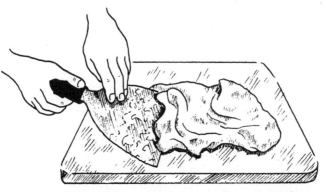

WORKING FONDANT WITH A SCRAPER

Easy No-cook Fondant

This method is very easy for producing fondant (as the name suggests), so this recipe is a good place to get your first taste of fondant, so to speak. You can make and store this fondant for use in other recipes, too.

Preparation time: *15 minutes*

Yield: *1½ pounds fondant (8 servings)*

⅓ cup softened butter	1 teaspoon vanilla extract
⅓ cup corn syrup	2 cups confectioners' sugar, sifted
½ teaspoon salt	

1 Place the butter, syrup, salt, and vanilla extract in a mixing bowl and mix with a stand mixer on slow speed for 2 to 3 minutes to blend well.

2 When the mixture is consistent and with the mixer on slow speed, slowly add the powdered sugar, allowing the sugar to blend with the mixture a little at a time, taking about 4 to 5 minutes to blend the sugar into the batch.

3 When you've mixed in all the powdered sugar, scrape the sides of the bowl with a rubber spatula to ensure even blending.

4 If you don't plan to use the fondant immediately, wrap it in plastic wrap to prevent drying and place it in an airtight plastic container for two to three months.

Per serving: Calories 222 (From Fat 68); Fat 8g (Saturated 5g); Cholesterol 20mg; Sodium 163mg; Carbohydrate 40g (Dietary Fiber 0g); Protein 0g.

The term "softened butter" occurs frequently in recipes like the previous one. When you see this ingredient, remove the butter from the refrigerator at least one hour before you need to use it. Open the wrapper, cut the needed portion into tablespoon-size pieces, and allow the butter to warm to room temperature. Softening allows the butter to blend smoothly throughout the mixture; it isn't a melting or liquefying process.

Basic Fondant

With this recipe, you do some basic cooking using techniques that large-scale candy makers in real candy kitchens use. After you make the fondant in this recipe, you'll be able to make a number of other products in this book. For example, you use fondant to make the mints in this chapter and the divinity and the nougat center for the pecan rolls, both in Chapter 8. Although fondant is considered a candy, for your purposes, fondant is also an ingredient for making other candies.

Tools: *Small marble slab*

Preparation time: *20 to 25 minutes plus 50 minutes of cooling time*

Yield: *1½ pounds of fondant (8 servings)*

Approximately 1 tablespoon butter to grease pan

2½ cups sugar

½ cup corn syrup

1½ cups water

1 Lightly butter a 9 x 13-inch baking pan and dampen it slightly with water. Set aside.

2 Combine the sugar, syrup, and water in a medium saucepan over medium heat, stirring occasionally with a wooden spoon.

3 When the sugar dissolves (usually after about 10 minutes), cover the pan for 5 minutes to allow the sugar to wash down the sides.

4 After 5 minutes, remove the cover, clip a candy thermometer to the inside of the pan — being certain that the tip of the thermometer doesn't touch the bottom of the pan — and cook the mixture to 240 degrees. Total cooking time for the batch falls between 20 and 25 minutes.

5 Remove the pan from the heat and pour the contents into the greased 9 x 13-inch baking pan.

6 Lightly sprinkle water on top of the fondant and allow the fondant to cool at room temperature to 125 degrees. Cooling takes about 40 to 45 minutes in a 72-degree kitchen.

7 Place the fondant mixture on a small marble slab (one that measures at least 12 x 12 inches) and work the mixture with a metal scraper by folding, chopping, and refolding it until it becomes opaque and crumbly. Working the fondant on the slab usually takes about 7 to 10 minutes.

Per serving: Calories 312 (From Fat 13); Fat 1g (Saturated 1g); Cholesterol 4mg; Sodium 26mg; Carbohydrate 78g (Dietary Fiber 0g); Protein 0g.

I assume that you will occasionally make your fondant for use at a future date. When the fondant has cooled at room temperature, wrap it in plastic kitchen wrap and store it in a plastic storage container at room temperature for six to eight months. Although you may store the fondant for such a period, I like to think that you would use this small amount in a shorter period of time. Fondant stores well for an extended period and, because you're not making a huge batch at a time, I don't suggest freezing it.

Make Me More Mints

Sometimes you just have to have a mint. And it just so happens that I have a couple of very good mint recipes coming up right here. Both these recipes require that you coat the mints in chocolate, but is any combination more tempting to your taste buds than mint and dark chocolate? Okay, at some point in the book, I may imply that nothing beats the combination of chocolate and peanut butter. But for right now, we're talking about mints, so I don't want to hear about your peanut butter fetish.

The mint is a symbol of freshness, of the outdoors, or of a beautiful spring morning. Can peanut butter conjure up feelings of the great outdoors? I don't think it does. Can the lowly goober freshen your breath before a kiss? Get serious. In the following sections, I tell you everything you need to know about making delightful, fresh mints.

Looking at the ingredients of mints

As delightful a flavor as mint is, always keep in mind that a little mint goes a long way. When I use mint oil — which is an excellent source of flavor that you can purchase from one of the suppliers I list in Chapter 24 — I use ¼ teaspoon or even less for 2 to 2½ pounds of chocolate. So when measuring mint oil, use it sparingly and taste to be certain that the amount you use is what you want in the final product.

Of course, with a little practice, you can substitute fresh mint as a flavor in some candies. In Chapter 18, I show you a steeping process to infuse cream with a natural mint flavor into truffles.

When flavoring a candy, what matters is the taste that pleases you. If you desire a milder flavor, use oil flavors accordingly. They're your taste buds, so don't be afraid to experiment to find what you like better.

Another ingredient I often mention in these recipes is invertase. *Invertase* is an enzyme that controls bacterial growth and acts as a preservative. It extends the shelf life of many candies, including mints.

Sometimes you can make a type of candy using more than one method or even using different ingredients. For example, I previously mentioned that the three primary ingredients of fondant are sugar, corn syrup, and water (see "A Fondness for Fondant" earlier in this chapter). However, I show you a recipe that isn't based solely on those ingredients because I want you to understand that there are different means of achieving a similar end. Take one of the mint recipes — which is really a type of fondant candy — in this chapter; it contains no corn syrup. Instead, it uses gelatin, which simply gives the mint a little structure (similar to what corn syrup would do) to keep the center from becoming crumbly.

Piping your mint centers

You can easily form your mint centers using a technique called piping. To *pipe,* you simply fill a paper or plastic cone-shaped bag that has a hole on the end (a *piping bag*) with your mixture so you can squeeze the mixture out of the bag into a shell or for a variety of other purposes. For instance, piping is a useful way to write on candy, using chocolate as the "ink." You can also pipe fillings for mints and other fancy chocolates (see Chapter 18).

You can purchase piping bags from most of the suppliers that sell other candy-making or baking supplies. I list some of these suppliers in Chapter 24. I recommend getting the simplest piping bags: fairly inexpensive, disposable, plastic cone-shaped bags. Suppliers usually sell these bags in small packages of 25 or so. When you use a piping bag, use scissors to cut a small hole in the bottom of the bag so you can squeeze the contents out through the hole.

If you need to pipe something and simply don't have any piping bags or the time to go get any, fill a closable freezer bag with the filling, seal the bag, and snip off one corner — but be sure you make a small snip.

To pipe like a pro, just follow these easy steps and check out Figure 6-2:

1. **Use a disposable cone-shaped plastic bag that's about 12 to 14 inches in length for the greatest ease.**

2. **Cut off the tip of the bag to create a tiny hole.**

3. **Place your mint mixture in the bag, filling the bag (halfway to ⅔ full), and twist the bag closed.**

4. **To pipe the mixture evenly, use one hand to hold the bag and the other to guide the tip.**

5. **To refill the bag for continued piping, set the bag down so the mixture doesn't run out the little hole as you fill from the top.**

Figure 6-2:
You can use a plastic piping bag with a hole in the tip to easily pipe mints.

FORMING WAFERS WITH A PIPING BAG

Creating marvelous mints

Okay, enough talking about mints and how good they are. I think it's time for you to make some delicious mint candies. Before you start, be sure to check out Chapter 14 on tempering chocolate and Chapter 15 on dipping methods because the following two recipes require hand-dipping your mint delights in chocolate.

Fondant Mint Wafers

For those occasions when you want a delicious little mint, this recipe is really quite nice. It shows you how a basic fondant recipe with a few additions becomes a truly delicious candy.

Tools: *Piping bag for making wafers*

Preparation time: *20 to 25 minutes plus at least 30 minutes for cooling*

Yield: *35 to 40 wafers*

1 tablespoon butter

2 tablespoons plus 1 cup water

¼ teaspoon unflavored gelatin

4 cups sugar

⅛ teaspoon mint oil

⅛ teaspoon invertase

Green food coloring as desired

About 1½ pounds dark chocolate, chopped and melted for tempering

1 Lightly butter a 9 x 13-inch baking pan and sprinkle it with water to slightly dampen it. Set aside.

2 Put 2 tablespoons of water into a small cup; sprinkle the gelatin into the water and set aside.

3 Put the sugar and 1 cup of water in a large saucepan and bring the ingredients to a boil, stirring occasionally to dissolve the sugar. Cover the saucepan for 3 minutes to allow the water to wash the sugar down the sides of the pan.

4 Remove the lid and clip a candy thermometer to the inside of the pan, being sure that the tip doesn't touch the bottom of the pan. Cook the mixture to 245 degrees for about 15 to 20 minutes. Then remove from heat, remove the thermometer, and stir in the gelatin.

5 Pour the mixture into the baking pan; sprinkle water lightly on top. Cool to 105 degrees, which takes about 1 hour to 1 hour and 15 minutes at room temperature.

6 Work the mixture with a scraper on a marble slab until the batch is opaque and crumbly; this step takes about 7 to 10 minutes.

7 Line a large cookie sheet with wax paper and set aside.

8 In a microwave, warm the mixture in a microwaveable bowl on high to 150 degrees, stopping every 45 seconds to stir. This step should take about 3 minutes, but microwaves vary.

9 Add the mint oil and a couple of drops of green food coloring to make green mints. Stir about 1 minute and add the invertase; then stir again for about 1 minute.

10 Put the mixture into a piping bag and pipe it into discs approximately 1½ inches in diameter onto a lined cookie sheet.

11 When the wafers are firm — after usually about 1 hour at room temperature — remove them from the cookie sheet. Now you're ready to hand-dip them in dark chocolate.

12 Temper the chocolate (see Chapter 14) and then hand-dip the mints using the technique I describe in Chapter 15. Place each piece on a wax-paper–lined cookie sheet to dry for about 5 minutes at room temperature, but allow another 10 minutes for the chocolate to set.

Tip: If you don't have time to complete the whole recipe, you can easily store the mint mixture until you're ready to dip it into the chocolate. Just place the mixture in an airtight plastic container and store it for up to one week at room temperature. If you want to store the undipped mints longer, carefully place them in a freezer bag before placing them in the plastic container, and freeze for up to three weeks.

Per serving: Calories 107 (From Fat 23); Fat 3g (Saturated 1g); Cholesterol 1mg; Sodium 0mg; Carbohydrate 23g (Dietary Fiber 0g); Protein 1g.

Fondant Mint Cream Centers

The fondant mint cream I describe in this recipe is of the same type as the cream centers in Chapter 17. But I placed the recipe here to show how you can combine fondant and mint to create a delightful cream candy.

Preparation time: *1 hour plus 1½ hours to cool and 10 minutes for chocolate to set after dipping*

Yield: *Approximately 60 centers*

1½ pounds fondant from Basic Fondant recipe earlier in this chapter	Green food coloring as desired
⅛ teaspoon mint oil	1 pound dark chocolate, chopped and melted for tempering
⅛ teaspoon invertase	

1 Line the top of a counter with about a 3-foot to 4-foot sheet of wax paper for the finished chocolate-coated mints.

2 Place the fondant in a microwaveable bowl and carefully warm it to 150 degrees on a candy thermometer in the microwave on high power, stopping every 35 seconds to stir, for a total of about 3 minutes.

3 Add the mint oil and food coloring. Then stir the ingredients with a hard rubber spatula to mix. Add the invertase and work it into the batch until the mixture is blended smoothly.

4 Allow the mixture to cool to room temperature for about 1½ hours. Then form it into centers approximately ¾ inch in diameter, rolling into balls in your hands.

5 Temper the dark chocolate (see Chapter 14 for tempering information).

6 Dip the candies into tempered dark chocolate. Then place them on the counter lined with the wax paper and allow them to set for about 6 minutes. Allow another 5 to 10 minutes before eating for a better set of the chocolate.

Per serving: Calories 69 (From Fat 17); Fat 2g (Saturated 1g); Cholesterol 1mg; Sodium 4mg; Carbohydrate 14g (Dietary Fiber 0g); Protein 0g.

Keeping your mints safe

The chocolate-coated mints you make using this chapter's recipes have an excellent shelf life when kept at room temperature (about four to five weeks when stored in a plastic container at room temperature). If you stack the mints, you need to separate the layers with wax paper. You don't need to refrigerate them; instead, place your mints in a plastic container or even a simple box for two weeks to protect them from the elements. If one of the elements is your husband, you want to hide them as well to extend your batch's life.

Refrigerating — as many folks think you should do — can cause more harm than good. When you store candies in the refrigerator, you risk condensation problems and, when the chocolates aren't stored properly, they pick up odors from other foods. Chocolate is a natural sponge that absorbs the odors of the neighborhood.

If you need to store candy for a long period of time, freezing is better. Carefully place the mints in a freezer bag, and place small sheets of wax paper between the layers. Then place the candies in another freezer bag and freeze. You can usually freeze candies for up to six months in this fashion. Personally, I've never been able to hide something from myself for that long.

To thaw your mints, allow them to sit at least eight hours at room temperature. After the candy thaws, remove it from the freezer bags. This procedure prevents condensation from forming during the thawing process.

Mastering Meltaways

If you've ever bitten into a piece of chocolate, and the inside was a creamy, rich, delicious center that you knew wasn't a cream or a truffle, well, it may have been a meltaway. These pieces have several names (including "velvets"), but a meltaway is really a very simple piece of candy. Chocolate or peanut butter chips or some similarly textured piece is melted and combined with a liquid fat to make a piece that literally melts in your mouth.

Now that I told you that bit about the fat, I want you to forget about it. Good candies are delightful to bite into and to savor in our mouths, and that mouthfeel comes from the pleasant sensation derived from the texture derived from fat. Well, I know I said to forget about it, and there I go talking about it again — sorry.

A primer on mixing up meltaways

Putting together a meltaway batch is pretty simple. Most meltaway recipes involve the combination of two primary ingredients: chocolate and fat. To get a yummy meltaway, you need to

- **Liquefy and slightly warm the fat portion.** The added fat in meltaways can come from several sources, including cocoa butter and coconut oil. (Confectioners commonly use coconut oil.) What fat source you use is usually a matter of price because cocoa butter is more expensive than coconut oil. Coconut oil is sold as 76-degree coconut oil or 92-degree coconut oil, the names of which reflect the melting points of the oil. I recommend using the 76-degree oil because that's what I use in my candies. You can purchase small quantities of this product at health-food stores.

- **Chop some chocolate.** In a meltaway, the ratio of chocolate to fat is 4 to 1. When a recipe calls for chopped chocolate, use a kitchen scale to weigh the chocolate. If you want, you can carefully microwave the chopped chocolate to add to the fat because you don't use tempered chocolate in a center.

Some recipes, like the one for Peanut Butter Meltaways, don't call for chopped chocolate as part of their base. However, all the recipes in this section do call for tempered chocolate for dipping, so be sure to review Chapter 14 on tempering and Chapter 15 on dipping before you try any of the recipes.

I show you two different methods to create these meltaways: microwaving and melting in a double boiler. When using a double boiler to liquefy the coconut oil, as you will frequently do when making a meltaway, remove the top pot of the double boiler carefully and wipe the bottom with a dry towel before pouring the mixture into a pan. Doing so prevents water from getting into your candy. You surely don't want water to get into your chocolate because it causes the chocolate to *seize,* meaning that the chocolate instantly turns into an ugly thick blob that's virtually unusable.

From there, blend the chocolate with the melted coconut oil in the double boiler and pour this mixture into a pan, allowing it to cool before cutting and dipping it. You can cut a batch of meltaways with a kitchen knife by lightly scoring marks about 1 inch apart on each side of the batch and simply cutting straight lines across both ways (see Figure 6-3). Cutting your meltaways like this produces 64 squares in an 8 x 8-inch pan.

SCORING AND CUTTING MELTAWAYS

1. USE A STRAIGHT KNIFE TO SCORE LINES, 1" APART.

2. CUT THE LINES CAREFULLY!

Figure 6-3:
You can use a kitchen knife to carefully score and cut meltaways.

To store meltaways, follow the same procedure as you used in mint storage (see "Keeping your mints safe" earlier in this chapter for the scoop). Once again: Keep away from the husband unless, of course, the wife is the problem. Then the kids may like candy as well . . .

Tasty meltaways to try

Some folks call these candies "velvets" or maybe other smooth-sounding names, but I call them meltaways. Whatever the name, this piece melts in your mouth, delivering a most pleasant *mouthfeel* (the sensation of something melting in your mouth).

You produce this candy's mouthfeel by adding fat to the chocolate. I know, "adding fat" isn't a particularly pleasant expression; nevertheless, this addition gives this candy its tasty sensation. As a rule, I recommend having about 20 percent added fat by weight (based on the weight of the chocolate), or 4 ounces of fat added to every pound of chocolate. However, not all meltaways have chocolate centers. Peanut butter meltaways are among the most popular, and peanut butter brings its own fat to the party, so you shouldn't feel so guilty about adding fat to the chocolate centers.

Peanut Butter Meltaways

Certainly one of the most popular candy-flavor combinations is peanut butter and chocolate. (If I tell you somewhere in this chapter that chocolate and mint are one of the most popular combinations, get over it. We're talking about chocolate and peanut butter now — everybody's *real* favorite.) This pairing is available in a number of ways, but one of the most delicious is the chocolate-covered peanut butter meltaway (shown in the color section).

One special ingredient that this recipe calls for is popcorn salt. *Popcorn salt* is a very fine salt, and it's great for making such a smooth piece of candy. You can find popcorn salt in your grocery store. So now that you have your popcorn salt in hand, get ready to make this delightful candy.

Preparation time: *1 hour plus 30 minutes to cool*

Yield: *64 pieces*

12-ounce package of peanut butter chips	*1½ pounds of milk chocolate, chopped and melted for tempering*
1 cup creamy peanut butter	
1 teaspoon popcorn salt	

1 Line an 8 x 8-inch baking pan with wax paper and set aside. Place a sheet of wax paper that's about 3 feet long on the counter; you'll use the paper when dipping the pieces in chocolate and cooling them.

2 Place the peanut butter chips in a microwaveable bowl and melt them in a microwave, heating on high power for about 50 to 60 seconds. Stir the chips at 25 seconds and at the end until they have a smooth consistency.

3 Add the peanut butter and salt to the melted chips and mix with a rubber spatula until consistent; mixing takes about 1 minute.

4 Using a hard rubber spatula, scrape the mixture into the 8 x 8-inch baking pan and allow the mixture to cool in the refrigerator for 30 minutes. Remove the mixture from the refrigerator and test it with your finger to be certain that it's firm.

5 Grasp the corners of the wax paper in the pan and lift the entire slab out for easier cutting, and cut into 64 pieces.

6 Temper the milk chocolate (see Chapter 14).

7 Hand-dip the candies in the milk chocolate.

8 Allow the candies to cool at room temperature for 30 minutes, although the chocolate should be set in about 6 minutes.

> ***Tip:*** *For a different consistency, use chunky peanut butter rather than creamy or use creamy peanut butter and add 2 ounces of crisp rice cereal.*

Per serving: *Calories 80 (From Fat 46); Fat 5g (Saturated 3g); Cholesterol 0mg; Sodium 71mg; Carbohydrate 7g (Dietary Fiber 1g); Protein 3g.*

Mint Meltaways

Just as peanut butter and chocolate go great together, so do dark chocolate and mint. Try the following recipe to see for yourself.

Preparation time: *1 hour plus 30 minutes of cooling*

Yield: *64 pieces*

¼ cup 76-degree coconut oil

1 pound dark chocolate, finely chopped

¼ teaspoon mint oil

1½ pounds dark chocolate, chopped and melted for tempering for dipping the pieces

1 Line an 8 x 8-inch baking pan with wax paper and set aside. Be sure the paper is smooth to prevent unsightly wrinkles on the bottom of the pieces. Then line the top of the counter with about 3 feet of wax paper for the dipped pieces to set on.

2 Place the coconut oil in a double boiler and slowly melt it over low heat until the oil liquefies, which takes about 30 minutes. (You can speed the process by first placing the oil in a microwaveable bowl and microwaving it in 10-second increments; then stir it at each stop for 30 seconds. Do not let your oil reach more than 100 degrees.) Then place the oil in the top of the double boiler.

3 Slowly add the chopped chocolate to the oil and gently whisk to blend; the chocolate should melt in about 7 minutes. Stir in the mint oil, and stir 30 seconds to blend well with the chocolate mixture.

4 Remove the top of the double boiler and dry the bottom to prevent any water from falling into the pan with the chocolate mixture when you pour.

5 Using a hard rubber spatula, scrape the mixture into the baking pan, and allow the mixture to cool or place it in the refrigerator for 20 to 30 minutes.

6 When the mixture is firm (not hard), score the edges and cut it into 64 pieces.

7 Temper the chocolate as I describe in Chapter 14.

8 Hand-dip the candies in dark chocolate to coat and place the pieces on wax paper to set. Allow 15 minutes for a nice firm set.

Per serving: Calories 69 (From Fat 54); Fat 6g (Saturated 4g); Cholesterol 0mg; Sodium 0mg; Carbohydrate 6g (Dietary Fiber 0g); Protein 1g.

Chocolate Meltaways

Sometimes you just want a piece of chocolate that melts in your mouth like an ice cube in the desert sun. Well, this candy is that piece. When you make this simple little melt-away batch and coat it in chocolate, you'll think that you're an all-pro candy maker.

Preparation time: 1 hour plus 30 minutes for cooling

Yield: 64 pieces

¼ cup 76-degree coconut oil

1 pound milk chocolate, finely chopped

1 pound milk chocolate, chopped and melted for tempering to coat pieces

1 Line an 8 x 8-inch baking pan with wax paper and set aside. Place a 3-foot piece of wax paper on the counter to set dipped pieces on.

2 Place the coconut oil in a double boiler and slowly melt it over low heat until the oil liquefies, which takes about 30 minutes. (You can speed the process by first placing the oil in a microwaveable bowl and microwaving it in 10-second increments; then stir it at each stop for 30 seconds. Do not let your oil reach more than 100 degrees.) Then place the oil in the top of the double boiler.

3 Slowly add the chopped chocolate to the oil and gently whisk to blend ingredients; whisking takes about 7 minutes.

4 Remove the top pan of the double boiler and dry the bottom to prevent any water from falling into the pan with the chocolate mixture when you pour.

5 Using a hard rubber spatula, scrape the mixture into a baking pan and allow it to cool or place it in the refrigerator for 20 minutes.

6 When the mixture is firm (not hard), score the edges and cut it into 64 pieces.

7 Temper the chocolate as Chapter 14 describes.

8 Hand-dip the candies in tempered milk chocolate to coat. Then place the candies on wax paper to set. Allow them to set for about 15 minutes for a nice firm set.

Per serving: Calories 70 (From Fat 40); Fat 5g (Saturated 3g); Cholesterol 0mg; Sodium 9mg; Carbohydrate 8g (Dietary Fiber 0g); Protein 1g.

Chocolate Orange Bites

This recipe is similar to the previous one, but this recipe has a delightful orange flavor and an orange marking. Don't worry — I show you a simple technique to *string* (or drizzle) colors or contrasting chocolate on a piece.

Preparation time: *1 hour plus 30 minutes to cool*

Yield: *64 pieces*

¼ cup 76-degree coconut oil

1 pound milk chocolate, finely chopped

¼ teaspoon orange oil

1½ pounds milk chocolate, chopped and melted for tempering for dipping

3 ounces white chocolate, chopped

Orange food coloring as desired

1 Line an 8 x 8-inch baking pan with wax paper and set aside. Place a 3-foot piece of wax paper on the counter where the finished pieces can dry.

2 Place the coconut oil in a microwaveable bowl for two 10-second increments to nearly melt the oil. Place the oil in top of a double boiler over low heat to liquefy it.

3 Slowly add the chocolate to the coconut oil and gently whisk the ingredients for about 7 minutes to melt the chocolate and to blend. Stir in the orange oil to blend.

4 Remove the top pan of the double boiler and dry the bottom to prevent any water from falling into the chocolate pan when you pour.

5 Scrape the mixture into a baking pan using a hard rubber spatula and allow the mixture to cool or place in the refrigerator for 20 minutes.

6 When the mixture is firm (not hard), score the edges and cut into 64 pieces.

7 Temper the milk chocolate as Chapter 14 describes.

8 Hand-dip the candy in tempered milk chocolate to coat. Place the pieces on wax paper to set for about 6 minutes.

9 In a microwave, melt the white chocolate in a microwaveable bowl to about 94 degrees, which takes about 50 to 60 seconds on high. Do not overheat the chocolate.

10 Add the orange food coloring as desired to the white chocolate; stir to blend. Drizzle thin lines over the dipped pieces using a salad fork and quickly shake the orange-tipped fork back and forth to mark the pieces (see Figure 6-4).

11 Place the pieces on wax paper to cool. They should set in about 10 minutes.

Vary it! *To make Raspberry Delights, use raspberry flavoring and red food coloring instead of orange.*

Per serving: *Calories 78 (From Fat 44); Fat 5g (Saturated 3g); Cholesterol 1mg; Sodium 10mg; Carbohydrate 9g (Dietary Fiber 0g); Protein 1g.*

Figure 6-4:
A fork is a
simple and
easy tool to
use to string
(drizzle) the
white
chocolate
on a
meltaway.

Chapter 7

Caramel Contentment

Even a short list of the most popular candies found in any candy assortment would have caramels near the top. You find caramel in so many different types of candy, and it's used in so many ways that I can't comprehend how I could make any assortment without including caramel.

Caramel use has grown as manufacturers have found new and easier ways to present this wonderful candy to you in ever-more-tempting confections. Nothing compares to biting into a simple-looking piece of chocolate and discovering that chewy center, so rich and buttery. How many apples have you eaten that have been coated with that same tasty goodness? And I don't believe a nut exists that hasn't been draped with sticky caramel. Caramel is literally the connecting confection that makes so many favorite candies possible!

Suffice it to say that caramel is a superstar in the world of confections, and you don't have to have dozens of recipes to enjoy the variety of results it produces. In my business, we use one recipe for virtually everything we make with caramel. So in this chapter, I introduce you to a few methods and applications of caramel that especially stress its versatility.

Cooking Up Caramels Slowly but Surely

Although variations exist from batch to batch in any confection, some of the primary ingredients in a caramel batch include sugar; corn syrup; shortening (one source of fat in the candies); and some form of milk, cream, and butter or all three. The milk products, which are the most important ingredients, are a primary source of fat in a caramel, which gives the confection that delightful texture, and the cooking of the milk solids gives caramel its color.

In caramel recipes, the proportion of corn syrup to sugar is usually 1:1 or higher. Typically, a recipe has to contain more syrup than sugar for the simplest of reasons: The excess syrup prevents the caramel from graining, which causes a visible gritty, unattractive appearance in the caramel. You can also get a graining effect in your caramel even with proper proportions if some of the sugar crystals don't dissolve in the cooking process. For this reason, I recommend washing down the inside of a pot at boiling (see Figure 7-1) so any undissolved sugar crystals on the sides of the pot mix with the rest of the batch. Covering the pot for a minute or two has the same effect because the steam generated within the pot dissolves any remaining crystals.

Figure 7-1:
Wash down the sides of a saucepan using a pastry brush and a cup of hot water.

WASHING DOWN SUGAR

☆ KEEP A CUP OF WATER + A PASTRY BRUSH NEAR THE STOVE.

1. WHEN THE SUGAR HAS DISSOLVED, 'WASH DOWN' ANY CRYSTALS THAT REMAIN. DIP THE BRUSH IN WATER.

2. PLACE ON THE SIDE OF THE PAN JUST ABOVE SYRUP AND GENTLY 'PUSH' CRYSTALS DOWN ↓ WITH WATER.

3. WET BRUSH AS NEEDED. CONTINUE ALL THE WAY AROUND THE PAN.

When washing the inside of a pot, be aware that boiling candy is very volatile, and it may splash your hands — especially when you introduce water to the solution. To avoid burning yourself, you may want to put a glove on your hand during the washing process.

When measuring the ingredients for the recipe you're making, measure carefully. Don't estimate the amounts of your ingredients because cooking is a system of chemical reactions. If you don't have the proper proportions in your ingredients, you may generate the wrong reaction.

Large candy factories and even smaller candy kitchens cook their caramel in some type of kettle, usually a large copper kettle. But the typical household doesn't usually have space for such a large cooking utensil; at least, that's true of the folks whom I know. Nevertheless, not having such equipment doesn't preclude you from producing a wonderful caramel. Instead of using a 50-gallon copper kettle, you can produce your candy in a large 4- to 5-quart saucepan on your stove

When cooking your caramel, you also need to pay attention to your temperature. You want to cook your caramel to a final temperature of 234 degrees, and I recommend using a candy thermometer because accuracy in your temperature is important. By cooking on low or medium heat, you allow for a gradual rise in the temperature. This gradual rise lets you remove the pot from the heat with the candy at the proper temperature and prevents scorching. You don't want to cook your caramel too quickly. Ideally, you want to cook it for 20 to 25 minutes after the batch comes to a boil to allow a good full flavor to develop. But if you cook your caramel too fast, you can overshoot your target temperature simply because the extremely hot candy continues to cook a little even after you remove the pot from the heat source due to the ambient heat of the batch and the hot pot. Cooking a little slower allows you to stop the cooking at the end point. A higher temperature results in a tougher, harder-to-chew candy that you may not enjoy. So be a little patient, and your palate will be pleased with the results.

Constantly stirring your caramel as you cook it is essential once the batch reaches the boiling point. Without proper agitation, the high milk content in a good batch of caramel can cause scorching because milk products burn very easily. Stirring the caramel by hand is adequate, but you must continue stirring throughout the entire cooking process once the batch has reached boiling. Of course, you could learn the hard way — but you don't want to do that, right?

When a batch reaches its target temperature, remove it from the heat source because the batch will continue cooking even if you've turned off the heat. Even the ambient heat of the pot continues to cook the caramel.

Trying Your Hand at Basic Caramels

The joy of biting into a piece of candy with that rich caramel flavor is such a pleasure. How many people have gone through a box of chocolates, biting pieces trying to find that caramel center? Maybe the solution to that problem is to buy a box with nothing but caramels. But maybe an even better solution would be to make your own caramels. Fortunately for you caramel lovers, I show you how to make your own caramels in this section. To add more satisfaction to your caramels, you can coat them in rich milk chocolate (not to fear; I tell you how to dip in chocolate in Chapter 15).

The following caramel recipes include shortening, but if you want your caramels to have an even richer taste, substitute an equal amount of butter for the shortening, and cook the caramels to a temperature that's 2 degrees higher than the recipe specifies.

Caramels

This caramel has a *short bite,* meaning that it doesn't string when you bite into it, and it's delicious to eat just as it is. But most folks will want to go at least one step further with this recipe. For instance, you can make caramel dessert apples and caramel pecan clusters (I provide these recipes later in this chapter), or you can use it in any other recipes that call for a basic caramel.

Preparation time: 40 minutes plus 1 hour to cool

Yield: 1.6 pounds or about 75 pieces when cut

1 cup sugar	½ cup whipping cream
1 cup light corn syrup	1 ounce shortening
1 can (12 ounces) evaporated milk	Pinch of salt

1 Line an 8 x 8-inch baking pan with nonstick paper. The pan may be smaller for thicker pieces; the ideal depth is about ¾ inches.

2 Combine the sugar, corn syrup, evaporated milk, cream, shortening, and salt in a 4- to 5-quart saucepan. Bring to a boil over low heat, stirring with a wooden spoon to blend and to ensure that the sugar dissolves.

3 When the batch comes to a boil (about 25 minutes), the batch will boil up in the pot due to the milk and cream. Use a pot of water and a pastry brush to wash sugar crystals down the inside of the pot and clip a thermometer on the side of the pot, being sure that the tip doesn't touch the bottom of the pot. Continue to boil over low heat.

4 After the ingredients boil up, they boil back down to the cooking level. This process takes about 10 minutes. Stir continuously after the batch lowers, and do not allow it to scorch.

5 When the batch reaches 234 degrees (after about another 15 minutes of boiling), remove it from the heat and remove the thermometer.

6 Pour the batch into the baking pan and let the mixture cool for 1 hour at room temperature. Cut the batch into ¾-inch squares, which makes about 75 pieces.

Per serving: Calories 37 (From Fat 11); Fat 1g (Saturated 1g); Cholesterol 4mg; Sodium 12mg; Carbohydrate 7g (Dietary Fiber 0g); Protein 0g.

Chocolate Caramels

Incorporating chocolate into this recipe adds a delightful chocolate flavor to an already-delicious caramel. This recipe follows the previously listed basic caramel recipe but adds baking chocolate, which is pure, unsweetened chocolate, to make a chocolate caramel. This tasty treat requires an adjustment in temperature to allow for the addition of the chocolate and to maintain the same texture. See these caramels dipped in chocolate in the color section.

Preparation time: *40 minutes plus 1 hour to cool*

Yield: *1.7 pounds or about 75 pieces*

1 cup sugar	*1 ounce shortening*
1 cup light corn syrup	*Pinch of salt*
1 can (12 ounces) evaporated milk	*2 ounces unsweetened baking chocolate, chopped*
½ cup whipping cream	

1 Line an 8 x 8-inch baking pan with wax paper or use a smaller pan to make thicker pieces; the ideal depth is about ¾ inches.

2 Combine the sugar, corn syrup, evaporated milk, cream, shortening, and salt in a 4- to 5-quart saucepan. Bring the ingredients to a boil over low heat, stirring with a wooden spoon to blend and to ensure that the sugar dissolves.

3 When the batch comes to a boil (after about 25 minutes), it will boil up due to the milk and cream content. Wash the inside of the pot with water and a pastry brush to wash away sugar crystals. Then clip on the candy thermometer, being careful not to allow the tip to touch the bottom of the pot, and continue to boil over low heat.

4 After the batch boils up, it will boil back down. Stir continuously after the batch lowers. Do not allow the batch to scorch.

5 When the batch reaches 234 degrees (after another 15 minutes of cooking), remove it from the heat, remove the thermometer, and stir in the chopped chocolate to blend. The blending and melting take 2 to 3 minutes.

6 Pour the mixture into the baking pan and allow it to cool for 1 hour at room temperature. Cut the batch into approximately ¾-inch squares, making about 75 pieces.

Per serving: Calories 41 (From Fat 15); Fat 2g (Saturated 1g); Cholesterol 4mg; Sodium 12mg; Carbohydrate 7g (Dietary Fiber 0g); Protein 0g.

Pumpkin Caramels

Pumpkin is a seasonal flavor, and you expect certain flavors and aromas to accompany certain times of the year. Few things say fall, especially the latter part of fall, like pumpkin. In the fall, my company produces a couple of pumpkin-flavored caramel candies, and these caramels are quite popular.

I derived this recipe from a much larger one that I use and, unfortunately, I don't know of a smaller can of pure pumpkin than the 15-ounce can, but this recipe calls for only part of the can. Either plan to make a really small pumpkin pie with the rest of the pumpkin or waste a little. On the bright side, pumpkin isn't very expensive.

Preparation time: *40 minutes plus 1 hour to cool*

Yield: *2 pounds or about 85 pieces*

1 cup sugar	*½ teaspoon cinnamon*
1 cup light corn syrup	*⅛ teaspoon nutmeg*
1 can (12 ounces) evaporated milk	*⅛ teaspoon ginger*
½ cup whipping cream	*⅛ teaspoon sage*
1 ounce shortening	*Pinch of salt*
7½ ounces (½ of 15-ounce can) pure pumpkin	

1 Line a 9 x 13-inch baking pan with nonstick paper. You can use a smaller pan to make thicker pieces; the ideal depth is about ¾ inches.

2 Combine the sugar, corn syrup, evaporated milk, whipping cream, shortening, pumpkin, salt, and spices in a 4- to 5-quart heavy saucepan. Bring to a boil over low heat, stirring with a wooden spoon to blend and to ensure that all the sugar dissolves.

3 When the mixture comes to a boil (after about 25 minutes), it will boil up because of the milk and cream content. Then wash the inside of the pot with a pastry brush and water to wash away any remaining sugar crystals. Clip thermometer to the side of the pot, being sure that the tip doesn't touch the bottom of the pot, and continue to boil over low heat.

4 The batch will boil up and then back down to its cooking level. Stir the mixture continuously after the level lowers. Don't allow the batch to scorch.

5 When the batch reaches 234 degrees (after another 15 to 16 minutes, but watch the thermometer), remove it from the heat and remove the thermometer.

6 Pour the batch into the baking pan. Allow the batch to cool for about 1 hour or more at room temperature; then cut it into ¾-inch squares.

Tip: *This recipe produces an excellent caramel that's delicious just as it is, or you may use it for dipping apples or for a cluster with pecans (I cover both of these recipes later in this chapter). In my store, I don't cover this caramel with chocolate because I don't have any real affinity for a chocolate-pumpkin combination. But nothing says that you can't cover this caramel in chocolate!*

Per serving: Calories 34 (From Fat 10); Fat 1g (Saturated 1g); Cholesterol 3mg; Sodium 11mg; Carbohydrate 6g (Dietary Fiber 0g); Protein 0g.

Wrapping and Storing Basic Caramels

Caramel is a *hydroscopic candy,* which means that it attracts moisture, so protecting your caramel from humid air is of paramount importance. The problem isn't evident when the caramel is warm but, as it cools, if the humidity is high, the attraction becomes unavoidable.

If you want to save caramel to eat later or to dip in chocolate later (see Chapter 15 for details on dipping), you must protect it from the elements. To do so, you want to store the caramel in an airtight container at or below 50 percent humidity. (To measure humidity, get an inexpensive thermometer that has a humidity gauge on it.) When storing caramel using this method, be careful not to let the pieces touch because they'll become inseparable friends in a short period of time. Before you fill your container, place a sheet of wax paper in the bottom and, as you're filling it, place a sheet between the layers of caramel.

If you use this method, you should keep the caramels at room temperature. Refrigerating them isn't a good idea because more harm than good befalls them due to the condensation that forms inside the containers, which leads to very sticky caramel.

If you want to freeze your caramel, don't cut the caramel. Wrap the uncut caramel in nonstick paper, and place it in a freezer bag and then in another freezer bag. You can freeze it for up to six months. To thaw it, place it on the counter at room temperature for at least eight hours (overnight is good). When thawed, remove from the packaging and treat as fresh caramel.

Putting Caramel to Good Use in Fancier Treats

In this section, I tell you all kinds of ways to use caramel so you can enjoy this delicious confection to the fullest. Although caramel squares are wonderful and are such a nice addition to any candy assortment, other uses of caramel await you!

For instance, in recent years, the lowly caramel apple has been elevated to the level of a full-blown dessert. In bygone times, a plain caramel apple or a caramel apple with chopped roasted peanuts was pretty much the caramel-apple menu. But then some wise candy maker somewhere out there decided that the apple could stand for a bit of a skin lift, so to speak.

Although caramel apples are still quite popular in their original forms, nowadays apples have gone just a little further. Today's caramel apple has gained a chocolate coating and, on top of that, just about anything that can stick to chocolate. One of the wonderful things about the dessert apple and, something that has accounted for its growth in appeal to the masses, is the seemingly limitless concoctions. You're limited by only your imagination.

Caramel Dessert Apples

For this recipe (featured in the color section), you need 2 pounds of tempered chocolate (for details on how to prepare tempered chocolate, see Chapter 14 before you dig into the following recipe). You also need skewers, either wooden or paper. I prefer wooden skewers, but they're very sharp. Always be aware of the pointed end because you'd be surprised how easily you can forget to look before you stick an apple. The point will go through you about as easily as it will go through an apple.

Which end of the apple you stick is up to you; I've seen people stick them using either end. I prefer putting the stick in the bud end, making the end that had the stem the bottom.

Tools: 5¼ inch-long skewers

Preparation time: 1½ hours plus at least 1 hour cooling time for caramel and 10 minutes for chocolate to set on the apples

Yield: 6 apples

6 Granny Smith apples (100-count size; your produce person knows)

1 warm batch of caramels (see the Caramels recipe earlier in this chapter)

2 pounds chocolate for tempering to coat caramel apples

2 cups each of at least 2 types of toppings, such as chopped pecan pieces, almond slices, fresh coconut, chocolate chips, and peanut butter chips

1 Wipe the apples with a clean, damp cloth and dry them. Remove the stems of the apples; you can use tin snips or another cutting tool, or twist the stems off by hand.

2 Line two cookie sheets with wax paper.

3 Set one apple on one of the cookie sheets lined with wax paper and carefully grasp a skewer (with the pointy side facing away from you) with a small cloth in your hand for padding. Place the point on the apple core, and slowly press it into the apple. You can press the stick completely through the core but, by stopping short of complete penetration, you slow oxidation to the core, making the apple last longer.

4 Make a batch of caramels using the basic caramel recipes (as I describe how to do earlier in this chapter). Remove the pot from the heat.

5 Grasp the end of the skewer and, while allowing the apple to rest in the pot of warm caramel, spoon caramel over the apple until it's coated. Then lift the apple out of the caramel, but still keep it within the confines of the pot; gently roll the skewer between your fingertips, spinning the excess caramel back into the pot. (See Figure 7-2 to get an idea of how to do this technique properly.)

Don't spin too hard because you can spin caramel out of the pot and onto you, among other things. Just spin enough to remove the excess caramel, and place the apple on a cookie sheet lined with wax paper.

6 When the caramel-coated apples have completely cooled (about 1 hour), replace the wax paper on the cookie sheets to receive the chocolate apples. Temper the 2 pounds of chocolate as I describe in Chapter 14.

7 Dip an apple into the tempered chocolate and use a spoon to make sure that you cover the caramel and apple completely. Lightly spin the excess chocolate off as you did with the caramel in Step 5.

8 Place your toppings in a small bowl that's big enough to hold about 2 cups of topping with room to roll the apple. Roll the chocolate-coated apple into the coating, and hold the apple by the stick over the bowl, allowing the excess toppings to drop off. You'll get a little chocolate in the bowl, but that's not a problem.

Vary It! *For a regular nutty caramel, simply follow the first five steps of the recipe, hold the end of the skewer, and roll the caramel-coated apples in a bowl of nuts. Try chopped peanuts, chopped pecans, walnut pieces, or sliced roasted almonds.*

Tip: *This item has a fairly short life because the combination of the extreme heat and the core's being skewered contribute to a shorter life. Store your caramel apples uncovered on the counter for four to five days.*

Per serving: Calories 664 (From Fat 383); Fat 43g (Saturated 9g); Cholesterol 8mg; Sodium 52mg; Carbohydrate 75g (Dietary Fiber 10g); Protein 7g.

SPINNING AN APPLE

A simple marshmallow becomes a special treat in the following recipe with the addition of hot caramel and nut pieces.

Caramel-coated Marshmallows Rolled in Nuts

In this recipe, you take the basic Caramels recipe from this chapter and use it to make a simple treat that you're certain to enjoy. I mean, you'll enjoy this recipe if you like caramel, nuts, and marshmallows — and who doesn't?

When making this confection, the caramel is very hot and, occasionally, small drippings fall into the nuts. You may want to wear leather gloves to protect your hands, if you choose. If you encounter hot caramel, immediately put your hand under cold water. Do not put your hand in your mouth, which is the first instinct, because then you'll burn your lip, too.

If you want only a few of these puffs, make them using the still-warm leftover caramel that you have after dipping caramel apples. The caramel will be a little cooler, and these pieces are a great use for the leftovers.

Preparation time: 55 minutes plus 45 minutes for cooling

Yield 30 to 35 pieces

3 to 4 cups chopped pecans or sliced almonds

1 warm batch of caramels (see the basic recipe earlier in this chapter)

1-pound bag large marshmallows

1 Line a 9 x 13-inch cookie sheet with wax paper, and place the nuts in an 8 x 8-inch baking pan. Set both items aside.

2 When the caramel has completed cooking and you have removed it from the heat, let the batch set for about 5 to 6 minutes to cool a little because the hot caramel may cause the marshmallows to melt on contact. You can actually dip the marshmallows until the caramel temperature drops to about 130 to 140 degrees, so a little cooling is fine.

3 Drop the marshmallows into the warm caramel one by one; quickly use tongs to remove the marshmallows from the caramel and roll them in the pan of nuts. Try not to get nuts on the tongs because they'll transfer to the caramel. Dip the marshmallows until they're completely covered. As you dip, place the pecan puffs or almond puffs on the lined cookie sheet to cool at room temperature

4 As the puffs cool, turn them every few minutes to prevent them from flattening on one side. I have found that by placing the puffs very close together, you prevent them from spreading as they cool. As you rotate the pieces, be sure they aren't stuck together. If they do get stuck together, you can easily unstick them.

Tip: When you drop the marshmallows on the tray, carefully gather a pile of the nuts over the caramel-coated piece to completely cover. Then remove the marshmallow.

Tip: If you want to keep these treats for a while, simply place them in a large plastic container with wax paper underneath. If you have more than one layer, place a sheet of wax paper between the layers. You should be able to store the puffs for three weeks in this manner.

Per serving: Calories 168 (From Fat 68); Fat 8g (Saturated 2g); Cholesterol 8mg; Sodium 32mg; Carbohydrate 25g (Dietary Fiber 1g); Protein 2g.

Caramel Pecan Clusters

You have several preparations to make but, otherwise, this recipe follows fairly simple procedures. When you complete this recipe for Caramel Pecan Clusters, you'll have a piece of confection to rival that of many fine candy stores. This particular candy (which you can see in the color section) is by far the best-selling piece of candy that my little company has ever made.

This recipe calls for tempered chocolate, which I cover in detail in Chapter 14. Be sure to read that chapter before you proceed with this recipe.

Preparation time: 1¾ hours plus at least 1 hour to cool the caramel before applying the chocolate

Yield: 60 pieces

1 warm batch of caramels (see the recipe earlier in this chapter)

6 cups medium or raw large pecan halves

2 pounds milk chocolate, chopped and melted for tempering for coating

1 Line three 9 x 13-inch cookie sheets with nonstick paper and completely cover them with a thin layer of fresh pecan halves and put aside. Place a sheet of wax paper about 3 feet long on the counter for placing the chocolate-dipped pieces after you dip them.

2 Make the basic caramels batch (as I describe earlier in this chapter). Remove the pot from the heat.

3 Using a tablespoon, spoon silver-dollar–size dollops of caramel onto the nuts as closely as possible without allowing them to touch. (Caramel will spread some and, if the pieces run together, cut them apart with a small knife.)

4 Cool the caramel for at least an hour. When the caramel is cool (touch the candies to feel whether they're still warm), lift the clusters off the trays, removing any loose pecans, and place them on wax paper on the counter. Remove the pecans from the cookie sheets, but keep the lined sheets for the chocolate clusters.

5 Temper 2 pounds of milk chocolate as described in Chapter 14, and hand-dip the clusters in the chocolate by holding each piece in your hand and dipping with the caramel side down into the chocolate. Then place each piece on wax paper on the counter to cool. The chocolate should set in about 6 minutes. Allow them to cool for another 15 minutes at room temperature to form a nice firm set.

Tip: You can place the finished clusters in a plastic container with waxed sheets between the layers and keep for up to three weeks at room temperature.

Per serving: Calories 123 (From Fat 90); Fat 10g (Saturated 2g); Cholesterol 2mg; Sodium 12mg; Carbohydrate 9g (Dietary Fiber 1g); Protein 2g.

Chapter 8

Doctoring Divinity

*W*hen you think of the South and Southern candies, you immediately think of candies such as *divinity* (a light, fluffy confection) and pecan rolls, which have divinity centers. These candies have been popular since the turn of the 20th century, and people still enjoy them today. Over the years, the market for such delightful confections has spread. But I like to think that the way these candies are made in the South is still something special.

This chapter is devoted to a very specialized part of the world of candies: divinity. With the recipes in this chapter, you produce divinity, which is a confection made with sugar, corn syrup, and egg whites. The egg whites, beaten during the process of making divinity, provide the air that makes this candy so light. But I don't make you crack any eggs to make divinity: Instead, use powdered egg whites.

Divinity is the basis of the pecan roll. Don't worry, I include a recipe for that tasty treat in this chapter, too. These candies share a Southern heritage, but you can enjoy them wherever you live.

Delving into Divinity Production

Divinity is a very sweet confection, which isn't surprising considering the ingredients. To make this candy, you primarily use sugar, including *invert sugar* (a sugar that's about 20 percent sweeter than regular sugar that gives candy a smoother texture), sugar, corn syrup, and egg whites.

Invert sugar has a crystal structure that enhances the enjoyment of the candy by producing a smoother texture, and this smoothness gives a pleasant mouthfeel. You can purchase invert sugar — a brand name is Nulomoline — from bakery suppliers (see Chapter 24 for a list).

In the event that you're unable to acquire any invert sugar, try substituting honey for the invert sugar. Honey is another form of invert sugar and imparts a similar sweetness.

Another ingredient in divinity is egg whites. The egg whites, of course, provide the fluffiness for which divinity is known. I'm sure you can find divinity recipes that use fresh eggs, but I prefer using powdered egg whites — which are really quite easy to reconstitute by adding water to your batch — because I don't like handling fresh eggs when I make candy. I also really don't like the separating process to get fresh egg whites. Powdered egg whites also are available from baking suppliers.

Two other key ingredients in divinity are *invertase,* a natural enzyme that helps candy retain moisture, and fondant, which I show you how to make in Chapter 6. In the event that you cannot or choose not to locate invertase, you may leave it out, but be aware that the candy may become dry a little faster. The divinity will still be excellent a couple of days after you make it.

Divinity involves a two-part production: First, you beat your combination of invert sugar and egg whites into a nice, light, almost meringue-looking state. Next, you cook the second part — a granulated sugar, syrup, and water portion — to the proper temperature. This step is the key to making a batch that *stands up,* by which I mean that the final product easily forms round dollops that retain their shape and don't fall flat. If this part of the batch isn't cooked properly, no amount of beating will save the batch.

When the weather is humid, you may have a hard time getting divinity to stand up when you're beating it. Typically, the cooking process boils off a lot of water but, if the air is humid, the batch may give off less moisture. When a batch gives off less moisture, it may not stand up when beaten, and water retention may be the cause. (For years, I've heard folks say that they can't make divinity in rainy weather. They say that when they beat their batches, the divinity doesn't stand up. I always tell them that my shop makes divinity in all types of weather, and the South is a very humid part of the country.)

You can solve this problem in one of two ways. You can

- ✔ Beat the batch a little longer at the end, assuming that you've cooked the batch to the right temperature.
- ✔ Cook the batch a couple of degrees higher to remove more moisture, assuming that the weather is rainy or excessively humid.

Of those two solutions, I prefer cooking to a higher temperature to remove the extra moisture. But don't adjust the temperature by more than a degree or two; when making such adjustments, make small changes.

Many things can happen to a batch of candy during the cooking process, and one of these things is graining. You want smoothness in your divinity. When the syrup, sugar, and water portion of divinity comes to a full boil, wash down the inside of the pot by dipping a pastry brush in hot water and brushing the inside of the pot down to the cooking line. This washes down any sugar crystals that may have splashed onto the side of the pot, which prevents unwanted crystallization from taking place and assures you that your divinity will be enjoyable.

Making a good batch of divinity may be as simple as knowing the proper way to pour one part into the other. After you master this step, the rest should be a snap for you. One of the first points I stress when training a new confectioner is patience. You cannot rush some things, and divinity is one of those things.

With the mixer running on medium speed, *slowly* pour the hot liquid (the invert-sugar-and-egg-white combo) into the syrup mixture, and allow the two parts to blend (see Figure 8-1). When I show a new cook how to pour the mixture, I tell him or her to pour the liquid like water running slowly from a faucet. You cannot dump the second part into the first part because doing so causes the batch to lose its aeration, and you will never get the batch back to a fluffy state. So pour the contents of the pot slowly into the mixer, and beat the mixture until you see that the batch doesn't fall when you stop the beater.

Figure 8-1: Slowly pour your cooked syrup into your egg-white mixture with the beater running on slow speed to ensure your divinity's fluffiness.

MIXING DIVINITY

With a little practice, you'll recognize the proper appearance of divinity that has been beaten the proper amount of time. When you stop the beater, watch how the batch reacts. Early in the process, you'll notice that the mass falls heavily when the beater stops. As you get closer to the end, little pieces may break off and fly out of the bowl, indicating near-readiness.

Stop the mixer and observe; the bulk of the batch should hold its shape when the beater stops. At this time, turn the beater to slow speed and add the vanilla extract, invertase, and nuts, if included. Mix for 20 to 30 seconds; then stop the mixer and remove the bowl for dipping your candies.

A divine Southern tradition

Contrary to popular belief, divinity probably didn't originate in the South. In fact, no one knows for sure exactly when or where this confection began. Although the name *divinity* wasn't officially given to the candy until the late 1930s, the candy was most likely made in its current form shortly after the turn of the century. Corn syrup is a main ingredient, and this product was developed in the early 1900s; in fact, a major corn syrup manufacturer included a recipe for divinity on its containers.

Early reports of divinity often refer to the candy as "divinity fudge," a term that you sometimes still hear. In the context of divinity as I make it, I don't see any correlation between fudge and divinity. Divinity and fudge are two very different, delicious candies. Divinity, which includes egg whites among its ingredients, is light and quite airy because of the beating process that is used to make the confection, whereas fudge is a heavier candy with a very different texture.

Although divinity most likely wasn't made first in the South, Southerners certainly were the folks who made the first pecan divinity. Who first put the pecans in divinity or when they first did so isn't clear, but recipes from the early 1900s refer to nuts without specifying which nut to use. However vague this history may be, at some point, pecans became the nut of choice for divinity, and the rest is pecan history.

Whatever the source of this delicious candy, you're certain to enjoy it for years to come. Divinity remains one of those traditions of the sweet South that's as southern as a Southern accent.

Sampling Southern Divinity Treats

If I had to name one candy that my shops never seem to have in sufficient supply, divinity would be the one. My staff seems to make it constantly, but we always seem to need more. Maybe this confection is just that good. Make some, and you be the judge.

Plain Divinity

In the event that you like your divinity without nuts — quite a few folks like theirs naked — you can try this recipe. However you choose to make it, you still make a honey of a piece of candy.

Tools: *Ice cream scoop*

Preparation time: *30 to 40 minutes plus 10 to 15 minutes to dip*

Yield: *45 to 50 kisses*

¼ cup invert sugar

1½ tablespoons powdered egg whites

½ cup plus 1½ tablespoons water

2 cups sugar

½ cup honey

¼ cup Basic Fondant, cut into bite-size pieces (see Chapter 6)

½ teaspoon vanilla extract

⅛ teaspoon invertase

1 Line a cookie sheet with wax paper.

2 Combine the invert sugar and egg whites in a mixing bowl, and stir lightly with fork to blend; add 1½ tablespoons of water.

3 Start the mixer on low speed to begin blending using the paddle attachment. Then beat on high speed for about 3 to 5 minutes until the mixture forms light peaks (looks like meringue on a pie) that stand when you stop the mixer. Stop the mixer, and leave the bowl in place for the second part to be added when cooked.

4 Combine the sugar, honey, and ½ cup of water in a 5-quart saucepan and cook over medium heat until the ingredients come to a boil. Occasionally stir the mixture with a wooden spoon.

5 Wash down the inside of the pan with a pastry brush and hot water to wash down the sugar crystals. Clip a candy thermometer on the side of the pan, making sure that the tip of the thermometer doesn't touch the bottom of the pan, and continue boiling to 250 degrees without stirring. Remove the mixture from the heat and remove the thermometer. Total cooking time is about 25 minutes, but watch your thermometer.

6 Start the mixer on medium speed and slowly pour the cooked syrup into the egg-white mixture.

7 Immediately and steadily add the fondant, a piece at a time to blend, to the mixture.

8 Beat on medium speed until the batch thickens and begins to stand up when you stop the mixer. With the mixer on slow speed, add the vanilla extract and invertase; when blended, stop the mixer and remove the bowl, scraping the excess off the beater into the bowl with a spatula.

9 With a small ice cream scoop, dip level scoopfuls of divinity onto a cookie sheet lined with wax paper (see Figure 8-2). Every several dips, rinse the scoop in a pot of water.

10 You can set divinity on the kitchen counter overnight or all day to dry. I usually like to allow eight hours for the divinity to set properly.

Tip: *As you drop the pieces of divinity onto a lined cookie sheet, dipping your scoop into a pot of hot water is very useful because it prevents the scoop from clogging. Periodically rinse the scoop and work the mechanism in the water to prevent jamming.*

Per serving: Calories 50 (From Fat 0); Fat 0g (Saturated 0g); Cholesterol 0mg; Sodium 3mg; Carbohydrate 13g (Dietary Fiber 0g); Protein 0g.

SCOOPING DIVINITY

Figure 8-2:
Make sure that your scoops of divinity are even before you drop them onto a cookie sheet.

Divinity with Pecans

Whenever you make this recipe, you're certain to enjoy it. I observe my guests as they sit on benches in front of my shop. The pure pleasure they derive from that first bite into a piece of my divinity gratifies me. They savor the combination of a light, sweet confection with just the right texture to make the bite pleasurable, and the initial bite is followed by the delicate crunch of fresh pecans. See these treats in the color section.

Tools: *Small ice cream scoop*

Preparation time: *30 to 40 minutes plus 10 to 15 minutes to dip*

Yield: *45 to 50 kisses*

¼ cup invert sugar

1½ tablespoons powdered egg whites

1½ tablespoons plus ½ cup of water

2 cups sugar

½ cup corn syrup

¼ cup Basic Fondant, cut into bite-size pieces (see Chapter 6)

½ teaspoon vanilla extract

⅛ teaspoon invertase

1 cup small pecan pieces

1 Line a cookie sheet with wax paper.

2 Combine the invert sugar and egg whites in a mixing bowl; stir the ingredients lightly with a fork to blend and add 1½ tablespoons of water.

3 Start the mixer on low speed using the paddle attachment to begin blending; then beat on high speed until the mixture forms light peaks (like meringue on a pie) that stand when you stop the mixer. Beating takes about 3 to 5 minutes. Stop the mixer and leave the bowl on the mixer, awaiting the second part of the batch.

4 Combine the sugar, syrup, and ½ cup water in a 5-quart saucepan. Cook the mixture on medium heat, stirring occasionally with a wooden spoon, until the contents come to a boil (about 10 minutes).

5 Wash down the inside of the pan with a pastry brush and hot water to wash down the sugar crystals. Clip a candy thermometer to the side of the pan, making sure that the tip of the thermometer doesn't touch the bottom of the pot. Continue boiling the mixture, without stirring, to 250 degrees (about another 15 minutes), but watch your thermometer. Remove the mixture from the heat and remove the thermometer.

6 Start the mixer on medium speed, and slowly pour the cooked syrup into the egg-white mixture.

7 Immediately and steadily add the fondant, a piece at a time to blend, to the mixture.

8 Beat the mixture on medium speed until the batch thickens and begins to stand up when you stop the mixer. With the mixer on slow speed, add the vanilla extract and invertase, and mix until blended (which takes about 30 seconds).

9 Add the pecans and, as soon as you've mixed them in (about 30 seconds), stop the mixer and remove the bowl from the mixer. Use a spatula to scrape the excess off the beater and back into the bowl.

10 With an ice cream scoop, dip level scoopfuls of divinity onto the cookie sheet lined with wax paper. Every several dips, rinse the scoop in a pot of hot water.

11 Typically, you can set divinity on the kitchen counter overnight or all day to dry. About eight hours is usually sufficient.

Vary It! *You can substitute walnuts or almonds for the pecans in this recipe.*

Per serving: *Calories 55 (From Fat 14); Fat 2g (Saturated 0g); Cholesterol 0mg; Sodium 3mg; Carbohydrate 10g (Dietary Fiber 0g); Protein 0g.*

Divinity with Dried Fruits

Certain occasions call for a change in tastes, and you may decide that you want a variation in the taste and texture of your divinity. Sometimes adding fruit to your candy helps put you in the spirit — say, for the holidays. I offer a variation using the Plain Divinity recipe (which I show you earlier in this chapter) with a couple of changes that are sure to put you in the holiday spirit. Hey, sometimes you just feel like a little taste of fruit.

Tools: *Small ice cream scoop*

Preparation time: *25 to 30 minutes plus 10 to 15 minutes to dip*

Yield: *45 to 50 pieces*

¼ cup invert sugar

1½ tablespoons powdered egg whites

1½ tablespoons plus ½ cup water

2 cups sugar

½ cup corn syrup

¼ cup (4 ounces by weight) Basic Fondant, cut into small pieces (see Chapter 6)

½ teaspoon vanilla extract

⅛ teaspoon invertase

1 cup candied cherries or mixed candied fruits, chopped into small pieces

1 Line a cookie sheet with wax paper and set aside.

2 Combine the invert sugar and egg whites in a mixing bowl and stir lightly with a fork to blend; add 1½ tablespoons of water.

3 Start mixing on low speed; then beat on high speed for 3 to 5 minutes until the mixture forms light peaks that stand (like meringue on a pie) when you stop the mixer. Stop the mixer and leave the bowl on the mixer for the next part to be added.

4 Combine the sugar, syrup, and ½ cup of water in a 5-quart saucepan and cook over medium heat, stirring occasionally with a wooden spoon until the contents come to a boil (about 10 minutes).

5 Wash down the inside of the saucepan with a pastry brush and hot water to wash down the sugar crystals. Clip a candy thermometer on the side of the pan, making sure that the tip of the thermometer doesn't touch the bottom of the pot. Continue boiling without stirring to 250 degrees; reaching this temperature takes about another 15 minutes, but watch your thermometer. Remove the mixture from the heat and remove the thermometer.

6 Start the mixer on medium speed, and slowly pour cooked syrup into the egg-white mixture.

7 Immediately and steadily add the fondant, a piece at a time to blend, to the mixture.

8 Beat the mixture on medium speed until the batch thickens and begins to stand up when you stop the mixer. With the mixer on slow speed, add the vanilla extract and invertase, and mix until blended (usually about 30 seconds).

9 Add the chopped fruit and, as soon as you've blended it in with the mixture, stop the mixer and remove the bowl. Use a spatula to scrape the excess mixture off the beater and back into the bowl.

10 Dip level scoopfuls of divinity onto a cookie sheet lined with wax paper. Every few dips, rinse the scoop in a pot of hot water.

11 Typically, you can set divinity on the kitchen counter overnight or all day to dry before placing in white paper candy cups. About eight hours to set is typical.

Per serving: Calories 63 (From Fat 0); Fat 0g (Saturated 0g); Cholesterol 0mg; Sodium 8mg; Carbohydrate 16g (Dietary Fiber 0g); Protein 0g.

I brake for pecan rolls

The pecan roll is a true symbol of the South. In the 1950s and 1960s, a drive through the South on any main highway (and a lot of side roads) included a stop at a roadside stand where these delicious rolls were readily available. Several major retailers of these candies lined the highways with huge billboards for miles in either direction from their stores, so that driving past one without stopping was virtually impossible. With such a buildup, surely the family demanded that Dad stop and purchase some pecan candy. And, of course, he did.

People made fortunes with these clever highway promotions, and the marketing had a lot to do with establishing the South as the home of great pecan candies, just as citrus fruit sellers established their hold on the same travelers in Florida. Today, the highways of the South are wider, and traffic moves faster. As a result, the number of vendors has dwindled over the years, but a few are still there. Nowadays, you can enjoy those delicious candies made in your own kitchen.

Pecan Rolls

The nougat center in this candy is a close cousin of the fluffy white divinity from this chapter. To make a pecan roll, you need to make the basic caramel from Chapter 7. Or, if you desire, you can melt store-bought caramels to coat your centers before rolling them in chopped pecans. Check out these candies in the color section.

Preparation time: 25 to 30 minutes plus 20 to 25 minutes to make rolls when the divinity mixture has dried

Yield: 15 to 18 pecan rolls

¼ cup invert sugar

1½ tablespoons powdered egg whites

1½ tablespoons plus ½ cup of water

1⅔ cups sugar

½ cup corn syrup

¼ cup Basic Fondant, cut into bite-size pieces (see Chapter 6)

½ teaspoon vanilla extract

⅛ teaspoon invertase

½ box confectioners' sugar for rolling centers

1 batch of caramels using the basic Caramels recipe in Chapter 7 or 1 pound store-bought caramels to melt

1 cup small pecan pieces

2 to 3 cups small pecan pieces for coating pecan rolls

1 Line a cookie sheet with wax paper.

2 Combine the invert sugar and egg whites in a mixing bowl and stir lightly with a fork to blend; add 1½ tablespoons of water.

3 Start the mixer on low speed to begin blending; then beat on high speed until the mixture forms light peaks that stand (like meringue on a pie) when you stop the mixer, about 3 to 5 minutes. Stop the mixer and set the mixture aside.

4 Combine the sugar, syrup, and ½ cup water in a 5-quart saucepan and cook over medium heat, stirring occasionally with a wooden spoon until the contents come to a boil, which takes about 10 minutes.

5 Wash down the inside of the pan with a pastry brush and clip a candy thermometer on the side of the pan, making sure that the tip of the thermometer doesn't touch the bottom of the pan. Continue boiling the mixture, without stirring, to 253 degrees (which takes about 16 minutes). Remove the mixture from the heat and remove the thermometer.

6 Start the mixer on medium speed, and slowly pour the cooked syrup into the egg-white mixture.

7 Immediately and steadily add the fondant, a piece at a time to blend, to the mixture.

8 Beat the mixture on medium speed until the batch thickens and begins to stand up when you stop the mixer. With the mixer on slow speed, add the vanilla extract, invertase, and nuts to blend; stop the mixer and remove the bowl.

9 Scrape the contents of the bowl about 1½ inches thick onto a cookie sheet lined with wax paper and allow the candy to dry overnight or approximately eight hours.

10 When the divinity is dry, cut it into pieces that are big enough to make centers approximately 3 to 4 inches in length and 1 to 1½ inches in diameter when rolled. Each piece will weigh about 1½ to 2 ounces. Dust your hands with confectioners' sugar to prevent sticking when you roll the centers.

11 Make a basic batch of caramels (see Chapter 7) or melt the caramel in a microwave to 160 degrees, measuring with a candy thermometer. Using the tongs, drop a center into the caramel; roll the center in the caramel to coat well and shake off the excess caramel.

12 Using the tongs, drop the roll into a bowl of pecan pieces, and cover it completely with pecans. (See Figure 8-3 to see how to carefully coat the rolls.) I like to cover the roll by using my hands to sweep the pecans over the caramel-coated roll, avoiding the hot caramel. Then carefully remove the roll from the nuts, and place it on the cookie sheet.

13 Place the rolls on a paper-lined cookie sheet with the rolls side by side, touching so that they don't spread. Rotate the rolls every few minutes until they're cool; rotation prevents spreading while the caramel cools. The pecan rolls usually cool in about 25 to 30 minutes, depending on room temperature.

Per serving: Calories 290 (From Fat 94); Fat 11g (Saturated 2g); Cholesterol 2mg; Sodium 73mg; Carbohydrate 50g (Dietary Fiber 1g); Protein 3g.

Figure 8-3:
Carefully roll
your
caramel-
coated
nougat in a
bowl of
pecans.

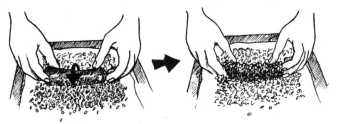

COATING PECAN ROLLS

Wrapping and Storing Your Divinity

Now that you have your divinity in hand (and maybe some in your belly), you need to store whatever remains. When the divinity is set and ready for you to handle, put each kiss in a #6 white paper candy cup. (The #6 cup may go by different names from supplier to supplier but, if you ask for a sleeve of #6 white cups, you'll get what you want. I explain in Chapter 24 where to find the cups.) You don't have to use white, but this appearance pleases the eye. Using these cups gives your candy a professional appearance and keeps the sides and bottoms of the kisses moist.

If you intend to keep the candy around for more than a day or two, you may want to store the pieces in an airtight plastic container. You can make two layers with wax paper between, but be careful not to mash the lower layer. You can even place the divinity on plates and cover it with plastic kitchen wrap.

Although you want the fresh candy to dry overnight when you first make it, letting the candy sit out unprotected for an extended period of time causes it to dry out and become hard. I don't recommend storing divinity for more than a week in this manner because it will gradually harden.

If you need to store divinity for an extended period, carefully place it in a freezer bag, and place that within another freezer bag. Do not layer the divinity pieces. Carefully place in the freezer, and freeze for up to six months. To thaw, remove the candy from the freezer and allow it to thaw in the bags overnight (at least eight hours) on the counter. Then remove from the bags and enjoy.

Chapter 9

Whipping Up Quick and Easy Fudges

Fudge is a category of candy that most folks can identify, and just about everyone has enjoyed it at one time or another. Plus everyone's mother or grandmother seems to have a special recipe for fudge. But somehow, you always have room for a few more fudge recipes so, after a quick overview of the fudge-making process, I show you a number of ways that you can produce this delicious confection: in the microwave, with and without chocolate, and as the centers for other candies. I also share some easy wrapping and storage tips with you so that your fudges stay fresh and delicious.

Touring the Fudge-making Process

So just what is fudge? I'm afraid that strict definitions elude this candy, so it's no wonder that people are frequently confused by what is fudge and what isn't. People often confuse fudge and chocolate. Chocolate can be in fudge, but plenty of differences exist between the two confections. In fact, many fudges aren't chocolate at all (see "Trying Out Nonchocolate Fudges" later in this chapter).

Fudge is an American confection that's been around for about a century. The suspicion is that someone who was making a batch of caramel probably ended up with a batch of fudge (see Chapter 7 for more about caramels). As a matter of fact, fudge has been called a "grained caramel." When you enjoy a buttery bite of caramel or a rich piece of fudge, you'll note that they have quite different textures and provide different mouthfeels.

Mouthfeel is exactly what the word sounds like: how a food feels in your mouth. You can define a food by its coarseness, smoothness, and the general all-around sensation that it creates. Caramel is chewy and soft with a smooth texture. Fudge has a grainier texture, but you control this graininess in the cooking process and in how you handle the fudge while it's cooling.

Producing fudge is a rather simple sugar crystallization process. This process begins when you heat the fudge batch to about 234 degrees on your candy thermometer. The heating times vary by recipe because stovetop ranges and interpretations of low, medium, and high heat vary. Batches usually come to a boil in a few minutes and have to boil for a few minutes.

After the batch reaches 234 degrees, you usually let it cool undisturbed to about 110 degrees (the procedure in different recipes varies). No stirring occurs during the cooling process because agitation initiates the crystallization process too early and causes the fudge to become excessively grainy and even crumbly.

After the fudge reaches 110 degrees, you stir it in the pan with a wooden spoon until it lightens in color and becomes thicker.

Because of variations in atmospheric conditions, room temperatures, sizes of the batches, and any number of other factors, the exact time required to complete the crystallization process is a variable, but it usually takes from 10 to 15 minutes.

In the microwave recipes in this chapter, don't be concerned with the graining so much, because you aren't boiling granulated sugar; you're simply heating confectioners' sugar or blending chocolate with milk, butter, or whatever to make a creamy confection. You don't have to worry about the mixture's temperature.

After you stir a batch of fudge, you almost always pour it into a buttered pan because it makes getting the fudge out of the pan much easier. After all, you don't want your fudge to stick to the pan. Lining a pan with nonstick paper produces the same result. With a paper-lined pan, you can lift the fudge from the pan and peel the paper off or cut the fudge and lift the fudge off the paper.

When greasing your baking pans, a tablespoon of butter is plenty. Use butter softened at room temperature. To soften the butter, cut it into tablespoon-size pieces and leave it on the kitchen counter for about an hour at room temperature. A simple method for buttering the pan is to blot soft butter on a paper towel and rub the inside of the aluminum baking pan to give it an even coat of butter (see Figure 9-1 for the right technique).

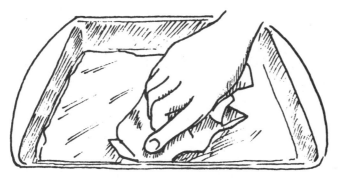

Figure 9-1:
Use a paper towel to effectively and evenly butter an aluminum baking pan.

BUTTERING A PAN

I like my finished fudge to have a sort of dull appearance and a texture like butter when it's cut. Fudge with an appearance that's too shiny indicates that a portion of the mixture wasn't completely cooled. The batch is fine, but I strive for perfection.

Starting Off Easy with Microwave Fudges

Over the years, you've probably learned that few things are easier than cooking with a microwave. And so is the case with fudge. You can actually produce a pretty tasty fudge this way, and no one has to know how easy the process is, so let 'em think that you toiled away in the kitchen making the candy.

Simple Microwave Fudge

This recipe makes a very simple chocolate fudge, and it's a good beginning for the novice home candy maker. Ruining this fudge is really difficult, so give this recipe your best shot.

Preparation time: *10 minutes plus one hour of cooling*

Yield: *64 1-inch pieces*

1 tablespoon butter for buttering pan plus
½ cup butter

3⅔ cups confectioners' sugar

½ cup pure unsweetened cocoa

¼ cup milk

1 tablespoon vanilla extract

1 Butter an 8 x 8-inch aluminum baking pan using 1 tablespoon of butter.

2 Combine the confectioners' sugar, cocoa, ½ cup butter, and milk in a large microwave-able bowl. Heat the mixture in the microwave on high power until the butter melts (usually about 2½ to 3 minutes). Stop and stir the mixture once during this process.

3 Remove the mixture from the microwave and, using a rubber spatula, stir it until it's smooth. Stir in the vanilla extract.

4 Pour the mixture into the baking pan and use a spatula to smooth it; allow it to cool at room temperature for about an hour.

5 When the batch is cool, use a butter knife to cut it into 64 1-inch squares.

Per serving: Calories 43 (From Fat 16); Fat 2g (Saturated 1g); Cholesterol 4mg; Sodium 1mg; Carbohydrate 7g (Dietary Fiber 0g); Protein 0g.

Microwaves vary, of course, so cooking times can vary. Just remember that 30 seconds too much or too little can make a big difference in the final product. You always can add a few seconds, but you can't subtract time; overcooking your fudge can dry out or overcook your candy. If you do overcook your fudge, you can add a tablespoon of water or milk to the fudge and stir to regain the consistency. Simply check your fudge frequently — even every 10 seconds with a candy thermometer — when it's nearing the right temperature.

Microwave Chocolate Pecan Fudge

In the previous recipe, you made a quick fudge using cocoa. In this recipe, you use chocolate chips to make a fudge with its own distinct taste. Even though you use different ingredients, you achieve similar results.

Preparation time: *12 minutes plus one hour of cooling*

Yield: *64 1-inch pieces*

1 tablespoon butter for buttering pan	*¼ cup butter*
2 12-ounce bags semi-sweet chocolate chips	*1 cup chopped pecan pieces*
1 14-ounce can sweetened condensed milk	

1 Butter an 8 x 8-inch aluminum baking pan using 1 tablespoon of butter.

2 Combine the chocolate chips, condensed milk, and butter in a large microwaveable bowl. Microwave the mixture on high until the chocolate chips melt (usually between 3½ and 5 minutes). Make sure to stir the mixture with a spatula at the 2-minute mark and the 3-minute mark. Melting chips hold their shape, so stirring is important to see how much they've melted.

3 Remove the mixture from the microwave and stir in the pecans.

4 Pour the mixture into the greased pan, smoothing the mixture with a spatula. Put the batch into the refrigerator for 30 minutes to cool or allow it to cool at room temperature for at least one hour.

5 Use a butter knife to cut the batch into 64 1-inch squares.

Vary It! *Replace 2 cups of chocolate chips with 2 cups of peanut butter chips for a delightful chocolate peanut butter fudge.*

Per serving: *Calories 92 (From Fat 54); Fat 0g (Saturated 6g); Cholesterol 5mg; Sodium 9mg; Carbohydrate 10g (Dietary Fiber 1g); Protein 1g.*

Microwave Rum Walnut Fudge

This recipe is great for someone who has a taste for rum, but you can substitute amaretto, hazelnut, coffee, or Irish cream liqueurs for the rum. (When making liquid substitutions, be sure that the liquid volumes are the same.) You also can substitute pecan halves or sliced almonds for the walnuts.

The basic recipe contains rum and rum flavoring. The flavoring is an oil that simply reinforces the taste of the real rum. You can make this fudge without the oil, or you can make the batch with only the oil if you don't care for the real thing. Any of these variations still produces a good fudge. Without the extra liquid, the fudge may be a little firmer.

Preparation time: *10 minutes plus one hour of cooling*

Yield: *64 1-inch pieces*

1 tablespoon butter for buttering pan

1 12-ounce package semi-sweet chocolate chips

1 14-ounce can sweetened condensed milk

¼ cup your favorite rum (or other favorite spirit)

1 teaspoon rum flavoring oil (optional)

¾ cup walnuts, halves and pieces (or appropriate substitution)

1 Butter an 8 x 8-inch aluminum pan using 1 tablespoon of butter.

2 Combine the chocolate chips and sweetened condensed milk in a large microwaveable bowl. Microwave the mixture on high for 3 minutes and stir halfway through the heating. At the end of the 3 minutes, the chips should be melted and should blend easily when stirred.

3 Remove the mixture from the microwave and stir with the spatula until the mixture is smooth.

4 Blend in the rum and, if you like, the rum flavoring oil. The rum provides plenty of flavor, and the rum oil only enhances the flavor. Stir in the walnuts, and pour the mixture into the buttered pan.

5 Let the batch cool at room temperature for about one hour; then cut it into 64 1-inch squares with a butter knife.

Per serving: *Calories 58 (From Fat 29); Fat 3g (Saturated 2g); Cholesterol 3mg; Sodium 9mg; Carbohydrate 7g (Dietary Fiber 0g); Protein 1g.*

Focusing on Favorite Chocolate Fudges

You have a few options for making fudge that doesn't involve chocolate (see the next section) but, at some point, you're going to want to make a serious batch of good old chocolate fudge. After all, chocolate is most folks' favorite flavor, and you can satisfy your cravings with the recipes in this section.

TIP

When making the recipes in this section (and the nonchocolate fudges in the next section), you come across a step instructing you to wash down the inside of the pot after the batch comes to a boil. This step is an important one because a few sugar crystals often splash against the inside of the pot during cooking and don't dissolve. Washing down the inside of your pot is a simple procedure that solves this problem. For more details, see Chapter 7.

Donna's Best Fudge

The chocolate in a good chocolate fudge can come from a variety of sources —semi-sweet chocolate chips, cocoa powder, and baking chocolate, to name a few. I've seen variations of a basic chocolate fudge everywhere, but I include this one because my sister-in-law Donna has made this one for years to please family and friends. She says that if you make this fudge recipe in rainy weather, it will grain, so use your best judgment.

Preparation time: 1 hour and 20 minutes plus one hour cooling time

Yield: 64 1-inch squares

1 tablespoon butter for buttering pan	*1½ cups half and half*
3 cups sugar	*¼ cup butter, cut into 4 pieces*
⅔ cup pure cocoa powder	*1 teaspoon vanilla extract*
⅛ teaspoon salt	

1 Butter an 8 x 8-inch aluminum baking pan with 1 tablespoon of butter.

2 Combine the sugar, cocoa, and salt in a 4-quart saucepan and stir in the half and half using a wooden spoon. Cook the mixture over medium heat, stirring constantly until it comes to a full boil (about 16 minutes). Using a pastry brush and water, wash the inside of the pan to wash down the sugar crystals.

3 Clip a candy thermometer to the inside of the pot; don't allow the thermometer to touch the bottom of the pot. Allow the mixture to continue boiling, without stirring, until it reaches 234 degrees on the candy thermometer, which takes about 15 minutes.

4 Remove the mixture from the heat and add ¼ cup of butter. Do not stir the mixture. Allow the mixture to cool at room temperature to 110 degrees and then add the vanilla extract.

5 Remove the candy thermometer and beat the fudge with a wooden spoon until it thickens and becomes smooth; this step takes about 3 minutes.

6 Using a spatula, spread the batch into the greased baking pan. Allow the fudge to cool at room temperature for about an hour. Then cut the fudge into 64 1-inch squares or 36 larger pieces with a butter knife.

Per serving: Calories 54 (From Fat 15); Fat 2g (Saturated 1g); Cholesterol 5mg; Sodium 7mg; Carbohydrate 10g (Dietary Fiber 0g); Protein 0g.

Chocolate Nut Fudge

This recipe is for chocolate pecan fudge, but you can make it using English walnuts, macadamias, or sliced almonds. The choice is yours. Check out a photo of this fudge in the color section.

Preparation time: *35 to 40 minute plus 30 minutes to cool*

Yield: *36 pieces 1½ inch squares*

1 tablespoon butter for buttering pan	*4 cups sugar*
4 ounces unsweetened baking chocolate	*½ cup butter*
½ cup evaporated milk	*1 cup pecan halves (or other nuts)*
¼ teaspoon salt	

1 Butter an 8 x 8-inch aluminum baking pan with 1 tablespoon of butter.

2 Place the baking chocolate in a saucepan and melt it slowly over low heat; melting takes about 4 minutes. Add the evaporated milk and salt and stir well with wooden spoon to mix. Blend in the sugar and bring the ingredients to a boil while stirring about 10 minutes over medium heat.

3 Wash down the inside of the pan with a pastry brush and water to wash down sugar crystals, and clip a candy thermometer to the inside of the pan, being sure that it doesn't touch the bottom of the pan.

4 Stir a couple of times until the temperature reaches 234 degrees; then remove from heat.

5 Add 1 stick of butter and stir to blend. Add pecans and stir. Beat the mixture well (about 5 to 10 minutes) with a wooden spoon, adding the vanilla extract as the batch thickens.

6 Pour the mixture into the buttered pan and spread it with a spatula.

7 Refrigerate the fudge until it's cool (30 minutes or so). Using a butter knife, cut the fudge into approximately 1½-inch squares.

Per serving: Calories 153 (From Fat 63); Fat 7g (Saturated 3g); Cholesterol 9mg; Sodium 21mg; Carbohydrate 24g (Dietary Fiber 1g); Protein 1g.

Mississippi Mud Fudge

Because pecans grow all across the South, quite a few candies in the South feature pecans. And my recipe for Mississippi Mud Fudge is no different.

Preparation time: *35 minutes plus one hour cooling time*

Yield: *About 36 1½-inch squares*

1 tablespoon butter for buttering pan

1 5-ounce can evaporated milk

1⅔ cups sugar

½ teaspoon salt

1½ cups chocolate chips (about 8 to 9 ounces)

2 cups plus ½ cup mini-marshmallows

1 cup pecan halves

1 teaspoon vanilla extract

1 Butter an 8 x 8-inch aluminum baking pan with 1 tablespoon of butter.

2 Combine the evaporated milk, sugar, and salt in a 4-quart saucepan and cook over medium heat to boiling, which takes about 11 minutes; stir occasionally.

3 Using a pastry brush and water, wash down the inside of the saucepan to wash away the sugar crystals. Clip a candy thermometer to the saucepan, keeping the tip off the bottom of the pan.

4 Constantly stir the mixture using a wooden spoon and cook the mixture to 234 degrees (which takes about 9 minutes). Then remove it from the heat and remove the thermometer.

5 Add the chocolate chips, 2 cups of marshmallows, and pecans, and stir with a wooden spoon until the chips and marshmallows melt (about 3 minutes). Add the vanilla extract and stir.

6 Pour the mixture into the buttered baking dish and immediately sprinkle the remaining marshmallows on top. Using a spatula, press them into the fudge until the marshmallows are covered with fudge.

7 Allow the fudge to cool at room temperature for one hour. Then use a butter knife to cut the fudge into 36 pieces that are about 1½-inches square.

Vary It! *Walnuts are a favorite in other areas of the United States, and you often find this nut in Rocky Road Fudge. To make the Rocky Road variation of this recipe, simply substitute walnuts for pecans.*

Per serving: *Calories 109 (From Fat 44); Fat 5g (Saturated 2g); Cholesterol 2mg; Sodium 39mg; Carbohydrate 17g (Dietary Fiber 1g); Protein 1g.*

Trying Out Nonchocolate Fudges

Since the 1970s, fudge shops have popped up all over the place, from board-walks to theme parks, from tourist towns to malls. As a result, quite a few folks are fully aware that fudge comes in almost any flavor that you can think of (and, frankly, probably a lot of flavors that you would never think of). Suffice it to say that a lot of fudge flavors that have nothing to do with chocolate are available to your palate.

Some of the most popular nonchocolate flavors include vanilla (also known as *opera fudge*), peanut butter, and penuche. When you master making a good vanilla fudge, you can make any number of fudges from that base — like the following recipes.

Opera Fudge

Opera fudge (shown in the color section) is a fancy name for vanilla fudge. If you can make a simple batch of opera fudge, you can make a whole variety of other fudges using variations of additional ingredients, such as fruits, nuts, coffee, and other flavors. For instance, you can take this basic recipe and, with a little practice, add peanut butter when the batch is cooling at about 160 degrees to make a very good peanut butter fudge (see the next recipe).

You can even stir in chocolate chips at 110 degrees to make a vanilla chocolate chip fudge (if you get that out of the pot pretty quickly, the chips retain most of their shape and give a nice effect). You can make pretty much any fudge you can dream up.

Preparation time: *35 to 40 minutes plus one hour to cool*

Yield: *36 pieces, approximately 1½-inch squares*

1 tablespoon butter for buttering pan	¼ teaspoon salt
2 cups sugar	2 tablespoons butter
⅔ cup milk	1 teaspoon vanilla extract
2 tablespoons light corn syrup	

1 Butter an 8 x 8-inch aluminum baking pan with 1 tablespoon of butter.

2 Combine the sugar, milk, corn syrup, and salt in a 2-quart saucepan. Cook the mixture over medium heat, stirring it constantly with a wooden spoon until it boils, which takes about 11 minutes.

3 Wash down the inside of the pan with a pastry brush and water to wash down the sugar crystals and clip a candy thermometer on the side, being sure that it doesn't touch the bottom.

4 Heat the mixture — without stirring it — to 234 degrees, which takes about 9 or 10 minutes.

5 Remove the mixture from the heat, and stir in 2 tablespoons of butter to melt and blend.

6 Allow the mixture to cool to 110 degrees without stirring (about 35 to 40 minutes).

7 Add the vanilla extract and beat the mixture with a wooden spoon until it becomes smooth (about 10 minutes).

8 Pour the mixture into the buttered aluminum baking pan and smooth the mixture with a spatula. Allow the fudge to cool at room temperature for at least one hour before cutting it into 36 1½-inch squares with a butter knife.

Per serving: *Calories 58 (From Fat 10); Fat 1g (Saturated 1g); Cholesterol 3mg; Sodium 20mg; Carbohydrate 12g (Dietary Fiber 0g); Protein 0g.*

Peanut Butter Fudge

One of the favorite nonchocolate-flavor fudges is peanut butter fudge. In the United States, most folks seems to love peanut butter in candy, and fudge is one of the most popular places to find it.

Preparation time: *35 to 45 minutes plus 20 minutes for cooling*

Yield: *36 1½-inch squares*

1 tablespoon butter for buttering pan	*½ cup premium creamy peanut butter*
2 cups sugar	*1 tablespoon butter*
1 cup milk	*1 teaspoon vanilla extract*
¼ teaspoon salt	

1 Butter an 8 x 8-inch aluminum baking pan with 1 tablespoon of butter.

2 Combine the sugar, milk, and salt in a 2-quart saucepan. Bring the mixture to a rapid boil over medium heat (about 11 minutes), constantly stirring.

3 Wash down the inside of the pan with a pastry brush and water to wash down the sugar crystals.

4 Reduce the heat slightly but maintain a boil; clip a candy thermometer to the side of the pan, not allowing the tip to touch the bottom of the pan. Cook without stirring the mixture to 234 degrees; this step takes about 9 to 10 minutes.

5 Remove the mixture from the heat, and allow it to cool to 160 degrees, which takes about 25 to 30 minutes.

6 Add the peanut butter, 1 tablespoon of butter, and the vanilla extract. Then beat the mixture with a wooden spoon until it's smooth (approximately 3 or 4 minutes should be fine to mix the peanut butter in well).

7 Pour the mixture into an aluminum baking pan and spread with a spatula.

8 Chill the fudge until it's firm (about 20 minutes or so) and, using a butter knife, cut it into squares of approximately 1½ inches.

Per serving: Calories 74 (From Fat 24); Fat 3g (Saturated 1g); Cholesterol 3mg; Sodium 36mg; Carbohydrate 12g (Dietary Fiber 0g); Protein 1g.

Penuche Fudge

Penuche fudge is made with brown sugar and has a taste that some find similar to maple fudge. *Penuche* can be spelled several ways, but no matter how it's spelled, the recipes all have brown sugar in them.

Preparation time: *35 to 40 minutes plus one hour to cool*

Yield: *36 squares 1½-inch squares*

1 tablespoon plus ½ teaspoon butter	¼ teaspoon salt
2 cups dark brown sugar, packed	⅓ teaspoon vanilla extract
½ cup light corn syrup	½ cup milk

1 Butter an 8 x 8-inch aluminum baking pan with 1 tablespoon of butter.

2 Combine the brown sugar, milk, corn syrup, ½ teaspoon of butter, and salt in a 2-quart saucepan. Cook the mixture over medium heat, stirring it constantly until it boils (about 11 minutes).

3 Wash down the inside of the pan with a pastry brush and water to wash down the sugar crystals. Then clip a candy thermometer to the side of the saucepan, being sure not to let the tip touch the bottom of the pan.

4 Heat the mixture without stirring it to 234 degrees, which takes about 9 to 10 minutes.

5 Remove the mixture from the heat, and allow it to cool at room temperature until it reaches 110 degrees. Cooling should take 35 to 45 minutes.

6 Add the vanilla extract and beat the mixture with a wooden spoon until it's creamy (about 5 to 10 minutes).

7 Pour the mixture into the buttered 8 x 8-inch aluminum pan and smooth the mixture with a spatula.

8 Allow the fudge to cool at room temperature for about an hour and, using a butter knife, cut the fudge into approximately 1½-inch squares.

Vary It! *To make maple fudge instead of penuche fudge, simply substitute granulated maple sugar for the dark brown sugar. See Chapter 24 for a list of suppliers.*

Per serving: *Calories 64 (From Fat 4); Fat 0g (Saturated 0g); Cholesterol 2mg; Sodium 28mg; Carbohydrate 16g (Dietary Fiber 0g); Protein 0g.*

Zeroing In on Fudge Centers

Sometimes you just have to mix peanut butter and chocolate. One popular way to do this is to make a peanut butter fudge and roll the fudge into bite-size balls. Then you coat the peanut butter balls with rich milk chocolate and stand back while your tongue beats your brains out. It's that good. I illustrate how to dip more items in chocolate in Chapter 15.

Peanut Butter Balls

This recipe is so easy that you'll find yourself making it all the time just to have some tasty treats around the house. This recipe requires tempered milk chocolate, which I show you how to whip up in Chapter 14.

One nice thing about this recipe is that you can make the balls and store them in an airtight plastic container until you're ready to dip them. However, when storing them, there's always the possibility of someone eating the undipped balls, so you may have to put them under lock and key.

Preparation time: 1½ hours

Yield: 40 to 50 pieces

2 cups creamy peanut butter

¼ cup butter

½ teaspoon popcorn salt

2 cups confectioners' sugar

1½ pounds milk chocolate, chopped and melted for tempering

1 12-ounce bag peanut butter chips (you will use about 50 chips for the topping; optional)

1 Line a cookie sheet or a countertop with wax paper.

2 Combine the peanut butter, butter, and salt in a microwaveable bowl. Heat the ingredients in the microwave for 1 to 2 minutes until they're soft, checking and stirring every 20 seconds. Heat the mixture until it's warm to the touch, or about 100 degrees.

3 Mix in the confectioners' sugar and blend it into the mixture with a spatula until the mixture is doughlike.

4 Pinch off a piece of the dough and roll it into equal-size balls. Make the balls a little smaller than a walnut in its shell.

5 Temper the chocolate as described in Chapter 14. Dip the balls into the tempered milk chocolate and place a peanut butter chip on top (if you like). Then place the ball on a paper-lined cookie sheet or similar flat surface to dry. If the room isn't at about 70 degrees or if you feel your kitchen is a little damp, place the balls in the refrigerator for 5 minutes to set the chocolate. If you leave them in too long — an hour or more — it may cause condensation to form on your candy.

Per serving: Calories 115 (From Fat 70); Fat 8g (Saturated 2g); Cholesterol 3mg; Sodium 71mg; Carbohydrate 10g (Dietary Fiber 1g); Protein 3g.

Wrapping and Storing Your Fudge Properly

As you master the art of making fudge, you can produce such good results that storing your fudge may not be a problem for you because you'll eat it all! But for those rare occasions when you need to store your candy for a while, I have good news: You can store it easily!

To store fudge for less than a week, simply put the candy in a plastic storage container. Easy enough, right? When storing fudge in this manner, place a waxed paper sheet between the layers of fudge to prevent the pieces or slices from sticking to one another and damaging your candy.

Most fudges don't take to refrigeration very well because it dries out the fudge. You probably already have Aunt Betty's fruitcake for the doorstop, so keep your fudge at room temperature at a range of 70 to 75 degrees.

If, for any reason, you need to store your fudge for more than a week, you can freeze it. Freezing fudge for up to six months is usually all right. Because freezers vary, I can't guarantee exactly how long you can freeze your fudge, but six months is a good general rule.

To keep your fudge in tip-top shape, follow these tips when you freeze fudge:

- ✔ Place serving-size portions or smaller pieces of fudge in a freezer bag. Place that bag in another freezer bag and freeze.

- ✔ For larger portions of fudge, place waxed paper between the fudge pieces and wrap everything in plastic wrap. Place this package in a freezer bag and freeze.

To thaw the fudge, remove it from the freezer and allow it to come to room temperature before removing it from the bags. Letting it thaw overnight is best because it prevents condensation from occurring and spoiling your candy.

Clockwise from top: Cappuccino Truffles and Grand
Marnier Truffles (Chapter 18); Peanut Butter Meltaways
(Chapter 6); Caramel Pecan Clusters (Chapter 7)

From top: Caramels dipped in chocolate (Chapter 7);
Caramel Corn with Peanuts and Chocolate (Chapter 13);
Almond Butter Toffee (Chapter 11)

From top: Caramel Dessert Apples (Chapter 7);
Peanut Brittle and Pecan Brittle (Chapter 12);
Chocolate-dipped Pretzels (Chapter 15)

Clockwise from left: Pecan Rolls (Chapter 8);
Divinity with Pecans (Chapter 8); Pecan Pralines
(Chapter 11)

From top: Easy Raspberry Fruit Jellies (Chapter 10);
Donna's Best Fudge (Chapter 9); Opera Fudge (Chapter 9);
Basic Marzipan dipped in chocolate (Chapter 10)

From top: Chocolate Apricots, Chocolate Orange Peels, Chocolate Strawberries, and Chocolate Cherries (Chapter 15)

From top: Hand-dipped Nut Clusters (Chapter 16); Almond Bark (Chapter 16); Butter Creams Decorated with Sprinkles and Nuts (Chapter 17)

From top: Dipped and Decorated Rice Cereal Bars
(Chapter 21); Skewered Marshmallows (Chapter 21)

Chapter 10

Making Magic with Marshmallows, Fruit Jellies, and Marzipan

Some candies are simply fun. Such a candy is marshmallow. I love biting into a thin chocolate shell and sinking my teeth into a fluffy piece of marshmallow. I don't know which I find more pleasing: the fluffy marshmallow or the contrast between the chocolate and the light center. But something about that combination makes my taste buds happy.

Another candy that's really popular is the *fruit jelly.* This gelatin-based candy is pretty simple to produce, and you can coat jellies in sugar or leave off the sugar coating and go straight to the chocolate. Dipping a fruit jelly in chocolate produces a completely different effect.

The last fun candy I tell you how to make in this chapter is *marzipan,* which is a candy made of almond paste and sugar that is shaped like fruits and vegetables (but you don't have to get that fancy if you don't want to). Marzipan is one of those candies you either love or . . . well, you don't.

In this chapter, I show you how to make delicious, light marshmallows; tasty fruit jellies; and excellent marzipan that's wonderful when coated with chocolate, especially dark chocolate. I enjoy making these fun candies, and I hope that you do, too!

Making Marshmallows from Scratch

Everybody knows what a marshmallow is, but do they know what it's actually made of? A primary ingredient in marshmallows is gelatin, which gives the candies their texture by acting as a thickening agent. When a marshmallow recipe calls for gelatin, be precise in your measurements because erring with gelatin will spoil your batch: Using too much gelatin gives a candy a tough consistency, and using too little gelatin produces a marshmallow that's too soft.

You don't simply add gelatin to a marshmallow recipe: First, you must soak it in water to soften it. This soaking causes the gelatin to perform its thickening magic in your candy. Then you add the gelatin to the rest of the ingredients, which typically include granulated sugar, light corn syrup, and vanilla extract.

For the best texture in a marshmallow (or a fruit jelly, which I cover later in this chapter), gelatin is difficult to top. But if you're a vegetarian, you probably don't wish to use something made from animal hooves and horns like gelatin. Occasionally, cooks substitute Agar Agar for gelatin. This product, which is available at health-food stores, is made from seaweed.

The second part of marshmallow production involves beating your mixture to create the candy's fluffiness. You pour the cooked and beaten marshmallow into a paper-lined pan to be cut when it has set. After your marshmallow has set, you cut it, powder the pieces with enough confectioners' sugar or cornstarch so that you don't notice any stickiness, and place them in an airtight plastic storage container until you're ready to enjoy them. Place a sheet of wax paper between layers for added protection, and leave the container on the counter at room temperature.

Protected in this manner, your marshmallows should remain fresh for about six weeks at room temperature. I have never frozen marshmallow, but I don't know why you can't freeze yours, if you desire. Place the pieces in a freezer bag, layered with wax paper, and place that in another freezer bag. Freeze for up to six months. When you're ready to thaw, let the bags sit on the counter overnight at room temperature. When the marshmallow is thawed the next day, remove it from the bag and enjoy.

Homemade Marshmallows

You may wonder why someone would want to make homemade marshmallow if you can buy very good marshmallows at the store. Well, purchased marshmallows limit you because they pretty much come in two sizes: large and mini. And they also usually come in one color: white. But sometimes you just have to have a bigger hunk of marshmallow, or you may want a different color and flavor — like strawberry marshmallow. All you have to do is take the basic recipe, add flavor and color, and you satisfy your taste.

Preparation time: *40 minutes plus overnight to set*

Yield: *30 to 35 pieces*

½ cup plus ½ cup water

1-pound box confectioners' sugar (you won't need the entire box; just keep plenty of sugar handy)

3 1-tablespoon envelopes unflavored gelatin

2 cups granulated sugar

1 cup light corn syrup

¼ teaspoon salt

2 teaspoons vanilla extract

1 Place ½ cup of cold water in a mixing bowl, sprinkle 3 gelatin envelopes into the water, and put aside for about 5 minutes to soften the gelatin.

2 Line a 9 x 13-inch glass baking dish with parchment paper, and generously sprinkle the lined dish with about 3 tablespoons of confectioners' sugar using a sieve (doing so helps marshmallow release from the paper).

3 Place the granulated sugar, ½ cup water, corn syrup, and salt in a 2-quart saucepan, and cook over medium heat until the sugar dissolves and the solution comes to a boil (about 15 minutes). Cover the mixture with a lid for about 3 minutes to allow any sugar crystals to dissolve from the sides of the pan. Remove the lid, place a candy thermometer on the side without allowing it to touch the bottom of the pan, and cook on high heat until the mixture reaches 240 degrees (about another 11 minutes). Remove the pan from the heat.

4 With the mixer on medium speed, slowly pour the cooked syrup into the gelatin mixture. When you've poured all the syrup into the pot, beat the mixture on high speed, using the whisk attachment for about 15 minutes until it becomes white and quite thick. During the beating process, stop the mixer to scrape the sides of the bowl because marshmallow thickens on the sides. Beat in the vanilla extract on slow speed.

5 When the mixture is thick like a thick crème of marshmallow, scrape it into a lined baking dish and spread it with a rubber spatula (see Figure 10-1). The marshmallow is quite sticky and thick at this stage, so simply do your best to spread it in the dish. Sprinkle the top with 2 to 3 tablespoons of confectioners' sugar (using a sieve is best to spread the sugar).

6 Allow the marshmallow to set uncovered overnight at room temperature; then remove the marshmallow from the dish by lifting the paper lining by the corners. Peel off the paper and cut the marshmallow into 30 to 35 1½ to 2-inch squares.

Per serving: *Calories 78 (From Fat 0); Fat 0g (Saturated 0g); Cholesterol 0mg; Sodium 29mg; Carbohydrate 20g (Dietary Fiber 0g); Protein 1g.*

Figure 10-1:
Pour your
marsh-
mallow
carefully,
and use a
rubber
spatula to
spread it in
your dish.

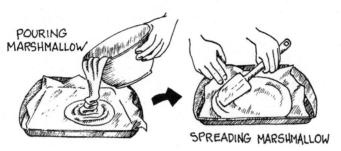

POURING MARSHMALLOW

SPREADING MARSHMALLOW

Easy No-cook Marshmallows

With this recipe, you make a nice light marshmallow that has a very chewy quality. This recipe is technically a no-cook recipe because no boiling is involved: You just heat your combined ingredients to 160 degrees.

When you handle the marshmallow, I recommend using a 50-50 ratio of cornstarch and sugar mixture to prevent the marshmallow from sticking to your hands. In the previous recipe, I recommend using confectioners' sugar for the same purpose. Frankly, you can use either option because both work just fine; I simply like to offer alternatives when I can to present you with options that serious confectioners use.

Preparation time: *55 minutes plus overnight to set*

Yield: *117 1-inch marshmallows*

¼ cup plus ¼ cup cornstarch	*2½ cups granulated sugar*
¼ cup plus ¼ cup confectioners' sugar	*2 cups light corn syrup*
3 envelopes unflavored gelatin	*1 teaspoon vanilla extract*
½ cup plus ½ cup water	

1 Sprinkle a mixture of ¼ cup cornstarch and ¼ cup confectioners' sugar into a 9 x 13-inch glass baking dish and set aside.

2 Place ½ cup of water in a small bowl and let the gelatin soak for 30 minutes or longer.

3 Combine ½ cup water, the granulated sugar, and corn syrup and heat in a 2-quart saucepan until the sugar dissolves — approximately 160 degrees. If you want to be really accurate, clip a thermometer onto the pan when the solution comes to a gentle, lightly bubbling boil. Don't let the tip touch the bottom of the pan.

4 Add the gelatin/water mixture and vanilla extract to the saucepan and stir until it dissolves into the mixture.

5 Place the mixture in a mixing bowl and beat it on high speed with a mixer using the whisk attachment until it's white and fluffy. The volume of the mixture will double.

6 Pour the marshmallow into a 9 x 13-inch glass baking dish and spread the marshmallow with a rubber spatula. Using a sieve, sprinkle the mixture of ¼ cup of confectioners' sugar and ¼ cup of starch on top of the marshmallow and let it set at room temperature for 24 hours before cutting it into 1-inch squares.

Per serving: Calories 37 (From Fat 0); Fat 0g (Saturated 0g); Cholesterol 0mg; Sodium 7mg; Carbohydrate 10g (Dietary Fiber 0g); Protein 0g.

To go one step beyond plain marshmallows, why not try coating your treats in milk chocolate? I often say that I don't know of many things that aren't improved with the addition of chocolate, and I especially believe that statement to be true of marshmallow because I simply love the snap created by biting into the thin chocolate shell and the joy of finding that delightful white confection hiding inside.

To chocolate-coat your marshmallows, first review the tempering information in Chapter 14 and the hand-dipping information in Chapter 15. To coat a batch the size of the marshmallow recipes in this chapter, you need to temper between 2 and 3 pounds of chocolate. Line one or two cookie sheets (depending on how many marshmallows you dip) with wax paper, or place a section of wax paper on the counter. Place the dipped marshmallows on the wax paper to dry; at room temperature, the chocolate should set in about 5 to 6 minutes. If you're worried that the room is a little warm, just place the marshmallows cookie sheet in the refrigerator for 5 minutes.

A name with ancient (plant) roots

The name *marshmallow* is derived from the food's origin — ancient Egypt. More than 4,000 years ago, the Egyptians enjoyed a treat made from the mallow plant *(Athaea officinalis),* which, oddly enough, grew in the marshes of Egypt. Thus, the name *marshmallow* came to be. (However, I wonder what the name was in Egyptian. Maybe we're lucky, because the name could have been *athacinalis,* so maybe *marshmallow* is okay.)

Despite the name, today marshmallow is made with gelatin, which people began substituting years ago for the mallow plant, even though mallow grows in marshes and other bodies of water in the United States. Gelatin is an animal protein that's derived from various parts of animals, primarily hooves, horns, and skin. For vegetarians, an alternative gelatin form is produced from Agar Agar, which is made from seaweed. You can find this alternative at health-food stores. Agar Agar and gelatin produce similar results.

Jamming with Fruit Jellies

One of the most popular candies I make is the fruit jelly. I produce *sanded* (or sugar-coated) jellies and chocolate-covered jellies. As a sanded candy, jellies produce a very nice, slightly tart piece. When I leave off the sugar coating and make a chocolate-covered piece, the result is a completely different confection with a different appeal. You may find that you enjoy one more than the other; then again, you may like them equally. You get the opportunity to make a choice later in this section.

In the following recipe, I show you how to make your fruit jellies. One key ingredient is gelatin, which you can easily find in grocery stores. I recommend purchasing a box containing four envelopes for the following recipe. If you wish, you can substitute Agar Agar, available at health-food stores, for gelatin.

This fruit jelly recipe also includes coloring and flavors to make it look and taste like raspberry as well as another important ingredient I use in jellies: citric acid. The citric acid acts as a natural preservative, but mostly it brings a little tartness to the candy. You can locate the flavors, citric acid, and food colors at the suppliers listed in Chapter 24.

When coloring and flavoring jellies, a little bit goes a long way. Use powdered food coloring and essential oils sparingly because you want to suggest the flavor, not overpower the eyes and taste buds.

Easy Raspberry Fruit Jellies

The fruit jelly is a very special piece of candy. In my shop, we make this jelly in five flavors: raspberry, cherry, orange, lemon, and lime. We settled on those five flavors, but you can make other flavors, too. Here I show you one recipe, but you can substitute other flavored oils and food colorings for other pieces. Check out these jellies in the color section.

Preparation time: *35 to 40 minutes plus 1½ to 2 hours to cool*

Yield: *45 pieces, about 1 inch square*

1½ cups corn syrup	¼ teaspoon red powdered food coloring
1¼ cups sugar	1 teaspoon raspberry oil flavor
1 ounce unflavored gelatin (usually 1 box of 4 packets)	¼ teaspoon citric acid
2½ cups water	2 cups granulated sugar

1 Take a piece of nonstick paper that's about 11 x 7 inches and, from the corners, cut in about 3 inches at a 45-degree angle. Press the paper into a 5 x 9-inch loaf pan, and press around the bottom of the pan to crease (see Figure 10-2). Set the lined pan aside.

2 In the top pan of a double boiler, warm the corn syrup to 100 degrees (use a candy thermometer to check). You simply want the syrup warm enough to pour easily.

3 In a 6-quart heavy saucepan, combine the sugar and gelatin and mix with a spoon to blend the two dry ingredients. Add water and bring to a boil over medium heat, occasionally stirring with a wooden spoon for 10 to 12 minutes.

4 When the sugar mixture comes to a boil, pour the corn syrup into the pan with the sugar and add the food coloring. Then wash down the inside of the saucepan with a pastry brush and water. Clip on a candy thermometer, being sure that the tip doesn't touch the bottom of the pan, and continue heating over medium heat and stirring constantly until the temperature reaches 228 degrees (in about 15 minutes).

5 Remove the batch from the heat and add the flavoring and citric acid; stir the batch for about 15 seconds to blend. Pour the mixture into a lined pan, and allow it to cool uncovered for 1½ to 2 hours at room temperature.

6 Cut the jellies into 1-inch squares and toss them into a small bowl filled with 2 cups of granulated sugar; coat each piece well. Each jelly takes as much sugar as needed and no more. Be sure to coat all sides.

Tip: *You may occasionally note that the tops of the jellies aren't sticky. If you encounter this situation with your jellies, before cutting, simply sprinkle a few drops of water on the tops and rub them lightly with your fingertips to create a slight stickiness. Then cut and coat them in sugar.*

Tip: *Store your sanded jellies in an airtight container. Although the sanding process should prevent most sticking problems, place a sheet of wax paper between the layers if you stack them. You can store them at room temperature for six to eight weeks this way. I would not freeze them because you don't make that many pieces at a time and because room-temperature storage life is so long.*

Per serving: Calories 90 (From Fat 1); Fat 0g (Saturated 0g); Cholesterol 0mg; Sodium 15mg; Carbohydrate 23g (Dietary Fiber 0g); Protein 1g.

Figure 10-2:
Properly prepping your loaf pan is essential for jellies.

PRESS PAPER AROUND THE
BOTTOM OF THE PAN TO CREASE IT.

Instead of coating your jellies in sugar, you may want to dip them into milk or dark chocolate. To coat your batch in chocolate:

1. **Dust the jellies you plan to coat in chocolate with cornstarch (have 1 cup of cornstarch in a small bowl), and cut them into 1-inch squares, being certain to cover all the sides with cornstarch.** When you're done dusting them well with cornstarch, shake the pieces in a sieve or a colander to remove as much excess as possible. The pieces will retain as much of the starch as they need and no more.

2. **Temper 1½ pounds of milk or dark chocolate immediately.** See Chapter 14 for details on tempering.

3. **Hand-dip the pieces in the chocolate and place the pieces on wax paper to dry for 30 minutes.** Be sure to coat your pieces evenly because the starch sometimes causes the chocolate to miss a spot. If you find any bare spots, simply rub chocolate on the spot with your finger.

4. **When the pieces are dry, place each piece in a #6 brown paper cup.** These cups are available from the suppliers I list in Chapter 24.

Store your chocolate-coated jellies in an airtight container at room temperature for up to three weeks. You can place wax paper between the layers, but the jellies won't stick together once they're completely coated with chocolate. I always recommend enjoying your candy as soon as possible. (I'm sure you won't argue with that advice.) You can always make some more another day!

Having Fun with Marzipan

Marzipan is a delightful and quite versatile candy. When making marzipan, Europeans probably start with raw almonds and roast them, grind them, and make their own almond paste. In America, some candy makers like to cut the occasional corner — me included — so I like to start with a canned almond paste (which is available in most grocery stores) and add sugar, flavoring, and a few other ingredients to it to make a wonderful basic marzipan. This marzipan makes an excellent center.

The batch of marzipan you make with the following recipe is quite simple: It involves just a bit of mixing and a bit of cooling time, which allows the marzipan mixture to set properly before you cut it.

When making marzipan, just like with the marshmallow in this chapter, keep a box of confectioners' sugar handy and rub it liberally on your hands and on the surface of the marzipan before handling.

After the marzipan is prepared, I like coating it with dark chocolate (milk chocolate is just a little too sweet for this center). Of course, no one says you *can't* use milk chocolate to coat your marzipan; I mean, no candy police will come to your house and take you away for a coating violation. Well, anyway, to coat your marzipan after you've cut it into pieces about ¾-inch square, hand-dip it in tempered chocolate (see Chapter 14 for tempering info) and place each piece on a small sheet of wax paper to dry. After dipping, allow about 30 minutes for the chocolate to dry before storing your candies.

You should store your marzipan in an airtight container at room temperature for up to four weeks. If you layer the pieces in a container, place wax paper between the layers.

If you don't want to dip your marzipan in chocolate right away, let it cool; then wrap the small, uncut loaf in plastic wrap, and store it in the refrigerator. You should be able to safely store it for two months.

Basic Marzipan

Okay, this recipe is one where, if you blink, it's done. This recipe is very simple and gives you a basic idea of what marzipan is. You will be able to experience the unique flavor of this delightful confection, which has a slight amaretto, some even say cherry-like, flavor. At any rate, you should enjoy making and coating this candy and, if you should put together an assortment of chocolates, this piece would be a nice addition.

Preparation time: *50 minutes*

Yield: *About 40 to 45 pieces*

2 8-ounce cans almond paste

1 ½ cups confectioners' sugar

1 teaspoon amaretto flavoring or almond extract

Additional confectioners' sugar to help when rolling finished batch

1 Line an 8 x 8-inch aluminum pan with wax paper and set aside.

2 Combine the almond paste, sugar, and amaretto flavoring or almond extract in a mixing bowl and beat on low speed for about 5 minutes until the mixture forms a uniform paste.

3 Using a rubber spatula, scrape the dough into a lined pan, and cover it with wax paper. Place the dough in the refrigerator to set for about 45 minutes.

4 Take the dough from the refrigerator and dust it with confectioners' sugar; roll the dough with a rolling pin until it's about a ¼-inch thick slab (see Figure 10-3). This rolling and kneading of the dough give it a cohesiveness that allows you to form and cut the dough into pieces.

5 Cut the dough into ¾-inch-square pieces.

Per serving: *Calories 63 (From Fat 25); Fat 3g (Saturated 0g); Cholesterol 0mg; Sodium 1mg; Carbohydrate 9g (Dietary Fiber 1g); Protein 1g.*

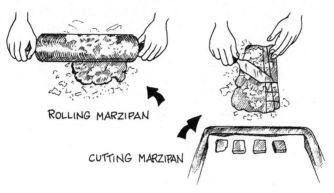

Figure 10-3:
Use a rolling pin to flatten your marzipan before you cut it.

ROLLING MARZIPAN

CUTTING MARZIPAN

Part III
Getting a Little Nutty

The 5th Wave   By Rich Tennant

"Homemade peanut brittle? I left the screen door
open while it was cooling, so just eat around
the insects."

In this part...

As the title of this part implies, you get a chance to make some nutty confections. What did you think the title meant? If you're one of those folks who likes a few nuts in your candy, you can have a ball here.

In this part, you find some of the most popular candies, including toffee that'll make your tongue beat your brains out. This toffee is *that* good. You also need to try one or more of the delicious brittle recipes. If crunches or pralines are more your thing, you get a chance to try your hand at those recipes, too. Or perhaps you crave something that involves popcorn. Whatever your sweet tooth aches for, this part has plenty of opportunities to satisfy you.

Chapter 11

Taking On Crunches, Toffees, and Pralines

*I*n this chapter, I tell you all about crunches, toffees, and pralines and show you how to make all three of these crispy, delicious treats. The biggest difference in making crunches, toffees, and pralines involves the temperature to which you cook the batches.

First up is the butter crunch, also known as a butter crisp. A *butter crunch* is a crunchy confection that you cook to at least 290 degrees. This candy is similar to toffee (a crispy confection that contains a lot of butter and sugar), but it contains slightly less butter. If you drop the butter content of a crunch even lower, you produce a butter crisp — but really, these names are purely a designation.

I also tell you how to prepare *toffee,* another crunchy candy that has a buttery-rich flavor. You cook this confection to about 300 degrees. The signatures of a good toffee are high butter content and, not to be left out, a nearly equal amount of sugar.

The final candy you can whip up using the recipes in this chapter is the *praline,* a confection that consists of sugar, corn syrup, butter, pecans, and a few other small ingredients that you cook to 238 to 243 degrees. Pralines are a tender, creamier candy than crunches or toffees, and you can make this confection using different sugars, including granulated sugar, brown sugar, or even maple sugar.

Now that you have the scoop on these candies, it's time to get down to some candy-making business. Just follow my lead.

Getting Down to Crunch Time

To make this butter-crunch recipe, you combine butter, sugar, nuts (almonds or pecans), and corn syrup as the main ingredients and cook them to at least 290 degrees. When cooking up a batch, make sure you use a thermometer to determine the precise temperature of the candy.

When cooking candies like crunches to such high temperatures, errors occur quickly. Temperatures rise, even after you've removed the pot from the heat source, because the pot and the internal heat of the batch can cause a slight rise in temperature. Anticipate your target temperature, and you can avoid scorching your crunches, which are none too tasty.

After you cook and cool the crunches, you coat them with chocolate. You can use tempered chocolate (see Chapter 14) as the coating for the following recipe but, because you cover the chocolate completely with nuts, not tempering your chocolate doesn't affect the showmanship or taste of your candy. What I'm saying is, tempering your chocolate isn't essential for this recipe. Besides, not tempering your chocolate saves you time. (You're welcome.)

When you finish your crunches, place them in a plastic container. If you plan to keep your crunches for a couple of weeks, place the finished product in an air-tight plastic container and store at room temperature. This product does contain butter, so you don't want it sitting around on the counter for a long time.

If you want to store your crunches for an extended period of time, freeze them. To prepare them for freezing, place the pieces in a freezer bag using wax paper to separate the layers. Then place the first freezer bag in a second freezer bag, and put the bag of crunches in the freezer. You can freeze them for up to six months. To thaw your crunches, remove them from the freezer, and allow the candy to thaw overnight at room temperature before you remove them from the freezer bags. This method of thawing protects the candy from condensation, which can damage your candy.

Nutty Butter Crunch

Candy makers have different methods for cooking toffees and toffeelike candies, such as crunches. Some cooks add toasted nuts at the end, and some cooks add raw nuts during the cooking. I like cooking the nuts along with the rest of the batch because I feel that it adds more nut flavor. You can make this recipe with raw chopped almonds or raw medium pecan pieces, and you get the same results.

Coarsely chop the nuts that you use to cook in the crunch with a large knife, and finely chop the nuts that you use to cover the crunch at the end.

Preparation time: 2 hours, including cooling time

Yield: 30 to 35 large pieces

1 cup (2 sticks) butter plus enough butter for coating the baking pan heavily

2 cups raw almonds or pecans

1½ cups granulated sugar

3 tablespoons light corn syrup

3 tablespoons water

12 ounces milk chocolate, chopped, for coating

1 Heavily butter a 9 x 13-inch aluminum baking pan and set aside.

2 Chop 1 cup of nuts into medium pieces using a large knife; set them aside for use in cooking the crunch. Using a food processor, finely chop 1 cup of almonds for topping the finished crunch; put them aside.

3 In a 4-quart saucepan, combine 1 cup of butter, the granulated sugar, corn syrup, and water. Cook over medium heat and stir constantly until the batch comes to a boil (about 11 minutes).

4 When the batch comes to a boil, attach a candy thermometer to the side of the pan, being sure not to let it touch the bottom of the pan.

5 When the temperature reaches 250 degrees, stir in 1 cup of chopped nuts and continue stirring. When the temperature reaches 300 degrees, remove from heat, pour into a baking pan, and spread quickly and evenly with a rubber spatula.

6 Allow the batch to cool for about an hour at room temperature (it should be cool to the touch); then remove it from the pan by hand and place it on wax paper.

7 In a microwaveable bowl, melt the chocolate on high until it reaches about 100 degrees (about 2 minutes). Stop the microwave every 30 seconds to stir. On the third stop, check the temperature with a chocolate thermometer to see how close to 100 degrees the chocolate is. Don't heat the chocolate past 115 degrees because you don't want to scorch it.

8 Pour about half the chocolate on one side of the crunch, and use an offset spatula to spread it to create a thin chocolate layer. Then heavily sprinkle about half the finely chopped nuts on top immediately. Cover the candy completely (see Figure 11-1) and place wax paper on top of it.

9 Carefully turn the crunch over, trying not to spill loose nuts, and repeat the chocolate/nut coating on that side.

10 Place the candy in the refrigerator for about 15 minutes until the chocolate sets. Remove the candy from the refrigerator and break it by hand into large pieces.

Per serving: Calories 183 (From Fat 112); Fat 13g (Saturated 5g); Cholesterol 15mg; Sodium 12mg; Carbohydrate 18g (Dietary Fiber 1g); Protein 3g.

Figure 11-1:
After you
spread the
melted
chocolate
on your
crunch with
a spatula,
make sure
you
completely
cover it with
finely
chopped
nuts.

1. USE A SPATULA TO SPREAD CHOCOLATE ON ONE SIDE.

2. COVER THE CHOCOLATE COMPLETELY WITH NUTS. REPEAT ON THE OTHER SIDE.

COATING CRUNCHES

Trying Terrific Toffee

Toffee is a buttery rich, very crunchy creation. A good toffee has equal or nearly equal amounts of butter and sugar and a large helping of nuts to impart their special flavor.

A special ingredient for this toffee recipe is soy lecithin. In toffee, soy lecithin prevents the fats from separating and creating an oily residue. This ingredient is available from the suppliers I list in Chapter 24.

To make toffee, you cook the batch to the 300-degree range, which is just short of burning the candy to a crisp. (But don't worry: You produce a wonderful candy with this recipe.) Toffee sets up pretty quickly after you pour it, so you need to pour it out of the pan fairly quickly because, at 300 degrees or so, you can scorch it.

After your toffee cools, you need to coat it with chocolate immediately (melted chocolate, not tempered) or place it in a very cool, dry area until you're ready to coat it. After the toffee cools for a couple of hours, you can break it into pieces.

You may choose to store your toffee for two or three days before you coat it with chocolate. If so, place the candy in an airtight plastic container. Just remember that this product is made to be coated, and waiting doesn't do anything to improve the candy. This candy is about enjoyment, so finish the coating, and get on to the enjoyment.

Almond Butter Toffee

This recipe contains a higher percentage of butter, which makes it a toffee rather than a crunch. You can call your candy anything you want; I just have to adhere to a higher standard, so this recipe makes a toffee. If desired, you can make this recipe with pecans or raw cashews. This recipe produces a very buttery, very crunchy piece of candy; see it for yourself in the color section.

Preparation time: *2 hours, including cooling time*

Yield: *55 to 60 pieces*

2 cups (1 pound) butter, cut into pieces, plus enough butter to heavily coat a baking pan

2 cups almonds

¼ cup warm water

¼ teaspoon salt

2 cups granulated sugar

1 teaspoon lecithin

12 ounces milk chocolate, chopped and melted for coating

1 Heavily butter a 9 x 13-inch aluminum baking pan and set aside.

2 Using a food processor, finely chop 1 ½ cups of almonds for the topping and put aside. Also, using a knife, coarsely chop ½ cup of almonds for cooking.

3 In a 5-quart heavy saucepan, bring the butter to a boil (which takes about 11 minutes) over medium heat, and add warm water. Continue cooking the mixture on medium-high heat for about 11 more minutes, stirring occasionally.

4 When the pan returns to a boil, add the salt, and slowly stir in the sugar; continue stirring and boiling. When the sugar dissolves, clip a candy thermometer to the side of the pan, being certain that the stem doesn't touch the bottom of the pan. Add 1 teaspoon of soy lecithin.

5 When the temperature reaches 240 to 250 degrees, add ½ cup of coarsely chopped nuts.

6 When the temperature reaches 285 degrees, reduce to low heat, and cook to 310 degrees. Remove the mixture from the heat and pour it into the buttered aluminum baking pan.

7 Cool the batch for about one hour at room temperature; remove it from the pan by hand, and place it on wax paper.

8 Melt the chocolate in the microwave on high in a microwaveable bowl until the chocolate reaches 100 degrees (slightly warm to the touch) on a chocolate thermometer (about 2 minutes). Stop the heating process every 30 seconds to stir the chocolate and check the temperature.

9 Pour half the chocolate onto the toffee and spread it with an offset spatula. Heavily sprinkle the finely chopped nuts on top of the chocolate immediately. Place wax paper on top of the candy and turn it over; repeat the chocolate/nut coating on the other side.

10 Place the toffee in the refrigerator for about 15 minutes until the chocolate sets; remove the candy from the refrigerator, and break it by hand into large pieces.

Per serving: Calories 138 (From Fat 93); Fat 10g (Saturated 5g); Cholesterol 17mg; Sodium 16mg; Carbohydrate 11g (Dietary Fiber 1g); Protein 2g.

Store any leftover toffee in an airtight plastic container. Toffee, like its relative butter crunches, contains a lot of butter, but it contains even more butter than butter crunches. You can store the coated toffee at room temperature for two weeks. For longer storage, I recommend freezing the toffee. To do so, place the toffee pieces in a freezer bag with wax paper between layers to keep them separate. Place the first freezer bag in a second freezer bag (I always recommend double bagging), and keep in the freezer for up to six months. To thaw, remove the candy from the freezer, and allow it to thaw overnight at room temperature before removing it from the bags. This method prevents condensation from ruining your candy.

Perfecting Pralines

The word *praline* means different things to people in different parts of the world. In Europe, the praline is a candy with a pureed nut center that has a consistency similar to some peanut butter products in the United States. The center is most commonly made with hazelnuts (filberts) and is a staple in quite a few of the candies from that continent. In the United States, a traditional praline combines sugar, brown sugar, or both with butter, cream, or both and corn syrup to help stabilize the sugar. Of course, plenty of pecans are incorporated as well.

Praline has at least two different pronunciations in America, depending on whom you talk to. Some people say PRAH-leen, and some say PRAY-leen, but both are traditionally made with pecans. Now that nut is either pe-CAHN or PEA-can. I prefer the French pronunciation: PAY-canh. However you pronounce these words, the candy and the nut are pretty darn good.

This chapter provides two praline recipes. You can experiment with numerous combinations of ingredients, changing up your sugar and types of cream. You may discover that you prefer a little lighter piece or a little darker piece. While you're learning, you may produce a variety of textures: Some pralines may be crumbly, and some may be sticky. If you're willing to take recipe guidelines and experiment just a little, you can create your own recipe. Ultimately, you'll have more fun when you push the envelope a bit. Never be afraid to take cooking chances with the guidelines you receive. Heck, you may get it right on the first try.

When your pralines are cool, the best way to store them is to individually wrap them in plastic wrap and place them in an airtight plastic container at room temperature. You can store them with wax paper between the layers for about four days. And don't be alarmed: Pralines usually start to take on a sugary appearance after a few days because the sugar crystals continue forming.

Pecan Pralines

Pecan pralines (shown in the color section) are a real Southern favorite, and the presence of so many pecan trees in the South has made them a relatively inexpensive candy to make. Traditional pralines combine sugar (granulated or brown), corn syrup, butter, and pecans as the main ingredients.

Pralines are fairly easy to make. The process involves cooking the ingredients to around 240 degrees, adding the butter, stirring until you get just the right consistency, and then dipping them out. If you make them a few times, you learn the tricks of the trade.

Preparation: *1 hour and 45 minutes, including cooling time*

Yield: *About 2 dozen pralines*

1 ¼ cups granulated sugar	2 cups raw pecans, halves or large pieces
¾ cup light brown sugar, packed	¼ cup butter (1/2 stick), cut into small pieces
½ cup light corn syrup	2 teaspoons vanilla extract
½ cup water	

1 Line two cookie sheets with nonstick paper and set aside.

2 In a 5-quart saucepan, combine the sugars, corn syrup, water, and raw pecans and heat over medium heat until the sugar dissolves (about 10 minutes). Clip a candy thermometer onto the side of the saucepan, being certain that the stem doesn't touch the bottom of the pan.

3 Continue heating the mixture until the temperature reaches 240 degrees; heating takes about 11 to 14 more minutes. When the temperature reaches 240 degrees, remove the mixture from the heat, and add the butter pieces and vanilla extract; stir in the ingredients using a wooden spoon.

4 Allow the batch to set for 2 minutes in the pot; then beat the mixture with a wooden spoon until it loses its gloss and takes on a slightly dull appearance.

5 Using a tablespoon or an ice cream scoop, spoon the mixture onto the paper-lined cookie sheets into pieces about 2 to 2½ inches in diameter (you should make between 22 and 25 pieces).

6 Allow the candy to cool at room temperature for one hour.

Per serving: Calories 165 (From Fat 75); Fat 8g (Saturated 2g); Cholesterol 5mg; Sodium 11mg; Carbohydrate 24g (Dietary Fiber 1g); Protein 1g.

Pralines: A chameleon of the candy world

Although New Orleans (N'awlins, to locals) is famous for the pecan praline, neither the name nor the candy originated there. The word *praline* comes from a Frenchman by the name of Cesar de Plessis Praslin (1598–1675). Depending on whom you talk to, he wanted something to aid in digestion or desired a delicious treat to offer his lady friends when he went courting or they came calling.

As a romantic, I prefer the courtship version of the story but, actual facts aside, his chef created a combination of syrup and almonds and, with that, the praline was born. Years later, when travel across the ocean to the New World became common, the concept made its way to our shores, where a rebirth occurred, and the pecan praline was conceived.

No matter how the piece changed from a syrupy almond confection to a sugary pecan piece, the name stuck, and the praline is known far and wide. The praline is a wonderful piece of candy and is pretty easy to make. Pralines are made all across the South, but each section seems to have its own version.

In N'awlins, they swear by the PRAW-leen, which is a firm and very sweet confection with which most people can identify. But if you travel to other sections of the South — to Texas, for example — you find the chewy praline. Now these two pieces are almost as different from each other as the Southern praline is from the original piece produced by that French chef hundreds of years ago. Some things just don't have rules in the candy world; sometimes what's right boils down to what you want. And boiling down is just what praline production is all about.

Chewy Caramel Pralines

Folks in the Deep South like their pralines nice and firm, but a lot of people in Texas and a few other places prefer theirs chewy. I have friends in Texas who've built quite a reputation with their chewy pralines. This recipe is one adaptation of the chewy caramel-like praline that you may enjoy.

Preparation time: *1 hour and 10 minutes*

Yield: *80 to 85 pieces*

1½ cups granulated sugar

½ cup light brown sugar, tightly packed

2 cups light corn syrup

2 cups (1 pound) butter, cut into pieces

2 cups half and half

1 tablespoon vanilla extract

7½ cups raw pecan pieces

1 Line three cookie sheets with nonstick paper and set them aside.

2 In a 5-quart heavy saucepan, combine the sugars and corn syrup. Cook over medium-low heat, and stir constantly until the solution comes to a boil (about 10 minutes); clip a candy thermometer on the side of the pan, being careful that the tip of the thermometer doesn't touch the bottom of the pan.

3 Continue cooking until the batch reaches 250 degrees on the candy thermometer (about another 11 minutes); then remove from heat.

4 Add the butter, and stir to melt it. Then add half and half in a slow stream, and return the mixture to heat. Stir constantly until the batch reaches 241 degrees.

5 Remove the batch from the heat, and stir in the vanilla extract and pecan pieces.

6 Use a small ice cream scoop or spoon the mixture with a wooden spoon onto the paper-lined cookie sheets. Then allow it to cool for about one hour at room temperature.

Per serving: *Calories 152 (From Fat 107); Fat 12g (Saturated 4g); Cholesterol 14mg; Sodium 13mg; Carbohydrate 12g (Dietary Fiber 1g); Protein 1g.*

 You may freeze pralines for six months by placing them in a freezer bag and then in another freezer bag. To thaw, let them set overnight at room temperature (at least eight hours) to thaw completely before removing them from the bag.

Chapter 12

Breaking Out the Brittles

In This Chapter

▶ Dishing up basics on making brittles

▶ Trying delicious brittle recipes

▶ Putting away your brittles for safekeeping

Recipes in This Chapter

▶ Peanut Brittle

▶ Pecan Brittle

▶ Coconut Brittle

▶ Cashew Brittle

I can thank brittles for introducing me to the world of candy making. I have a special affinity for peanut brittle because it was the first candy that my wife Janet and I made many years ago. We had no concept of candy making, but someone taught my wife and me to make peanut brittle and, within a few years, we were serious candy makers. In those days, we made the brittle in our little home, so I have an appreciation of what cooking in your own kitchen at home is like.

Over the years, we added candy making of all types to our repertoire, but we still make peanut brittle in our store almost every day of the year. In this chapter, I show you how to create delicious peanut brittle as well as a few other variations of this yummy, crispy candy.

The Basics of Brittle Making

Simplicity is the key to brittles. Brittles are made primarily of sugar, nuts, and corn syrup, and the proportions of these ingredients are quite simple, too. When reading recipes for brittle, you may see variations, but I always use the same *volume* of sugar and nuts in brittle. Because of density, the sugar may weigh a little more than the nuts, but the volumes are the same in these brittles.

I find that maintaining the equal sugar-to-nuts ratio creates the perfect blend of nuts and brittle. Some folks prefer fewer nuts, though, and making brittle their way is fine. The nuts don't control the chemistry of the batch; the sugar/syrup ratio is more important. You can increase or decrease the amount of nuts that you use according to your personal taste or preference of appearance.

Whatever the amount of sugar you use in the recipe, the volume of corn syrup you use should be about half as much as the volume of the sugar. This ratio is of prime importance because the corn syrup controls the grain of the brittle. If the ratio of corn syrup to sugar is too low, the brittle can be quite grainy and unattractive when it cools. If the ratio of corn syrup to sugar is too high, the brittle may be stringy and sticky when it cools.

The other typical ingredients are a little salt, butter, and baking soda. The amounts you use of those ingredients also influence the outcome of your brittle. Salt enhances the flavor of the candy, and the more butter you add, the more buttery the brittle tastes. However, you don't need to add a lot of butter; the prescribed amount is fine. Baking soda causes the brittle to aerate and to rise a little, making the final product crunchy instead of brutally hard.

Because you usually add baking soda, salt, and butter at the end of the batch, place them in a small (5-ounce) paper cup with the butter on top. When the time comes to dump these ingredients into the batch, everything goes in all at once — when timing is important. And be sure to take a moment to sift the soda; if a lump goes into the batch, it usually doesn't break apart.

You cook brittles to a high temperature — about 300 degrees. You must constantly stir brittles to prevent scorching. When you cook to such high temperatures, you may be surprised at how inaccurate your candy thermometer is if you don't stir your mixture. The inaccuracies occur because, without agitation, pockets of heat build up in the batch, so keep the batch moving during the boiling process (which is about 25 minutes in a typical batch)!

Whenever you cook candy, you need to beware of getting burned. The high temperatures at which you cook brittles create a very volatile solution that spews small, boiling globules out of the pot. If these globules touch your skin, they can cause severe burns, and you should place the affected area under cold water and treat it as soon as possible. Resist the urge to touch the burned spot to your mouth because doing so causes a second, more severe burn to your lips.

During the cooking process, the nuts settle to the bottom of the pan or pot because of their weight. When the candy is boiling, constant stirring is of primary importance because, if you allow the nuts to lie on the bottom, they will scorch. And you really don't want that burned taste in your candy, do you?

I've seen thousands of recipes for various candies, and I'm aware of the differences in cooking methods. For example, quite a few people believe that you should add peanuts later in the process — adding roasted nuts at about 250 to 260 degrees and allowing them to cook for the last 40 degrees or so.

If you add roasted nuts, you should do so late in the batch because, if you put them in at the start, they overcook and can give your candy a scorched taste.

Although I respect others' cooking methods, I put the raw peanuts in at the beginning and allow them to cook during the entire process, thus imparting (I believe) more flavor to the syrup. I've used this method since the beginning of my candy-making days, and I haven't had any complaints about the taste. Some nuts, such as cashews (see the recipe later in this chapter), are okay to put in later in the process, but I have my feelings about peanut brittle.

When the batch reaches the target temperature, you usually take the batch off the heat and add a few ingredients (including the baking soda, butter, and salt), which you need to stir into the batch. Then you take the candy out of the pot because setting occurs pretty quickly once the cooking process is complete. From that point, you pour the brittle into pans, onto a cookie sheet, or onto a marble slab and stretch it. How you finish the batch is a matter of preference.

In the recipes in this chapter, I suggest pouring your brittle onto buttered cookie sheets because you may not have a marble slab. Or if you have a slab, it may not be large enough for the brittle. A marble slab sprayed with cooking spray is preferable, but a large cookie sheet will work quite well.

When you want to stretch peanut brittle, you must do so while the candy is still hot (see Figure 12-1). To protect your hands, you can purchase a pair of leather work gloves to wear just for this reason. Otherwise, use a couple of buttered salad forks: one to hold the brittle and one to pull to thin the brittle.

Hot brittle is quite elastic. If you're using gloved hands, grasp the sides of the brittle mass and gently pull it until it becomes a thin sheet. Pull along all the sides until the entire mass is spread thin. If you use forks, stick the forks into opposite sides of the brittle and pull. Repeat this process along the sides until the brittle is spread thin.

Figure 12-1:
You can
stretch your
brittle by
hand if you
wear
protective
gloves.

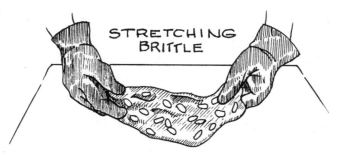

STRETCHING BRITTLE

Beckoning Brittles

In this section, I show you four different brittles. And if you ever need to make any other type of brittle, you can adjust one of these recipes to suit your needs. If the macadamia is your nut of choice or if you like almonds, you can make the appropriate substitutions.

Just be aware that if you make a recipe using whole almonds, they're somewhat harder than most other nuts, so they may not produce as good a candy as the nuts listed in the recipes.

Peanut Brittle

Peanut brittle is kind of like a peanut toffee (see Chapter 11 for more about toffee), except brittle doesn't have the butter content of toffee, just the high cooking temperature. Despite changing tastes over the years and the introduction of all sorts of fancy confections, peanut brittle hangs on as one of the favorite confections. Simplicity of production and inexpensive ingredients may have something to do with its popularity, but its rich taste is hard to beat. You can see this brittle in the color section.

Preparation time: *35 minutes plus 30 minutes to cool*

Yield: *About 2 pounds (serves 6)*

¼ cup plus ¼ cup butter

2 cups granulated sugar

2 cups raw peanuts

1 cup light corn syrup

1 cup water

1 teaspoon salt

1 tablespoon baking soda

1 Use ¼ cup of butter to coat two cookie sheets and set aside. Put the baking soda, salt, and remaining butter in a small (5-ounce) paper cup with the butter on top, and set aside.

2 Combine the sugar, peanuts, corn syrup, and water in a 5-quart saucepan. Bring the ingredients to a boil over medium heat, using a metal spoon with a plastic handle to stir constantly. Cover the pan with a lid for about 1 minute to allow the sides to wash themselves down and dissolve sugar crystals; remove the lid. Clip a candy thermometer to the side of the saucepan without allowing the tip to touch the bottom of the pan; continue cooking the mixture over medium heat, and stir constantly.

3 When the temperature reaches about 295 degrees (if you listen carefully, you'll hear peanuts "pop," which means they're ready), remove the mixture from the heat, and stir in the salt, remaining butter, and baking soda; stir hard to mix. The batch immediately begins to expand, but stirring keeps it at bay until you stop. Stir about 25 to 30 seconds to mix well.

4 Pour the batch onto two buttered cookie sheets and, before the brittle hardens and while it's still pretty hot, use your gloved hands to stretch it. If you want to make a thinner brittle, use two buttered forks to stretch the mixture. If you desire a thicker brittle, don't stretch it. Let the brittle cool to room temperature for about 30 to 35 minutes.

5 When the brittle is cool, remove it from the cookie sheet by hand and break it by hand into about 3- to 4-inch pieces, and store in an airtight container or enclose in freezer bags and seal. This prevents sticking.

Vary It! *Although many experts disagree about the best method for brittles, you can substitute pecans in this recipe and produce an excellent brittle. (I provide a separate pecan brittle recipe later in this chapter.)*

Per serving: Calories 822 (From Fat 352); Fat 0g (Saturated 39g); Cholesterol 41mg; Sodium 675mg; Carbohydrate 116g (Dietary Fiber 4g); Protein 13g.

A brief history of the peanut

Though one might assume that peanuts have always been in the United States, the fact is that peanuts originated in South America thousands of years ago. Spanish traders discovered peanuts in the New World and carried them back to Europe on their ships. The Spanish eventually carried the peanuts to Africa, where they traded them. When African slaves were brought to America, the peanuts were brought along and eventually were grown in America.

Peanuts, which are legumes, not nuts, grow best in sandy soil, so the Southern U.S. became fertile ground for cultivation, especially after the boll weevil destroyed a lot of the cotton crop in the 20th century. The Southern U.S. still leads the country in peanut production; most of peanuts are used to manufacture peanut butter, and peanuts remain a great source of protein in the diet (including a very delicious part of many candies). Although the United States is a big producer of this wonderful legume, India leads the world in peanut production, producing about 50 percent of the world's peanuts.

Pecan Brittle

Pecan brittle reminds me a little of a hard praline (see Chapter 11 for more about pralines). You cook the pecan's rich flavor into a crispy brittle, and the effect is quite nice — especially if you like pecans. This recipe (shown in the color section) really delivers a great taste, but I think that it also produces one of the best aromas of any candy.

Preparation time: *35 minutes plus 30 to 35 minutes to cool*

Yield: *About 3 pounds (serves 8)*

¼ cup plus ½ cup butter	1½ cups light corn syrup
3 cups granulated sugar	1½ cups water
3 cups pecan halves, chopped into medium pieces (slightly larger than whole coffee beans)	1 teaspoon salt
	1 tablespoon baking soda

1 Use ¼ cup of butter to coat two cookie sheets and set aside.

2 Combine the sugar, pecans, corn syrup, and water in a heavy 5-quart saucepan and cook over medium heat, occasionally stirring with a metal spoon with a plastic handle until the mixture comes to a boil (about 15 to 16 minutes). Place a cover on the pan for about 1 minute to allow the sugar crystals on the inside walls of the pan to dissolve.

3 Remove the lid, and clip a candy thermometer to the side of the saucepan; don't allow the tip of the thermometer to touch the bottom of the pan. Cook the ingredients over high heat, stirring constantly until the temperature reaches 295 degrees. Remove the pan from the heat. Add the baking soda, salt, and remaining butter; stir in to blend well.

4 Pour batch onto two buttered cookie sheets, evenly splitting the batch between the two trays.

5 While the batch is still warm, stretch the mixture with your hands or with two buttered forks or simply allow the mixture to cool at room temperature for 30 to 35 minutes. When the batch cools, break it into medium pieces by hand, place it in freezer bags, and seal to keep it from getting sticky.

Tip: Medium pieces of pecans are better in brittle than pecan halves because the pieces spread through the batch better than the halves, making a prettier brittle. Halves are too large, and small pieces are too small.

Per serving: Calories 894 (From Fat 416); Fat 46g (Saturated 13g); Cholesterol 46mg; Sodium 840mg; Carbohydrate 128g (Dietary Fiber 4g); Protein 4g.

Coconut Brittle

This brittle combines the nice crunchy Spanish peanut with the delightful texture of fresh coconut to create a very delicious, quite crunchy brittle. When you add the coconut at the end, be ready to stir and get the candy out of the pan; this candy sets up quickly because the coconut thickens the batch and lowers the temperature.

Preparation time: 35 minutes plus about 30 minutes to cool

Yield: 3½ pounds (serves about 10)

¼ cup plus 1 tablespoon butter	2 cups Spanish peanuts
2 cups granulated sugar	1 tablespoon baking soda
1 cup light corn syrup	1 teaspoon salt
1 cup water	3 cups medium-shred coconut, unsweetened

1 Use ¼ cup of butter to coat two cookie sheets and set aside.

2 Combine the sugar, corn syrup, water, and peanuts in a heavy 5-quart saucepan and cook over medium heat, occasionally stirring with a metal spoon with a plastic handle until the batch comes to a boil (in about 15 to 16 minutes). Place the lid on the saucepan for 1 minute to allow the sides to wash down and dissolve the sugar crystals; remove the lid, and clip a candy thermometer, being sure that the tip doesn't touch the bottom of the pan.

3 Continue cooking over high heat until the batch reaches 295 degrees and remove from heat. Add the baking soda, salt, and remaining butter and stir well. Then stir in the coconut.

4 Pour the brittle onto the buttered cookie sheets and, while the batch is still warm, stretch the brittle with gloved hands or using forks. Allow the batch to cool for at least 30 to 35 minutes.

5 When the batch is cool, break the brittle by hand into medium pieces. Store the brittle immediately in freezer bags to prevent stickiness because it absorbs moisture.

Per serving: Calories 549 (From Fat 254); Fat 28g (Saturated 13g); Cholesterol 15mg; Sodium 662mg; Carbohydrate 73g (Dietary Fiber 5g); Protein 9g.

Cashew Brittle

Of the brittle recipes in this chapter, the cashew brittle has the most delicate flavor by far. Cashew brittle creates a very light, very subtle nut flavor, but this recipe has an interesting contrast: It has a little added flavor (from vanilla extract and cinnamon) to boost the cashew.

Preparation time: *40 minutes plus 30 to 35 minutes to cool*

Yield: *3½ pounds (serves about 10)*

¼ cup butter plus 2 tablespoons butter	1 teaspoon vanilla extract
2 cups granulated sugar	½ teaspoon cinnamon
1 cup light corn syrup	¼ teaspoon salt
1 cup water	1 tablespoon baking soda
2 cups roasted, salted cashew pieces	

1 Use ¼ cup of butter to coat two cookie sheets and set aside.

2 Combine the sugar, corn syrup, and water in a heavy 5-quart saucepan and cook over high heat, stirring occasionally, until the sugar dissolves and the batch comes to a boil (about 15 minutes). Place the lid on the pan for 1 minute to dissolve the sugar crystals on the inside walls of the pan; remove the lid, and clip on a candy thermometer, being sure that the tip doesn't touch the bottom of the pan. Continue cooking and stirring until the temperature reaches 240 degrees (which takes about 10 to 12 minutes).

3 Add the cashew pieces and continue stirring until the batch reaches 298 degrees (about another 10 minutes). Remove from heat, and dump in 2 tablespoons of butter, the vanilla extract, cinnamon, salt, and soda. Quickly stir in these ingredients; then pour the mixture onto two buttered cookie sheets. While the batch is still hot, stretch the brittle with gloved hands or with forks. Allow the brittle to cool at room temperature for about 30 to 35 minutes.

4 When the brittle is cool, break it into medium pieces by hand and immediately store it in freezer bags to prevent the brittle from getting sticky from humidity.

Per serving: *Calories 460 (From Fat 173); Fat 19g (Saturated 6g); Cholesterol 18mg; Sodium 499mg; Carbohydrate 73g (Dietary Fiber 1g); Protein 5g.*

If you want to give your brittle as a holiday gift, you can place it in an airtight bag and place it in a decorative tin to make a lovely presentation. You only need to disguise your bag, and this task shouldn't be too difficult. (Check out Chapter 22 for more tips on how to present your tasty creations as beautiful gifts.)

Storing Your Brittles Safely

 Brittles fall into the category of candy that is extremely *hydroscopic,* which means that it attracts moisture. Be prepared to store your confection as soon as it cools to protect it from humidity.

I recommend having a box of plastic freezer bags available, probably in the quart-size or even the pint-size bags. As soon as the brittle cools (or even when it's still slightly warm), place roughly ½-pound amounts in these bags, and close them. Storing brittle in plastic bags at room temperature protects your candy for two to three weeks. Even wrapped in this way, you may eventually see some degradation after a couple of weeks, but two weeks should be long enough for you to consume the amount you produce!

Chapter 13

Discovering Amazing Uses for Popcorn

*P*opcorn is a snack that's pretty much linked with one activity: movie-watching. Separating one activity from the other can be quite difficult. I can't imagine watching a movie without a huge barrel of popcorn in one hand and an enormous container of soft drink in the other.

The average American consumes 15 gallons of popcorn per year — that means that the total U.S. population wolfs down more than a billion pounds a year! While you're enjoying your share of that 15 billion pounds, you may as well sweeten the corn a little and put a different taste in your crunch, so to speak, with the recipes in this chapter. After all, I wouldn't want you getting bored with the same old taste.

Getting the Scoop on Popcorn Basics

When you make a recipe that includes popcorn as one of the ingredients, you can produce a lot of volume with very little weight; that is, one ounce of unpopped corn produces a quart of popcorn, so four ounces of unpopped corn makes about one gallon of popcorn.

You may want to pop your own popcorn. Or, if you're making a large batch of caramel corn, you may want to pick up prepopped popcorn at the grocery store. However you manage to get your popcorn is up to you. Because how to pop popcorn or going to the store to purchase popped popcorn isn't rocket science (at least for most people), I don't include it as part of the recipes in this chapter. But frankly, I prefer to pop my own popcorn, and I bought a popcorn machine for one of my stores just for that purpose.

When you want to add a little something special to your popcorn, try nuts. Where nuts are involved, I suggest the nut volumes and types of nuts based on my experience. I put raw nuts into batches of popcorn, and the stages at which the recipes add them and the amounts that they state are also based on my experience. (I like to put in a total of between 2 and 2½ cups of nuts for every 10 cups of popped corn. But you can use as many nuts as you want.) You can increase the volume of nuts and make nut substitutions, if you want; just remember that certain nuts cook faster than others, and you don't want to scorch them!

If you substitute nuts in one of the recipes, take into consideration the relative cooking times of the nuts. I determine this by the "bite rule." If a nut is harder to bite, that nut needs to cook longer than a softer nut does. A nut that's softer to the tooth, such as a pecan, will require less time to cook. Add the hardest nuts to the batch at about 240 degrees; add the softer nuts at about 285 degrees. Other nuts fall somewhere in between hard and soft. In those cases, just experiment based on how hard the nut is and based on the time the recipe includes.

Everything else involved in making sweetened popcorn is pretty basic. You simply cook the liquid topping of your choice (such as caramel, chocolate, or both), and mix it with your popcorn.

For best results, cook caramel batches in a heavy 6-quart saucepan. Ideally, you cook the batches in a large copper pot, but I don't expect you to have that at home (I don't have one at my house, either). Instead, you can use a heavy aluminum pot, which you can purchase at a store that sells cookware. Depending on the recipe, you temper the chocolate for coating popcorn (see Chapter 14 for the scoop) using a double boiler or melt it in the microwave.

When you're making a batch of caramel corn, the liquid gets very hot because you're cooking it to around 300 degrees. Believe me when I say that anything that gets on you at that temperature will damage your skin. These batches don't tend to be terribly volatile, but you don't want to touch the caramel!

I recommend having a large stainless steel bowl available to mix your topping with the popcorn. I suggest using a bowl at least 2 feet in diameter, capable of containing at least 2 gallons, to provide ample space to fold the popcorn into the hot topping.

So what makes corn pop, anyway?

As you enjoy your popcorn, you might have wondered what makes the corn pop in the first place. And if one type of corn pops, why doesn't another? Does the answer lie in the legend that a spirit dwells inside the kernel and, when the spirit is heated, it bursts out in anger?

Okay, here's the real reason: The corn pops because of the water inside the kernel. The amount of water required to produce a "pop" is fairly precise, so not all types of corn will pop. I'm not sure about the "angry spirit" thing, but that's a lovely thought. . . .

In reality, a perfect popcorn kernel contains between 13.5 percent and 14 percent water.

Even then, all kernels don't pop because even a tiny hole in the hard shell can allow enough leakage to prevent a proper buildup of steam. Also, if the percentage of water is too low, the pressure isn't sufficient to cause the little explosion and, if the water percentage is too high, the production will most likely be one of those hard, half-popped duds you sometimes see (or eat).

Given all the possibilities, most brands of popcorn pop at least 99 percent of their kernels, so I guess we shouldn't complain about the few "old maids" at the bottom of a bag or bowl.

I also recommend purchasing a pair of leather work gloves, which you use to break up the popcorn after you mix it with the caramel or other hot toppings. Caramel popcorn batches tend to form large clumps, and you need to break these clumps apart while the caramel is still quite hot. Without protection gear on your hands, you'll burn them. You want to avoid using forks or tongs to separate the clumps because you risk damaging the kernels.

The rest of the "cooking" involves the cooling process. When the batch cools, you have one fine treat at your disposal. So be prepared to enjoy.

If you can find a strainer large enough for a corn kernel to pass through, you should use that to sift out the unpopped kernels in your corn. Otherwise, hand-sort as well as you can because you really don't want to bite one of those kernels when you're enjoying your sweetened corn.

Putting Delicious Finishing Touches on Popcorn

Perhaps you associate caramel corn with something you've enjoyed at carnivals and fairs. Maybe you recall having chocolate popcorn at Halloween or on another holiday. Whatever your associations, you have the opportunity to enjoy these delicious treats in your own home any time you want with just a little preparation!

Closely follow the steps in the following recipes, and you'll be on your way to making a great snack. Don't hesitate to make one of these treats for a party; you'll find them a fairly inexpensive treat and fairly easy to produce.

Nutty Caramel Corn

This tasty treat includes three different nuts, and it's bound to please you and anyone you know who likes the rich flavor and crunch of caramel corn!

Preparation time: 20 to 30 minutes plus 20 to 30 minutes for cooling

Yield: 8 servings

10 cups popped corn	*1 cup raw whole almonds*
1½ cups granulated sugar	*½ cup whole raw cashews*
½ cup dark brown sugar, packed	*¾ cup raw pecan halves*
½ cup corn syrup	*2 teaspoons salt*
½ cup water	*2 teaspoons baking soda*
2 tablespoons butter	

1 Rinse a large stainless steel bowl with hot water and dry well (this step is to heat the bowl). Put the popped corn in a bowl.

2 Combine the granulated sugar, brown sugar, corn syrup, and water in a heavy 6-quart saucepan and cook on medium heat with occasional stirring until the batch comes to a boil; place a lid on the pot for 1 minute to allow the sugar crystals to wash down inside the pan. Remove the lid, and clip a candy thermometer to the side of the pot without allowing the tip to touch the bottom of the pot. Continue cooking and stirring.

3 When the temperature reaches 240 degrees, add the butter and almonds and continue stirring. At 270 degrees, add the cashews and continue stirring. At 285 degrees, add the pecans and cook to 300 degrees. Remove the mixture from the heat.

4 Stir in the salt and baking soda; then pour the mixture over the popcorn in a stainless steel bowl and mix thoroughly with two hard rubber spatulas to coat completely. Spread the popcorn mixture over aluminum foil, and break the clumps apart with your hands while wearing leather utility gloves.

Per serving: Calories 473 (From Fat 149); Fat 17g (Saturated 3g); Cholesterol 8mg; Sodium 934mg; Carbohydrate 80g (Dietary Fiber 4g); Protein 7g.

Caramel Corn with Peanuts and Chocolate

Like so many candies nowadays, caramel corn has been getting a little fancier, and this recipe is one for the chocolate-lover (you can see the finished treat in the color section). I prefer using dark chocolate with this recipe because of the contrast in tastes, but you may use milk chocolate if you like. This recipe combines the sweet taste of caramel, salty popcorn, and the rich dark chocolate atop it all. I threw the peanuts in for good measure. You can make this delightful treat with or without peanuts.

Preparation time: *50 to 60 minutes plus 20 minutes of cooling*

Yield: *10 to 12 servings (2¾ pounds)*

10 cups popped corn	*½ cup water*	*2 teaspoons baking soda*
1½ cups granulated sugar	*2 tablespoons butter*	*1 pound dark chocolate, chopped and melted for tempering*
½ cup dark brown sugar, packed	*1 cup raw Spanish peanuts (optional)*	
½ cup light corn syrup	*2 teaspoons salt*	

1 Rinse a large stainless steel bowl in hot water to preheat it and dry it thoroughly. Put the popped corn in a bowl.

2 In a heavy 6-quart saucepan, combine the granulated sugar, brown sugar, corn syrup, and water. Cook over medium heat, stirring with a stainless steel spoon with a plastic handle. Bring the mixture to a boil and cover the pan with a lid for 1 minute to allow the sugar to wash down the inside of the pan. Remove the lid, and clip a candy thermometer to the side of the saucepan without allowing the tip of the thermometer to touch the bottom of the pan. Continue stirring and, when the temperature reaches 240 degrees, add the butter and raw peanuts (if desired).

3 Stir the batch until it reaches 300 degrees. Remove the mixture from the heat; add the salt and baking soda, and then mix. In a large bowl, pour the mixture over the popcorn, and use two large hard rubber spatulas to completely coat the corn with caramel. Spread the mixture onto aluminum foil to cool at room temperature (about 15 minutes).

4 When the caramel corn is cool, temper the dark chocolate (or the chocolate of your choosing) using one of the methods I describe in Chapter 14. Drizzle the chocolate over the corn, being certain to get chocolate on all the corn (see Figure 13-1). When the chocolate sets (20 to 25 minutes), use your hands to break it up into clumps.

Tip: *I prefer using premium chocolate, but you can substitute 2 12-ounce packages of semi-sweet chocolate chips, melted. You can use all the chips — even though the weight is more than 1 pound — because why would you want leftover chips? Melt the chips in a microwave-able bowl on high to 94 degrees, stopping every 30 seconds to stir to check the temperature with a chocolate thermometer. Melting should take about 2 minutes, but microwaves vary.*

Per serving: *Calories 394 (From Fat 129); Fat 14g (Saturated 9g); Cholesterol 8mg; Sodium 618mg; Carbohydrate 67g (Dietary Fiber 4g); Protein 2g.*

Finding a real gold mine

In the world of confections and snacks, perhaps the most important man in history is Hernando Cortez, the Spanish explorer. Cortez traveled to the Americas looking for gold in 1519. He saw the Aztecs drinking a dark brown liquid and noticed them using cacao beans, the source of this chocolate drink, as currency. He developed plantations to grow the cacao beans because he saw it as a means of producing "currency."

Eventually, the Spanish took the beans back to Spain and, by adding spices, they made the chocolate drink palatable to Spanish taste buds.

Efforts to cultivate the trees in Europe led the Spanish to develop chocolate plantations in an area of West Africa. Today, that area produces more than 40 percent of the world's chocolate.

Cortez also observed the Aztecs using popcorn. Not only did the Aztecs eat popcorn, but they also wore strings of popcorn as part of their ceremonial headdresses. Cortez had the opportunity to return to Spain with both chocolate and popcorn, but he apparently saw no real value to popcorn. How wrong he was!

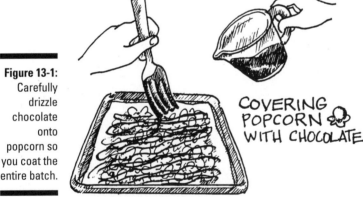

Figure 13-1:
Carefully drizzle chocolate onto popcorn so you coat the entire batch.

COVERING POPCORN WITH CHOCOLATE

White Chocolate Popcorn

This recipe is really quite easy, and it doesn't involve making any caramel. For this recipe, you have only the popcorn and white chocolate. As simple as that sounds (and it is), this treat is delightful and makes a nice snack on a hot day. (For a holiday suggestion with a similar recipe, see Chapter 20.)

Preparation time: *5 minutes plus 30 to 45 minutes for cooling*

Yield: *2 pounds or 8 4-ounce servings*

½ pound (2 gallons) popcorn, popped   *1½ pounds white chocolate*

1 Preheat the stainless steel bowl by rinsing it in hot water to preheat it and drying it thoroughly. Put the popped corn in the bowl.

2 In a microwaveable bowl, melt the white chocolate on high power for about 3 minutes, stopping every 45 seconds to stir and check the temperature. After the third stop, check the temperature after you stir. If the temperature is approaching 95 degrees, stop the microwave every 20 seconds. Heat to about 95 degrees on a candy thermometer. If you have an assistant, have one person stir the corn and one pour the melted white chocolate over the popcorn and work the chocolate thoroughly into the corn with a spatula to mix all the popcorn with the coating.

3 When you're done mixing the popcorn and chocolate, pour the batch onto aluminum foil to allow the white chocolate to set on the popcorn at room temperature for about 30 to 45 minutes. When the white chocolate has set up, break the clumps apart by hand. Often, when you stir the white chocolate into the corn, the kernels begin to separate, but you may have some clumps left after cooling.

Tip: *You can increase or decrease this batch, keeping the proportions of coating by weight 3 to 1. For example, if you want twice as much popcorn, use 1 pound (4 gallons) of popped corn and 3 pounds of white chocolate, melted. Your melting time for the white chocolate would be a little longer — maybe 4 minutes. From that point, simply follow the same procedures, and stop to stir and check the temperature every 45 seconds. As the white chocolate approaches 95 degrees, stop, stir, and check more often.*

Per serving: *Calories 608 (From Fat 258); Fat 29g (Saturated 18g); Cholesterol 30mg; Sodium 92mg; Carbohydrate 74g (Dietary Fiber 5g); Protein 10g.*

Packing Away Your Popcorn

Now that you have mounds of popcorn, you need to find a place to store it. Caramel corn by its very nature is *hydroscopic,* meaning that it absorbs moisture from the air. Now, you don't want that to happen. As soon as the batch cools, put the caramel corn in a large plastic container (or containers) or be prepared to make up eight or ten cellophane bags or freezer bags for later enjoyment. You can store the corn at room temperature for up to two weeks. Store the caramel corn with chocolate the same as the regular caramel corn. If you leave the caramel exposed to humid air, you can literally create a sticky situation. Due to a long shelf life and the stability of the product at room temperature, I don't recommend freezing caramel corn.

The white chocolate popcorn doesn't absorb as much moisture, Nevertheless, as soon as the white chocolate sets up, put the popcorn in a plastic container or in freezer bags. I prefer using freezer bags because you can bag the corn in serving-size portions. You can store this popcorn for three to four months at room temperature — if you can resist it for that long.

If you need help throwing back the popcorn, here's a hint: It makes a nice gift. You can get some attractive cellophane bags and close them with some colorful ribbon.

If you prepare this treat for a party, I recommend simply letting the crowd dig in. I'd tell you what to do with the leftovers in that case, but I doubt that you'll have any leftovers from a partygoing crowd.

Part IV

Becoming a Chocolate Artist

The 5th Wave   By Rich Tennant

© RICHTENNANT

TROUBLE AT THE CHOCOLATE PLANT

"Okay - there's been a meltdown in cooling tower 9! Chocolate syrup's leaking everywhere! This is why you signed up for this job. Now grab your sliced fruit and your fondue forks and let's go to work!!"

In this part...

For many folks — including yours truly — their favorite part of the book is the one that covers chocolate and its many uses. To get you started, I tell you the right ways to chop and melt chocolate. I also demystify the process of tempering chocolate; my intention is for every one of you to understand this key technique of the candy-making world.

In this part, I provide you with recipes for chocolate-dipped treats, chocolate barks and clusters, chocolate-covered creams, chocolate truffles, and molded chocolates. After you master the simple tasks you find here, many hours of pleasurable candy making await you.

You'll love becoming a chocolate artist, and everyone you know will love the results. So, roll up your sleeves and jump in! Well, not literally, although a lot of visitors offer to get into my chocolate pot nude. Sorry, but I have to draw the line somewhere.

Chapter 14

Chopping, Melting, Tempering, and Storing Chocolate

Chocolate is such a wonderful product and, surprisingly, this seemingly simple food is one of the most complicated substances you deal with in candy making. Some folks think you just melt some chocolate, put on a little of whatever you want to coat, and you have a chocolate-coated candy. Well, chocolate isn't quite that simple.

Fortunately, more experts are writing books on the subject of chocolate (you picked a good one), and countless TV shows explain a lot of the techniques for handling chocolate. A lot of the confusion surrounding the working with chocolate has been resolved, and you find that by following basic steps, you can make excellent chocolates.

The secret to producing beautiful chocolate pieces has much to do with how you handle and store them and with following simple procedures to assure that your finished products have a nice gloss. In this chapter, I give you the secrets to chocolate success — including how to chop, melt, temper, and store it.

Chopping Chocolate Correctly

You don't have to break any eggs to make the candies in this book, but you need to break a lot of chocolate. Chopping chocolate is almost always the first step in preparing chocolate for use in candy making. Chopping chocolate properly enables you to melt and temper your chocolate faster and more evenly. Whether you're melting the chocolate or *tempering* (a controlled process of heating and cooling chocolate using movement to achieve the proper temperature and crystal structure so that your candy has a nice, glossy finish) the chocolate, you want to chop it into fairly small pieces about the size of a fingernail.

The terms *melting* and *tempering* are not interchangeable. You must melt chocolate to temper it, but you don't always temper your melted chocolate; sometimes you only need to melt chocolate to include it in a recipe. If you're a bit confused about that now, don't fret: I make the distinction quite clear in this chapter.

The chocolate you're chopping is in perfect temper and ready to use. The only problem you have at this point is that the chocolate is in solid form, and you must have it in liquid form for dipping. Remarkably, the difference between the solid and the liquid forms is only a few degrees, but so much can go wrong between the two states of chocolate.

If the chocolate you choose is of the small-bar variety (3 ounces or so), breaking it is pretty simple because the bars are usually thin and easy to break. If you're using bigger bars of chocolate, you're not going to be able to break the bars; you need to chop them using a large knife, preferably a butcher knife. I also recommend using a large two-handled knife, like a butcher knife with handles on both ends of the blade. This knife, which you find in commercial kitchen-supply stores, is good for chopping the 10-pound blocks of chocolate (available from bakery suppliers) that you may encounter if you make a lot of chocolate.

Don't let the sight of a large chocolate bar intimidate you. You can use a little of it and keep the rest for a year or so with proper storage (which I cover later in this chapter).

So how do you chop chocolate properly?

1. **Give the chocolate a good whack with a rubber mallet, taking care not to break the bag.** Repeat this step several times, and the bar will break into several pieces.

2. **Remove one or two of the pieces, depending on how much chocolate you need at the time, and keep the rest in the bag to retain its freshness.** To determine how much to cut, see whether the recipe calls for a certain weight; if so, weigh your chocolate on a small kitchen scale.

3. **Place the chocolate on a cutting board, and cut the chocolate with a heavy knife, shaving off fingernail-size pieces until you chop all the chocolate that you need (see Figure 14-1).** You aren't cutting the chocolate into chunks; you're shaving equal-size pieces off the bar. If you use a butcher knife, which is preferable, you may want to lightly hammer the back of the knife with a rubber mallet as you chop to make the process as easy as possible.

CHOPPING CHOCOLATE

1. LARGE CHUNKS OF CHOCOLATE NEED TO BE CUT INTO SMALL PIECES FIRST, THEN USING A CHEF'S KNIFE WITH A LARGE BLADE ON A CUTTING BOARD....

2. ....CHOP THEM INTO TINY PIECES. WORK WITH A SMALL AMOUNT AT A TIME.

3. TRANSFER THE CHOPPED PIECES TO A BOWL. KEEP THE CUTTING BOARD FREE FOR CHOPPING!

KEEP CHOPPING!

Figure 14-1:
Chop the chocolate into small pieces using a large knife.

You'll quickly have plenty of chocolate chopped and ready to melt. Just be sure that the pieces are uniform in size because uniformity allows for consistent melting and helps prevent lumpiness as you temper your chocolate.

Melting Chocolate in Preparation for Tempering

When you start with chocolate in the solid form — as you probably will — you must melt it before you can use it as a coating or in a recipe that calls for tempered chocolate. Tempering (which I cover in the next section) is necessary only when you're using the chocolate as a coating because only tempered chocolate sets properly with a beautiful gloss that's desired when making chocolates.

When making chocolate centers, such as truffles (which Chapter 18 covers), tempering isn't necessary because you're not concerned with a glossy appearance in a center. Plus chocolate, when used in the production of centers, doesn't bloom. (When chocolate gets warm — as it does when you put chocolate in your pocket — and then sets up again, light streaks form in the chocolate. In that case, the cocoa butter in the chocolate has melted and, when cocoa butter melts, separation occurs. This separation is called "bloom" or "fat migration.")

The following sections cover two handy techniques for properly melting chocolate for tempering: using a double boiler and microwaving. (In Chapter 18, I cover a third technique you can use exclusively in making truffles: blending chocolate with cream to form truffle centers.)

Do not allow any water, even a drop, to come into contact with the chocolate during the process of storing, chopping or melting, because this will cause the chocolate to seize into a hard mass of gunk. But you don't have to throw this chocolate away; you can chop this mass into small pieces, melt it, and use it for making truffle centers.

Using a double boiler

I don't like the term "double boiler" when melting chocolate, because the last thing you want near chocolate is water — especially boiling water. To melt chocolate using a double boiler, you use hot water (about 140 degrees or so) to bring the chocolate to a liquid state, placing the water in the bottom pot and the chocolate in the top pan. (Chapter 3 gives you the complete scoop on double-boiler setups.)

When using a double boiler to melt chocolate, you must be careful because of the problem of potentially mixing water with chocolate. If you're melting chocolate and the water from the bottom pot splashes into the top pot where the chocolate is, the chocolate seizes up into a thick mass. You don't want the chocolate to form a thick mass because you won't be able to use it for tempering. To prevent this from happening, don't heat the water in the bottom pot to more than 140 degrees.

When I use a double boiler, I use a 5-quart saucepan for the bottom pot and a large stainless steel bowl for the top because I like using a wider pan for the chocolate. Make sure that the top pan fits tightly over the bottom saucepan, because you don't want steam to escape and form droplets in the top where the chocolate is melting. For the same reason, don't put any type of cover over the chocolate because it can create condensation and, thus, water.

Here's how to melt chocolate using a double boiler:

1. **Put enough water in the bottom pot so that the water level is just at the bottom of the top pot.** Before you put the top pot in place, heat the water in the bottom to about 140 degrees on medium heat, and turn the heat off when the water reaches 140 degrees. Use a candy thermometer to check the temperature. You heat the water before putting the top pan in place because you don't want to risk overheating the water, causing steam to escape and get into the top pan with the chocolate.

2. **With the water at a stable temperature — about 140 degrees — place the top pot or bowl, with a few ounces of the chopped chocolate, over the bottom pot, and allow the chocolate to melt.** As the chocolate melts, stir it lightly with a hard rubber spatula to blend until all the chocolate melts. Melting 4 ounces of chopped chocolate using this method should take 5 to 7 minutes.

3. **Add a little more chopped chocolate, and slowly blend it with the melted chocolate.** Continue adding more chocolate until all the chocolate is almost completely melted. Do not allow the chocolate to reach a temperature higher than 115 degrees because heating your chocolate too high can cause it to scorch, and you really don't want that taste in your chocolate. Keep your chocolate thermometer handy because you want the liquid chocolate to reach at least 110 degrees to be certain that all the cocoa butter crystals melt.

Melting the chocolate to a temperature of 110 degrees is necessary because the purpose of tempering is to melt the crystals in the cocoa butter and then recrystallize them at a lower temperature to stabilize the cocoa butter. Just melting the chocolate doesn't create this controlled crystallization.

4. **When the chocolate has melted, remove the top pan from the double boiler and carefully dry the bottom of the pot with a towel.** Do not allow any water to get into the chocolate. Place the bowl on the counter, and continue to stir the chocolate until it has a creamy, smooth appearance.

5. **You can use the chocolate in any recipe that doesn't involve using it as a coating or for molding.** You can use this chocolate as part of a center because it's ready for that use. If you need to have tempered chocolate, you can take steps to temper the chocolate, but I explain how to temper it later in this chapter in the section "Tempering Chocolate with Ease."

Microwaving with care

A microwave is useful for melting chocolate, as long as you're careful about how long you heat the chocolate. Quantity is also an important factor in whether you choose to use a microwave; a microwave works best for small amounts of chocolate (about 6 to 8 ounces of chocolate at a time).

Follow these instructions when microwaving your chocolate:

1. **Put the chopped chocolate in a microwave-safe bowl, and place the bowl in the microwave.** When melting your chocolate in this manner, be sure that you chop the chocolate into fingernail-size pieces. You want fairly small, uniform-size pieces so that the chocolate melts evenly.

A good microwave-safe plastic bowl is preferable to using a glass bowl because a glass bowl gets hot and can cause the chocolate to scorch. Also, if you're going to temper the chocolate, the hot bowl can make tempering difficult.

2. **Heat the chocolate on 50 percent power for about 2½ to 3 minutes, stopping midway through the heating process to stir it with a hard rubber spatula.** You can melt your chocolate using 50 percent or high power on your microwave, as long as you watch the chocolate carefully and stop to stir it and check the temperature with a chocolate thermometer frequently (30 to 45 seconds). I like to melt on high because it requires less time, but I am very aware of my temperature and use a chocolate thermometer.

3. **If the chocolate hasn't melted in the allotted time, reheat it on 50 percent power in 15-second increments until most of the chocolate melts.**

When microwaving, you don't need to completely melt the chocolate before removing it from the oven because microwaved items continue cooking after you remove them from the microwave, which can create a scorching problem. By stopping early, you can check the temperature and texture. If you need to melt the chocolate a little more, you may do so.

4. Remove the bowl from the oven, and stir the chocolate until it's smooth and shiny. If you need to melt the chocolate a little longer, put the chocolate back into the oven for 10 seconds at a time, stirring every time you stop.

With a little practice, you can figure out how long your oven takes to melt a particular amount of chocolate. Make this notation in your book for future use.

If you need more chocolate, repeat the process or use a double boiler for larger chocolate amounts. Because a larger bowl of chocolate retains heat longer, you have to melt more chocolate than you need to keep what you use warm.

Tempering Chocolate with Ease

Simply melting chocolate is important for some center recipes, but any time you need to use chocolate for coating or for molding, you need to temper the chocolate. In the tempering process, you heat and cool chocolate using movement to achieve the proper temperature and crystal structure. Though many methods can get you where you need to go, the goal is to have chocolate that has a nice glossy finish when it's set and that has a nice "snap" when you bite into the candy.

Tempering is a matter of three elements: time, temperature, and agitation. Chocolate must spend a certain amount of time warm and a certain amount of time cooling, and must end up at the right temperature. You must accomplish all these steps while you keep the chocolate in motion because, through agitation, you keep a constant temperature throughout the chocolate, assuring yourself that the cocoa butter crystals are heated and cooled completely.

Lots of candy companies refuse to use chocolate in their candy making because of a fear of tempering, but I teach young people how to temper quite often. Tempering is a procedure to learn, and it isn't difficult. In the following sections, I describe several tempering methods and give you some details that you need to know before you start tempering.

Checking out guidelines before you temper

Tempering chocolate requires some preparation, even after you've chopped and melted your chocolate. The following sections show you how to keep an eye on cocoa butter and how to adjust your room temperature and humidity to create the ideal tempering conditions.

Understanding cocoa butter's role in tempering

So what's tempering all about? Well, a number of substances make up chocolate, and one of the most complicated (and important) is cocoa butter. Cocoa butter contains the fat that gives chocolate its wonderful *mouthfeel,* which is how a food is perceived by your taste buds. Fine chocolate has a very good mouthfeel because you enjoy the pleasant texture, taste, and aroma.

Multiple crystals with different melting points make up cocoa butter. These crystals have a complex structure that must be maintained if you want chocolate to have a shiny appearance like you see in fine candy shops. Chocolate bars, even the 10-pound bars I describe frequently in this book, are in temper when you receive them, assuming proper handling during shipping and storage. To use the chocolate, you have to melt it, and it loses that temper when you do so. By a process of heating and cooling while adding tempered chocolate to the melted chocolate, the crystals in the cocoa butter form again in their proper structure. The result is tempered chocolate in a liquid state at about 88 degrees for milk chocolate and 90 degrees for dark chocolate. Folks are often amazed by the low temperature of chocolate in its liquid state, assuming that it must be very hot, but chocolate is *never* hot. If you simply melt the chocolate until you have a brown liquid, the crystals of the cocoa butter will never properly align themselves.

Only through tempering can you achieve this proper alignment of the crystals. The process requires that you raise the temperature of the chocolate to at least 110 degrees (115 degrees for dark chocolate). Do not exceed 120 degrees. After you've heated the chocolate to 110 degrees and held it at that temperature for a few minutes, you're ready to cool the chocolate, re-form those crystals, and complete the tempering process.

Controlling room temperature and humidity

Perhaps some elements are easier to control in a business situation than they are at home; nevertheless, temperature and humidity in the chocolate workspace — no matter where that workspace is — are of primary importance. You simply cannot properly temper chocolate and dip chocolate items in an environment that's too warm, too damp, or both.

I have chocolate production areas that are always 68 degrees and about 40 percent to 42 percent humidity. This percentage of humidity is ideal for chocolate work because you're assured a relatively dry environment. You don't want to work in a damp environment; at least, your chocolate doesn't want to be exposed to such humidity because the moisture can damage the chocolate. At the very least, chocolate exposed to high humidity during the cooling (post-dipping) stage will spot or take on other unattractive characteristics.

Although you may not always be able to maintain ideal standards in your home kitchen, try to work in as cool and as dry an environment (within those guidelines) as possible. See Chapter 2 for more details on creating a proper candy-making environment.

Tempering by hand

Many candy makers still enjoy tempering chocolate by hand instead of using any other method. Perhaps the thrill of getting their hands into the chocolate and doing it the old-fashioned way has something to do with it, but candy makers make a great deal of candy in this manner. Figure 14-2 depicts the classic hand-tempering method, which I cover in the following steps:

1. **Chop and melt the chocolate using one of the methods I discuss earlier in this chapter, and have a bowl with 1 pound of chocolate melted to 110 degrees on a chocolate thermometer.** You don't need the chocolate to be much warmer than 110 degrees, but you need to reach that temperature to melt the cocoa butter crystals.

2. **Pour about ⅔ of the chocolate onto a marble slab, and work the chocolate back and forth on the slab using an offset spatula and a trowel until the chocolate reaches 82 degrees on a chocolate thermometer (84 degrees for dark chocolate).** This back-and-forth motion exposes the chocolate to the marble (if you're using marble), which helps in the cooling process. You'll notice the chocolate becoming thicker as it cools.

3. **Add the chocolate from the slab back into the chocolate in the bowl, and stir the chocolate together.** Combining the cooler and the warmer chocolate will elevate the temperature to about 88 degrees. The chocolate should now be in temper, and you're ready to start dipping your candies (see Chapter 15 for details on dipping methods).

If the chocolate begins to thicken even a little on the side of the bowl while you're dipping your candies, scrape it back into the chocolate. The batch will slowly cool and will need *gentle* reheating. To reheat, place the chocolate in the microwave for 5 seconds at a time. Do not exceed 91 degrees, or you lose the temper. Although you temper chocolate to about 88 degrees, it can stand a slight elevation in temperature, but don't exceed 91 degrees. Getting the knack of this process may take a while, but you'll feel like a real candy maker!

CLASSIC TEMPERING

1. WITH AN OFFSET SPATULA, SPREAD THE CHOCOLATE OUT ONTO A MARBLE SURFACE. SPREAD INTO RECTANGLE.

2. USE A PLASTIC SCRAPER TO SCRAPE IT UP INTO A 'POOL' IN THE CENTER. REPEAT THESE STEPS 3 OR 4 TIMES.

3. TAKE THE TEMPERATURE OF THE CHOCOLATE USING A CHOCOLATE THERMOMETER. THE TEMPERATURE SHOULD READ BETWEEN 82°+84°F

Figure 14-2:
Hand-tempering requires a spatula and a marble slab for best cooling results.

I recommend using a heating pad to maintain the chocolate temper. Use this method for only 2 or 3 minutes at a time so you don't get the chocolate too hot. Remove the bowl of chocolate from the heating pad, and place the bowl on a clean towel. If you notice your chocolate becoming thicker, repeat this process until you finish.

Although some people swear by hand-tempering as the only true way to temper chocolate, the truth is that the chocolate doesn't know the difference. However you temper the chocolate, if you have followed good practices, you will have fine tempered chocolate. You can simply reach this destination (tempered chocolate) in more than one way.

Chunk tempering

The "chunk" or "block" method of tempering is a process by which you temper chocolate using chunks of chocolate as "seed" for the heated chocolate. In this method, you heat the chocolate to 110 degrees and mix it with large chunks of chocolate, which melt slightly while the chocolate is cooling. In fact, the melting chunks cool the chocolate while they provide tempered chocolate. The chunks should be large enough to be easily removed when you reach 88 degrees. Follow these instructions to chunk temper:

1. **Chop your chocolate, and melt 12 ounces of it to 110 degrees.** You can melt your chocolate using a microwave or a double boiler.

2. **Break or cut several 1 x 2-inch chunks off the bar of chocolate to use as seed.** Take the bowl of 110-degree chocolate, place three or four chunks of chocolate into the bowl, and stir until the temperature on your chocolate thermometer reads 88 degrees (90 degrees for dark chocolate).

3. **Remove the chunks, and put them aside.** The chocolate should be in temper. Place the chunks aside for future use; they'll be fine for reuse if no streaks of discoloration have formed during the process. Store in an airtight container until needed again. If the chocolate develops some bloom, just melt it next time and repeat the chunk process with fresh in-temper chunks.

If you want to check whether your chocolate is in temper, take a small piece of pretzel or a small spoon and dip it into the chocolate. Put it aside, and check what time it is. In 5 minutes, the chocolate should have a nice gloss and be set completely. The optimum time frame for a good set is between 4 and 6 minutes, but 5 minutes is ideal.

If the chocolate is still wet, it isn't in temper. Put another 2 x 3-inch block in, stir a few minutes more, and repeat the process. If the chocolate sets in less than 4 minutes, your chocolate may be a little too cool. Add just a little (a couple of ounces) warm chocolate melted to 110 degrees, and stir for about 2 minutes to temper. Repeat the test.

Tempering by machine

Some folks may tell you that chocolate is better when you hand-temper rather than use chocolate that's machine-tempered. Well, tempered chocolate doesn't know from whence it came, and you won't know the difference in the final result. Shops like mine sometimes have to temper hundreds of pounds a day, and machines simplify that process.

If, at some point, you discover that you're making a lot of chocolate and none of the previous methods in this chapter satisfies your needs, you can always purchase a machine to temper your chocolate. You can purchase a small chocolate-tempering machine that holds about 1½ pounds of chocolate at a time (see Figure 14-3). This item may seem like a luxury, but a lot of people buy these for home use. You can find machines from less than $400 to more than $1,000, and all of them will be useful to you if you want to make a pretty steady supply of chocolate at home. You find information about these machines in Chapter 24, where I reveal supply sources.

Figure 14-3:
A chocolate-tempering machine is useful for making a lot of candies.

CHOCOLATE-TEMPERING MACHINE

I actually have two of the higher-end models, which I use for lab work (I do a lot of research and development to create new pieces) in my candy kitchen, and they're wonderful. In addition, I have two machines that produce 600 pounds each per day and six machines that produce 240 pounds each per day. But I don't have them all running at once.

Tempering is very simple when you use a machine. With these machines, you can use the same methods you do when tempering without a machine. With machines, you add chocolate to the back of the machine to melt and use the tempered chocolate that comes out in front. With a machine, you have access to about 12 pounds of tempered chocolate a day.

To temper using a machine:

1. **Melt 1 pound of chocolate by placing one to two chunks in the back of the machine, and set the machine's thermostat at 110 degrees.** Let the machine run for about 5 minutes at this temperature. The machine has a divider and, as chocolate melts in the back, liquid chocolate flows to the front.

2. **Place 2- to 3-inch chunks of chocolate in the back of the machine, and turn the thermostat down to 84 degrees.** When the temperature reaches 84 degrees (after about 10 to 15 minutes), remove the chunks from the back. Then turn the thermostat up to 88 degrees.

3. **When the temperature reaches 88 degrees, your chocolate is in temper.** You may dip chocolates as described in Chapter 15 and other recipes throughout the book.

Storing and Reusing Chocolate Properly

In some ways, chocolate is a sponge. How you store it and what it's close to when being shipped can affect the flavor of the chocolate. So when you have to store large or small chocolate bars at home, *do not* place them in the pantry next to the onions. Yuck — onion truffles. Chocolate is best kept in an airtight plastic container in a dark area at room temperature. You can store chocolate for a year in this manner.

Keeping your chocolate away from any heat source is also of primary importance. I have a friend in Canada who puts labels on her bags in the summertime with a recipe for Chocolate Soup. Roughly, the recipe is: Take 1 pound of chocolate; leave it in the car in the sun for 15 minutes — and you get Chocolate Soup. I may have misquoted a bit, but she makes her point: Chocolate doesn't like heat, before or after you've used it. If you store chocolate in temperatures that are more than 94 degrees, melting will occur for sure. But even at a lower temperature, you can do damage. Keep in mind that chocolate held in liquid form in tempering machines is being held at 88 to 89 degrees, so you know that it won't do well in a hot, closed car in the summer!

If your chocolate is exposed to heat or direct sunlight for even a short period of time, it suffers damage. Once this damage occurs, you initially notice a light streakiness on the surface, which comes off when you run your finger across it. This streakiness is bloom (to find out more about bloom, see the earlier section, "Melting Chocolate in Preparation for Tempering"), which means your chocolate is now losing its temper.

Ideally, you need to keep your chocolate in a cool, dry, dark place. In other words, keep your chocolate out of direct sunlight and store it at a temperature between 70 and 72 degrees. You may not be able to achieve that ideal temperature, but try to store it as closely as you can to that temperature.

Don't refrigerate the chocolate because doing so can cause condensation, which brings water into your chocolate. In this book, you will occasionally see recipes that require you to cool your chocolate for a few minutes in the refrigerator, but I never recommend refrigeration for chocolate storage.

You can freeze the chocolate, if necessary, but if you need to freeze your chocolate, you may be buying too much. Considering that you can keep chocolate for a year in an airtight container at room temperature, freezing it for six months seems pointless. You can purchase chocolate in fairly small quantities and, even if the price is higher per pound, you would do well to buy less at a time.

Perhaps you're unable to control your room temperature to allow keeping chocolate for an extended period of time. To freeze chocolate, double-bag it in plastic storage bags, and freeze for up to six months. To thaw, remove the chocolate from the freezer, and allow it to reach room temperature before removing it from the bags. Letting it thaw overnight is best, and allowing it to thaw completely before removing it from the bags prevents condensation.

When storing leftover used chocolate (as opposed to unused bars), use the same precautions as far as light and temperature go. Just be sure to place it in a plastic container. Next time you make something using leftover chocolate, melt the leftover chocolate, and follow the procedures I outline earlier in this chapter for melting and tempering. You want to have some chocolate that you haven't used before, though, so always have some nice chunks of unused chocolate available when you start candy making.

Chapter 15

Dipping Delicious Treats into Chocolate

In This Chapter

▶ Getting a grip on dipping methods

▶ Coating cookies and crackers

▶ Getting into chocolate pretzels

▶ Covering fresh, candied, and cordial fruits

*A*nything you enjoy can surely be improved with the addition of chocolate. I'm sure some wise person must have said that sometime in the past, and it's true. One method of adding chocolate to your favorite treats is dipping.

You're probably familiar with some foods that are routinely chocolate-dipped; for instance, strawberries are certainly very popular. Most folks have seen chocolate-covered pretzels — the combination of salty snacks and chocolate is quite popular.

Or maybe you've always wondered how liquid gets inside the chocolate in a cordial cherry. In this chapter, I explain a few myths and provide you with all the tips and tricks you need to know to dip cookies, crackers, pretzels, and fruit like a pro.

In Chapter 14, I cover several methods for tempering chocolate, which is a necessary step when preparing to dip the items in this chapter. All the items in the following recipes involve the use of tempered chocolate, so you need that knowledge before you dive in.

Mastering Dipping Methods

The key elements to dipping are tempered chocolate; a fairly cool, dry room; and whatever you care to dip, whether it's a cream center or a ready-to-go snack. In this chapter, you'll see that if you can dream it up, you can dip it in chocolate.

When dipping items, you have two dipping methods you can use: You can dip treats by hand or use special dipping tools. As a bonus, you can decorate your dipped pieces as you desire. So roll up your sleeves, and get ready to put some chocolate on your favorite treats!

Patience is the key to quality chocolate. You don't rush chocolate. Chocolate must be tempered, as I explain in Chapter 14, and the tempering process requires that you warm chocolate to a certain point and then cool it while "seeding " it with tempered chocolate. The process involves time, temperature, and agitation. You can't rush this process, and if you try to do so, you can find yourself starting over again because you will not have achieved temper. Take your time, follow the instructions, and enjoy your chocolate.

Dipping by hand

As far as hand-dipping goes, my theory is to wash your hands well, dry them well, and get your fingers into the chocolate. Many chocolate-makers still dip that way.

To dip by hand, the only tool you need handy (besides your tempered chocolate and dipping treats) is a tray. I usually ask you to line a tray or a cookie sheet with wax paper when you're dipping chocolates. A tray or a cookie sheet can be useful because, once you dip a tray of chocolates, you can move the tray and fill another, if necessary.

When I teach my dippers to hand-dip a flat-bottomed piece, such as a caramel square or a square jelly, I show them a little trick to prevent "feet" from forming under the dipped piece. *Feet* describes the appearance of a piece when you lay the piece on a tray and spreading occurs. If you apply the chocolate too heavily to a piece, the chocolate spreads away from the piece because of the weight, and the result looks unprofessional. And you don't want that, do you?

So what's that trick I was talking about? To prevent the chocolate from spreading when dipping, follow these steps:

1. **Hand-dip your candy into the chocolate, tumbling it around so you completely coat it.** Shake the piece gently to get rid of heavy dripping chocolate.

2. **Turn the piece over so it's on top of your fingers. Using your thumb, lightly wipe any excess from the exposed top of the chocolate.** Doing so still leaves plenty of chocolate on what will be the bottom of the candy. With a little practice, you can easily master this technique.

3. **After you wipe away the excess chocolate, turn your hand over just above the tray, and lay the piece on the tray.** The piece slowly releases from your fingers. (The viscosity — which is a measure of the rate of flow of the chocolate — results in a slow release when you invert your hand during dipping.) Try this technique a few times, and you will be surprised how easy it is to do. Don't press down on the piece as you release it, because doing so produces the same result as excess chocolate: "Feet" will appear. If your kitchen is about 70 to 72 degrees and fairly dry, the pieces should set in about 5 to 6 minutes. Let them stay on the tray about 15 minutes longer.

Dipping with the method I describe gives your chocolates a very professional appearance. (See Figure 15-1 for more details on how to properly hand-dip candies.)

HAND-DIPPING CANDIES

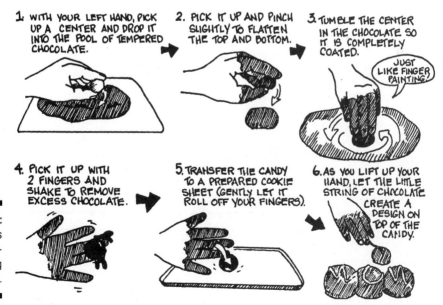

1. WITH YOUR LEFT HAND, PICK UP A CENTER AND DROP IT INTO THE POOL OF TEMPERED CHOCOLATE.

2. PICK IT UP AND PINCH SLIGHTLY TO FLATTEN THE TOP AND BOTTOM.

3. TUMBLE THE CENTER IN THE CHOCOLATE SO IT IS COMPLETELY COATED.

JUST LIKE FINGER PAINTING!

4. PICK IT UP WITH 2 FINGERS AND SHAKE TO REMOVE EXCESS CHOCOLATE.

5. TRANSFER THE CANDY TO A PREPARED COOKIE SHEET (GENTLY LET IT ROLL OFF YOUR FINGERS).

6. AS YOU LIFT UP YOUR HAND, LET THE LITTLE STRING OF CHOCOLATE CREATE A DESIGN ON TOP OF THE CANDY.

Figure 15-1:
The basics
of hand-
dipping
candies.

When dipping, there's a fine line between a chocolate coating that's too heavy and one that's too thin. If the coating is too heavy, spreading occurs; if the coating is too thin, you get a *leaker,* or a piece whose center cracks the chocolate shell. Leakers occur when you dip an item and the center is considerably cooler than the chocolate coating. What happens is that the chocolate slightly warms the center, which causes the center to expand. This expansion creates just enough energy to slightly crack the chocolate shell.

When you're hand-dipping chocolate, the chocolate will cool while you're dipping. If you're dipping quite a few pieces, you need to resupply yourself with more warm chocolate. You can reheat the chocolate you are using slightly (don't exceed 91 degrees on your chocolate thermometer), or you can reheat some chocolate that you have on hand and add a little to your working bowl. Practice makes this routine for you.

Dipping with tools

In my shops, a lot of the chocolate production involves hand-dipping or dipping with small tools designed just for that purpose. Some pieces are simply easier to dip using a tool, and the same goes for at-home dipping. A set of dipping tools typically includes one of each of the following: a four-prong fork, a three-prong fork, a two-prong fork, a spiral-tipped piece for holding a piece of candy, and several tools with various loops for dipping individual nuts and smaller pieces. These sets are available from the suppliers I list in Chapter 24, and they range in price from $8 to $17, depending on how nice a set you want. I recommend getting the least expensive unless you plan to do a lot of dipping.

Some pieces are easier to dip with these pronged forks. For example, pretzels and cookies are two items that do well on the forks because they're wider items, and you can slide the dipped pieces off the fork onto a lined tray.

When you dip a pretzel or other large flat piece:

1. **Use the fork of your choice to press the pretzel into the chocolate to coat completely.** You can easily move the piece in the chocolate.

2. **Lift the piece out of the chocolate with the fork and tap the fork lightly on the side of the bowl to remove the excess chocolate.** You want plenty of chocolate on the piece, just not a runny excess.

3. **Lightly drag the fork across the rim of the bowl to remove bottom excess that drips through.** By dragging, you prevent the puddling of feet under the piece.

4. **Point the fork downward just above the tray to allow the piece to slide off, placing the edge of the dipped piece on the paper.** Then slide the fork away.

You'll master this method with practice, and you'll learn not to leave little tails beside the pieces. If you get a set of forks (and you should), experiment and find what's easiest for you. See Figure 15-2 for more dipping details.

USING DIPPING TOOLS

1. USE YOUR DIPPING TOOL TO GENTLY LOWER THE CANDY INTO THE TEMPERED CHOCOLATE.

2. REMOVE THE CANDY AND SKIM THE SURFACE OF THE CHOCOLATE TO REMOVE THE DRIP.

3. GENTLY DROP THE CANDY ONTO A PIECE OF PARCHMENT PAPER.

YOU CAN USE THE TOOL TO DRIZZLE A PATTERN ON TOP!

Figure 15-2: Dipping tools are a useful alternative to hand-dipping.

Decorating dipped pieces

Most of the items I show you in this chapter have a distinctive shape or enough of the undipped portion exposed to make recognizing what candy is what easy. However, a few dipped candies, such as creams, aren't very distinctive, and decorating them is an easy way to identify what each one contains. Of course, you can decorate candies just for the fun of it, too.

When you see an assortment of candies, different markings provide a nice visual. Some pieces are sprinkled, some have nuts, some have fork marks, and others have drizzles. When you group the pieces, these variations make for an eye-appealing assortment.

How you decorate your chocolates may be nothing more than whatever you care to do to identify your chocolates. You have no rules to follow, and no one says that you can't leave every piece in a box a surprise. In general, you'll probably find identification of your candies important, so whatever you decide, be consistent.

If you're applying any type of topping, do so when the chocolate is still wet so the topping sticks to the chocolate. If you're using a drizzle, you can apply it while the chocolate is wet, but you don't have to. Drizzling or "stringing" onto a dry piece of chocolate works just fine.

The following decorating ideas are a few of my favorites:

- ✔ Some of the simplest decorations to put on pieces to distinguish them are sprinkles, such as jimmies. Jimmies are great because they're available in so many colors, and they're usually available in grocery stores. These decorations come in little bottles with openings, which make decorating easy.

- ✔ You can use coconut in a number of ways to decorate pieces that have nothing to do with coconut on the inside. For example, I love to sprinkle toasted coconut on chocolate pretzels.

- ✔ Nut pieces make nice toppings for some pieces. What you put on the chocolate should visually complement the chocolate; in other words, don't sprinkle something on just to coat the piece. For instance, peanut pieces on a strawberry cream could be a little confusing.

- ✔ Additionally, you can use a salad fork to string a contrasting color or chocolate on top of a piece. Stringing involves dipping a fork into melted white chocolate mixed with food coloring and shaking your hand back and forth over the chocolates. This technique helps identify a piece as well as give it a nice appearance. The secret to stringing is to create as thin a string as possible because it gives the piece a richer appearance. With just a little practice, you'll master this technique in no time.

- ✔ One especially creative method for decorating candies is to make an imprint, either by hand or using a utensil. Methods for making imprints abound. For instance, you can use your finger to make an initial of the first letter of a center's flavor. Some pieces that look good with a finger-marker initial are creams because these pieces have identical appearances with a variety of center flavors (see Chapter 17 for details on creams). Such similar-looking pieces are why finger markings are necessary.

As soon as you've dipped a piece, the chocolate is still quite liquid. Touch the top of the piece without applying any pressure (you don't want to create spreading underneath the piece), and the chocolate should stick to your finger. Quickly finger-write a letter on top of the piece (see Figure 15-1).

To practice making letters with your fingertip, pour a little chocolate onto a piece of waxed paper and practice making small letters. Soon you will master the technique. Tempered chocolate retains its shape when you "write."

✔ A related method of marking is to use the dipping forks as markers. The forks have a variety of ends: two-pronged, three-pronged, spiral ends, and more. You can use each of these ends as a marker. Place a just-dipped piece of candy on the paper and simply touch the top of the piece lightly with the dipping fork and lift straight up (see Figure 15-2). This leaves a distinct imprint on the top of the piece.

Again, with a little practice, you will become quite adept at this technique. Some pieces that look good with this type of marking include chocolate sandwich cookies and chocolate caramel pecan clusters. Aside from marking the piece, the ridges and markings add to the appearance of the piece, affecting how light creates shadows.

Choosing Cookies and Crackers to Dip

You can dip nontraditional items, such as cookies and crackers, in chocolate, too. Folks are often surprised to see salty crackers and chocolate paired up, but chocolate-covered pretzels have been popular for years. Take a couple of buttery crackers with peanut butter between them, cover them in chocolate, and you have a real treat. For something sweeter, there are always chocolate-dipped sandwich cookies. You can easily dip either of these items (which are wider pieces) in chocolate yourself using the forks from a dipping utensil set. All you need are a package of crackers or cookies, forks, a tray, some tempered chocolate in a bowl, and a healthy appetite for dessert!

Taking the plunge with cookies

An item that has found its way into quite a few candy shops in recent years is the dipped sandwich cookie. Most commonly, candy makers dip chocolate sandwich cookies with white filling, but you can also coat vanilla sandwich cookies or even peanut butter cookies with chocolate. Any of these combinations has wide appeal, so just go with what you like!

Dipped Chocolate Sandwich Cookies

For sandwich cookies, select a dipping fork with three or four prongs. For this size piece, I prefer using a three-pronged fork because of the similar width of the cookie and the fork, but either type is fine.

The chocolate sandwich cookie is wonderful when covered with chocolate because of the nice crunch that it provides when you bite into it. Of course, you can use other kinds of cookies, too. Whatever cookie you use, this item is a real treat for chocolate- and cookie-lovers.

When making this confection, I recommend using a heating pad to keep the chocolate warm, but use the pad sparingly (a minute or two at a time) because you don't want to overheat the chocolate.

Tools: *Three-prong dipping forks and a heating pad*

Preparation time: *45 to 60 minutes*

Yield: *24 pieces*

2 pounds milk chocolate, chopped and melted for tempering	*2 dozen sandwich cookies*

1 Spread a large sheet of wax paper on the countertop. Temper the chocolate using one of the methods I describe in Chapter 14.

2 Place a bowl of tempered milk chocolate on a heating pad occasionally to maintain its temperature. Beside the larger bowl, place a small bowl of dark chocolate on the heating pad for a minute, as needed, to maintain temperature. Put a cookie into the milk chocolate and, using the dipping fork, press the cookie into the chocolate, completely coating the cookie.

3 Using your fork, lift the coated cookie out of the chocolate, and lightly tap it on the side of the bowl to shake off the excess chocolate, being careful not to drop the cookie back into the bowl. (If you drop it, start over.) Lightly scrape the fork on the side of the bowl to remove the excess chocolate on the fork.

4 Hold the cookie just above the wax-paper sheet, angle the cookie downward, and allow it to slide gently off the fork onto the paper. As the cookie is almost off the fork, lightly slide the cookie away from the fork so that the cookie sits in its own little chocolate puddle. Lay the fork lightly on top of the cookie and lift straight up to leave a three-ridge marking. Repeat the process with the rest of the cookies.

5 Let the cookies cool for 30 minutes at room temperature before eating or storing.

6 Store the dry, dipped cookies in a plastic container for up to two weeks. If you layer the cookies in the container, put a sheet of wax paper between layers.

Per serving: Calories 130 (From Fat 59); Fat 7g (Saturated 3g); Cholesterol 3mg; Sodium 83mg; Carbohydrate 16g (Dietary Fiber 0g); Protein 2g.

You can decorate dipped cookies according to your personal taste. For instance, you can make a light impression on top of a dipped cookie by laying a dipping fork gently on the cookie as soon as you put the cookie onto the tray or, when finished, stringing all cookies with dark chocolate using a salad fork and tempered dark chocolate. Each adds its own appearance to the finished piece.

If you're marking cookies with a fork, your finger, or another utensil, the chocolate must be as wet as possible because you want the chocolate to be pliable enough to take the marking. If the chocolate is drier, you simply leave a fingerprint or an ugly mark.

If you want to dip different types of cookies, you can mark one flavor with a fork and another by stringing. If you dip more than two flavors, you can use different marks. Experiment and create different appearances. For instance, if you use peanut butter cookies, melt peanut butter chips and use them as a string.

Crunching on dipped crackers

In this book, I frequently present an idea for combining peanut butter and chocolate, and the reason is simple: People love that combination. This combination of buttery crackers, peanut butter, and chocolate is simply delightful.

Dipped Chocolate Peanut Butter Crackers

This procedure requires a little time to put together the crackers before you dip them — and I mean just a *little* time. You probably know that you can purchase ready-made crackers and peanut butter, but would you really want to do so when you're going through all the trouble to dip them yourself? I find that assembling the crackers and peanut butter doesn't require too many skills, and I believe you can save money, too. Besides, if you're like me, you'll want to put more peanut butter on your crackers.

Tools: *Three- or four-pronged dipping forks and a heating pad*

Preparation time: *1 hour*

Yield: *24 pieces*

1 pound milk chocolate, chopped and melted for tempering	48 buttery crackers
2 pounds white chocolate, chopped	¾ cup creamy peanut butter (more for thicker centers)

1 Temper 1 pound of milk chocolate using one of the methods I describe in Chapter 14; if the temperature of the chocolate drops during dipping, place it on the heating pad for 1 minute and stir.

2 Melt 2 pounds of white chocolate for about 2½ to 3 minutes in a microwave on high power, stopping every 30 to 45 seconds to stir and check temperature with a chocolate thermometer. To hold the temperature at 92 to 94 degrees, occasionally place the bowl of chocolate on a heating pad.

3 Make 24 cracker sandwiches with about ½ tablespoon of peanut butter in the center. Give the crackers a gentle twist to spread the peanut butter. You should apply the peanut butter heavily enough so that you leave no space around the cracker center. Wipe around the cracker to give the peanut butter a smooth edge.

4 Spread a large sheet of wax paper on a countertop. Using a three-prong or four-prong dipping fork, completely coat each double peanut butter cracker in white chocolate. Tap the fork lightly on the side of the bowl to knock off the excess chocolate; scrape the bottom of the fork on the side of the bowl to get off the excess chocolate, and place the piece on wax paper to dry. When sliding the piece off the fork, allow the cracker to slide off and gently nudge the cracker so that it rests in its own small pool of white chocolate, preventing feet from forming under the cracker.

5 When the white chocolate cools (about 15 to 20 minutes), hold one side of the cracker and dip half the cracker into milk chocolate, scraping some excess on the rim of the bowl. Place the cracker on wax paper to cool for about 25 to 30 minutes at room temperature.

6 Store the crackers in a plastic container for up to two weeks. If you layer the stored crackers, place wax paper between the layers.

Tip: If you don't want so much white chocolate on your cracker, dip half the double cracker into white chocolate and, when it's dry, dip the other half into milk chocolate. When dipping this way, be certain that you dip the underside of the cracker at least halfway. Always dip into white chocolate first; you don't want to hold the milk-chocolate side in your hand because it melts too easily and leaves fingerprints.

Per Serving: Calories 182 (From Fat 101); Fat 11g (Saturated 4g); Cholesterol 3mg; Sodium 141mg; Carbohydrate 18g (Dietary Fiber 1g); Protein 4g.

The following recipe is a surprisingly delicious little treat, made up of chocolate and graham crackers. If you're looking for something to delight the family, this one idea certainly will please them.

Chocolate Graham Crackers

You can buy something similar to this treat in a grocery store, but those treats usually use imitation chocolate. You'll find that taking a little time to use real chocolate is worth the little extra work. You can top chocolate-coated graham crackers, while still wet, with coconut, sliced almonds, or chopped pecans for nutty variations.

Tools: *Four-prong dipping forks*

Preparation time: *45 to 60 minutes*

Yield: *24 pieces*

2 pounds milk chocolate, chopped and melted for tempering	*6 ounces dark chocolate, chopped and melted for tempering*	*24 graham cracker halves*

1 Temper 2 pounds of milk chocolate and 6 ounces of dark chocolate using one of the methods I describe in Chapter 14. Keep a heating pad handy for use a minute at a time to prevent the chocolate from cooling.

2 Spread out a large sheet of wax paper on the countertop. Dipping the cracker using a four-prong dipping fork, completely coat each graham cracker with tempered milk chocolate; scrape the excess chocolate on the side of the bowl before placing the coated cracker onto wax paper to dry. Let dry for about 25 to 30 minutes at room temperature.

3 Using a salad fork, string the dark chocolate over each dipped cracker. Let them cool for about 15 minutes at room temperature to allow the "strings" to set.

4 Store the dipped graham crackers in a plastic container for up to two weeks. If you layer the stored crackers, place a sheet of wax paper between the layers.

Vary It! *You can reverse the chocolates, dipping the graham crackers in dark chocolate and stringing them with milk chocolate. You can also melt 3 12-ounce bags of peanut butter chips in the microwave for about 2½ to 3 minutes, stirring every 30 seconds. Check the temperature with a chocolate thermometer. Dip the graham crackers in the peanut butter. Then string them with milk chocolate. Dipping the crackers in white chocolate and stringing them with a contrasting chocolate also creates a cool effect.*

Per Serving: Calories 112 (From Fat 49); Fat 6g (Saturated 3g); Cholesterol 0mg; Sodium 52mg; Carbohydrate 16g (Dietary Fiber 0g); Protein 2g.

Putting Chocolate on Pretzels and Pretzel Rods

Nowadays, all sorts of foods are covered in chocolate, and people have learned to appreciate combinations they once thought would have never worked — like really zesty spices and rich chocolates, even flower petals and chocolate. But I'm not going that far here.

One of the most popular nonconfectionery items you can cover with chocolate is the pretzel. In this chapter, I mention how popular the salt-and-chocolate combination is, and the pretzel is at the top of this list. Pretzels primarily come in three sizes and two shapes (I know there are more, but you find three main pretzels): large and mini-pretzels in the traditional shape and pretzel rods. The regular pretzels are easy to coat in chocolate and decorate in numerous ways. I string them, shake sprinkles on them, top with coconut, or top with small nut bits. You can dip the pretzel rods into the chocolate and string them with a contrasting chocolate or any of a variety of toppings.

When you make chocolate-coated pretzels, be aware that they tend to form cracks in their shells a couple of days after you dip them. If you leave the pretzels out overnight before dipping them and allow them to get just a little soft, this cracking shouldn't occur. The softening of the pretzel doesn't affect it in any discernable way — except to prevent cracking.

Chocolate-dipped Pretzels

When purchasing pretzels by the bag, check the bags as well as possible while you're at the store. I've found that getting enough unbroken pretzels from one bag is quite difficult. When you get home, be sure to sort through the bag and choose unbroken, uncracked pretzels for dipping. The pieces are fine to dip; they just aren't as pretty.

I usually use toasted coconut and colored sprinkles for toppings on pretzels, but you can use sliced almonds, pecan pieces, or granulated roasted peanuts as toppings, too. See these treats in the color section.

Preparation time: *1 hour and 15 minutes*

Yield: *48 pieces*

2 pounds milk chocolate, chopped and melted for tempering

6 ounces melted dark chocolate, chopped and melted for tempering

1 small container of assorted color sprinkles

8 ounces toasted coconut

1 Lay out the pretzels on a sheet of wax paper at room temperature overnight before coating them. Doing so allows the pretzels to become a little soft, which will help prevent cracking in their chocolate shells.

2 Temper both chocolates using one of the methods I describe in Chapter 14.

3 Place a bowl of tempered milk chocolate and a small bowl of dark chocolate on a heating pad for 1 minute at a time to maintain temper. Drop a pretzel into a bowl of milk chocolate and, using your hand or a dipping fork, completely coat it with milk chocolate. Shake the excess chocolate into the bowl, and lay the pretzel on a wax-paper sheet. Dip a salad fork into the tempered dark chocolate, and string the pretzels with dark chocolate. You can dip pretzels in dark and string with milk chocolate, too.

4 After you dip about six to eight pretzels, sprinkle them with assorted sprinkles or coconut, making sure that the chocolate is still wet. Continue this process until you've dipped and topped all the pretzels. Use only one topping on each piece of paper, and recycling the leftover topping will be simple. Let pretzels cool for about 20 minutes at room temperature.

5 Store the pretzels in a plastic container for up to two weeks. Line the layers with wax paper to prevent scratching.

Vary It! *To make white-chocolate pretzels, melt 1½ to 2 pounds of white chocolate in a microwave on high for about 2 to 2½ minutes, stopping every 30 seconds to stir. Check the temperature with a chocolate thermometer. Another great variation is to melt 3 12-ounce bags of peanut butter chips in a microwave for about 1 minute and 45 seconds, stopping and stirring every 30 seconds until the temperature reaches 94 degrees. Dip the pretzels in peanut butter and string them with tempered milk chocolate.*

Per Serving: *Calories 89 (From Fat 41); Fat 5g (Saturated 3g); Cholesterol 0mg; Sodium 109mg; Carbohydrate 12g (Dietary Fiber 1g); Protein 1g.*

When the pretzels are set and you can move them, transfer them to a clean piece of wax paper or to a plastic container. Dump the loose topping you used to coat the pretzels back into the appropriate topping container for continued or future use. You will think that you're using a lot of topping, but most of it will be left over on the wax paper.

Chocolate-dipped Pretzel Rods

Chocolate-covered pretzels and pretzel rods are made using the same ingredients, but how you dip them and their respective tastes seem quite different. When making chocolate-dipped pretzels, you submerge the entire pretzel in chocolate but, when making chocolate-dipped pretzel rods, you leave one end of the pretzel rod uncoated.

The bowl you use to melt your chocolate won't be deep enough to dip the pretzel rods straight into, so you need to dip the rods at an angle and use a spoon to pour the chocolate over the rod. Just be sure to leave about 2 inches exposed for a handle.

Preparation time: *45 to 60 minutes*

Yield: *30 pieces*

2 pounds milk chocolate, chopped and melted for tempering

6 ounces white chocolate, chopped

1 bag (30 pieces) pretzel rods

1 Spread out a large sheet of wax paper on a countertop. Temper the milk chocolate using one of the methods I describe in Chapter 14.

2 Hold one end of the pretzel rod and dip the other end into the milk chocolate, leaving about 2 inches exposed on the end you're holding. Roll the rod around in the chocolate using a spoon to thoroughly coat the pretzel. Remove the rod from the chocolate and hold the pretzel vertically, allowing the excess chocolate to drain into the bowl. When most of the excess has run off, hold the pretzel horizontally, and turn it to allow the chocolate to coat the rod evenly. Lay the rod on wax paper to dry. Continue until you've coated all the pretzels in this manner.

3 Melt the white chocolate in the microwave, stopping every 30 seconds to stir and take its temperature with a chocolate thermometer, until it reaches 95 degrees. Reaching 95 degrees takes about 1 minute and 20 seconds.

4 Using a salad fork, string white chocolate across the pretzel rods. Allow the chocolate to dry for 30 minutes.

5 Store the pretzel rods in a plastic container. Place a sheet of wax paper between layers of pretzels.

Per Serving: *Calories 69 (From Fat 20); Fat 2g (Saturated 1g); Cholesterol 0mg; Sodium 127mg; Carbohydrate 11g (Dietary Fiber 0g); Protein 1g.*

The preceding recipe is the basic way to coat a pretzel rod. From here, you can produce any number of variations, including dipping the rods in white or dark chocolate and using a contrasting string. If those little touches aren't enough for you, you can

✔ Dip the rods in chocolate and string them with peanut butter by melting a 12-ounce bag of peanut butter chips in a microwave for about 1 minute and 30 seconds.

✔ Dip the rods in white chocolate and sprinkle chocolate jimmies on the wet coating.

✔ Dip the rods in melted peanut butter chips and string them with milk chocolate.

✔ Dip the rods in melted caramel and roll them in medium pecan pieces. When they're cool, string them with milk chocolate or dip the entire nut-coated portion into milk chocolate and let them cool on wax paper.

All the above produce scrumptious pieces and are great variations on a simple idea.

Flavoring Fruits with Chocolate

Not surprisingly, fruits dipped in chocolate or completely coated with chocolate are big items in the candy business, so I imagine that you'd enjoy finding out the simple tricks to making these treats at home.

Picking the best berries

I decided years ago that as long as we were able to find good berries, my stores would sell chocolate-covered berries year round. The recipes in this section include dipped strawberries and maraschino cherries.

Farmers grow strawberries in hothouses, so they're available year round — though sometimes for a steep price. You may want to make chocolate-dipped berries only when they're in season (springtime), when you can get the very best berries. (I have friends who dip fresh strawberries only at certain times of the year, and they sell an awesome volume of them.)

But you should know a few things about strawberries before you dunk them in your beautiful tempered chocolate:

✔ Look for strawberries with fresh green stems because the stem will be your handle in the dipping process. If the stem is dry, the berry may separate when you dip it into the chocolate. In the spring, you can find berries as big as monkey fists, just another reason to dip strawberries in the springtime.

✔ Strawberries are prewashed so, before you stick a basket of beautiful red berries under the faucet to wash them, remember that fact. If you think that your berries aren't clean enough, wash them in cold water, but allow them to drain completely before dipping them into chocolate because you don't want to introduce water to chocolate; the combination of a few drops of water and chocolate causes the chocolate to form a thick mass.

Strawberries are fat red sponges, and they store water like a camel. So try not to soak them. If you must clean the berries, you can usually wipe them carefully with a dry towel or even a slightly damp towel.

Chocolate Strawberries

Now that you've selected some nice berries, the time has come to take the plunge; at least, the strawberry will take the plunge. These delectable treats (shown in the color section) are especially great for special occasions: weddings, fancy parties, and don't forget Valentine's Day.

Preparation time: *45 to 60 minutes*

Yield: *24 berries*

2 pounds milk chocolate, chopped and melted for tempering

3 small baskets of strawberries (select the best 24 berries)

1 Spread out a large sheet of wax paper on a countertop.

2 Temper the chocolate using one of the methods I describe in Chapter 14.

3 After blotting the berries with a dry towel, they're ready to dip. Take the berries by the stem, one at a time, and dip them in the chocolate, leaving about ⅓ of an inch exposed on the stem end. Wipe the bottom of the berry lightly on the edge of the bowl and set the berry on wax paper to dry.

4 Allow the chocolate to set for about 5 minutes.

Tip: *This item isn't one you want to make and use the next day because the berries are perishable and, although you may on occasion refrigerate them overnight, don't count on doing so. Enjoy them the day you dip 'em!*

Per Serving: *Calories 78 (From Fat 37); Fat 4g (Saturated 2g); Cholesterol 0mg; Sodium 10mg; Carbohydrate 11g (Dietary Fiber 1g); Protein 1g.*

The preceding recipe is for a basic chocolate strawberry; of course, variations abound. For instance, you can

✔ String the chocolate berries with melted white chocolate

✔ String the chocolate berries with tempered dark chocolate

✔ Dip the berries in white chocolate and leave them plain or string them with tempered milk chocolate

✔ Dip the berries in dark chocolate and leave them plain or string them with milk chocolate.

✔ Coat the chocolate berry, while still wet, with coconut

✔ Cover the wet chocolate with almond slices or pecan pieces

✔ Make a "tuxedo" berry, which you do by dipping in such a way as to leave a *v* on one side; using a toothpick, dot studs on the shirt and draw a bow tie, all with tempered milk chocolate.

Chocolate Cherries

I explain cordial cherries in this chapter, but this recipe is even simpler. You need a large jar of maraschino cherries with stems for this treat, which you can see in the color section.

Preparation time: *20 minutes*

Yield: *About 45 pieces*

1 10-ounce jar of maraschino cherries   *1 pound milk or dark chocolate, chopped and melted for tempering*

1 Drain the cherries by pouring them into a sieve and letting the excess juice drain away.

2 Spread a large sheet of wax paper on a countertop. Temper 1 pound of chocolate using one of the methods I describe in Chapter 14. Occasionally place the chocolate on a heating pad for 1 minute at a time to maintain chocolate temperature of 88 to 90.

3 Holding the cherry by the stem, completely coat the cherry in chocolate. Lift the cherry out of the pot, and gently wipe the bottom on the rim of the bowl; set the cherry on wax paper, and hold the stem for a couple of seconds to make sure that the cherry stands up straight. Sometimes the cherries fall over — and nothing's hurt by their falling — but they look prettier standing up straight.

4 Let the chocolate cherries set for 10 minutes at room temperature.

5 Store your chocolate cherries in a plastic container for up to two weeks.

Vary It! *Other than milk or dark chocolate, you can dip cherries in white chocolate. When the white chocolate has set, dip the cherry in milk chocolate but leave about ¼ inch exposed — the candy looks very nice and gives dual tastes.*

Per Serving: *Calories 36 (From Fat 14); Fat 2g (Saturated 1g); Cholesterol 0mg; Sodium 4mg; Carbohydrate 6g (Dietary Fiber 0g); Protein 0g.*

The preceding recipe is for a basic milk-chocolate cherry, but you can make a few variations on this theme. For example, you can

- Dip cherries in tempered dark chocolate.
- Dip cherries in white chocolate.
- Dip cherries in white chocolate and allow them to set for about 30 minutes while you temper 12 ounces of milk chocolate. Then dip the white cherry in the milk chocolate, leaving the top ¼ inch exposed to show the white.
- You can make any of these cherries and add a tempered contrasting string for a great look.

Dipping dried and candied fruits

If you visit fancy chocolate shops, you see apricots dipped in chocolate with a portion of the fruit exposed. You may notice that these fruits are pretty expensive, but you can buy these apricots at a variety of places, including a lot of grocery stores and major discount stores.

With this recipe, I show you how to dip apricots, but you also can try candied pineapple slices, orange slices, or even kiwi slices. Although candied fruits and dried fruits aren't the same thing, you should be able to have great results with either, using them interchangeably.

Chocolate Apricots

One of those simple chocolates that has a certain cachet is the chocolate apricot. You can purchase these treats online for quite a few bucks or you can make them yourself in just a few minutes. By now, you may have guessed that tempering chocolate opens the door to many fine chocolate products. You just must be patient and take the time to temper your own chocolate. You can purchase dried apricots in 1-pound bags at a number of stores, including "big box" stores. See these treats for yourself in the color section.

Preparation time: *40 to 50 minutes*

Yield: *36 apricots*

1 pound milk chocolate, chopped and melted for tempering　　　*1-pound bag dried apricots*

1 Spread a large sheet of wax paper on a countertop. Temper the milk chocolate using one of the methods I describe in Chapter 14. Keep a heating pad handy or put the chocolate in a microwaveable bowl that allows you to heat the chocolate a few seconds at a time.

2 Hold an apricot between your finger and your thumb and dip it into the chocolate, leaving the area around your fingers exposed. Set the piece on wax paper to dry. Repeat this step until you dip all the apricots.

3 Let the dipped fruit and chocolate set for about 20 minutes at room temperature.

4 You can store your dipped apricots in a plastic container for up to two weeks. Line the bottom of the container with wax paper, and place a sheet between layers of the fruits.

Per Serving: Calories 65 (From Fat 16); Fat 2g (Saturated 1g); Cholesterol 0mg; Sodium 5mg; Carbohydrate 12g (Dietary Fiber 1g); Protein 1g.

Chocolate Orange Peels

Although you dip a lot of the fruits in such a way that you expose a portion of the fruit, some pieces are better completely covered. One such piece is the candied orange peel. These peels are the rinds of the orange that have been cut into slices about ¼-inch wide and candied to preserve and tenderize them. They can be hard to find, but they're usually available wherever varieties of dried fruits and nuts are sold.

The recipe I provide uses dark chocolate, but you can substitute other coatings, if you want. This piece also requires no decoration to identify it because it has such a recognizable appearance (see the color section).

Tools: *Three-prong dipping forks*

Preparation time: *45 to 60 minutes*

Yield: *32 pieces*

1½ pounds dark chocolate, chopped and melted for tempering	8 ounces candied orange peel

1 Spread a large sheet of wax paper on a countertop. Temper the dark chocolate using one of the methods I describe in Chapter 14. Keep a heating pad handy for brief warming spells or put the chocolate in a microwaveable bowl that you can heat in 5-second intervals to maintain the temper of the chocolate.

2 Using a three-prong dipping fork, drop an orange peel into the bowl of dark chocolate; move the piece around with the fork to coat completely. Remove the peel and, while holding the fork, tap the side of the bowl lightly to remove excess. Lightly drag the fork across the side of the bowl to remove the excess chocolate and set onto the wax paper to dry for about 15 minutes.

3 Store the chocolate-covered peels for two weeks in a plastic container. Place a sheet of wax paper between the layers.

Vary It! *You can dip candied orange slices, candied ginger, or even candied kiwi slices using the same method. You can dip any of these items in dark chocolate or white chocolate.*

Per Serving: Calories 50 (From Fat 17); Fat 2g (Saturated 1g); Cholesterol 0mg; Sodium 8mg; Carbohydrate 9g (Dietary Fiber 1g); Protein 0g.

Trying cordial fruits

The cordial cherry recipe in this section answers the age-old question, "How do they get the juice inside the chocolate?"

Of course, as you discover here (if you don't already know), you don't put the juice in the chocolate cherry; the juice forms there with a little help. The few ingredients included in the cordial cherry are sugar, cherries, cherry juice, and invertase, which is an enzyme that assists in the cordial process.

If you want to make many of the recipes in this book, keep a small bottle of invertase in the refrigerator, because you will use it quite a few times. You can find it at some of the suppliers I list in Chapter 24. You can purchase a small bottle, which you store in the refrigerator.

After the cherries are coated in chocolate, the process that creates the liquid may take a few days to complete, but the process starts almost immediately. If you were to coat the cherries with the fondant sugar coating and leave them on a tray, you would have little puddles on your tray the next day. You want to be ready to dip these cherries within an hour.

Chocolate Cordial Cherries

A cordial cherry is one of those great little pieces of candy. I couldn't believe that I had made them the first time I tried my hand at it, but the technique is quite easy. The worst-case scenario leaves you with a bunch of leaky chocolate cherries.

For this recipe, you use a stainless steel bowl as half of a *pan* (a rotating device that candy makers use to coat a wide variety of candies). For your purposes, making a small batch of cherries, you can roll the cherries around in the bowl to adequately coat them. For a small number of cherries, as in the following recipe, the bowl works.

Because of the weight of the pieces relative to the strength of the chocolate to support it, I recommend placing a little spot of chocolate on the wax paper you use to let the pieces dry. Then set the cherry on the little spot before the spot dries. This spot provides a stronger base so that the cordial doesn't leak out the bottom.

Tools: *Small plastic refillable spray bottle and a heating pad*

Preparation time: *1 hour and 15 minutes*

Yield: *36 to 40 cherries*

1 pound milk or dark chocolate, chopped and melted for tempering

1 10-ounce jar maraschino cherries, without stems

1 teaspoon invertase

8 ounces fondant sugar, sifted

1 Spread a large sheet of wax paper on a countertop. Temper the chocolate using one of the methods I describe in Chapter 14. Then place the bowl on a heating pad occasionally and briefly (1 minute at a time) to maintain the chocolate's temper.

2 Drain the cherries using a strainer, and keep the cherry juice. Mix 4 ounces of cherry juice and 1 teaspoon of invertase in a measuring cup and pour into a small plastic spray bottle.

3 Place half the fondant sugar in a small stainless steel bowl and toss in half the cherries (about 18 to 20). Roll the cherries around in the sugar and, as the cherries pick up sugar, lightly spray them with the cherry juice. Occasionally sprinkle the unused sugar onto the cherries, but let them get most of their sugar from what's in the bowl. Continue sugaring and spraying the cherries until they acquire a nice, thick coating of sugar (they will have a pink color). Cherries can nearly double in size.

4 Remove the cherries from the bowl, and repeat the previous step with the last half of cherries, adding the rest of the sugar as needed. Remove these cherries from the sugar to a piece of wax paper.

5 Immediately hand-dip the cherries one by one in the chocolate, being sure to completely coat each cherry. Make small spots on the wax paper with dabs of chocolate, and set the cherry on the spot. Repeat until you've dipped all the cherries. Let the cherries dry for 25 to 30 minutes.

6 When the cherries are dry, put each one in a #6 brown candy cup, and place the cherries in a plastic container for up to two weeks. The cherries are not immediately ready to eat. Give them at least a week to complete the liquefying process while stored in an airtight container at room temperature.

Vary It! *Dark chocolate is excellent with cherries. I believe white coating is too sweet, but you can substitute white chocolate if you prefer. You temper the dark chocolate as described in Chapter 14. To melt the white chocolate, place it in a microwave for about 2½ minutes on high power, stopping every 30 seconds to stir and check the temperature. Heat the chocolate to 95 degrees and coat the cherries.*

Per Serving: Calories 58 (From Fat 15); Fat 2g (Saturated 1g); Cholesterol 0mg; Sodium 7mg; Carbohydrate 11g (Dietary Fiber 0g); Protein 0g.

Although cordial cherries are quite common, you don't often see other cordial fruits. Nevertheless, a couple of fruits that cordialize quite nicely are strawberries and raspberries. Although these berries have a very short shelf life when partially dipped in chocolate, they do quite well when completely covered.

Because these fruits don't come with their own juice, you can use some of the cherry juice from the maraschino cherries. The juice is a small part of the piece and doesn't overpower the natural fruit flavor when it cordializes.

If you use raspberries, follow the exact procedure you do to make cordial cherries. If you use strawberries, remove the stem from the strawberry and then follow the procedure for making cordial cherries.

I don't recommend keeping strawberry and raspberry cordials in a plastic container for more than a week because they break down faster than cherries do.

Chapter 16

Taking a Bite Out of Barks and Clusters

Chocolate comes in many forms, and people seem to enjoy chocolate in a thousand different ways. But as good as chocolate is, you'd probably get bored with it if you always had it the same way. Chocolate is available in so many forms that becoming bored with it is difficult to do. Sometimes you simply need a good solid piece of pure delight. Sometimes you want a bar of chocolate that you can hold in your hand. (If it melts, you can always lick your fingers.) Sometimes you just want a chocolate cluster or chocolate bark. Don't worry, I've got your back. In this chapter, I give you the lowdown on barks and clusters.

Clusters and bark are made from the same combination of chocolate and nuts *Chocolate clusters* are just what they sound like: bite-size pieces of chocolate goodness wrapped around a few of your favorite nuts. *Bark* is composed of chocolate and nuts, too, but it is made in tray-size sheets and cut into more manageable pieces about the size of a commercial chocolate bar. These two treats taste the same — but don't tell that to someone who prefers either version over the other. Cluster folks don't like bark, and bark-eaters won't touch clusters. Go figure.

Mixing Nuts and Tempered Chocolate with Care

An essential ingredient in barks and clusters is tempered chocolate. Any time you work with real chocolate (which contains cocoa butter) and you're using it for molding, for coating a piece, or as a stand-alone piece — such as bark or clusters — you must temper the chocolate. If you don't temper the chocolate, your finished pieces won't have the fine gloss, and it will develop streaks and spots soon after it cools. I explain the tempering process in detail in Chapter 14.

Another key ingredient common to barks and clusters is nuts, either raw or roasted. I use both kinds in my stores: I use roasted salted peanuts, roasted and unsalted almonds and cashews, and raw pecans. But what I do is a matter of taste. I know candy makers who use roasted salted pecans, and the overall perception is different because a roasted pecan imparts a different taste from a raw pecan. I let you decide which taste you prefer and allow you to make your candies accordingly. In addition, the amounts I suggest in this chapter's recipes are only suggestions. You may, of course, add more nuts or fewer, if you want. The amount of nuts suggested is just that — a suggestion.

Always add room-temperature nuts to chocolate for the best results. If the nuts are too cool, the chocolate cools too quickly. If the nuts are too hot, your chocolate loses its temper because the heat from the nuts causes the temperature of the chocolate to rise above its tempered range of 88 to 91 degrees.

When you add nuts to tempered chocolate, your chocolate may begin to lose its temper, so you need to work quickly or be ready to heat the chocolate slightly. Any time you heat chocolate that you've already tempered and cooled slightly, take small steps. If necessary, heat the cooled chocolate in the microwave — just don't let the temperature exceed 91 degrees on a chocolate thermometer because you risk losing the temper. Microwave your chocolate in bursts of 3 to 5 seconds, stir, and observe. If you make small adjustments, your chocolate should be safe.

This slight warming is especially helpful when you're hand-dipping clusters. Unlike making bark, which involves putting the nuts in and getting the bark out, making clusters can be more time consuming because you make one cluster at a time. (For more details, see "Pulling Together Chocolate Clusters," later in this chapter.)

Peeling Away the Layers of Bark Basics

I've always assumed that the name "chocolate bark" was derived from the product's appearance because it is so similar to the bark of a tree. If you picture tree bark in your mind and look at a cut piece or even a broken piece of chocolate bark, you don't need much imagination to see the similarities. So I'm going to let that description suffice, and now you may always think about chocolate every time you look at a tree.

Spreading and cutting different kinds of bark

In my stores, I make most of the candy in small batches — larger than you'd make at home, but still small batches. I make the bark in sheets of 3 to 4 pounds, so those batches aren't much larger than the ones here. But, although my batches are fairly small, I set up to make a lot of batches back to back, so my overall production is good.

Another theory on bark's humble beginnings

An alternate theory of how bark got its name is attributed to a young candy maker named Richard Swilligen, who was an apprentice in a little chocolate factory in New England in 1923. The story goes that young Richard worked for a gentleman by the name of Alan Hampton, who was a little tight with the bucks. Hampton supposedly knew where every penny he had ever made went; he didn't suffer fools lightly, and he didn't have any patience for waste.

One morning, the young apprentice was tempering some chocolate for use that day. He was carrying a small bucket of almonds from the nut-roasting area to the area where the nuts were bagged for sale and, as luck would have it, he slipped on a wet spot on the floor and spilled the nuts into the tempered chocolate.

He hurriedly tried to separate the nuts from the chocolate, but he quickly realized that it was a losing proposition. So he did the next-best thing: He mixed the nuts with the chocolate, spread it out, let it cool, and cut the whole thing into candy-bar–size pieces.

Just as he was cutting his creation, Hampton walked past and saw what he was doing. "What the heck is that?" he boomed. (At least, this is how I imagine the story would have gone.)

"This is my new creation. I call it chocolate almond . . . chocolate almond, uh . . . " he stammered.

"What is chocolate almond uh?" the old man wanted to know.

As luck would have it, a dog was scratching at the back door at that exact moment, crying and barking for a bone.

"It's chocolate almond . . . bark," Richard said proudly.

Apparently, Hampton didn't fire the apprentice for his mistake, and the rest is history. At least, that's one legend. I don't know whether the tale is true or not, but it sure does make an entertaining story.

When making batches of candy like the ones in this chapter, making small repeatable, controllable batches is a good idea because you don't want to try to do more than you can handle at once. The chocolate — especially white chocolate — can set before you're ready.

I have a pattern (see Figure 16-1 for details on the full process) that I use when I make bark, and it works well for me. Just follow these steps:

1. **Line a cookie sheet with wax paper for use later and temper your chocolate using one of the methods I outline in Chapter 14.** I usually include 30 to 40 minutes for tempering chocolate as part of the preparation for the recipes in this chapter that include milk or dark chocolate. This time frame is only a reference; you may temper your chocolate much faster than that time.

2. **With your chocolate in temper, add the nuts and stir them in, mixing well and spreading the nuts throughout the bowl.** Don't forget that the added nuts start cooling the chocolate, so stir quickly to blend and be ready to pour the bark.

3. **Pour your chocolate in a mound on the center of the wax paper.** A 2-pound batch of bark makes a sheet approximately 18 inches x 10 inches, depending on how thick you spread the chocolate.

4. **Make the mound about 14 to 18 inches long, using a hard rubber spatula to spread the chocolate from the center into a sheet about ¼ to ⅓ inch thick.** Be sure to include the nuts with the chocolate as you spread the bark. If nuts stand on end or clump together, quickly move them with the tip of the spatula because the clumps are cooler than the chocolate, and they set faster.

5. **Wait about 10 to 15 minutes for the bark to set and become firm enough to cut or break.** To determine the stage that the bark is in, touch the bark with a fingertip. If the surface feels sticky or gooey, don't cut or break it yet because your pieces will be messy. By the same token, don't wait until the bark is completely set, because it'll break when you attempt to cut it.

6. **Cut or break the bark with your hands into smaller pieces.** You don't want to store the sheets uncut or unbroken because the bark will harden, making cutting it very difficult. To break the bark with your hands, simply grasp the sides of the sheet of thin bark and snap it into pieces. But cutting your bark makes packaging easier and makes it look neat.

If you want to cut your bark into neat squares, use a large knife to cut it as soon as the bark becomes firm, not hard. I like using a double-handled large knife because the knife is wider than the bark, which facilitates cutting.

You can cut the pieces to any size you want. I like cutting the bark into pieces that are approximately 3 x 4 inches, but you can cut yours larger or smaller. I don't recommend cutting them too small, though, because you'll make clusters to satisfy small, bite-size needs. When you cut the bark, think in terms of small candy bars with nuts.

Figure 16-1:
Spread the bark carefully, and use a knife to cut it when it's cool.

SPREADING BARK ON A LINED SHEET

CUTTING BARK WITH A KNIFE

Pecan, Peanut, and Almond Bark

Making your own milk-chocolate, white-chocolate, or dark-chocolate nutty bark is quite simple. You can make these nutty barks, cut them into a size that you feel is appropriate as a snack for the family, and store them in an airtight container for special treats.

As far as the nuts you use in this recipe go, I use raw pecans, roasted unsalted almonds (this variation appears in the color section), and roasted salted Spanish peanuts. Whichever nut you choose is a matter of personal taste. You can add more nuts than the recipe specifies because how nutty your bark is a matter of personal taste, too.

Preparation time: *1 hour including cooling time*

Yield: *24 pieces when cut into 2-inch or 3-inch squares*

2 pounds chocolate (milk, white, or dark), chopped and melted for tempering

1½ cups whole nuts (roasted salted peanuts, raw or roasted pecans, or roasted unsalted almonds)

1 Line a 13 x 18-inch cookie sheet with wax paper or place a similar size piece of wax paper on the counter for the bark.

2 Temper the chocolate (see Chapter 14 for tempering) or melt the white coating to 95 degrees in a microwave and add the nuts. Use a hard rubber spatula to stir the nuts into the chocolate until you've blended evenly; cover all the nuts with chocolate.

3 Pour the mixture onto a cookie sheet lined with wax paper or wax paper rolled out on the counter. Using a hard rubber spatula, spread the mixture to a thickness of about ½ inch or the thickness of the nuts.

4 If you want to cut your bark into squares, allow the mixture to cool at room temperature for 8 to 10 minutes until it's firm but not hard. Then cut with a large knife. If you cut and the knife comes out wet from the chocolate, wait 5 more minutes and try cutting again. If you want to break the bark into pieces, allow the mixture to cool for one hour and then break it into pieces by hand.

Per serving: Calories 351 (From Fat 220); Fat 25g (Saturated 7g); Cholesterol 0mg; Sodium 149mg; Carbohydrate 30g (Dietary Fiber 3g); Protein 10g.

Tiger Butter

I never seem to be too far from the peanut-butter-and-chocolate combination. This recipe derives its name from its appearance; when made properly, the swirls should remind you of a tiger's coat. Okay, maybe if you squint a bit; nonetheless, this candy has a really good taste and is easy to make. In this recipe, timing is important because you want the white chocolate and peanut butter to be soft enough for the chocolate to swirl and create the "tiger" effect.

Preparation time: *1 hour including cooling time*

Yield: *32 pieces cut into 2-inch squares*

1 pound white chocolate, chopped, or 2½ 12-ounce bags of white chips

½ cup creamy peanut butter

1 12-ounce bag semi-sweet chocolate chips

1 Line a 13 x 18-inch cookie sheet with wax paper or place a similar-size sheet on the counter.

2 In the microwave, melt the white chocolate in a microwaveable bowl on high power for about 2 minutes, stopping and stirring with a hard rubber spatula every 30 seconds. After that, stop and stir every 10 seconds until the temperature reaches 95 degrees on a chocolate thermometer. Immediately melt the semi-sweet chocolate chips in a smaller bowl, checking every 15 seconds or more often, to melt about 1½ minutes at most.

3 Using a hard rubber spatula, stir the peanut butter into the white chocolate until the mixture is smooth. With your spatula, spread the mixture to between ¼-inch and ⅓-inch thickness on a cookie sheet or wax paper placed on the counter.

4 Immediately drizzle the melted semi-sweet chocolate on top of the white chocolate and swirl it with a paper lollipop stick or similar-size utensil. Be sure that the stick or utensil completely penetrates the bark as you swirl, creating a sort of paisley look that gives Tiger Butter its name. You want the swirl to be all through the bark, not just on the top.

5 Allow the bark to cool at room temperature for 30 to 45 minutes. Then cut it into whatever size pieces you prefer.

Tip: *If your bark turns out too soft, increase the amount of white chocolate and slightly lower the amount of peanut butter. You don't want the pieces to be too soft to pick up!*

Vary It! *You can use chunky peanut butter in place of the creamy peanut butter, if you prefer.*

Per serving: *Calories 151 (From Fat 88); Fat 10g (Saturated 5g); Cholesterol 3mg; Sodium 33mg; Carbohydrate 16g (Dietary Fiber 1g); Protein 2g.*

Crunchy Rice Bark

This chocolate concoction resembles a famous chocolate bar. This recipe calls for only two ingredients: milk chocolate and crispy rice cereal. The trick is to mix the rice cereal into the chocolate and to spread the chocolate before the mixture sets. Doing so isn't difficult, but be prepared to spread the chocolate when you add the rice cereal.

Preparation time: *35 to 45 minutes*

Yield: *24 pieces*

1 pound milk chocolate, chopped and melted for tempering   *½ cup rice cereal*

1 Line a 13 x 18-inch cookie sheet with wax paper and set aside.

2 Temper the milk chocolate (see Chapter 14 for tempering instructions). Add the rice cereal to the chocolate and stir for about 30 seconds with a hard rubber spatula until you've mixed all the rice with the chocolate.

3 Using the spatula, spread the mixture to about ¼-inch thickness on the lined cookie sheet.

4 Allow the mixture to cool at room temperature for about 20 minutes. Then cut it with a knife into whatever size pieces you prefer. If you like the rough look, break into pieces by hand. (I prefer the neat look of the cut.)

Vary It! *You can also make this recipe with white chocolate or dark chocolate. Follow the same procedure, but melt 2½ 12-ounce bags of white chips to about 95 degrees in a microwave (see the earlier Tiger Butter recipe for melting instructions). If you're using dark chocolate, temper 1 pound of dark chocolate as I describe in Chapter 14 and follow the recipe's instructions.*

Per serving: *Calories 96 (From Fat 48); Fat 5g (Saturated 3g); Cholesterol 0mg; Sodium 19mg; Carbohydrate 13g (Dietary Fiber 0g); Protein 1g.*

After you've made a few basic barks, you can try a variety of other additions to make different barks. You can try

- White chocolate bark with dried cranberries or raisins rather than nuts.

- Bark with chopped maraschino cherries or diced candied orange peels rather than nuts, using melted white chocolate or tempered dark or milk chocolate.

- Bark with a combination of fruits and nuts, keeping the total volume the same as the original amount of nuts that the recipe calls for. Use melted white or tempered milk or dark chocolate.

✔ Milk or dark chocolate bark with white chocolate liberally drizzled over the bark before cutting. Just melt a few ounces of white chocolate in a small bowl to 95 degrees. Drizzle the white liberally over the chocolate bark. You can leave it like that or you can swirl the white.

✔ Milk-chocolate pecan bark with ⅓ cup of miniature marshmallows added. Stir in the marshmallows before you spread the mixture. Use raw pecan halves or pieces.

✔ Tempered milk or dark chocolate and add ¼ cup roasted salted pistachios; ¼ cup roasted unsalted hazelnuts; and ¼ cup diced, drained maraschino cherries. Stir the nuts and fruit into the chocolate, and pour the mixture into a sheet.

✔ Nut bark that uses macadamia nuts in place of the other nuts.

This list should give you a few ideas to broaden your bark recipes. You'll undoubtedly think up your own ideas, too.

Peppermint Bark for Christmas

Peppermint bark brings the scent of mint to the Christmas season, but you can enjoy this candy any time of the year. (You can find other holiday ideas in Chapter 20.)

Preparation time: *30 minutes*

Yield: *2¼ pounds or about 32 pieces*

12 peppermint sticks or about 2 dozen individual peppermint pieces	*2 pounds white chocolate, chopped*

1 Line a 13 x 18-inch cookie sheet with wax paper or place a similar-size piece of wax paper on the counter.

2 Crush the peppermint sticks or pieces in a blender or food processor or place them in a freezer bag and crush them with a rolling pin or other heavy object to a pretty fine consistency. Having a few slightly larger pieces is okay.

3 In a microwaveable bowl, melt 2 pounds of white chocolate to a temperature of about 95 degrees. Melt on high for 2 to 3 minutes, stopping every 30 seconds and then every 15 seconds to stir and check with a chocolate thermometer. Do not overheat, because you want the coating to be about 95 degrees. You should be able to touch the coating to your lips and not burn yourself; the coating should feel just about the same as your body temperature.

4 Remove the mixture from the microwave and stir with a hard rubber spatula until it's smooth. With a small sifter, sift the peppermint into the white chocolate; put the larger pieces of peppermint aside. Stir the mixture to blend the peppermint.

5 Using the spatula, spread the mixture about ¼-inch thick on a cookie sheet lined with wax paper or on wax paper on the counter. Sprinkle the larger peppermint pieces over the entire sheet of bark, and press lightly with an offset spatula to press into the white coating.

6 Allow the bark to cool at room temperature (70 degrees or so); it should be firm enough to cut in about 15 minutes, but the time varies according to room temperature and humidity. If you prefer to break the bark into pieces, allow it to cool for one hour. Then break it into pieces by hand.

Vary It! *You can make this recipe with tempered dark chocolate. Temper the chocolate (see Chapter 14 for instructions) and follow the preceding procedure with the peppermint. For dark chocolate, I recommend adding ⅛ teaspoon of peppermint oil when stirring in the peppermint pieces because dark chocolate has a stronger natural flavor that can overpower the peppermint pieces.*

Per serving: *Calories 168 (From Fat 81); Fat 9g (Saturated 6g); Cholesterol 6mg; Sodium 27mg; Carbohydrate 21g (Dietary Fiber 0g); Protein 2g.*

Storing your bark safely

If you're going to store your entire bark production or most of it, use a plastic storage container. Put sheets of wax paper between the layers of bark in the container to prevent the layers from scratching one another.

You can store the bark in the plastic containers for two to three weeks at room temperature. The chocolate stores fine, but you have to worry about storing nuts for extended periods. You don't want to store your nuts for longer than three weeks because they become rancid after a while. How soon the nuts go bad depends on the freshness of the nuts, the dampness in the air, and the storage temperature.

If you want to freeze your bark, you can. Simply place it in a freezer bag with wax paper between layers. Put that freezer bag inside another freezer bag, and freeze the bark for up to six months. When you want to thaw the bark, remove it from the freezer and allow it to thaw on the counter at room temperature overnight (eight hours). Then remove the chocolate from the freezer bags. This method prevents condensation from forming because you don't want water spots on your chocolate.

Pulling Together Chocolate Clusters

All clusters and cluster-type chocolates aren't created equally: You can find more than one way to make a cluster, including hand-dipping and molding. Some clusters end up with a rough exterior appearance, and others are smooth because of the molding process.

When you produce a variety of candies, the variations in shapes and textures add a lot to the eye appeal of the assortment. You really don't want every piece to look the same. Don't worry: In the following sections, I provide you with several cluster recipes.

Dipping clusters by hand

The only difference between chocolate bark and chocolate clusters is the shape of the candies. With bark, you spread it into sheets and cut it into large pieces, whereas you usually hand-dip or spoon clusters into bite-size pieces.

I prefer hand-dipping to spooning because when you use a spoon, you tend to include more liquid chocolate in the piece, which makes the piece spread more. I think clusters look better when they stand up with a nice blend of chocolate and nuts. When you hand-dip, you tend to allow some of the excess chocolate to drain away, leaving a nice piece of nutty chocolate (see Figure 16-2).

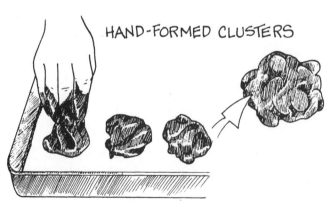

HAND-FORMED CLUSTERS

Figure 16-2:
Clusters look great when you hand-dip them.

As with most suggestions I make throughout this book, hand-dipping is only my opinion; you certainly can do as you please.

So what's the basic process of making a hand-dipped cluster?

1. **Temper the chocolate as I describe in Chapter 14.** You can temper milk or dark chocolate or melt white chocolate to 95 degrees. If chocolate cools during the dipping, reheat it for 5 seconds in the microwave.

2. **Line a 13 x 18-inch cookie sheet with wax paper.** You can place a similar-size piece of wax paper on the counter instead, if you wish.

3. **Stir the nuts of your choice into the chocolate, and mix well with a spatula.** Be certain that all the nuts are mixed well with the chocolate.

4. **Dip the clusters by hand, and place them on the wax paper, creating mounds about the equivalent of a teaspoonful.** Each mound should contain at least two or three nuts to create a bite-size piece.

5. **Allow the clusters to cool at room temperature for about 20 minutes to achieve a good set.** When they are set, put each cluster into a #4 or a #6 brown paper cup, available from the suppliers listed in Chapter 24.

When you hand-dip a cluster, you want to include two or three nuts with the chocolate; the result should be a piece that's about 1¼ inches in diameter at the base and less than 1 inch tall, slightly rounded or even peaked at the top. Tempered chocolate with several nuts should create a cluster that forms a rounded mass, not one that spreads into a puddle. If you get too much chocolate with the nuts, the candy can spread but, generally, the cluster holds its shape. Gravity plays a big part in the shape of your candy.

As you dip the clusters, you may notice the tempered chocolate getting cooler. If you have the chocolate in a microwaveable bowl, heat it in the microwave for 5 seconds at a time. Or you can keep a heating pad wrapped around the bowl; just be sure that the temperature isn't too high (no more than 91 degrees) because you don't want the chocolate to get out of temper. You can check the temperature with a chocolate thermometer.

When you stir the chocolate, don't try to scrape chocolate from the sides of the bowl if it has already set. This chocolate simply thickens your tempered chocolate. Just leave the set chocolate on the sides until you finish. Or wait until you reheat for 5 seconds to loosen the set chocolate.

And always have some extra nuts available because you tend to use the nuts up before you use up all the chocolate. When you finish making the clusters, let them set at least 20 minutes at room temperature before cupping and storing.

Instead of putting nuts in your clusters, you can make clusters using mini-marshmallows. Simply put three mini-marshmallows at a time into the bowl of chocolate; with your fingertips, coat them with chocolate and deposit them onto wax paper. Repeat until the chocolate is gone. A 10½-ounce bag of mini-marshmallows produces about 40 to 45 clusters.

Hand-dipped Nut Clusters

Sometimes a simple chocolate piece is just what you need, and I don't think many pieces are much easier to make than a nut cluster (you can see some clusters in the color section). To make a nut cluster, you combine chocolate (milk, dark, or white) and a nut of your choice to make a crunchy piece of chocolate goodness. Sure, you have to temper chocolate to make this piece, but I explain that process in Chapter 14. The rest is a matter of deciding which chocolate you want to use and selecting the nut you want in your chocolate. I recommend using raw large pecan pieces or roasted salted or unsalted whole almonds. The choice, of course, is yours.

Preparation time: *40 to 50 minutes*

Yield: *45 pieces*

1½ pounds milk chocolate, chopped and melted for tempering

1½ cups nuts (large raw pecan pieces or roasted salted or unsalted whole almonds)

1 Line a 13 x18-inch cookie sheet with wax paper or place a similar-size piece of wax paper on the counter.

2 Temper the chocolate (see Chapter 14 for instructions) and put it in a microwaveable bowl. Pour the nuts into the bowl of chocolate and stir with a hard rubber spatula to blend.

3 Using your fingers, shape the clusters with two or three nuts each, and deposit them on a cookie sheet lined with wax paper.

4 Dip the clusters until you use up all the chocolate and nuts.

5 Allow the clusters to cool at room temperature for at least 20 minutes. When they are cool, you can place them in #4 brown paper cups, available from suppliers listed in Chapter 24.

Vary It! *You can use white or dark chocolate to make clusters, too. If you use dark chocolate, follow the same procedure for tempering. If you use white chocolate, melt it in a microwave until it's 95 degrees. The melting process for 1½ pounds of white chocolate takes about 2 minutes in the microwave on high power. Stop and stir every 30 seconds, and check the temperature with a chocolate thermometer. Then follow the preceding dipping procedure.*

Per serving: *Calories 100 (From Fat 62); Fat 7g (Saturated 2g); Cholesterol 0mg; Sodium 11mg; Carbohydrate 10g (Dietary Fiber 0g); Protein 1g.*

Using molds to create clusters

Another way to make clusters is to mold them. This method involves putting the chocolate and nuts directly in a brown paper cup. Here's how you make molded clusters:

1. Temper the chocolate as I describe in Chapter 14 and select the nut you want to use in your cluster.

2. Place a #4 brown paper cup in each cavity of your cup molds.

3. Add the nuts to the tempered chocolate, and stir with a spatula to mix well.

4. Spoon a teaspoonful of the mixture into each cup, and use a second spoon to scrape the mixture off the first spoon.

5. Place the molds in the refrigerator for 20 minutes to cool; then lift the paper cups with the clusters from the mold.

Molded Clusters

To make molded clusters, you use the same ingredients you do in the hand-dipped clusters (see the previous section) but, instead of hand-dipping onto a cookie sheet, you spoon the cluster into a mold. This method produces a nice piece without the messy fingers!

Tools: 6 small peanut butter cup molds with 8 cavities lined with #4 brown paper cups

Preparation time: 40 to 50 minutes

Yield: 48 pieces

1½ pounds milk chocolate, chopped and melted for tempering

1½ cups unsalted nut pieces of your choice

1 Temper the milk chocolate (see Chapter 14) and line the cavities of your molds with #4 brown cups.

2 Pour the nuts into the tempered chocolate and stir with a hard rubber spatula to blend well.

3 Using a teaspoon, spoon the mixture into the cups in the molds. Be sure to include enough nut pieces in each cluster to create a rough top surface on the mold (looks like it's full of nuts).

4 When you've filled a mold (peanut butter cup molds usually have eight cavities), place the mold in the refrigerator for about 20 minutes to set the chocolate. Remove the mold from the refrigerator, and remove the cups from the molds.

Vary It! *For Crunchy Rice Clusters, use the same ingredients that the Crunchy Rice Bark recipe calls for, substituting rice for nuts. You can also use two 12-ounce bags of peanut butter chips; melt them in a microwave to about 95 degrees, stopping every 30 seconds to stir and check the temperature with a chocolate thermometer (total time is about 1½ to 2 minutes). Or try making rice cereal clusters with melted white chocolate, which you melt to 95 degrees using the same procedure you do for the peanut butter chips.*

Per serving: *Calories 93 (From Fat 58); Fat 6g (Saturated 2g); Cholesterol 0mg; Sodium 10mg; Carbohydrate 10g (Dietary Fiber 0g); Protein 1g.*

Peanut Butter Cups

I recommend making this recipe at the same time that you make the Peanut Butter Meltaways in Chapter 6 because you use the meltaways as the center for this piece. The meltaways, once they have set, are quite soft and are easy to shape to make these centers.

Tools: *6 peanut butter cup molds with 8 cavities lined with brown paper cups. If you use large peanut butter cup molds, line with #6 brown paper cups; if you use small peanut butter cup molds, line with #4 brown paper cups.*

Preparation time: *40 to 50 minutes*

Yield: *48 pieces*

48 pieces of Peanut Butter Meltaways (see Chapter 6)

1 pound milk chocolate (use ½ pound more for larger cups), chopped and melted for tempering

1 Temper milk chocolate (see Chapter 14), and line the cavities of your molds with the appropriate-size cups.

2 Shape the 48 meltaway pieces into ½-inch–thick discs by hand.

3 Using a teaspoon, spoon the chocolate into the paper cups in the molds, filling each cup about halfway. Place a Peanut Butter Meltaway disc in each cup, and press down lightly. Spoon enough chocolate on top of the disc to bring the level to just below the top of the cup, covering the disc.

4 When the tray is full, tap the tray lightly to spread the chocolate in the cup, and put it in the refrigerator for 20 minutes to cool.

5 When the candy is cool, remove it from the refrigerator, and remove the cups from the molds.

Vary It! *You can make this recipe using white chocolate. Melt 1 pound of white chocolate in the microwave to 95 degrees, and follow the procedure in this recipe. Melt a little more white chocolate for larger cups.*

Per serving: Calories 126 (From Fat 70); Fat 8g (Saturated 4g); Cholesterol 0mg; Sodium 77mg; Carbohydrate 13g (Dietary Fiber 1g); Protein 3g.

Storing all types of clusters

You can store your clusters in an airtight container for up to three weeks. If you layer the container, place a sheet of wax paper between the layers. I don't like the candies to scratch one another, as they will if you just stack them.

If you want to freeze your clusters, you can do so or up to six months. To prepare them for freezing, place the clusters in a freezer bag, and put that bag in a second freezer bag. To thaw your candy, remove it from the package and allow it to thaw on the counter at room temperature overnight (eight hours) before unbagging. This method prevents condensation from forming on the chocolates.

These clusters are made in fairly small batches, and I recommend consuming them before freezing is necessary. Be aware that nuts can go bad over a period of time. You rarely know how long nuts have been around before you use them or how they have been stored, so I recommend enjoying your candy when you make it, if possible.

Chapter 17

Rolling Along with Wonderful Creamy Centers

*I*n the world of candy, a word can have multiple meanings. "Cream" is such a word, and folks can get a little mixed up sometimes about just what a cream is. So much cream is used in candy making to add richness and flavor to the candies, you might not realize that a cream, as in a piece of candy by the name, isn't named for the dairy product. A cream is a confection with a nice creamy center.

In this chapter, I focus on actual cream candies. Although production methods may vary, a cream center is predominately made with some form of sugar. Here I show you how to make creams in a variety of flavors and different textures, and none of them involves any real heavy-duty cooking. You'll enjoy the process of making creams.

Getting the Scoop on Making Creams

In the candy industry, creams pretty much fall into one of two categories: cooked creams and no-cook creams.

- *Cooked creams* are cooked in large kettles and cooled before being beaten on an apparatus called a cream beater. This process is involved, and I doubt that you have a cream beater in your house. Frankly, I don't have one, either.

- A lot of candy makers make *no-cook creams,* which are also known as *cold creams* or *cold-process creams.* These creams are made without using high temperatures and pretty much don't involve anything hotter than some melting of ingredients.

The no-cook process should attract you because this process is fairly easy. So have a little fun; make something new.

The key ingredient in the no-cook process is fondant sugar, which you can purchase from one of the suppliers I mention in Chapter 24. Unlike sucrose or granulated sugar, you can integrate fondant sugar into a recipe without any boiling. In fact, for a lot of recipes, you need only to blend fondant sugar and ingredients like corn syrup, water, salt butter, and flavors into a doughlike mixture and hand-shape the resulting batch into little balls, which you coat with chocolate. This process is sort of how you made candy when you were a kid playing in the mud. Oh, wait, maybe that was just me.

Another key ingredient in creams is *invertase,* an enzyme that helps keep the creams moist. You can purchase this ingredient from one of the suppliers I mention in Chapter 24. (See "Keeping Your Creams Fresh and Tasty" later in this chapter for more about preserving your creams.)

Precisely measuring these ingredients assures you of getting the results you want. You really shouldn't estimate with these recipes because being off just a little makes the difference between your batch having the right consistency to form a ball and falling flat. Because you want your creams to have a nice round appearance, carefully follow the recipe's directions.

All the creams I show you in this chapter involve a mixer. I like using a strong 4- or 5-quart mixer with easy-to-adjust variable speeds because mixing is key. In the following recipes, you create a nice doughlike mixture, and you want a good mixer for doing so.

You also hand-roll the results into balls to coat them with chocolate. So be prepared to roll up your sleeves and roll out some balls. Starting with the doughy mass, pinch off pieces a little smaller than an English walnut in the shell. Roll these into balls, repeating the process until all the mass has been used up (see Figure 17-1). You should get the knack of this fairly quickly, and you'll find this rolling useful in Chapter 18, when you need to roll truffle centers.

Figure 17-1:
Pinching and rolling creams into the right size are key steps in the process.

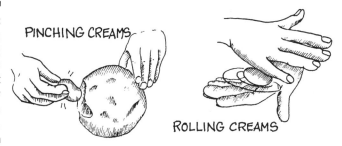

PINCHING CREAMS

ROLLING CREAMS

One last point: The recipes in this chapter require you to dip your creams into tempered chocolate. Be sure to check out Chapter 14 for all the details on preparing tempered chocolate before you try any of the recipes in the following sections. Chapter 15 has the scoop on dipping your treats properly.

Beginning with Basic Butter Creams

When I think of creams, the first one that comes to my mind is the butter cream. Few pieces hit me quite the way a butter cream does. Maybe the buttery-sweet taste is part of the attraction, but I think part of the reason I like a butter cream so much is the traditional nature of the piece. I think of the butter cream as a wonderful piece of candy that has been around for generations. Like a good caramel piece, the butter cream belongs in a typical assortment of chocolates. You can bet that you'll find butter creams in my best boxes.

Butter Creams Decorated with Sprinkles and Nuts

You can decorate butter cream pieces differently and create an assortment using only one center. I know candy makers who do so quite effectively, and the variety of textures, tastes, and appearances is remarkable. In this particular recipe, I show you how to put colored sprinkles and pecan pieces to work. You can change the toppings and use dark chocolate instead of milk chocolate as a coating, and you create a completely different flavor. Check out these treats in the color section.

Do not refrigerate these centers to accelerate the setting process because you risk a moisture problem; plus dipping cold centers will cause them to expand later, making your shells crack.

Preparation time: *45 minutes plus 8 hours overnight of cooling*

Yield: *45 to 50 centers*

2 cups plus 1½ cups fondant sugar

4 tablespoons light corn syrup

3 tablespoons water

¼ teaspoon salt

¼ cup butter, softened

¼ teaspoon vanilla extract

¼ teaspoon invertase

Confectioners' sugar for powdering hands to roll centers

2½ pounds milk chocolate, chopped and melted for tempering

Assorted toppings: Chocolate sprinkles, pecan pieces, assorted colored sprinkles, about ¼ cup of each (you won't use all of them completely)

1 Line two 9 x 13-inch cookie sheets with wax paper for the rolled centers; put aside.

2 Combine the 2 cups of fondant sugar, corn syrup, water, salt, butter, and vanilla extract in a mixing bowl and beat on slow speed for 20 to 30 seconds to blend the butter. Add the invertase and beat for 15 seconds to blend; then beat the mixture on high speed for 3½ to 4 minutes to blend to uniform consistency.

3 When the mixture is uniform and, with the mixer running on slow speed, slowly add the last 1½ cups of fondant sugar and beat until it has a uniform consistency (about 3 to 5 minutes).

4 Pinch off pieces of dough and roll them into balls of about 1 to 1½ inches in diameter; use confectioners' sugar to prevent the balls from sticking to your hands. As you roll each center, place it on the wax-paper–lined cookie sheets to set. For best results, let the centers set uncovered at room temperature for eight hours or overnight. You may dip them sooner, but they tend to be soft and will spread into thinner pieces as you coat them with chocolate.

5 Temper the chocolate as described in Chapter 14. Slide the wax paper with the centers onto the counter and reline the cookie sheets with wax paper for the chocolate-coated pieces.

6 Coat the balls in tempered milk chocolate using a hand-dipping method or a dipping fork, whichever you prefer, as described in Chapter 15. Decorate by sprinkling a few pecan pieces, chocolate sprinkles, or colored sprinkles on top while the chocolate is still wet. You can leave some candies plain, if you want. If you use all four options, you get four different appearances (see Figure 17-2).

7 Let the butter creams set at room temperature (70 degrees) for 45 to 50 minutes to attain a nice set.

Tip: For a slightly different appearance, carefully lay two or three sliced almond pieces on the cream while the chocolate is still wet. You should like the effect and the different appearance.

Per serving: Calories 80 (From Fat 25); Fat 3g (Saturated 2g); Cholesterol 3mg; Sodium 18mg; Carbohydrate 14g (Dietary Fiber 0g); Protein 0g.

Figure 17-2:
You can sprinkle butter creams with a variety of tasty toppings.

TOPPING BUTTER CREAMS

Chocolate Butter Creams

As good as regular butter creams are, some folks just have to have that taste of chocolate inside as well as on the outside of their creams. This recipe tells you how I like to put that combo together. I think you'll really like this one because it's one of those pieces that makes you think of the chocolates that have been loved for generations.

Preparation time: 45 minutes plus 8 hours of cooling

Yield: 45 to 50 pieces

2 ounces unsweetened chocolate, chopped into small pieces

2 tablespoons butter, softened

3½ cups fondant sugar

3¾ tablespoons water

¼ teaspoon salt

¼ teaspoon vanilla extract

¼ teaspoon invertase

Confectioners' sugar for powdering hands to roll centers

2 to 2½ pounds milk chocolate, chopped and melted for tempering

1 Line two 13 x 18-inch cookie sheets with wax paper for the hand-rolled centers.

2 In a double boiler, combine the baking chocolate and butter to slowly melt it; do not overheat, and stir occasionally for about 10 minutes.

3 In a mixing bowl, combine the fondant sugar, water, salt, and vanilla extract and beat on slow speed to blend for about 1 minute until it's uniform. Add the invertase and beat 15 seconds to blend..

4 Running the mixer on slow speed, slowly pour the chocolate/butter mixture into the sugar mixture, beating for about 3 minutes until it's uniform and scraping down the sides of the bowl once to blend.

5 Remove the bowl from the mixer, pinch pieces of dough off, and roll them into 1- to 1½-inch balls, using confectioners' sugar to prevent the balls from sticking to your hands. Place the rolled centers on the wax-paper–lined cookie sheets and allow them to set on the counter at room temperature for at least eight hours. You may dip the centers sooner, but they may spread after the chocolate goes on them.

6 When you're ready to dip the centers, slide the wax-paper sheets with the centers onto the counter and reline the cookie sheets with wax paper for the coated centers.

7 Temper the chocolate as described in Chapter 14.

8 Coat the balls in tempered chocolate by hand-dipping them or using one of the other methods I describe in Chapter 15. Place each piece on the lined cookie sheets as you dip them, and decorate each piece as you please or leave them plain.

9 Let the finished pieces set for at least one hour at room temperature (70 degrees) before storing.

Per serving: Calories 71 (From Fat 24); Fat 3g (Saturated 2g); Cholesterol 1mg; Sodium 16mg; Carbohydrate 12g (Dietary Fiber 0g); Protein 1g.

Unless a piece has a special topping (such as the ones I suggest in this chapter), you really can't identify a cream's contents. You never know which flavor is inside the candy. Candy makers usually use marks to distinguish among their pieces. Some of these marks are quite elaborate, and some are as simple as the first letter of the flavor of the contents, such as an *S* for strawberry, *C* for cherry, *L* for lemon, or *O* for orange.

With just a little practice, you'll get the hang of marking your candies. As soon as you put a piece on the cookie sheet, lightly touch the top of the piece with your fingertip so a little chocolate lifts up with your fingertip. One property of tempered chocolate is that it holds a shape when it is drizzled, which makes writing possible. Write the identifying letter on the chocolate with your finger. See Chapter 15 for more about decorating dipped candies.

Getting to the Heart of Richer and Fruitier Creams

After you get into making your own creams, you will want to make other flavors with slightly different tastes and textures. Slight variations in the recipes and the addition of different ingredients, such as evaporated milk, provide you with a richness that gives the cream the mouthfeel of a more expensive piece.

In this section, I show you how to produce a high-quality cream that you can add a few rather simple flavors to, like amaretto, rum, and maple flavorings. If your tastes run more to the fruit flavors, I show you how to make a delicious cherry cream. But you can just as easily make a strawberry, raspberry, orange, or lemon cream by changing the color and flavoring.

Like the other creams I show you in this chapter, these creams are at their best when allowed to set uncovered for three to four hours or, in some cases, overnight at room temperature (about 70 degrees).

Amaretto Kisses

This cream is almost as smooth and rich as a truffle (see Chapter 18 for more information on truffles). The evaporated milk is what gives this piece its richness.

Preparation time: *4 hours and 15 minutes plus 2 hours for cooling and setting chocolate*

Yield: *40 to 45 pieces*

8 ounces milk or dark chocolate, chopped

3 ounces unsweetened chocolate, chopped

1¾ cups fondant sugar

½ cup evaporated milk

1 tablespoon water

½ teaspoon almond extract or amaretto-flavor liqueur

½ teaspoon invertase

2 pounds milk chocolate, chopped and melted for tempering

1 8-ounce package of almond slices

1 Line an 13 x 18-inch cookie sheet with wax paper for the rolled centers.

2 Combine the milk or dark chocolate and the unsweetened chocolate in a double boiler and melt slowly, stirring occasionally, for about 10 minutes; the intent is to melt the chocolate, not overheat it.

3 Combine the fondant sugar, evaporated milk, and water in a mixing bowl and beat ingredients with a mixer on slow speed for 5 minutes; add the invertase, and beat for 15 seconds to blend.

4 Using a hard rubber spatula, scrape the melted chocolate into the bowl containing the sugar mixture; add the almond extract or amaretto-flavor liqueur and mix at slow speed until the mixture is uniform (about 1 minute).

5 Remove the bowl from the mixer and let the batch set for 30 minutes at room temperature (about 70 degrees).

6 Using a small ice cream dipper, scoop out balls and place them on a wax-paper-lined cookie sheet to set. Let them firm for 3 hours at room temperature, uncovered, before dipping them in chocolate.

7 Temper the chocolate as I describe in Chapter 14. Slide the paper with the centers off the cookie sheet and replace the wax paper for the chocolates.

8 Hand-dip the balls in tempered milk chocolate using one of the procedures in Chapter 15 and place on wax paper. While the chocolate is still wet, place an almond slice on top of each piece.

9 Allow the pieces to set for about 2 hours at room temperature to allow for a nice set.

Vary It! *As a substitution, use raspberry-oil flavoring (you can obtain flavors from the suppliers I list in Chapter 24) instead of amaretto. Leave off the almond slices, and leave the top unadorned or string with tempered dipping chocolate. To string or drizzle a piece, dip a salad fork into chocolate and shake the fork back and forth over the pieces. With a little practice, you'll master this little trick!*

Per serving: Calories 88 (From Fat 41); Fat 5g (Saturated 2g); Cholesterol 1mg; Sodium 11mg; Carbohydrate 12g (Dietary Fiber 0g); Protein 1g.

Bavarian Creams

You'll like the Bavarian creams. This candy is one of my absolute favorites because of the way it combines the different chocolates, producing an aftertaste that's less sweet than that of other chocolates. The process you use to make this piece is similar to the Amaretto Kisses recipe, with only a couple of variations. Get ready to dig in!

Preparation time: *4 hours and 15 minutes plus 2 hours for cooling and setting chocolates*

Yield: *40 to 45 pieces*

8 ounces milk or dark chocolate, chopped

3 ounces unsweetened chocolate, chopped

1¾ cups fondant sugar

½ cups evaporated milk

1 tablespoon water

½ teaspoon rum-oil flavor or rum extract (flavors available from suppliers listed in Chapter 24)

⅛ teaspoon ground ginger

¼ teaspoon invertase

2 pounds milk chocolate, chopped and melted for tempering

4 ounces dark chocolate, chopped and melted for tempering

1 Line an 13 x 18-inch cookie sheet with wax paper for centers when they are scooped.

2 Combine milk chocolate and unsweetened chocolate in the double boiler and melt slowly; do not overheat.

3 Combine the fondant sugar, evaporated milk, and water in a mixing bowl, and beat at a slow speed for 5 minutes to blend.

4 Pour the melted chocolate mixture into a mixing bowl containing the sugar mixture; add the rum flavor or rum extract and ginger; mix at a slow speed until the mixture is uniform (about 1 minute). Add the invertase and mix for about 15 seconds to blend.

5 Remove the bowl from the mixer and let the batch set for 30 minutes at room temperature (about 70 degrees).

6 Using a small ice cream dipper, scoop out the balls and set them on a cookie sheet lined with wax paper for 3 hours to firm at room temperature.

7 Temper the milk and dark chocolates as described in Chapter 14. Slide the wax paper with the centers off the cookie sheet and replace the wax paper on the tray for the chocolate pieces.

8 Hand-dip the balls in tempered milk chocolate using one of the methods I describe in Chapter 15 and place them on a cookie sheet lined with wax paper. Drizzle or "string" tempered dark chocolate over the candies. To string, dip a salad fork into the chocolate and shake it back and forth over the pieces. Let the candies cool at room temperature (70 degrees) for 2 hours for a nice set.

Tip: *You don't have to string the finished creams with the dark chocolate, but done well, it makes a special piece. The contrast between milk and dark always seems to make a smart-looking piece.*

Per serving: *Calories 105 (From Fat 49); Fat 6g (Saturated 3g); Cholesterol 3mg; Sodium 16mg; Carbohydrate 14g (Dietary Fiber 1g); Protein 2g.*

Maple Creams

The following recipe makes a delicious maple cream. Like the butter cream I discuss earlier in this chapter, the maple cream is a traditional piece that belongs in any true chocolate assortment. The full, rich, flavor of maple contrasted with the milk chocolate that encases it provides a taste that excites your taste buds.

This recipe, when made in my shops, uses maple emulsion and maple flavoring. You can find maple flavoring in your grocery store but, if you cannot find a substitute for the emulsion, double the amount of maple flavoring you use. You can also find a good assortment of flavorings available from the suppliers listed in Chapter 24.

Preparation time: *45 minutes plus 3 to 4 hours for cooling*

Yield: *30 to 35 creams*

2 cups plus 1½ cups fondant sugar	*1 teaspoon maple emulsion*
4 tablespoons light corn syrup	*¼ teaspoon invertase*
3 tablespoons water	*2 pounds milk chocolate, chopped and melted for tempering*
¼ cup butter, softened	
¼ teaspoon salt	*1 box confectioners' sugar for coating hands to roll centers*
1 teaspoon maple flavoring	

1 Line a 13 x 18-inch cookie sheet with wax paper for the rolled centers.

2 Combine 2 cups of fondant sugar, the corn syrup, water, butter, salt, maple flavoring, and maple emulsion in a mixing bowl and beat on slow speed for 20 to 30 seconds to blend the butter. Then beat on high speed for 3½ to 4 minutes to blend to a uniform consistency. Add the invertase and beat 15 seconds to blend.

3 When the mixture is uniform and with the mixer running on slow speed, slowly add the last 1½ cups of fondant sugar and beat until the mixture is uniform (about 10 minutes).

4 Remove the bowl from the mixer. Place about 1 teaspoon of confectioners' sugar in one hand and rub your hands together to prevent stickiness when rolling centers (repeat as needed). Pinch off a piece of the maple center mix (a piece smaller than an English walnut) and roll it into a ball between your hands. Place on the lined cookie sheet. Repeat until all pieces are rolled. Slide the sheet off the cookie sheet and reline the cookie sheet with another piece of wax paper for chocolate-dipped pieces.

5 Temper the chocolate as I describe in Chapter 14.

6 Coat the centers in chocolate (by hand-dipping or using one of the other methods I describe in Chapter 15). Place the pieces on the paper-lined cookie sheet and let them set at room temperature for about 2 hours.

Per serving: Calories 97 (From Fat 26); Fat 3g (Saturated 2g); Cholesterol 4mg; Sodium 24mg; Carbohydrate 18g (Dietary Fiber 0g); Protein 0g.

Cherry Creams

This recipe produces a center with bits of fruit to enhance the experience and is simply divine. Although this recipe contains butter like butter creams do, I refer to this recipe as fruit creams simply to differentiate between types of centers. The fruit flavors the center of this piece, and the butter provides texture by helping make the centers rich and smooth.

Preparation time: *45 minutes plus 4 hours cooling time for the creams to set for dipping*

Yield: *45 to 50 centers*

2 cups plus 1½ cups fondant sugar	*2 tablespoons pureed maraschino cherries*
4 tablespoons light corn syrup	*1 teaspoon cherry flavoring*
3 tablespoons water	*1 teaspoon citric acid*
¼ teaspoon salt	*Confectioners' sugar for powdering hands to handle rolling*
2 tablespoons butter, softened	
¼ teaspoon invertase	*2 pounds milk chocolate, chopped and melted for tempering*
¼ teaspoon vanilla extract	

1 Line a 13 x 18-inch cookie sheet with wax paper for the rolled centers.

2 Combine 2 cups of the fondant sugar, the corn syrup, water, salt, butter, and vanilla extract in a mixing bowl and beat on slow speed for 20 to 30 seconds to blend the butter. Then beat on high speed for 3½ to 4 minutes to blend to a uniform consistency.

3 When the mixture is uniform, slowly add the last 1½ cups of fondant sugar with the mixer running on slow speed and beat for 2 to 3 minutes until the mixture is uniform.

4 Add the pureed cherries, cherry flavoring, and citric acid; mix on slow speed until the batch is uniform (about 30 seconds). Add the invertase and beat for about 15 seconds to blend.

5 Remove the bowl from the mixer. Pinch off pieces of dough; roll them into 1- to 1¼-inch balls and place them on a cookie sheet lined with wax paper, using confectioners' sugar to prevent pieces from sticking to your hands. Let the finished rolled pieces set at room temperature for 4 hours.

6 Temper the chocolate as described in Chapter 14. Slide the paper with the centers off the cookie sheet and reline the cookie sheet with wax paper for the chocolate-dipped centers.

7 Coat the balls (by hand-dipping or other methods I describe in Chapter 15) in tempered milk or dark chocolate and place them on the paper-lined cookie sheet. Let them set for about 2 hours.

Vary It! *You can make other fruit centers using this recipe. Simply substitute the appropriate flavorings for the pureed cherries and cherry flavoring. Possible flavors include strawberry, orange, lemon, and peach.*

Per serving: *Calories 73 (From Fat 19); Fat 2g (Saturated 1g); Cholesterol 1mg; Sodium 18mg; Carbohydrate 14g (Dietary Fiber 0g); Protein 0g.*

Keeping Your Creams Fresh and Tasty

You want your finished chocolates to have that professional look of a chocolate shop. When your pieces have set according to the procedures set forth in the chapters, place each piece in a #6 paper cup. The cups you need are available in more than one size and color from the suppliers listed in Chapter 24.

To keep your chocolates for a while, you may place the cupped pieces in an airtight plastic container for four to six weeks. If you want to freeze the chocolates, carefully place the chocolates in double freezer bags and freeze for up to six months. To thaw the chocolates, remove them from the freezer and let them thaw on the counter overnight. When they're thawed, remove them from the plastic bags and enjoy.

You don't want to refrigerate your creams because refrigeration dries out your candy and can cause condensation. Condensation creates water spots on your candy, and you probably won't want to eat your candy if that occurs.

Chapter 18

Impressing with Incredible Truffles

*W*hen I think of fine chocolates, I think first of the truffle because few chocolates stimulate the taste buds or excite the eye the way a truffle does. If you're not familiar with truffles, the truffle is usually a bite-size piece of chocolate of the highest quality. The center is a combination of heavy cream and premium chocolate, and the outer layer is a thin layer of tempered chocolate (see Chapter 14).

In this chapter, I cover the basics of forming truffle centers and finishing them with a tasty outer coating. I also give you a wide variety of truffle recipes to enjoy. (Whether you share them is entirely up to you.)

Building Your Foundation with Ganache

The center of a truffle is commonly known as *ganache,* which is a smooth mixture of heavy cream and chocolate. (However, a truffle center, on occasion, contains no chocolate; instead, it may contain a caramel that has been thinned with extra cream to create a flowing caramel center. You may also find a truffle center made with peanut butter. Still, most centers are a combination of cream and chocolate.)

You can create ganache using different methods, but the goal is the same: to create a rich confection that excites all the senses. Opinions vary on the best method for combining the cream and the chocolate, but you ultimately wind up with a similar product. Some chocolatiers add the chopped chocolate to the hot cream; some add the cream to the chopped chocolate. Some even melt the chocolate and add that to the cream or vice versa. I choose to add melted chocolate to hot cream in my kitchens because I have access to hundreds of pounds of melted chocolate.

In the following sections, I cover the basics of making ganache: chopping and melting chocolate, scalding the cream, blending the two ingredients, and adding delicious flavors. I pretty much stick to blending scalded cream and melted chocolate (melted in a microwave) in the truffle recipes because I want you to get familiar with one method and become quite proficient at making centers one way.

Chopping and melting chocolate

When selecting which chocolate to make your truffles with, your primary consideration should be how much you enjoy the chocolate *before* you melt it. (My chocolate of choice is premium chocolate, commonly called *couverture*.) Chop off a small piece of chocolate and place it in your mouth; if you like the taste and mouthfeel, you will enjoy the chocolate when it becomes part of your finished truffle. Whether you're using the chocolate at your home or in a shop, the deciding factor is taste, so don't let price determine what you use — go for the taste.

Before you make ganache, you have to get your chocolate to a manageable size. To do so, use a large knife to chop your chocolate bars into very small, uniform pieces — about the size of a small fingernail is adequate. Chopping the chocolate into uniform pieces is important because the chocolate needs to melt evenly before you combine it with the hot cream (see "Blending and cooling ganache" later in this chapter). When you finish chopping the chocolate, the hardest part of the job is done.

Your next step is melting the chocolate for the ganache, which is a snap. Just place the amount of chopped chocolate that the recipe calls for in a microwaveable bowl and melt it in the microwave. For example, if a recipe calls for 8 ounces of melted chocolate, melt it on high power in 30-second intervals, stirring each time you stop. Melting the chocolate should take about 1 minute and 45 seconds, but microwaves vary. Keep a chocolate thermometer handy to be sure the temperature doesn't exceed 110 degrees. Check out Chapter 14 for full details on how to chop and melt chocolate.

Scalding cream

When making truffle centers, you have a choice of creams that you can use, from half and half to heavy cream. The difference in these creams is the butterfat content: Half and half is about 10 percent butterfat, whipping cream is about 30 percent butterfat, and heavy cream is at least 40 percent butterfat. The differences in butterfat content affect the texture, smoothness, and richness of the center. The more butterfat you add, the richer your centers will be. And the rich, smooth center is a trademark of a great truffle.

To make ganache, I strongly recommend using heavy cream, which is 40 percent butterfat. You may not find this cream in your grocery store; you may have to special order it or buy it from a bakery or a candy shop. Finding heavy cream may or may not be a simple task, but you need this cream for its high butterfat content. As a last resort, you can use unbeaten whipping cream, which is 30 percent butterfat, from your grocery. Your truffles will lose a little of the richness and texture that they would derive from the higher fat content.

When you make ganache, you need to scald the cream (a few recipes may say to boil it) so it's hot enough to blend with the chocolate. *Scalding* is the stage at which the cream begins to bubble up in the early stages of boiling. The cream boils at about 212 degrees, but it scalds at about 185 degrees.

To scald the cream, place it in a small saucepan and heat it over low heat to 185 degrees on a candy thermometer. When the cream starts to bubble around the edges of the pan, you need to remove the saucepan from the heat. If you feel that you need a thermometer to check the temperature, you certainly can use one; just remove the saucepan from the heat as soon as the temperature reaches 185 degrees. Let the cream set for about 30 seconds to a minute, allowing it to cool to about 160 degrees (you don't want the chocolate to get too hot). At that point, you're ready to blend the cream with the chocolate.

Blending and cooling ganache

Blending your chocolate and cream is a crucial point in the ganache-making process. You could simply scald the cream mix it with the chopped chocolate, and Step 1 would be complete. But I suggest melting the chocolate in the microwave in a microwaveable bowl because blending the melted chocolate with the cream is easier than blending and melting the chopped chocolate and cream (see "Chopping and melting chocolate" earlier in this chapter).

I don't see any reason to mix the chocolate in its chopped form with the cream when you can melt the chocolate in only a minute or two, depending upon the amount you're melting. (You typically use ½ cup of cream for every half pound of chocolate. When making a dark center, you may use a little less chocolate than you would use with milk chocolate because dark chocolate has a higher viscosity due to its higher cocoa content.)

When your chocolate is melted and your cream is scalded, you're ready to pour the cream over the chocolate. Immediately stir the mixture gently with a small whisk until blended, working from the center out (see Figure 18-1). Be careful not to create air bubbles as you stir because you don't want bubbles in your ganache (bubbles cause little holes in the chocolate and make the center less smooth). When the mixture is smooth and completely blended, you have a ganache.

BLENDING A CHOCOLATE GANACHE

1. DUMP THE CREAM INTO THE CHOCOLATE...

MAKE SMALL CIRCLES WITH THE WHISK UNTIL THE MIXTURE STARTS TO LOOK SMOOTH IN THE CENTER.

2. STIR THE OUT FROM CENTER GENTLY!

MAKE BIGGER + BIGGER CIRCLES UNTIL IT BLENDS AND IT ALL BECOMES SMOOTH.

Figure 18-1: Pour the cream into the melted chocolate and stir with a whisk to create a delicious ganache.

A few drops of liquid may cause your chocolate to seize up or form a clumpy mass and become virtually useless, but pouring in a lot of cream at once doesn't have that effect on your chocolate. This is simply the nature of chocolate and liquid.

The ganache needs to cool before you can use it to form the truffle centers. If you plan to hand-roll your ganache into balls, cool it uncovered first for three hours at room temperature. The centers should be firm enough to roll into balls and maintain their shape. If the centers are too soft, put them in the refrigerator for 10 minutes. (See "Trying Your Hand at Shaping and Coating Truffles" later in this chapter.) If you plan to pipe your ganache with a disposable plastic piping bag, cool the ganache to 91 degrees because you only need to get the ganache to a temperature that won't melt the chocolate shells you are filling. (For more details about piping, see "Piping Truffles into Cups and Shells" later in this chapter.)

Flavoring ganache with flair

When your ganache is cool, you can flavor it before you put the finishing touches on your truffles. You can flavor your ganache using two different methods: using flavored oils or *infusion,* which involves covering the saucepan and allowing the cream to blend with the flavoring.

Flavoring with oils

You can flavor your truffles using oils. Oil flavorings come in a wide variety of choices and, using these oils is quite simple: Put the small measurement called for in a recipe into the batch. If the flavor is too weak, add a little more. If the flavor is stronger than you like, make a note and use less next time. These flavorings are available from the suppliers listed in Chapter 24.

To add flavor to your centers:

1. **Put the bowl of ganache on the mixer and add the oil flavoring; beat the ganache for 2 minutes on high speed.**

2. **Add the *invertase* (an enzyme that prevents bacteria from forming in the moist center); then beat for another 15 seconds to blend.**

3. **Place the ganache in the refrigerator for 30 minutes or let it sit overnight at room temperature to set.**

4. **When set, scoop the centers with a small ice cream scoop and hand roll them for dipping.**

When using oil to flavor chocolate centers, use a little more than you believe is just right because, after you dip the piece in chocolate or otherwise coat it with chocolate, the center's flavor weakens in contrast to the amount of the chocolate. Make careful notes of the amounts you use and, if you need to make adjustments in amounts, make very small adjustments. Whatever you do, you still want to taste the chocolate because that flavor is what the piece is all about.

Flavoring using infusion

Although oil flavors provide an excellent flavor, infusing fruits, tea, or other items into your centers gives your truffle centers a more natural flavor. I have experimented with different combinations, such as the Orange Juice Truffles Piped into Shells, later in this chapter.

To infuse flavors into your centers:

1. **Scald your cream and remove it from the heat.**

2. **Add the flavoring (mint leaves, orange zest, or tea leaves, for example) to the cream and cover the saucepan with a lid for 5 to 8 minutes; then remove the lid and heat the cream to 160 degrees.**

3. **Remove the saucepan from the heat and strain the cream through a sieve to remove the leaves or zest.**

4. **Let the cream cool in the saucepan for about 5 to 10 minutes to 91 degrees before mixing with chocolate.**

With time adjustments for the infusion, you can infuse other citrus flavors, tea, or mint into your ganache. This produces a truly European type of truffle and a taste that's a cut above the oil flavors.

Trying Your Hand at Shaping and Coating Truffles

Early truffle-makers intentionally shaped the candy like the fungus truffle, which they gathered in the woods and included in their diets. The idea with the early candy truffles was to make them look like rough tubers that had been underground, so cooks coated the chocolate version in cocoa to give it the appearance of dirt. Some candy makers make truffles that way today for that very reason, but the majority of truffles are perfectly round balls, decorated in colorful ways to suggest what they contain.

You want your truffles to look professional, and they will if you follow the advice in the following sections. In this section, I tell you how to shape your centers into balls of roughly the same size. After you shape your truffles, you have to determine how to decorate and mark them.

Rolling your centers by hand

Don't let the perfectly round truffles you see in many boutiques intimidate you. Many of those truffles are made with a machine called a "one-shot," which creates the shell and the filling in "one shot." The one-shot machine is a remarkable and very expensive piece of equipment that major truffle producers use. The rest of us hand-roll (or pipe) our centers.

Hand-rolling produces a very nice round center and, when you coat the center with tempered chocolate, you have a very fine truffle. The process is easy:

1. **Lay a sheet of wax paper on the counter, and scoop out a piece of ganache about the size of a pecan in the shell.**

2. **Roll the ganache between your palms and place your rolled centers onto the wax paper until you're ready to dip them in chocolate.**

A key to making truffles is to keep your centers fairly small because they grow as you add the chocolate coating and adornments. I use a small ice cream scoop to get the right amount of ganache for my centers. Some folks use a melon baller for this part of the process, so whatever you prefer using is okay. Frankly, you can use your fingers to pinch a piece of the mass into the proper size and then hand-roll it, too.

If the ganache becomes slick and difficult to roll, you may need to chill the mass again for 10 minutes in the refrigerator. After chilling, these centers are ready to roll. For this reason, some people like piping their beaten centers onto wax paper in pecan-size pieces; then they let the centers set up before hand-rolling into balls (see "Piping Truffles into Cups and Shells" later in this chapter for more details). Allow these centers to set up at room temperature overnight or for 30 minutes uncovered in the refrigerator.

Coating and decorating to finish

Like so many facets of production, how you coat and decorate your truffles is a matter of preference. Before you start either task, decide whether you want a thin or thick coating of chocolate and how you want to decorate each different-flavored piece.

Just how heavy a coating you apply to your centers is up to you. I like a very thin chocolate coating, but you can also add a thicker layer to your truffles. Don't worry, I tell you how to achieve both results.

To give your truffles a thin coating:

1. **Place a small dollop of tempered chocolate in your palm and place a center in the middle of that little puddle.** (For complete details on tempering chocolate, see Chapter 14.)

2. **Roll the center around in the chocolate, using your fingertips to apply an even coating to the center.** This method produces a very thin coating.

3. **Place the piece on the wax paper and allow the candy to cool for about 15 to 20 minutes to get a good set on the coating.** This coat is so thin, the set doesn't take very long.

4. **After the dipped centers are cool, apply a second coat of chocolate to each piece using the same process.** As you lay the pieces on the wax paper this time, you can have an assistant help you decorate the still-wet pieces with nuts or finely chopped nuts. If you choose to drizzle a chocolate string on each piece, you may do so after the pieces have cooled for about 10 minutes at room temperature.

To give your truffles a thicker chocolate coating, you can do one of two things:

✔ Hand-dip the center directly into the bowl of tempered chocolate, as I describe for dipping creams in Chapter 17. This technique gives the center a thicker coating.

✔ After applying a thin coating using the "palm" method, allow the pieces to set for 15 minutes and apply a second coating, repeating the palm method.

I prefer the latter method because you achieve a nice coat of chocolate, but this coating is still thinner than hand-dipping into the bowl. How thick you coat your truffles is simply a matter of preference.

When you decorate your truffles depends on *how* you want to top them. For instance, if you want to decorate your truffles with pieces of nuts, chopped nuts, or jimmies (sprinkles), add the decorations while the chocolate is still wet. However, if you want to string (drizzle) the tops of your truffles, wait until the chocolate has dried (about 5 to 10 minutes) to decorate them.

Another popular way of decorating truffles is to dust them in cocoa (see Figure 18-2). Follow these instructions:

1. **After coating the center with a coat of chocolate, immediately drop the piece into a bowl containing 6 to 8 ounces of cocoa and be sure the piece is completely covered with the cocoa.** Wait about 2 minutes, and place the piece on a sheet of wax paper.

2. **Let the pieces set for about 20 to 25 minutes, and shake them lightly in a sieve over wax paper, salvaging the cocoa to use again, to remove the excess cocoa.** Store in an airtight container.

Another great method used to decorate truffles involves what we in the trade call *stringing,* which is simply lightly drizzling a contrasting color onto the just-dipped truffles. The "string" can be a color that indicates something about the nature of the center. No rules exist for the colors, so you get to determine how you want to mark your pieces.

Figure 18-2:
You can coat truffle centers with cocoa powder and shake off the excess.

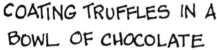

COATING TRUFFLES IN A
BOWL OF CHOCOLATE

To make colored chocolate to string over your truffles, melt 2 or 3 ounces of white chocolate in a microwave for about 1 minute and add ¼ teaspoon of powdered food coloring to produce a liquid coloring. You need to use the colored chocolate quickly because it sets up pretty fast.

You can also mark your pieces by grating a color onto the still-wet pieces:

1. **About an hour or so before you're going to decorate your pieces, make a white-chocolate coating by melting white chocolate in the microwave for about 1 minute; then add ¼ teaspoon of powdered food coloring to add color.** This produces a liquid coloring.

2. **Pour this chocolate onto wax paper and allow it to set up.** The coating will form a little puddle of color and become hard again.

3. **When you dip your truffles in the tempered chocolate and while they're still wet, grate fine specks of the color onto the truffles.** The specks will stick to the chocolate, making a beautiful marking for identification.

4. **Allow the pieces to dry for 10 minutes at room temperature.** If you have time, let them set a little longer.

If you need more decorating ideas, turn to Chapter 15.

Perusing Pure Chocolate Truffles

The following truffles are very basic recipes with no flavors added. These are for the lovers of pure chocolate in its highest form.

Milk Chocolate Truffles

This recipe is a basic formula for making truffles; you can take this basic recipe and make many variations using it. You can use any type of chocolate, both in terms of color (milk, dark, or white) or quality, you desire for the center; just remember that the better the chocolate, the better the results. After all, the taste will definitely reflect the quality.

Preparation time: *4 to 4½ hours including cooling time*

Yield: *60 pieces*

8 ounces milk chocolate, chopped	*½ teaspoon invertase (optional)*
½ cup heavy cream	*1 pound melted milk chocolate for tempering*

1 Melt the chopped milk chocolate in a microwaveable bowl in the microwave on high power for 30 seconds and then in 15-second increments until the chocolate measures 100 degrees on a chocolate thermometer. Melting the chocolate shouldn't require more than about 1 minute, but microwaves vary.

2 In a small saucepan over low heat, heat the cream to scalding (about 185 degrees on a candy thermometer), which is the point at which the cream begins to bubble around the edges. Remove from the heat and let the cream cool for about 30 seconds to 1 minute until it reaches 160 degrees.

3 Pour the cream onto the melted chocolate and whisk gently, blending from the center out. Do not create bubbles as you whisk. This mixture should become smooth in about 1 minute.

4 When the mixture is smooth, pour it into a mixing bowl of a 4- to 5-quart mixer and allow it to cool for 3 hours uncovered at room temperature.

5 When the mixture is cool, put the bowl on the mixer, add the invertase (optional), and beat on high speed for 2 minutes.

6 Place the mixture in the refrigerator to cool for 30 minutes. When it's done cooling, use a melon baller or sherbet scoop to scoop out the mixture and form the centers. Hand-roll the mixture into balls of equal size (about 1¼ inches in diameter) and place them on wax paper. If the centers feel too soft, refrigerate them for 30 minutes to allow them to firm before you dip them.

7 Temper the chocolate for coating as I describe in Chapter 14. Place a dollop of tempered milk chocolate in the palm of one hand and, with the other hand, place a center in the middle of the chocolate. Using your fingertips, roll the center around in the palm of one hand to coat it evenly with a very thin layer of chocolate. Place the ball on a sheet of wax paper to dry. Repeat with the other balls until you've coated them all with chocolate.

8 When you've coated all the pieces and they've set for about 15 minutes at room temperature, repeat the process to apply a second thin coating to each piece.

Per Serving: *Calories 63 (From Fat 35); Fat 4g (Saturated 2g); Cholesterol 3mg; Sodium 9mg; Carbohydrate 7g (Dietary Fiber 0g); Protein 1g.*

Dark Chocolate Truffles

This recipe is sure to please folks who believe that only dark chocolate is real chocolate.

Preparation time: *4 to 4½ hours including cooling time*

Yield: *60 pieces*

8 ounces dark chocolate, chopped

½ cup heavy cream

½ teaspoon invertase (optional)

1 pound melted dark chocolate for tempering

12 ounces unsweetened cocoa

1 In a microwave, melt the chopped dark chocolate in a microwaveable bowl on high power for 30 seconds and then in 15-second increments until the chocolate reaches 100 degrees on a chocolate thermometer. Melting shouldn't take much more than a minute, depending on the oven, but make sure you don't overheat the chocolate.

2 In a small saucepan over low heat, warm the cream to scalding (about 185 degrees on a candy thermometer), which is the point at which the cream begins to bubble around the edges. Remove the pan from the heat and let the cream cool for 30 seconds to 1 minute until it reaches 160 degrees on a candy thermometer.

3 Pour the cream into the bowl of melted chocolate and, using a small whisk, mix gently from the center out to blend into a smooth mixture. Do not stir hard enough to create bubbles. This whisking should produce a smooth mixture in about 1 minute.

4 When blended, pour the mixture into a mixing bowl of a 4- to 5-quart mixer, and allow it to cool for about 3 hours uncovered at room temperature.

5 When cool, put the bowl on the mixer. Add the invertase (optional) to the ganache and beat it for 2 minutes on high speed.

6 Place the uncovered ganache in the refrigerator to cool for 30 minutes. Then use a melon baller or a small ice cream scoop to scoop the ganache into walnut-size pieces, and place on wax paper to await their coating of chocolate. Hand-roll the ganache into balls of equal size, about 1¼ inches in diameter. If the centers are too soft to roll, place the ganache back in the refrigerator for 30 minutes to get firmer.

7 Temper the pound of melted chocolate using one of the methods I describe in Chapter 14. At this point, you may want to draft some help. Place a small amount of tempered chocolate in the palm of one hand; place a center in the middle of that dollop and, using your fingertips, roll the center in one hand until it's evenly coated. Drop the piece into the bowl of cocoa powder and have your assistant completely cover the piece with powder; leave it in the bowl for about 2 minutes until it's firm enough to move. Repeat this step with all the other pieces, having your assistant shake the excess cocoa off the pieces and move the cocoa-coated pieces to wax paper.

8 When the pieces are firm, gently roll them around in a small sifter or sieve to remove the excess powder. Let the truffles set for about 30 minutes at room temperature.

Per Serving: Calories 81 (From Fat 47); Fat 5g (Saturated 3g); Cholesterol 4mg; Sodium 2mg; Carbohydrate 10g (Dietary Fiber 3g); Protein 2g.

Filling Up on Flavored Truffles

Adding oils is a great way to impart flavors to your chocolate. I recommend finding high-quality essential oil flavorings because, like the chocolate you use, quality comes through. (See "Flavoring with oils" earlier in this chapter for more details.) Most of the recipes in this section use essential oils as a flavoring, and I recommend several good suppliers in Chapter 24. If you still can't find the oil flavorings you want, you may substitute other flavorings that you can find from the same suppliers. Your results will still be good.

Caramel Truffles

For a delightful chocolate caramel truffle, try out this recipe. Most truffles have some form of chocolate as part of their center, but the addition of caramel is a nice variation. This truffle has that great taste of chocolate and caramel with a thin chocolate shell that just barely contains the caramel goodness.

Preparation time: *1½ hour including cooling time*

Yield: *70 pieces*

8 ounces milk chocolate, chopped	*½ cup heavy cream*
4 ounces caramel, chopped into small pieces (try the recipe in Chapter 7 or use store-bought caramel)	*¼ teaspoon salt*
	1½ pounds melted milk chocolate for tempering

1 Melt the chopped milk chocolate in a microwaveable bowl on high for 30 seconds and then in 15-second increments, stirring each time until it reaches 100 degrees. Use a chocolate thermometer to check the temperature.

2 In another microwaveable bowl, microwave the chopped caramel on high, stopping every 30 seconds to stir, until it reaches 150 degrees on a candy thermometer. Melting should take about 1½ minutes.

3 In a small saucepan over low heat, cook the cream to scalding (about 185 degrees on a candy thermometer), at which point the cream begins to bubble up. Remove the cream from the heat and add the caramel and salt. Whisk gently for about 1 minute to blend the ingredients.

4 Add the caramel-and-cream mixture to the bowl of chocolate and whisk gently until the batch is smooth (about 1 minute). Allow the batch to cool for 3 hours. Alternatively, you can place the batch in the refrigerator uncovered to cool until firm if you need a faster cooling time than room temperature provides.

5 Using a large knife, cut the ganache into ¾-inch cubes and roll them into balls.

6 Temper the chocolate as described in Chapter 14. Place a small dollop of tempered chocolate in the palm of your hand and roll the ball around, using your fingertips to coat each piece evenly with the chocolate. Place the coated ball on a piece of wax paper to dry for about 10 to 15 minutes. Coat all the balls.

7 Follow the same coating process, giving all the balls a second coat of chocolate. Place them on wax paper and let them dry uncovered for about 30 minutes at room temperature.

Per Serving: *Calories 76 (From Fat 40); Fat 4g (Saturated 2g); Cholesterol 2mg; Sodium 22mg; Carbohydrate 10g (Dietary Fiber 0g); Protein 1g.*

Truffles from the ground up

Truffles have been around for thousands of years. Of course, that kind of truffle is a type of fungus that grows underground in the forest.

People hunt these difficult-to-locate truffles, which have a nutty taste and are considered a delicacy. These truffles are quite expensive. Some of the rarest truffles (Black Perigord) are often referred to as "black diamonds" due to their high cost. These walnut-size fungi command prices in excess of $2,000 a pound!

Once the truffle hunters have collected their delicacies from the wild, they put them to good use in various recipes. Their nutty taste supposedly is a nice addition to recipes, including salads.

From such humble beginnings sprang one of the most popular chocolate delicacies ever conceived: the chocolate truffle. The chocolate truffle came into being as an imitation of the one that grew underground. Through a love of chocolate, chocolatiers and pastry chefs started making chocolates that resembled the difficult-to-find fungi. Early chocolate truffles were covered with a healthy dose of cocoa powder, which gave the appearance of the real truffles, covered with dirt. Today, this appearance is still popular.

Coffee Truffles

This recipe is kind of fun because you get to eat a coffee bean, and that doesn't happen every day! The coffee truffle, with its dark center and the eye appeal of the coffee bean on top, is quite a luscious piece of candy. To make the best impression, turn the bean with its "belly button" up. You can substitute coffee crystals for the coffee-oil flavoring; either imparts a strong coffee flavor.

Preparation time: *4 to 4½ hours including cooling time*

Yield: *60 to 65 pieces*

8 ounces dark chocolate, chopped

½ cup heavy cream

½ teaspoon invertase (optional)

1 teaspoon coffee oil or 2 teaspoons instant coffee crystals

1 pound melted dark chocolate for tempering

1 ounce coffee beans for topping

1 In a microwave, melt the chopped dark chocolate in a microwaveable bowl on high power for 30 seconds and then in 15-second increments, stirring at each break, until the temperature reaches 100 degrees. Use a chocolate thermometer to check the temperature.

2 In a small saucepan over low heat, warm the cream and coffee crystals (if you're using those to flavor) to scalding (about 185 degrees), which is the point at which the cream begins to bubble up. Remove the cream from the heat and let it cool for about 1 minute.

3 Pour the cream into the bowl of chocolate and whisk gently from the center out for about 1 minute, being careful not to create bubbles.

4 When you've blended the mixture, pour it into a mixing bowl of a 4- to 5-quart mixer and allow it to cool for 3 hours uncovered at room temperature.

5 After the mixture cools, put the bowl onto the mixer and add the coffee oil (if you didn't use coffee crystals). Beat the mixture on high speed for 2 minutes. Stop the mixer, add the invertase (optional), and beat for 15 seconds. Place the mixture in the refrigerator uncovered for 30 minutes to cool.

6 Scoop out the ganache with a sherbet scoop or melon baller and hand-roll the ganache into balls.

7 Temper the melted chocolate as described in Chapter 14. To coat the balls with tempered chocolate, place a small dollop of the tempered dark chocolate in the palm of one hand and drop a ball in the puddle. Coat the ball in chocolate by rolling it with your fingertips. Place each coated piece on a sheet of wax paper to dry for about 15 minutes. Coat all the balls.

8 Repeat the chocolate-coating process to add a second coating to your candy. While the chocolate is still wet, place a coffee bean on each piece. Place the smooth side of the bean down and the grooved side (belly button) up. Let the pieces set for about 30 minutes.

Tip: When you eat the truffles, you can eat the bean — but you don't have to. The bean provides a nice crunch.

Per Serving: *Calories 64 (From Fat 37); Fat 4g (Saturated 3g); Cholesterol 3mg; Sodium 1mg; Carbohydrate 6g (Dietary Fiber 1g); Protein 1g.*

Grand Marnier Truffles

The Grand Marnier truffle (shown in the color section) is named for the liqueur of the same name. This flavor is a little more tart than orange, giving the center its own special flavor.

Preparation time: *4 to 4½ hours including cooling time*

Yield: *60 pieces*

8 ounces milk chocolate, chopped

½ cup heavy cream

1 teaspoon Grand Marnier oil flavor (or orange-oil flavoring)

½ teaspoon invertase (optional)

1 pound melted milk chocolate for tempering

¼ cup tiny chocolate squares or chocolate sprinkles to decorate

1 In a microwave, melt the chopped milk chocolate in a microwaveable bowl on high for 30 seconds and then in 15-second increments until the chocolate reaches 100 degrees. Do not overheat.

2 In a small saucepan, warm the cream over low heat to scalding (about 185 degrees on a candy thermometer), which is the point at which the cream begins to bubble up. Remove the cream from the heat and allow it to cool for 30 seconds to 1 minute until it reaches about 160 degrees.

3 Pour the cream into the bowl of melted milk chocolate and stir gently with a whisk, working from the center out to blend the cream and chocolate for about 1 minute to make it smooth. Do not stir hard enough to create air bubbles.

4 Pour the mixture into the mixing bowl of a 4- to 5-quart mixer and allow the mixture to cool uncovered at room temperature for 3 hours.

5 When the mixture is cool, put the bowl onto the mixer, add the Grand Marnier flavoring, and beat the mixture on high speed for 2 minutes. Add the invertase (optional) and beat for 15 seconds to blend. Put the mixture into the refrigerator uncovered for 30 minutes.

6 Remove the mixture from the refrigerator and scoop it with a melon scoop or a small ice cream scoop. Roll the mixture into balls.

7 Temper the milk chocolate as described in Chapter 14. Then place a small amount of tempered chocolate in the palm of one hand and place a ball in that hand. Using your fingertips, roll the ball around in your palm to coat it evenly with chocolate. Place the chocolate-coated ball on a sheet of wax paper. Repeat this process until you've coated all the pieces.

8 Let the pieces set for about 15 minutes, and repeat the coating process. This time immediately sprinkle tiny chocolate squares or chocolate sprinkles onto the still-wet chocolate. Repeat this process until you've coated all the pieces and decorated their tops. Let the finished pieces set for about 30 minutes to become completely firm.

Per Serving: *Calories 68 (From Fat 38); Fat 4g (Saturated 2g); Cholesterol 3mg; Sodium 9mg; Carbohydrate 8g (Dietary Fiber 0g); Protein 1g.*

Hazelnut Truffles

Hazelnut is one of the most popular flavors in Europe and has become quite popular in the United States, too. The way you make this truffle is quite similar to how you make the plain milk truffle — the recipes have only a few differences, one of which, of course, is the hazelnut flavoring.

Preparation time: *4 to 4½ hours including cooling time*

Yield: *60 to 65 pieces*

8 ounces milk chocolate, chopped

½ cup heavy cream

½ teaspoon invertase (optional)

1 teaspoon hazelnut oil

1 pound melted milk chocolate for tempering

4 ounces white chocolate, chopped

1 In a microwave, melt the chopped milk chocolate in a microwaveable bowl on high power for 30 seconds and then in 15-second increments, stirring each time, until the chocolate reaches 100 degrees. Use a chocolate thermometer to check the temperature.

2 In a small saucepan over low heat, warm the cream to scalding (about 185 degrees), which is the point at which the cream begins to bubble up. Remove the pan from the heat and let the cream cool for 30 seconds to 1 minute to about 160 degrees.

3 Pour the cream into the bowl of melted chocolate and use a small whisk to blend the mixture from the center out for about 1 minute. Do not stir hard enough to create bubbles, and stir only until the mixture is smooth.

4 Pour the mixture into a mixing bowl of a 4- to 5-quart mixer and let the mixture cool uncovered for 3 hours at room temperature.

5 When the mixture is cool, put the bowl on the mixer and add the hazelnut oil. Then beat on high speed for 2 minutes. Stop the mixer and add the invertase (optional); then beat for 15 seconds to blend. Let the ganache cool uncovered in the refrigerator for 30 minutes to cool.

6 After the ganache cools, use a small ice cream scoop or melon baller to scoop it into balls.

7 Temper the chocolate as described in Chapter 14. Hand-roll the centers into balls and coat them with tempered milk chocolate by placing a small puddle of chocolate in the palm of your hand. Then place a center in the chocolate puddle and coat the center, using your fingertips to coat it evenly. Place each piece on the wax paper, and repeat the process until you have coated all the balls.

8 Apply a second coat of chocolate to each piece using the same process. Place the pieces on wax paper to dry and set for 30 minutes.

9 While the pieces are drying, melt the white chocolate to 95 degrees in a microwaveable bowl on high for 1 minute, stopping at 30 seconds to stir. Use a chocolate thermometer to check the temperature. If the chocolate isn't heated to 95 degrees, heat in 10-second intervals until ready, stirring at each stop. Dip a salad fork into the melted white chocolate and shake it quickly back and forth over the truffles to create a series of thin lines across the tops of the pieces. Let the pieces set for 30 minutes.

Per Serving: Calories 69 (From Fat 39); Fat 4g (Saturated 2g); Cholesterol 3mg; Sodium 10mg; Carbohydrate 8g (Dietary Fiber 0g); Protein 1g.

Rum-flavored Truffles

This recipe uses nonalcoholic rum flavoring to make a tasty truffle. I like to use a small piece of walnut on top to decorate this truffle for a nice overall appearance.

Preparation time: 4 to 4½ hours including cooling time

Yield: 60 to 65 pieces

8 ounces dark chocolate, chopped	1 teaspoon rum oil
½ cup heavy cream	1 pound melted dark chocolate for tempering
½ teaspoon invertase (optional)	¼ cup of small walnut pieces for toppings

1 In a microwave, melt the chopped dark chocolate in a microwaveable bowl on high power for 30 seconds and then in 15-second increments, stirring until the chocolate reaches 100 degrees. Use a chocolate thermometer to check the temperature.

2 In a small saucepan over low heat, warm the cream to scalding (about 185 degrees), which is the point at which the cream begins to bubble up. Remove the cream from the heat and let it cool for about 1 minute.

3 Pour the cream onto the chocolate and stir gently with a whisk for about 1 minute, working from the center out, until the chocolate is smooth. Do not make bubbles when you stir.

4 When blended, pour the mixture into the bowl of a 4- to 5-quart mixer. Let the mixture cool for 3 hours uncovered at room temperature.

5 When the mixture is cool, put the bowl on the mixer and add the rum oil. Beat the mixture on high speed for 2 minutes. Stop the beater and add the invertase (optional); beat for 15 seconds to blend. Place the mixture in the refrigerator uncovered for 30 minutes to cool.

6 When the mixture is firm, use a small ice cream scoop to dip out the centers; then hand-roll the centers into balls.

7 Temper the dark chocolate as described in Chapter 14. To coat the balls with chocolate, put a small amount of the tempered dark chocolate in the palm of one hand. Drop one ball into the puddle and, using your fingertips, roll the ball in the chocolate. Place each piece on a sheet of wax paper. Repeat until you have coated all the balls. After the pieces set for 15 minutes, repeat the coating process.

8 Repeat the chocolate-coating process to apply a second coat of chocolate. This time apply a small walnut on the top of each piece while the coating is still wet. Let the pieces set for about 30 minutes for a good set.

Per Serving: Calories 66 (From Fat 40); Fat 4g (Saturated 3g); Cholesterol 3mg; Sodium 1mg; Carbohydrate 6g (Dietary Fiber 1g); Protein 1g.

Dark Mint Truffles

This truffle is a real special piece for mint-lovers. Something about mint and dark chocolate affects our senses unlike other candy combinations. A good, rich dark chocolate represents the essence of chocolate taste, and mint brings a sense of freshness. Together, you have one of the favorite combinations in the confection world.

You produce the mint flavor in this piece through the infusion process, whereby you steep the mint in the cream and then strain the mint leaves out of the cream, leaving the essence of the leaves. You may need a couple of tries to get the flavor just right, as the size and intensity of the leaves can vary a little.

Preparation time: 4 to 4½ hours, including cooling time

Yield: 60 pieces

8 ounces dark chocolate, chopped	*½ teaspoon invertase (optional)*
½ cup heavy cream	*⅛ teaspoon mint oil (optional)*
⅓ cup chopped fresh mint (snip 60 small pieces for toppings)	*1 pound melted dark chocolate for tempering*

1 Melt the chopped dark chocolate in a microwave on high power for 30 seconds and then in 15-second increments until it reaches 100 degrees. Use a chocolate thermometer to check the temperature.

2 In a small saucepan over low heat, warm the cream to scalding (about 185 degrees), which is the point at which the cream begins to bubble up. Remove the cream from the heat at 185 degrees and add the chopped mint. Cover the pan and let the ingredients steep for 8 minutes.

3 Remove the cover and reheat the mixture on low heat to 160 degrees. After the mixture reaches 160 degrees, remove it from the heat and pour it through a strainer into the bowl of melted chocolate to remove the chopped mint pieces. Whisk gently to blend, working from the center out for about 1 minute; do not make bubbles in the mixture as you stir. Let it cool uncovered for 3 hours at room temperature.

4 When cool, stir in the mint-oil flavoring (if the mint flavor isn't strong enough for your taste) and mix well with a spatula. Add the invertase (optional), and stir 15 seconds to blend. Place the batch in the refrigerator for 30 minutes to cool.

5 Remove the batch from the refrigerator, and use a small ice cream scoop to scoop into centers. Hand-roll the centers into balls.

6 Temper the dark chocolate as described in Chapter 14. To coat the balls with the tempered dark chocolate, place a small dollop of chocolate in the palm of one hand. Place a ball in the small puddle of chocolate and, using your fingertips, roll the center to coat it in chocolate. Place each piece on a piece of wax paper. Dip all centers in this manner. Let the dipped pieces set for 15 minutes before applying a second coat.

7 Repeat the chocolate-coating process to cover each piece with a second layer of chocolate. Then, while the chocolate is still wet, top each piece with a snip of mint leaf Let the truffles set for about 30 minutes.

Per Serving: Calories 68 (From Fat 40); Fat 5g (Saturated 3g); Cholesterol 4mg; Sodium 1mg; Carbohydrate 7g (Dietary Fiber 1g); Protein 1g.

Confetti Champagne Truffles

This recipe cooks up a white chocolate truffle with multicolored sprinkles on top, which gives it the look of confetti. I like the combination of the colored sprinkles with the champagne flavor because that taste and the "confetti" suggest New Year's Eve. This strikes me as a happy piece.

For this recipe, you can add 2 ounces more of the white chocolate because the viscosity of white chocolate is lower than milk chocolate and especially lower than dark chocolate.

Preparation time: *4 to 4½ hours including cooling time*

Yield: *60 pieces*

8 ounces white chocolate, chopped	*½ teaspoon champagne oil flavoring*
½ cup heavy cream	*1 pound white chocolate to melt for coating*
½ teaspoon invertase (optional)	*1 2-ounce bottle multicolored jimmies to top*

1 In a microwave, melt the chopped white chocolate in a microwaveable bowl on high power until it reaches about 95 degrees, stopping and stirring at least once. The heating shouldn't take more than about a minute to 1 minute and 30 seconds. Do not overheat. Check the temperature with a chocolate thermometer.

2 In a small saucepan over low heat, warm the cream to scalding (about 185 degrees), which is the point at which the cream begins to bubble up. Remove the cream from the heat at 185 degrees and let it cool for 1 minute.

3 Pour the cream onto the melted white chocolate and, using a small whisk, whisk gently from the center out for about 1 minute. Do not make bubbles.

4 Pour the mixture into the bowl of a 4- to 5-quart mixer and let it cool for 30 minutes in the refrigerator.

5 When the mixture is cool, put the bowl on the mixer, add the champagne flavoring, and beat on high speed for 2 minutes. Stop the mixer and add the invertase (optional).

6 Use a small ice cream scoop to scoop the mixture into centers. Hand-roll the centers into balls for dipping in chocolate.

7 Melt the 1 pound of white chocolate to 95 degrees in a microwave in a microwaveable bowl on high power. Stop every 45 seconds to stir. Heating to 95 degrees should take about 1 min-ute and 45 seconds. When you stir, check the temperature with a chocolate thermometer.

8 Coat the balls with melted white chocolate by placing a small dollop of white chocolate in the palm of one hand. Place a ball in the puddle and, using your fingertips, roll the ball around to coat it with chocolate. Place the ball on wax paper and sprinkle jimmies on it while the chocolate is still wet. Let the pieces set for about 20 to 30 minutes at room temperature.

Per Serving: Calories 77 (From Fat 42); Fat 5g (Saturated 3g); Cholesterol 7mg; Sodium 13mg; Carbohydrate 7g (Dietary Fiber 0g); Protein 1g.

Piping Truffles into Cups and Shells

Piped truffles are an extra-special treat for any chocolate lover. The piping process involves filling chocolate shells with chocolate, which allows you to create very soft, creamy truffle centers that would be too soft to hand-roll.

I use the piping method for a truffle center that's a bit more liquid than a firm ganache because sometimes you want a softer, more liquid center. Whereas many of the centers are hand-rolled into balls and dipped, near-liquid centers can be piped into preformed shells and closed through a process that I show you in Chapter 19.

The ratio between the chocolate and the cream determines the firmness of the ganache. For example, 8 ounces of chocolate blended with a ½ cup of scalded cream produces a firm center. This ratio produces a center that's easy to hand-roll into balls for coating with chocolate. However, I can also use the same ratio to produce a more liquid center for piping by simply adding juice or alcoholic spirits. I infuse the cream with the flavoring, mix it with the melted chocolate, and let it cool to about 91 degrees, so the cream doesn't melt the chocolate shell. When the mixture reaches 91 degrees, I stir in the liquid and pipe the mixture into shells. When I plan to add liquid to a center, I reduce the amount of cream in the recipe slightly, but I get a center that pipes easily into a prepared shell.

Despite the firmness of a ganache, you can definitely pipe any of the centers from the previous recipes in this chapter into cups and shells. You can pipe the centers as soon as you've beaten them for 2 minutes (with flavorings and invertase).

To pipe the truffle centers, you need (what do you know?) a piping bag and cups or shells of chocolate. I recommend using 12-inch disposable plastic bags for piping, available from suppliers listed in Chapter 24; they're relatively cheap and are a size that enables you to work easily, even if you've never piped before. You can purchase cups online from www.hauserchocolates.com or you can buy molds and make your own cups using shell-molding techniques (see Chapter 19 for more about molding).

When you use a piping bag:

1. **Have someone fold the bag down about ⅓ of the way and hold the bag open while you scoop the ganache into the bag using a large spoon or a hard rubber spatula.** Fill the bag about halfway and twist the bag closed, leaving enough room to hold the bag above the twist.

2. **Snip the pointed end with scissors, making a big enough opening to allow a slow flow.** Until you're certain, make small cuts, because you may always cut off more. Once you snip too much, you cannot go back.

3. **Pipe the walnut-size dollops of ganache into the cups or shells.** If you're filling cups, place the tip of the bag in the bottom and let the ganache flow (don't squeeze too hard), allowing the cup to fill from the bottom with no air pockets forming. Air pockets allow a different type of mold to form in your mold, if you catch my drift. Fill the mold as the recipe describes. Some shells get a topping; some require you to leave room for a chocolate backing to close the piece.

   If you're filling shells, place the tip in the bottom and ease the bag up as you fill the shell. Do not leave air pockets because these spaces allow for condensation to occur, which leads to bacterial growth. Leave enough room in the shell at the top (about ⅛ inch) to allow space to fill the back with chocolate to close the mold. When this chocolate sets, the piece appears to be solid, but it's really filled with ganache.

Cappuccino Truffles

The cappuccino truffle (shown in the color section) is quite an eye-appealing piece. It's made to look like a cup of cappuccino with white foam on top, sprinkled with cocoa. If you like cappuccino, if you like coffee, or if you like chocolate, you'll find something special in this piece. You need to do a little piping for this one, but don't worry, it's pretty easy.

Tools: *12-inch disposable plastic piping bag*

Preparation time: *1 hour*

Yield: *72 pieces*

½ cup butter, softened

½ tablespoon instant coffee crystals

1 tablespoon warm water

1 teaspoon plus 6 tablespoons unsweetened cocoa powder

2 ounces nut paste (hazelnut, almond, or peanut butter flavor)

10 ounces milk chocolate, chopped

6 dozen dark or milk chocolate cups

5 ounces white chocolate, chopped

1 Whisk the softened butter with a whisk until it becomes light in appearance (about 1 minute).

2 Dissolve the coffee crystals in 1 tablespoon of warm water; then add 1 teaspoon of cocoa to the mixture. Use a hard rubber spatula to blend this mixture with the softened butter.

3 Add 2 ounces of nut paste of your choice to the mixture and blend.

4 Melt 10 ounces of milk chocolate in the microwave on high power, stopping every 45 seconds and then every 30 seconds to stir and check the temperature with a chocolate thermometer. Melting takes about 1 minute and 45 seconds total.

5 Stir the butter mixture into the melted milk chocolate and blend.

6 Spoon the mixture into the piping bag. Pipe the mixture into chocolate cups, leaving about ⅛ inch at the top. If the piping causes peaks in the cups, flatten them with your fingertip.

7 Melt 5 ounces of white chocolate to 95 degrees in the microwave on high power, stopping every 45 seconds to stir and check temperature. Melting takes about 1 minute and 20 seconds total. Pipe or spoon the melted white chocolate onto the top of each piece to seal and lightly sprinkle the top with the remaining cocoa. This decoration is supposed to look like a cup of cappuccino with white foam and cocoa on top. Allow the white chocolate to set for about 15 minutes.

Tip: *To sprinkle the tops of the truffles with cocoa, fill an empty pepper shaker with cocoa and shake.*

Per Serving: *Calories 57 (From Fat 35); Fat 4g (Saturated 2g); Cholesterol 4mg; Sodium 5mg; Carbohydrate 5g (Dietary Fiber 0g); Protein 1g.*

Pecan Pie Truffles

This rather simple recipe produces a delicious piece. A lot of folks love a good pecan pie (okay, I never saw a bad pecan pie), and this piece combines some of the best elements of pecan pie: pecans, caramel sauce, and a little pie-shaped appearance. It's cute *and* it's delicious.

You also can make these truffles without a chocolate topping. You can apply the pecan pieces directly to the caramel, but if the pieces are laid on their sides, the caramel will slowly ooze out.

Tools: *12-inch disposable plastic piping bag*

Preparation time: *1½ hours including cooling time*

Yield: *35 to 40 pieces*

1 pound caramel from Chapter 7 or store-bought caramel

1 teaspoon maple flavoring

35 to 40 empty milk-chocolate cups

½ pound melted milk chocolate for tempering

½ pound small pecan pieces

1 In a microwaveable bowl, melt the caramel to about 115 degrees, stopping every 45 seconds to stir and check the temperature with a candy thermometer; melting usually takes about 1½ to 2 minutes.

2 Stir in the maple flavoring; mix together well. Cool the mixture to 90 degrees, which is just the right temperature so that when you pipe the mixture, you don't melt the chocolate cups.

3 Spoon the caramel mixture into a 12-inch disposable piping bag. Pipe the caramel mixture into the cups, leaving about ⅛ inch at the top.

4 Temper the milk chocolate as described in Chapter 14.

5 When you've filled all the cups, top them off by spooning tempered milk chocolate onto the cups to seal the tops. Immediately sprinkle the pecan pieces onto the wet chocolate and press them lightly to be sure that they stick. Let the pieces set at room temperature for 30 minutes to set.

Vary It! *If you decide to forgo the chocolate, you can apply the pecans directly to the caramel filling, making a topping of pecans without the chocolate. But you must keep the pieces upright because the caramel will ooze out if the pieces lie on their sides.*

Per Serving: Calories 121 (From Fat 65); Fat 7g (Saturated 2g); Cholesterol 1mg; Sodium 33mg; Carbohydrate 15g (Dietary Fiber 1g); Protein 2g.

Orange Juice Truffles Piped into Shells

I particularly like this recipe because the first time I made it, I calculated the proportions so well. When I tasted the truffle, I thought I was biting a chocolate orange!

Tools: *12-inch disposable plastic piping bag and scraper to scrape molds*

Preparation time: *3 to 3½ hours including cooling time*

Yield: *60 pieces*

8 ounces milk chocolate, chopped

3 ounces heavy cream

Zest of half an orange

½ teaspoon invertase (optional)

2 ounces fresh-squeezed orange juice

60 1⅛-inch-diameter, ¾-inch-deep chocolate shells in their molds (see Chapter 19 for instructions on how to make shells)

1 pound melted milk chocolate for tempering

1 In a microwave, melt the chopped milk chocolate in a microwaveable bowl on high power for 30 seconds and then in 15-second increments until the chocolate reaches 100 degrees. At each stop, check the temperature with a chocolate thermometer.

2 In a small saucepan over low heat, warm the cream to scalding (about 185 degrees on a candy thermometer), which is the point at which the cream begins to bubble up. Remove the cream from the heat at 185 degrees and add the orange zest; then cover the pot for 5 minutes.

3 After 5 minutes, put the mixture back on the heat until it reaches 160 degrees on a candy thermometer. Pour the mixture through a strainer into the chocolate, and whisk gently to blend, being careful not to make bubbles. Let the mixture cool to 90 degrees at room temperature and then stir in the orange juice. Add the invertase (optional) and stir to blend (about 15 seconds).

4 Spoon the mixture into a piping bag. Pipe the filling into the shells in their molds, leaving about ⅛ inch at the top of the shell. Place the molds in the refrigerator for 5 minutes to allow the centers to set and remove them from the fridge.

5 Carefully spoon the tempered chocolate over the shells, a process I call "backing off," which puts the back or bottom on the filled shell. Fill the bottoms and carefully scrape the mold with a triangular scraper to remove the excess chocolate from the molds without letting the filling leak out. Put the molds back into the refrigerator for 10 minutes.

6 Remove the molds from the refrigerator and tap the truffles out of the molds by turning them upside down and tapping the molds on the counter. The chocolates should fall out. Allow to set for about 15 minutes at room temperature or eat as soon as you finish.

Per Serving: Calories 108 (From Fat 58); Fat 6g (Saturated 3g); Cholesterol 2mg; Sodium 15mg; Carbohydrate 13g (Dietary Fiber 0g); Protein 2g.

Truffles with Spirits

Sometimes you just want a truffle made with more than a flavored oil, no matter how good that oil flavor may be. When that craving arises, you can make a truffle with alcoholic spirits. Just be careful whom you give them to. The alcohol content isn't enough to impair you, but you still wouldn't want to give these candies to young people.

Tools: *12-inch disposable plastic piping bag and a triangular scraper to scrape the molds*

Preparation time: *4 to 4½ hours including cooling time*

Yield: *60 pieces*

8 ounces milk chocolate, chopped

3 ounces heavy cream

½ teaspoon invertase (optional)

3 tablespoons dark rum

60 chocolate shells, about 1⅛ inch in diameter and ⅞ inch deep in their molds (see Chapter 19 for instructions on how to make shells)

1 pound melted milk chocolate for tempering

1 In a microwave, melt the chopped milk chocolate in a microwaveable bowl on high power for 30 seconds and then in 15-second intervals until the chocolate reaches 100 degrees. Use a chocolate thermometer to check the temperature. Do not overheat.

2 In a small saucepan over low heat, warm the cream to scalding (about 185 degrees), which is the point at which the cream begins to bubble up. Remove the pan from the heat and let the cream cool at room temperature until it reaches 160 degrees on your candy thermometer.

3 Pour the cream into the bowl of chocolate and whisk gently from the center out. Do not make bubbles. When the mixture is smooth, let it cool to 91 degrees (cooling takes only a few minutes). When the mixture reaches that temperature, add the dark rum and stir. Add the invertase (optional) and stir 15 seconds to blend.

4 Spoon the mixture into a piping bag, pipe the mixture into prepared shells (still in their molds), and put the shells in the refrigerator to cool for 8 minutes.

5 Temper the chocolate as described in Chapter 14. Remove the shells from the refrigerator and apply the tempered chocolate to the backs of the shells. Scrape the molds with a triangular scraper to smooth and remove the excess chocolate. Return the candy to the refrigerator for 10 minutes to set.

6 Remove the candy from the refrigerator and tap the molds on the counter to remove the chocolates. You may eat them immediately or enjoy them later.

Vary It! *Instead of rum, use coffee liqueur, orange liqueur, Irish Crème, or cognac.*

Per Serving: *Calories 109 (From Fat 57); Fat 6g (Saturated 3g); Cholesterol 2mg; Sodium 15mg; Carbohydrate 13g (Dietary Fiber 0g); Protein 2g.*

Protecting Your Truffles from the Elements

After you've dipped, decorated, and cooled your beautiful truffles, you want to protect them. To do so, place each finished truffle in a #4 or #6 brown paper cup, available from suppliers listed in Chapter 24, and store them in a plastic container for three weeks. (Or you can eat them as soon as they dry.)

If you used invertase in the recipes, you can store the truffles in an airtight container for two months at room temperature. Place wax paper between the layers of truffles. If you made your truffles without invertase, you should eat them in three weeks or less.

You also can freeze your truffles for up to six months. To prepare your truffles for freezing, place them in a double freezer bag. When the time comes to remove the truffles from the freezer, allow the chocolates to thaw completely (overnight is good) before you take them out of the bags to prevent condensation. Remember, condensation is the enemy of chocolate, so don't allow it to form.

But perhaps you don't plan to store any truffles at all — perhaps you're actually going to *give* them away. In Chapter 22, you find ideas about how to package your truffles to present as gifts. You certainly will want to share something as good as these truffles!

Chapter 19

Know How to Mold 'Em

. . . .

In This Chapter

▶ Choosing and using a variety of molds

▶ Making your finished molded candies look pretty

▶ Cleaning and protecting your molds

. . . .

The demand for molded chocolates in my business has grown tremendously in recent years, and I don't foresee that demand decreasing any time soon. Consequently, chocolate molding has become a big part of my candy-making operation. Because of molded chocolate's popularity, I figured you may want to give it a try yourself at home.

Working with molds is a lot of fun, and you can fashion any number of cute or unusual items out of milk, dark, or white chocolate. In this chapter, I cover the use of several types of molds, including solid molds, hollow molds, and shell molds (see Figure 19-1). I also give you advice on how to present your molded treats beautifully and how to clean up your molds so you can use them another day.

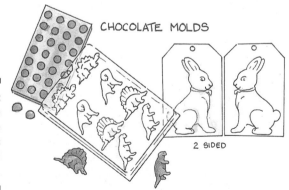

CHOCOLATE MOLDS

Figure 19-1:
Chocolate molds come in various sizes and shapes.

2 SIDED

Putting Different Molds to Great Use

You can mold your chocolate in three basic forms: solid molding, hollow molding, and shell molding. In the following sections, I give you a peek at all three of these forms as well as the variations on these types. I also cover a few guidelines that apply to all molding techniques.

In the beginning: Knowing a few molding basics before you start

To mold your chocolate, you can use metal or plastic molds. In the old days, molds were primarily metal, and some chocolatiers have preserved those molds over the years. Many of these molds are large with amazing details and, with proper care, the molds should last for generations. (I cover the general care and storage of molds later in this chapter.)

But nowadays, you're most likely to find plastic molds, ranging from hobby molds that are 0.30 gauge (30 gauge) to heavy polycarbonate molds that are nearly 1 inch thick with ¾-inch deep cavities (which are the parts you fill with chocolate).

Most candy-supply businesses that sell molds offer *hobby-type molds,* which are thin, pliable molds that aren't intended for long-term use. Hobby-type molds aren't as durable as the more heavy-duty polycarbonate molds that professionals use. (See Chapter 24 to get started with a list of suppliers.) These molds are wonderful for your at-home needs, and with proper care, they should endure quite a few uses.

One aspect of molding that gives you versatility is the range in sizes of the molds. Most recipes in this book produce candies of a fairly small, but molded pieces can be very tiny or quite large. You can produce a single molded piece that's a fraction of an ounce or you can mold a large hollow piece.

If you're interested in making small chocolate pieces, use the 12- to 24-cavity hobby molds that enable you to create little chocolate pieces that are about 1 inch x ¾ inch and about ½ inch deep. If you want to make three-dimensional pieces, you use two-piece molds that are held together by mold clips. Many of these molds are quite large, although you should be able to find some smaller options. When you clip two-piece molds together, they have an open bottom (for easy filling), which are used for solid molding, or they are closed (you usually fill one half before putting the two pieces together), which allows you to make a hollow molded chocolate piece. I tell you how to use all these molds later in this chapter.

When making three-dimensional chocolates with two-piece molds, you need about five to eight mold clips to hold the two halves of the mold together. Clips usually are available in bags of 100, and you can purchase them from the suppliers listed in Chapter 24. Experience will tell you if you need more or fewer clips. For instance, if you note leakage in certain areas, add a clip as needed.

Molding chocolate involves filling molds with chocolate, chilling the molds, and then turning the molds over (or opening two-piece molds) and tapping the molded pieces out of the molds. Before you fill the molds with chocolate, make sure the molds are at room temperature (70 to 75 degrees); if they're too cold, the chocolates won't release well from the molds.

 If you plan to reuse molds several times back to back, keep a hair dryer handy to warm the molds slightly and bring them back to room temperature. Just blow the warm air over the molds.

After you pour your tempered chocolate into the mold (see Chapter 14 for more on tempering), you clip your mold together and place it in the refrigerator so the chocolate sets. Chilling the molds causes the chocolate to shrink slightly and easily release from the mold. When you're ready to release the chocolate from the mold, take off the mold clips, and tap the chocolate piece out of the mold.

 Before you start molding your chocolate, I recommend purchasing inexpensive white cotton gloves because they keep you from transferring moisture from your fingertips and your fingerprints to the finished chocolate. The less you handle chocolate, the better the chance you won't have a melting problem — chocolate melts at about 98 degrees or lower. These gloves are usually available from bakery suppliers or see the suppliers I list in Chapter 24.

From beans to bars: Creating a chocolate bar

Virtually all the chocolate that small candy shops use has already been molded long before it ever arrived at those shops. Most candy makers — the ones who don't buy chocolate by the tanker truckload — get their chocolate in 10-pound bars, and the manufacturers molded that chocolate into bars at the very end of the chocolate-making process.

If you ever get a chance to visit a chocolate factory, you get to see this chocolate-bar molding process — where almost every step is mechanized and computerized. The process begins by dumping cacao beans into the machines. From there, everything is a blur of activity that includes roasting, shelling, pressing, and mixing the beans before they become chocolate. At the end of the production line, what were once little beans become 10-pound chocolate bars, chocolate drops, or liquid chocolate. And you use all three of these forms to produce candies — including molded chocolates.

So determine what you want to mold and the type of mold you need, and make your purchases. You may have a lot of fun and get a lot of smiles making chocolates for the kids (and for the adults, too)!

Filled to the brim: Solid molding

A solid-molded candy is about twice as heavy as the same-size hollow piece. Whereas you fill half a hollow mold with chocolate, you completely fill the solid molds with chocolate. (See "Empty on the inside: Hollow molding" later in this chapter for details on hollow molding.) Solid molding involves two different types of molds: flat molds and three-dimensional molds. Check out the following sections for the scoop on each type.

Flat molding

One type of solid molding is the *flat mold,* which consists of a cavity pressed into plastic that contains the details of the mold. In a finished chocolate, one side is the impression of the mold in all its detail, and the back of the candy is flat. This type of mold doesn't usually have a lot of fine detail, but you can produce some cute pieces nonetheless. People frequently use this mold to make chocolate lollipops, but plenty of other molds fall into this category, too.

Lollipop molds usually have three to six cavities. When filled, each cavity produces a 1-ounce piece of chocolate. A 1-ounce lollipop is about as small as you will find in these molds, but you can often find multicavity molds that produce little pieces that weigh only about 0.2 ounce, which is a piece about 1 inch x ¾ inch and ½ inch deep. In this chapter, I reference the 1-ounce chocolate lollipop, but the process is the same for other flat molds with one exception: Lollipop molds include a slot for the sucker stick.

To use flat molds (as shown in Figure 19-2):

1. **Lay the molds flat on the counter and temper your chocolate using one of the methods I describe in Chapter 14.** (Molding recipes specify how much chocolate you need; for instance, if you're making 30 1-ounce lollipops, you need about 2 pounds of tempered chocolate.)

2. **Spoon the chocolate into the mold cavities until it's level with the top of the cavity.** (If you're very neat and careful, you can pour the chocolate directly into the molds.) As you fill each cavity mold, tap the molds lightly on the counter to flatten the chocolate and to knock out air bubbles.

   For chocolate lollipops, insert a candy stick into the stick channel. When you insert each stick, give the stick a little twist to coat it with chocolate and angle the stick slightly downward into the body of the mold. Leave enough of the stick extended from the chocolate for a handle to hold the sucker. If you insert the stick straight into the chocolate, the stick doesn't embed deeply enough into the chocolate and may release from the chocolate when you remove it from the mold.

3. **Place the mold into the refrigerator to cool.** Leave the mold in the refrigerator for about 25 to 30 minutes.

4. **Remove the mold from the refrigerator and lift the suckers out of the molds.** At that time, the chocolates should release easily from the molds. If they don't, put them back in the refrigerator to chill for 5 minutes. For nonlollipop items, turn the mold over and tap lightly, and the chocolates should release and fall onto the wax paper.

When allowing time for chocolates to set up, remember that solid chocolates require more cooling time than filled chocolates (such as the creams, caramels, and truffles found in Chapters 17, 7, and 18, respectively) because the chocolate in a solid chocolate piece is more dense than in a filled piece.

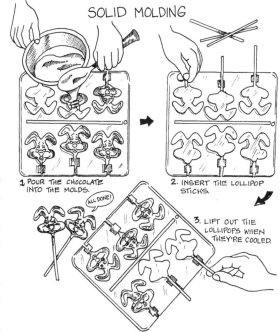

SOLID MOLDING

1. POUR THE CHOCOLATE INTO THE MOLDS.

2. INSERT THE LOLLIPOP STICKS.

3. LIFT OUT THE LOLLIPOPS WHEN THEY'RE COOLED.

(ALL DONE!)

Figure 19-2:
You can use the flat molding method to make yummy chocolate lollipops.

Three-dimensional molding

Another type of solid molding is *three-dimensional molding,* which involves clipping together two halves of a mold and then filling the mold with chocolate. You pour the chocolate into the mold via its open bottom and, when the chocolate is cool, you have a candy with details all around and with no flat side. Three-dimensional molding is similar to hollow molding, except you fill the entire mold with chocolate, and the result is a much heavier piece. (See "Empty on the inside: Hollow molding" later in this chapter for more about hollow molding.)

When making three-dimensional solid molds, the mold has to stand up in the refrigerator while the chocolate is cooling. Companies that sell molds also sell gizmos just for this purpose. But you have another option. Several years ago, I visited a shop that had a very clever way of handling the problem of standing molds up in the refrigerator. The staff's solution was to put small dried beans in plastic containers, deep enough and heavy enough so that the container wouldn't topple. Then they stood the filled mold in the beans with the open end up. You can easily duplicate this technique at home.

Okay, are you ready to make a three-dimensional molded piece? Follow these simple steps:

1. **Lay the molds flat on a counter and temper the chocolate using one of the methods I describe in Chapter 14.** (Molding recipes specify how much chocolate you need; for instance, two molds that are 5 to 6 inches tall require about 1½ to 2 pounds of tempered chocolate.)

2. **For 6-inch tall molds, fill plastic containers that are 3 x 3 inches and 3 inches tall half full with beans.** You can also use plastic containers that are 4 x 4 inches and 4 inches tall. Small plastic plant containers are ideal for this step.

3. **Clip the two halves of the mold together, using as many clips as you need to secure all possible leak points.** Most two-piece molds have points that mesh, so you'll see the best places to put the clips.

4. **With the halves clipped together, spoon the tempered chocolate into the mold, tapping the mold on the counter frequently to remove air bubbles.** You'd be surprised how easily bubbles form as you fill your mold and, sometimes they're difficult to get out, but they're easy to see.

5. **After you fill the mold and tap out as many bubbles as possible, stand the mold in a container of beans and put the mold in the refrigerator for at least 30 minutes.** Exact cooling times vary, but 30 minutes is a good rule of thumb for a mold that's 5 to 6 inches tall.

6. **Take the mold out of the refrigerator, remove the clips, and carefully remove the mold halves by taking off the clips; then lift one half of the mold off.** Next, turn the mold over and let the chocolate release into your hand. You should have a beautiful three-dimensional piece. If the mold seems to stick, put it back in the refrigerator for 5 minutes and repeat the process until the mold releases.

The bottom of the chocolate may or may not be flat enough for the mold to stand up. If it won't stand up, you can make a small base using some of the tempered chocolate and stand the finished chocolate piece in the center of the puddle. Brace the piece without melting it while the chocolate base sets. The base takes about 5 minutes to set, but it may be firm enough to release your grip before that.

Empty on the inside: Hollow molding

The primary visual difference between two-piece solid and two-piece hollow molds is pretty simple: The two-piece solid mold is open at the bottom, and the two-piece hollow mold is closed. When you join the two halves of a two-piece solid mold, you see a large opening at the bottom, which allows you to fill the mold with chocolate. Because the hollow mold doesn't have that opening when you join the two halves, the mold doesn't leak chocolate when you rotate it.

You can produce hollow molded chocolates in one of two ways:

- ✔ Clip together two halves of one mold and pour some chocolate inside. As the chocolate cools, you rotate the mold so that the chocolate fully coats the inside of the mold.

- ✔ You make two hollow halves with chocolate and fuse them together.

With either hollow-molding method, you may have to do a little trimming around the seams because buildup occasionally occurs there. For trimming, you need a sharp knife to carefully and quickly carve off any buildup. You shouldn't have to remove much excess. Hold the mold in your hand (with a cotton glove, if possible), and carve around the seam with the knife.

I prefer using the first method because of the relative ease of production. I've seen candy makers use the second method and achieve virtual perfection, and the effect is astounding. But the person I saw doing that masterful work was a virtuoso in the field, and he was set up to produce molds that way.

Molding by filling one half of the mold

For this method, you don't need any special tools beyond mold clips, which you can get from a mold supplier. You will need four to five metal clips for a 4- to 6-inch size mold and more if the mold is very large. Just be sure that you have enough clips to hold all the key points of the mold together; your eyes will tell you where you need to add clips. Before starting, also be sure that you have two halves of the mold that you want to make.

Just follow these directions to make a hollow chocolate by filling half of a mold (see Figure 19-3):

1. **Temper about 8 ounces of chocolate for a 6-inch high mold.** To temper your chocolate, use one of the methods I describe in Chapter 14.

2. **Fill half of the mold with chocolate.** You want to use enough chocolate to apply a nice coat to the inside of the mold when you rotate the assembled mold. The chocolate from the filled side will create the hollow shell. Place the other half of the mold on top of the filled half and clip the two halves together, as needed, to secure the two halves.

3. **Turn the mold over and allow the chocolate to completely fill the other half of the mold.** Let that set for about 30 seconds and then shake the mold to move the chocolate around inside. This step coats the inside of the two halves, but the contents, in terms of chocolate, are only half the volume of the mold.

4. **Place the mold in the refrigerator, laying the mold on the side you originally did not fill, for 5 minutes.** After 5 minutes, rotate the mold to the other side and let it set for 5 minutes. Repeat on each side for another 5 minutes per side and remove the mold from the refrigerator.

5. **Remove the clips and remove the plastic molds from the chocolate.** Hold the mold in one hand and lift one mold half off. Then turn the mold over, and the chocolate should release from the other mold half and fall into your hand. If you've done everything correctly, you will have a beautiful hollow chocolate.

Because most inexpensive molds aren't crafted to the highest standards, you usually get some buildup along the seam, but you can remove it with a sharp knife.

FILLING A HOLLOW MOLD

1. FILL ONE HALF OF A HOLLOW MOLD WITH CHOCOLATE.

2. CLIP THE OTHER HALF ON TOP. BE SURE THE BOTTOM OF THE MOLD IS CLOSED!

3. TURN THE MOLD OVER TO COMPLETELY COAT BOTH HALVES.

4. AFTER ROTATING AND LETTING THE MOLD SET IN THE FRIDGE, UNCLIP THE HALVES AND REMOVE THE CHOCOLATE CANDY.

Figure 19-3: You can simply fill one half of a mold to make a hollow chocolate.

Molding and joining two halves

The process of making two halves and putting them together requires a bit of handling and fusing the two pieces to form a two-dimensional piece. When you purchase a mold for this type of molding, you usually have two pieces: a front and a back of whatever you're molding.

Once you feel comfortable making hollow molds using the previous method, you may want to try your hand at making two halves and putting them together to form a hollow mold. To join the two molded halves, I recommend having two halves of a paired mold that's about 6 inches tall, a sheetrock trowel to scrape, and a 12-inch disposable piping bag. When you're ready to go, follow these instructions:

1. **Temper about 8 ounces of chocolate using one of the methods I describe in Chapter 14 and spoon it into half of the mold.** Fill the half completely, and allow the chocolate to completely coat the inside of the mold. Then tap the mold on the counter lightly to remove air bubbles. Be sure to get a good coating.

2. **Pour the chocolate out of the mold; a lining of chocolate will cling to the plastic.** Scrape the flat side of the mold to clean the excess chocolate from the mold and place in the refrigerator. Allow the chocolate to set for 10 to 15 minutes. Repeat this process with the other half of the mold. The thickness of the coating may vary, but you will learn after doing this process once or twice.

3. **Remove the molds from the refrigerator.** To connect the halves, apply a thin line of tempered chocolate along the edge of one molded half with the half still in the mold. You can apply this thin line of chocolate using a small parchment piping bag.

4. **Carefully attach the other molded half to the piece with the wet chocolate seal, being sure to align the pieces well**. Place a couple of clips on the mold to hold the halves in place. Return the mold to the refrigerator for 5 minutes.

5. **Take the mold out of the refrigerator, and remove the chocolate piece from the mold.** Carefully place the chocolate on a piece of wax paper and examine the seam for flaws. If you note any unsightly buildup on the seam, hold the molded piece in your gloved hand and trim off the excess with a sharp knife.

To add some fun to this type of molding, you can make a couple of dozen small solid molded pieces in advance. Place a few of these pieces inside the hollow mold before you seal it. This additional step provides a hidden treasure for the child (or adult) who enjoys the larger molded chocolate.

Truffle time: Shell molding

Shell molding has really come into vogue in recent years, and I have seen tremendous growth in my own business in this type of molding. In *shell molding,* you fill chocolate shells, usually with *ganache* (a very rich truffle center made with cream and chocolate; see Chapter 18). With shell molding, the chocolatier can add detail to a small piece of chocolate, so you can make pieces that look as professional as many of the expensive chocolates you find in the finest chocolate shops. Shell molding is also an excellent way to use softer, more liquid centers, such as caramel, which allows you to make a molded chocolate piece with a delicious caramel center.

Molds for shell molding are usually plastic molds with 18 to 24 cavities, although other cavity counts are available. The best shell molds are from Europe, quite often from Belgium, and are heavy polycarbonate molds that are about 1 inch thick. Such molds are commercial grade and are identical to the molds that professionals use. Finding these molds at a bakery-supply company may not be easy; you can find some of these molds at the suppliers listed in Chapter 24. But you don't have to have the $20 to $25 molds to make shells. In fact, you're more likely to find smaller, flat molds, and these are suitable for at-home candy making.

Before you attempt shell molding, check out Chapter 14 about tempering chocolate and Chapter 18 about producing truffle centers and piping. After you've absorbed that knowledge, this type of molding will be a lot of fun for you. All you need are some molds and a scraper. (See Figure 19-4 for additional details on the shell-molding process.)

Another reason for you to like shell molding is that you don't have to make the truffle centers when you make the shells; you make the shells and leave them in the molds until you need them. But you do need a place to store the shells at room temperature until you need them. Preferably, you will have an area that isn't too warm, such as a baker's rack in the coolest part of the kitchen. If you need to store the shells for an extended period, cover them with wax paper to keep dust out. Remember, you can keep chocolate for months at room temperature.

To make molded shells filled with ganache, follow these steps:

1. **Temper the chocolate using one of the methods I describe in Chapter 14.** About 1½ pounds of chocolate should be enough to fill three 24-cavity molds that are about 1 inch in diameter. (Truffle recipes specify the amount of tempered chocolate to use, of course.)

2. **Lay out a couple of feet of wax paper and, using a spoon, completely fill all the cavities of one mold and scrape the excess chocolate off with the scraper.** You may put the excess chocolate back into the bowl. Tap the mold on the counter to knock out as many air bubbles as possible. Don't worry — you'll always have a few bubbles left.

3. **Turn the mold upside down over the bowl of tempered chocolate and pour the chocolate back into the bowl.** Scrape the flat back of the mold with a wide scraper like a sheetrock trowel to remove the excess chocolate. Because of the viscosity, the chocolate leaves a coating on the

inside of the molds. Hold the mold up and, as the light comes through the chocolate, examine the bottom to see whether you can detect any bubbles. If you see bubbles, tap them out gently, and place the mold in the refrigerator for about 10 minutes. Remove the mold from the refrigerator and store the shells until needed.

4. **When you're ready to fill the shells, make the ganache as the recipes in Chapter 18 describe.** Fill the shells using the piping method I explain in Chapter 18. When you pipe the truffle center into the shells, leave about ⅛ inch at the top of the shell and put the mold in the refrigerator for about 5 minutes to allow the center to set.

   When piping truffle centers into shells, be sure to fill all the space from the bottom of the mold up because leaving space promotes the formation of condensation, which breeds bacteria.

5. **Remove the mold from the refrigerator and use a spoon to fill the cavities with tempered chocolate until the chocolate is level with the top of the mold.** Doing so puts the back on the piece.

6. **Scrape the back of the mold smooth using the sheetrock scraper.** Be sure that the back is as clean as possible and put the mold back in the refrigerator for about 6 minutes.

7. **Remove the mold from the refrigerator and tap the truffles out of the mold by tapping the mold upside down on wax paper.** You now have shell-molded truffles.

FILLING SHELL MOLDS

1. FILL THE MOLDS WITH CHOCOLATE.
2. POUR THE CHOCOLATE OUT OF THE MOLDS.
3. SCRAPE THE MOLDS CLEAN.
4. PIPE THE CENTERS INTO THE MOLDS.
5. SEAL THE MOLD WITH CHOCOLATE.
6. 'TAP' THE CANDIES OUT!

Figure 19-4: Shell molding is often used in making truffles.

Dressing Up Finished Molded Candies

You don't have to do a lot to give a piece of homemade chocolate gift appeal. When making molded pieces, you're making chocolate that already has visual appeal, so just a little flash completes the picture.

I don't assume that you'll make a gift of everything you make but, once you become an accomplished candy maker, you're going to want to give chocolate presents to the people you adore.

The process of making your candy presentable begins from the moment you start making the candy. I always stress to my chocolatiers and candy makers the importance of making each tray of candy look appetizing. Often, the public never sees these trays in their original form but, I believe that if you start out paying attention to little details, you will carry that mindset through to the final product.

Fortunately, the materials you need to dress up your candies to give them that chocolate-shop appearance are available from suppliers (see Chapter 24 for a handy list). Take a look at what you can do with some of your molded pieces, and be sure to flip to Chapter 22 for additional info on gift packaging.

Choosing paper cups

If you've ever bought chocolate at a fancy chocolate shop or have purchased a box of chocolates, the chocolates were probably cupped in brown or white paper cups. Well, you can dress up your homemade molded chocolates with paper cups, too.

The paper cups you need for your molded chocolates are available from bakery and candy suppliers in sleeves of 100 or a few hundred. When you make a small batch of chocolates, you will often produce more than 50 pieces, so you want to keep plenty of the little cups on hand.

Candy cups come in many sizes, but the two sizes you need to concern yourself with are the #4 (about 1 inch wide at the base) and #6 (about 1¼ inches wide at the base) sizes. If your supplier uses a different numbering system for cups, the supplier will usually know which cups you mean when you describe what you want. Additionally, the most common cup colors are brown and white, although you can also find seasonal cups for most holidays. I recommend having both colors on hand in at least the #6 size because those cups are the most commonly used.

When you make small molded pieces, you want to cup them in a brown #6 cup. When you take your molded chocolates out of the refrigerator, wet (very lightly) a paper towel or dishcloth, and lightly dampen your fingertip (unless you have naturally sticky fingers). Separate the cups and spread them on the counter. Place a chocolate in each cup, and store the chocolates in a plastic container for as long as you want.

Using foil wraps

As attractive and yummy as your pieces of freshly molded chocolate look, you can do a few more things to enhance their appearance. One of those decorative ideas is to wrap the individual pieces in foil.

Wrapping your molded chocolates in foil gives the piece a very classy appearance. When you produce an assorted box of your molded chocolates, a few pieces wrapped in gold, red, or another color of foil gives tremendous eye appeal to the box. And if you're making chocolates for a holiday, wrapping them in seasonal foils adds a lot to the festive appearance. Because decorative foils are available in virtually every conceivable color and seasonal idea, only your imagination limits you.

Foil squares usually come in bundles of 500, and they really aren't very expensive; they usually cost less than a penny each for small foils. I recommend buying foils that are about 3½ inches square (small) to 5 inches square (fairly large). You may find larger squares, but I don't think you would want much smaller squares because they might not fit most normal-size chocolates.

Wrapping your molded chocolates is pretty simple:

1. **Lay a piece of foil on the counter with the colored side down.**

2. **Place the piece of chocolate you want to wrap upside down on the foil and fold the foil over the chocolate, pressing the foil flat.**

3. **Turn the piece over and slide it around on the counter to press the foil, sealing the back of the piece.**

After applying the foil and sealing it, you can highlight the details of the mold by rubbing the top of the piece with a paper towel. Doing so causes the foil to fill in the impressions of the molded piece, and you will be able to see the details clearly through the foil. This trick is especially impressive when the mold includes printing, as many molds do.

Attractively packaging wrapped pieces

After you've prepared your molded chocolates, you may want to give some away as gifts. If that's the case, you want to find just the right box. Quite a few molds come with a box in which to package your candies but, if your mold doesn't come with a box, you can always purchase your own.

If you're unable to buy a box that fits the mold (many suppliers provide boxes that match the molds for easy packing), you can add a few items to the box to accommodate your piece. You can add plastic "grass," for example. Grass comes in colors other than green; in fact, you can get pink, red, and clear grass, to name a few colors. When you have your grass, place it in a box and arrange the larger molded piece in it like an egg in a nest. Using this form of packaging lets you create a gift with items other than candy, making a nice assortment.

Another alternative is to include your chocolate with another gift (that way, you double the impact). For instance, a nice coffee mug filled with foil-wrapped pieces makes a nice gift for any occasion. Or you can get a simple cellophane bag, place your molded chocolates in the bag, and put colorful stickers on the outside and tie a ribbon around the top.

Cleaning and Storing Molds with Care

When you're working with chocolate, you may use one type of mold over and over; you don't need to clean a mold every time you use it, nor is frequent washing particularly good for the molds. When large companies produce massive quantities of molded pieces, such as seasonal pieces, they may not wash the molds until they've completed their seasonal production.

One nice thing about proper chocolate molding is that the chocolate releases completely, so you have no residual chocolate inside the molds. You may have a little buildup on the flat surfaces of the molds, but you can usually scrape it off with a spatula.

Washing thinner plastic molds causes excessive wear on them. If you use them frequently, the plastic will eventually crack, and you will have to dispose of the molds you use most often.

If you want to wash your molds, never use soap because the soap can get into the crevices of the molds. Also, don't use hot water because the molds become cloudy; instead, use tepid water. You can clean your molds with a soft cotton cloth. Most chocolate, after drying, will simply wipe off, and the residues from chocolate, including cocoa butter, are beneficial to the next use.

If you use molds and have plans to use them again within a few days, place them somewhere out of the reach of dust. To store your molds for longer periods of time, put them in large freezer bags at room temperature for as long as you want.

Part V
Having Special Fun with Candy

"Don't blame us! The recipe clearly states, 'Add 4 tablespoons of sugar.'"

In this part...

For all those times you wished you could have made something for your friends at Christmas or for other holidays, well, your opportunity has arrived. In this part, you produce some special holiday pieces that are suitable for giving as gifts to the folks you really adore. (Of course, after you become proficient at making such gifts, you'll be expected to do so every year. But you won't mind such attention!)

Also in this part, your kids get to make some candies using marshmallows, cereal, and other tasty ingredients. Maybe they'll even give some of their finished products to you!

And, to top things off, I show you many inventive ways to present your candies as gorgeous gifts that your friends and family will adore.

Chapter 20

Creating Holiday Magic

- -

In This Chapter

▶ Loving Valentine chocolates

▶ Shaping chocolate Easter eggs and bunnies

▶ Getting into the Christmas spirit with various candies

- -

*E*very holiday has its own traditions, and nearly every holiday involves candy. When you think of Valentine's Day, heart-shaped boxes of chocolate come to mind. Easter, of course, suggests chocolate bunnies and chocolate eggs. And so many confections are associated with Christmas that singling out one or two is difficult, but I cover several ideas that are sure to get you into the holiday spirit.

If you're already in the holiday spirit, I try to keep you going in the right direction with the candies in this chapter. Part of the fun of giving holiday candies is the fun you have making the candies yourself. What better way to express your feelings than to make something special for a loved one?

Putting Your Heart into Valentine's Day Candy

In terms of candy sales, Valentine's Day isn't the biggest candy season, but few occasions are as married to candy — especially chocolates — as Valentine's Day. Pharmacies and chocolate shops start displaying beautiful heart-shaped boxes just about as soon as the confetti settles on New Year's Eve. Everyone seems to enjoy a little (or a lot of) chocolate in February.

If you're interested in making your own special candies for Valentine's Day, look no farther than the following sections. I give you a few creative ideas for yummy chocolates, provide advice on putting together an assortment that your special someone is sure to love, and help you choose the right container for all your delicious lovey-dovey creations.

Checking out different ideas for chocolates

For candy makers, Valentine's Day is a combination of candy, packaging, and marketing. The results are good business for candy makers and many happy recipients of Valentine goodies. But you can make the candies yourself and create your own packaging, giving your loved one a special gift that he or she will cherish.

In this section, I tell you how to make several Valentine specialties. You find a recipe for simple chocolate hearts that you can foil-wrap. For added elegance, I explain how to put an edible detailed transfer onto a chocolate piece or a sheet of chocolate. Finally, I show you how to paint little details into molds that transfer to chocolate, giving your simple pieces a look comparable to that of pieces made in fancy chocolate shops.

When making your Valentine's Day treats, you may need candy molds. A great source for candy molds of all kinds is www.jbprince.com. To find out more about molding techniques, see Chapter 19.

Solid Chocolate-molded Hearts

When cooling chocolates in the refrigerator, remember that solid pieces require more time to set than filled pieces due to the density of the solid chocolate. When you use a refrigerator to cool your chocolate, don't wander off and forget about them because, eventually, condensation occurs, and you don't want that because chocolate and water simply don't mix.

When making solid chocolate-molded hearts, I recommend using cherry oil to flavor the chocolate in the solid molded hearts. This flavor is available from candy and bakery suppliers (see Chapter 24). This recipe also requires the use of a sheetrock scraper, which you can get from a hardware store.

For an extra-nice presentation, wrap each finished chocolate heart in a 3¼ x 3¼-inch heart-print foil. (See "Getting into the Spirit with Christmas Candies" later in this chapter for more about decorative foils.)

Tools: *3 12-cavity heart molds with cavities approximately 1 x 1 inch and ⅔ to ¾-inch deep, plus a sheetrock scraper*

Preparation time: *1 hour and 15 minutes*

Yield: *36 pieces*

1 pound milk chocolate, chopped and melted for tempering   *1½ teaspoons cherry-oil flavor*

1 Temper 1 pound of milk chocolate using one of the methods I describe in Chapter 14; stir in the cherry oil with a hard rubber spatula.

2 Deposit the chocolate into the heart molds, tapping the molds as you fill them to remove air bubbles.

3 When you've filled each 12-piece mold, place the candy in the refrigerator to cool for 30 minutes.

4 When the molds have cooled, turn them over (with the chocolate side down) and tap them on the counter to knock out the chocolate pieces. Because the cold shrinks the chocolates, they should release easily from the mold. If the chocolates are hesitant to release, put the mold back in the cooler for 5 minutes.

Vary It! *You can try champagne flavoring, amaretto flavoring, or hazelnut flavoring in place of the cherry flavoring; oil flavors are available in small quantities from the suppliers listed in Chapter 24.*

Per serving: *Calories 64 (From Fat 34); Fat 4g (Saturated 2g); Cholesterol 0mg; Sodium 9mg; Carbohydrate 8g (Dietary Fiber 0g); Protein 1g.*

Something you see in candy shops are chocolate pieces with ornate designs that obviously weren't hand-painted on the chocolate. You may find yourself asking, "How'd they do that?" The answer? Edible transfer sheets.

Edible transfer sheets are usually made of cocoa butter and food coloring, and the effect they create on your hand-dipped chocolates is quite a nice touch. Nowadays candy makers can buy edible transfers in a wide variety of designs, colors, and sizes. These designs come in generic patterns and, of course, many seasonal designs. In my shops, I use a custom transfer — one that represents my logo. But you can find a variety of stock designs (including Valentine's Day themes) that you can use at home. You can find transfers at bakery-supply houses, and two good Internet sources are www.beryls.com and www.fancyflours.com. (For a list of additional candy-making suppliers, check out Chapter 24.) Depending on where you buy the transfers, they may cost from a little less than $2 to $7 a sheet.

Transfer sheets usually come in two sizes: 10 x 11 inches and 10 x 16 inches. A repeating design typically covers the sheets, so when you deposit a piece of wet chocolate on it, a random portion of the pattern transfers to the chocolate when it dries (see Figure 20-1). You may have a little wasted space between the chocolates, but careful placement produces a nice transfer to 40 to 50 pieces.

To add the edible transfers to your hand-dipped chocolates, simply:

1. **Place your hand-dipped chocolates on the sheets and let the transfer adhere to the chocolate.**

2. **Cool the chocolates in the refrigerator for about 15 to 20 minutes.**

3. **After the pieces cool, lift the piece off the sheet, and the transfer is on the bottom.** Turn the piece over, put it into a paper candy cup, and you have a beautiful piece with little effort.

Figure 20-1:
Edible transfers make a great impression on your hand-dipped chocolates.

Another method you can use with transfer sheets is to pipe the chocolate (see Chapter 18 to find out how to pipe properly). If you pipe the chocolate in discs onto the sheets, you have thin pieces to attach to the tops of other chocolates, which creates quite an effect.

Chocolate Discs with Edible Transfers

This recipe illustrates how to make small chocolate discs to place on a chocolate piece. Adding decorated discs adds some pizzazz to any candy.

Tools: *2 10 x 16-inch transfer sheets featuring Valentine designs, 12-inch disposable piping bag* **Preparation time:** *1 hour*

Yield: *80 to 90 pieces*

8 ounces milk chocolate, chopped and melted for tempering	*80 to 90 pieces dipped chocolates with fairly flat tops (caramels, fruit jellies, and meltaways are good candidates)*

1 Temper chocolate using one of the methods I describe in Chapter 14 and fill a small piping bag with the chocolate.

2 Lay several transfer sheets on the counter (be sure that the side with the design faces up — it's a little rougher than the wrong side) and cut a tiny hole in the end of the piping bag.

3 As neatly as possible — without dripping lines — make nickel-size circles (remember the chocolate will spread) as close to one another as possible without touching. Repeat this process until you have as many pieces as you wish.

4 To cool the discs, place them in the refrigerator for about 15 minutes. Then remove the sheets from the refrigerator and lift the discs off the sheets.

5 Apply a drop of tempered chocolate to the top of a flat-topped chocolate and carefully place a disc on top with the design facing up. Allow the piece to set at room temperature for 10 minutes.

Vary It! *You can spread chocolate bark (see the recipe in Chapter 16) over an entire transfer sheet. When you break or cut the bark, the design is on one side of the bark.*

Per serving: *Calories 83 (From Fat 46); Fat 5g (Saturated 3g); Cholesterol 0mg; Sodium 11mg; Carbohydrate 10g (Dietary Fiber 0g); Protein 1g.*

Another chocolate idea that takes a little practice but produces a really interesting effect is painting the inside of molds, especially bite-size piece molds with a thin veneer of color. The "paint" is made up of melted white chocolate mixed with the food coloring of your choice. You can paint with a brush or drop a couple of drops of color inside a mold and rub it with your fingertip to leave a very thin, translucent coating. This effect is more easily created if the "paint" is thinner because you want a thin veneer, not thick color. After you do this technique a few times, you get the hang of it. (See Figure 20-2 for details.)

Figure 20-2:
You can use
the colors of
your choice
to create
detailed
chocolate
candies.

PAINTING DETAILS ONTO MOLDS

1. PAINT DIFFERENT COLORS ONTO YOUR MOLDS.

2. THE FINISHED PRODUCTS HAVE COLORFUL DETAILS!

When you fill the mold with chocolate later, the chocolate picks up the details, which makes the molded piece appear as though you've painted it.

You can create an assortment of chocolate pieces with an assortment of colors on top, and you won't spend a fortune doing it. Fine chocolate shops charge a lot for this effect, and you can do it yourself. Practice this technique a few times with the following recipe, and you'll amaze your friends with your artistic chocolates.

St. Valentine: The man behind the holiday

As you make your Valentine's chocolates and concern yourself with packaging and such, take a few moments to ponder how this celebration came about. Valentine's Day takes its name from St. Valentine, or Valentinus, a priest in Rome who, in fact, was put to death on February 14, 269 A.D. (Stay with me — the story gets more romantic. I promise.)

So we know where the name originated, but how about the rest? February 14 had been the traditional day for a lottery in ancient Rome, during which Roman men drew the names of young ladies, whom they were matched up with for at least the length of the festival. In many cases, the couple was matched up for the entire year or longer. I can't imagine how a tradition like that ever went away. . . . Anyway, February 15 was the date that the Romans celebrated Lupercalia, to honor Juno, the goddess and protector of women who was concerned with their sexual activity. (I told you it got more romantic.)

All this stuff was going on during the reign of the cruel emperor Claudius II. Now, although mating lotteries were traditional, Claudius banned marriage because he felt married men would be reluctant to leave their families to fight his many wars.

St. Valentine defied Claudius and continued to perform marriages so, of course, he encountered the wrath of the antiromantic villain Claudius II. Claudius II sentenced St. Valentine to death, and the execution occurred on February 14. The Romans, not willing to give up their celebrating, decided to tie Valentine's martyrdom to their ongoing celebration, and February 14 became a holiday of sorts. The rest of the traditions simply grew over the years.

So when you enjoy your Valentine's chocolates, think kindly about St. Valentine, the ultimate romantic hero, who was simply unwilling to give up on marriage. At least, so goes the legend.

Painted Chocolates

Try this recipe, which creates painted cupids, to make a beautiful impression on Valentine's Day.

Tools: *6 4-cavity cupid molds with each cavity about 1½ inch x 1 inch and ½-inch deep, small paintbrushes for detail painting, and small bowls to contain the "paints"*

Preparation time: *45 to 60 minutes*

Yield: *24 chocolates*

4 ounces white chocolate, chopped

¼ teaspoon each of powdered food coloring in desired colors

½ teaspoon vegetable oil

1 pound milk chocolate, chopped and melted for tempering

1 Melt 2 ounces of the white chocolate in a small microwave-safe bowl on high for 45 seconds; then stop and stir. Melt another 20 to 30 seconds until it reaches 94 degrees on a chocolate thermometer.

2 Add powdered food coloring to the chocolate to create the color you want. Ideally, melting a little cocoa butter with the coating creates a nice paint texture and thins the "paint," but you can add a few drops of vegetable oil to get a similar effect. Use a heating pad to keep the "paint" at a temperature of about 94 degrees, but use it for only 2 minutes at a time. Continued use can cause the white chocolate to become warmer than 94 degrees. Keep a chocolate thermometer handy to check temperature.

3 Decide what you want to paint. If you want to paint a variety of molds with different colors, determine all the parts that have the same color on the different molds and carefully paint those parts in the one color.

4 Temper the milk chocolate using one of the methods I describe in Chapter 14, and fill the mold cavities with the chocolate. Tap the mold as you fill it to remove air bubbles.

5 Place the molded chocolates in the refrigerator for 30 minutes to cool.

6 Remove them from the refrigerator, turn the mold over with the chocolate side down, and tap the chocolates out of the mold by tapping on the counter or lightly twisting the mold to release chocolates.

Per serving: *Calories 121 (From Fat 63); Fat 7g (Saturated 4g); Cholesterol 2mg; Sodium 18mg; Carbohydrate 15g (Dietary Fiber 0g); Protein 2g.*

You can store chocolate for a year or more if you control ambient temperature and humidity (68 to 70 degrees and 42 percent or lower humidity are good areas). The molded chocolate should have a long shelf life, just like the original chocolate, as long as you aren't adding perishable centers to the chocolate.

Selecting special pieces and finding a beautiful box for your valentine

If you're interested in putting together your own beautiful gift box for Valentine's Day, you can do so using the recipes in this chapter and some of the other ideas in this book. For instance, you can take a few of the candies from the previous section and add chocolate caramels from Chapter 7; clusters from Chapter 16; creams from Chapter 17; and, of course, a handful of beautiful truffles from Chapter 18. Before you know it, you have an assortment of chocolates. If that doesn't do the trick for your valentine, be very surprised.

Your goal should be to take a couple of ideas at a time and put together small gifts, keeping the favorite candies of your loved one (whether they're chocolates or something else) in mind. Frankly, your loved one will appreciate it. If you find yourself doing a few of these things, you're well on your way to creating a splendid gift box.

You can find Valentine boxes at some bakery suppliers or candy suppliers (see Chapter 24 for a listing of several great suppliers). You may have to shop around a little to find just the right heart box, but you can also be creative with your packaging. No law says that your box has to be a heart-shaped box.

Another option is to find a box and decorate it yourself using your imagination. You can use red stick-on hearts and cupids, among other items, to get your Valentine point across. You put this together, and your loved one will never want a "store-bought" box again. For more gift-giving ideas, check out Chapter 22.

Crafting Easter Bunnies and Eggs

History states that Germany introduced the rabbit to Easter in the 1500s, and folks seem to have been making chocolate bunnies ever since. Well, actually, the chocolate bunny came along much later, but the whole bunny theme is based on the fertility of the rabbit.

The egg has been a symbol of life since ancient times and existed in many cultures, including the Chinese and Greek cultures. Early Christians tied the egg to the resurrection of Christ, and the Easter egg eventually came into being; people gave colored eggs as gifts during the Middle Ages.

However the symbols worked their ways into the holiday, today companies produce millions of chocolate bunnies and Easter eggs annually. You may as well become part of the tradition with the recipes in the following sections.

Molding chocolate bunnies

Few pieces of chocolate are more fun to eat than a chocolate bunny. In this section, I give you two options for making chocolate bunnies: solid molding and hollow molding. I cover both methods in detail in Chapter 19. (And yes, I know that everyone eats the ears first.)

Although three-dimensional solid and hollow molds come in two pieces (usually a front and a back), solid molds have an open bottom, and hollow molds have a closed bottom. For making solid pieces, you clamp the open-bottom mold halves together and fill the mold through the bottom opening. With this type of mold, you keep the mold upright and refrigerate it until the chocolate sets. When making hollow pieces, you have two pieces of a mold that fit together to form one closed plastic shell. You simply fill one of the shell halves, clamp the halves together, and then roll the closed mold around to coat the entire inside of the plastic shell. Then you chill the chocolate-filled mold and rotate it in the refrigerator to set the chocolate. When you remove the shell, you have a beautiful hollow chocolate bunny.

Solid Chocolate-molded Bunnies

When you use two-piece solid molds, as I discuss here, the molds use metal clamps. Keep these clamps out of the chocolate, and always know how many clamps you have because they don't add anything beneficial to the chocolate!

Tools: *2 pounds of very small, dried beans, 2 3- to 4-inch deep plastic containers to hold the beans; 2 2-piece open-bottom bunny molds that are 5 inches in length*

Preparation time: *1 hour and 15 minutes*

Yield: *2 solid bunnies*

1½ pounds milk chocolate, chopped and melted for tempering

1 Pour enough dried beans into the plastic containers to allow the molds to stand up and cool. Place each mold in a container, wedging the mold into the beans so that it remains level in the beans. Clamp the two pieces of the molds together, using as many clips as necessary to prevent leaking from the sides. Place the molds with the open ends up.

2 Temper the milk chocolate using one of the methods I describe in Chapter 14.

3 Using a spoon, fill the molds from the bottom, tapping as you fill them to remove air bubbles. Fill the mold completely; each mold should hold about ½ pound of chocolate. When the container is full, place the mold in the refrigerator for about 30 minutes to cool.

4 When the molds are cool, remove the clamps, and remove the two molds, which leaves a solid chocolate bunny. You probably will need to trim some excess around the seam, which is where the molds joined. Use a sharp knife to trim, and work quickly. When holding the chocolate to trim, you may want to wear white cotton gloves to prevent fingerprints and moisture from your skin from getting on your bunny.

Vary It! *You can use either white chocolate or dark chocolate in place of the milk chocolate.*

Per serving: *Calories 1,680 (From Fat 864); Fat 96g (Saturated 48g); Cholesterol 0mg; Sodium 240mg; Carbohydrate 216g (Dietary Fiber 0g); Protein 24g.*

In the following recipe, I describe an easy method of hollow molding. The method involves two halves of a mold clamped together with some chocolate inside. By rotating the mold as the chocolate cools, the chocolate coats the inside of the mold.

Hollow Chocolate-molded Bunnies

Hollow chocolates are fun to make and eat. When you learn to make these molded pieces, you're creating a chocolate delight that snaps when you bite it, and eating this piece is easy because the chocolate is more delicate than a heavier solid rabbit. Plus a hollow-molded bunny weighs about half as much as a solid-molded bunny because you use half as much chocolate.

Tools: *4 2-piece plastic bunny molds that are 5 inches in length with a closed bottom and clips*

Preparation time: *1 hour and 15 minutes*

Yield: *4 4½-ounce bunnies*

1½ pounds milk chocolate, chopped and
melted for tempering

1 Temper the milk chocolate using one of the methods I describe in Chapter 14.

2 Using a spoon, fill one side of a mold pair just short of full with tempered milk chocolate; attach the other half to the filled mold with the clips, being sure that the mold doesn't leak from the sides. Rotate the mold in your hands several times so that the chocolate flows from side to side inside the mold, coating the entire inside.

3 Place the mold in the refrigerator on the side you originally didn't fill (because the other side already was exposed to the chocolate). Five minutes later, rotate the mold to the other side to allow the entire mold to become coated with chocolate. Rotate twice more at 5-minute intervals. The hollow mold should be cool and set within 20 minutes.

4 Remove the mold from the refrigerator and remove the clips. Take the two mold pieces off your bunny.

Vary It! *You can mold using white chocolate or dark chocolate — just follow the same procedure.*

Per serving: *Calories 840 (From Fat 432); Fat 48g (Saturated 24g); Cholesterol 0mg; Sodium 120mg; Carbohydrate 108g (Dietary Fiber 0g); Protein 12g.*

You can put finished chocolate bunnies in plastic bags and tie them at the top with a colorful ribbon to give them a festive look. (See Chapter 22 for more ideas on how to give away your candies as gifts.)

One nice thing about chocolate is that when it's properly stored (in an airtight plastic container or in an airtight bag), you can keep it for a year. I don't know why you would need to, but just know that chocolate keeps very well at room temperature and low humidity.

Making an egg-cellent treat

Hand-shaping chocolate-covered eggs with cream centers can be a simple proposition, and you don't have to make the centers if you don't want. Plenty of manufacturers sell already-made centers, so you can buy your centers if you want. (See Chapter 24 for a list of several suppliers.) These centers are very good, and some candy-shop owners who don't want to take the time or don't feel that they have the time buy these premade centers. One advantage to buying premade centers is that you can get small amounts of a good variety of flavors, depending on where you find them. Of course, you also can use one of the cream recipes from Chapter 17 to make your own small batches of centers. The choice is up to you.

All that the following recipe involves is rolling your centers between your palms until the centers form ovals (see Figure 20-3), hand-dipping them in tempered chocolate, and decorating them with colored white chocolate in any way you like. For handy tips on hand-dipping candies, check out Chapter 15.

HAND-SHAPING 'EGGS'

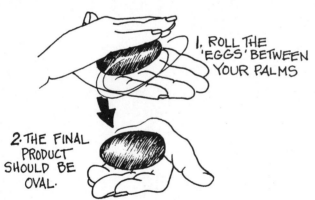

1. ROLL THE 'EGGS' BETWEEN YOUR PALMS

2. THE FINAL PRODUCT SHOULD BE OVAL.

Figure 20-3:
Roll your cream centers by hand before you dip them into the chocolate.

TIP

Take ½ cup of small flavored jellybeans. Roll one jellybean inside each cream when rolling and before you coat the candy with chocolate. This bonus provides a surprise "yolk."

Hand-shaped Eggs

Decorated chocolate Easter eggs are a real treat to folks of all ages, but you need to take good care of the eggs. Decorate the eggs while the coating of milk chocolate is still wet because decorations made from white chocolate tend to separate when applied to a dry chocolate surface.

Tools: *12-inch disposable piping bag*

Preparation time: *1½ hours*

Yield: *60 pieces*

2 pounds cream centers (either store-bought or from the recipe of your choice in Chapter 17)

6 ounces white chocolate, chopped

Powdered food coloring as desired, probably yellow and green

3 pounds milk chocolate, chopped and melted for tempering

1 Spread out a large piece of wax paper and hand-roll the centers into egg-shaped pieces. Simply roll the pieces (about the size of an English walnut) into balls about 1½ inches long and then roll them into slightly oval shapes that resemble eggs. Put the eggs aside and continue rolling until you have about five dozen eggs. The eggs don't have to be exactly the same size.

2 Melt the white chocolate in a microwave-safe bowl to about 95 degrees. This melting should take about 1½ to 2 minutes on high; stop every 45 seconds to stir and keep a chocolate thermometer handy. Blend in the food coloring as desired to make a colored decorating chocolate.

3 Hand-dip the eggs in tempered milk chocolate and coat them completely, shaking off the excess. Place the eggs on wax paper. Spoon the colored white chocolate into a piping bag, cutting as small a hole as possible in the bag that will still allow flow. Decorate the eggs while the chocolate is still wet.

4 Allow the decorated eggs to set at room temperature for 25 to 30 minutes and then store in an airtight container for three weeks.

Vary It! *You can drizzle plain white chocolate on the eggs using only a salad fork. Dip the fork in the white chocolate and shake the fork back and forth over the eggs to create a "string" design.*

Tip: *If you must stack the eggs in storage, place a sheet of wax paper between layers. Handle the eggs carefully, because the decorations are fragile.*

Per serving: Calories 106 (From Fat 38); Fat 4g (Saturated 2g); Cholesterol 2mg; Sodium 11mg; Carbohydrate 18g (Dietary Fiber 0g); Protein 1g.

You can place some of your Easter eggs in chocolate nests, which I tell you how to make in the following recipe. For this recipe, you need a small piece of marble that has been in the freezer, a small piping bag or parchment bag, a few ounces of tempered chocolate, and a small offset spatula.

Making chocolate nests takes a little practice, but you'll get the hang of it. When making your nests, you shape the chocolate strands as closely as possible into the shape of a bird's nest (perfection isn't a necessity) and place your chocolate eggs in and around it. If the nests are a little misshapen, don't worry. Your friends and family will eat them anyway along with your chocolate eggs.

Chocolate Nests

If you have a small piece of marble (you can find small to large scrap pieces at a cabinetmaker's shop because they cut out pieces when making countertops), this item is an easy one to make to amaze your family and friends.

Tools: *10- to 12-inch marble slab that's frozen, 12-inch disposable piping bag or a smaller parchment paper bag*

Preparation time: *35 minutes plus 2 hours for freezing the marble slab*

Yield: *4 nests*

4 to 6 ounces milk chocolate, chopped and
melted for tempering

1 Place the marble slab in the freezer for 2 hours.

2 Temper the milk chocolate using a method described in Chapter 14.

3 Remove the marble from the freezer; it should be very cold. Fill a 12-inch disposable piping bag halfway with tempered chocolate and quickly pipe a thin, continuous string of chocolate on the marble. Drizzle the chocolate back and forth, in circles, or however you like. As you drizzle, the chocolate is shocked to a set by the extreme cold. Using the spatula (because your hands can melt the thin strands), gently scrape the chocolate into nestlike formations (they don't have to be perfect). If you work quickly, you should have no problem building at least four nests from the chocolate.

4 When the nests are set — which takes only a few minutes — place the eggs in a small plate covered with green shredded plastic grass. Place your decorated chocolate eggs in and around the nests and give to your guests. Or place the nests in the refrigerator for 25 to 30 minutes; then remove from the refrigerator and place the eggs.

Tip: *Because of the nests' delicate nature, I recommend keeping them at room temperature and not trying to store them. Instead, make and serve them close together.*

Per serving: Calories 140 (From Fat 72); Fat 8g (Saturated 4g); Cholesterol 0mg; Sodium 20mg; Carbohydrate 18g (Dietary Fiber 0g); Protein 2g.

Getting into the Spirit with Christmas Candies

Christmas is a huge candy occasion in general and a grandiose chocolate holiday in particular. Those folks who do surveys say that Halloween is the biggest candy holiday and that Christmas is the second biggest. Others reverse the two holidays. But whatever the truth is, Christmas is an enormous time for candy production.

Christmas candy leans more toward nicer boxes and all sorts of specialty candies. Elsewhere in this book, you can find some candies that are appropriate for Christmas, such as holiday peppermint bark (see Chapter 16), and scads of fancy chocolates. I touch on a couple of items here that are also specifically for Christmas: Holiday Popcorn, Eggnog Truffles, and Christmas Molded Candies.

Holiday Popcorn

If you're looking for a sweet and simple treat that's easy to make and that provides for a small crowd, try coloring popcorn with seasonal colors. You can pop microwave popcorn or use store-bought popped corn. (Check out Chapter 13 for more details on popcorn production.)

Preparation time: *15 minutes*

Yield: *2 pounds*

½ pound popcorn or pop 3 bags of microwave popcorn according to instructions on bag (about 30 to 34 cups)

12 ounces plus 12 ounces white chocolate

1 teaspoon red powder food coloring as desired

1 teaspoon green powder food coloring as desired

1 Preheat a stainless steel bowl by rinsing it with hot water; dry it thoroughly. Spread out a large sheet of aluminum foil. Separate the popcorn into equal halves, which is about 1 gallon each. Put 1 gallon of the popcorn in the bowl and set the other gallon aside for later use.

2 In the microwave, melt half the white chocolate (12 ounces) in a microwaveable bowl, stopping every 45 seconds or so to stir. Heat the chocolate until it is 95 degrees. Then add red food coloring powder and stir it in to make the white coating slightly red.

3 With one person stirring and one person pouring, pour the melted chocolate over the popcorn, and work the chocolate thoroughly to mix all the popcorn with the coating.

4 Pour the mixture onto aluminum foil and separate the clumps as much as possible.

5 Repeat Steps 2, 3, and 4 with the other half of the corn, but make the coating green. When all the corn is cool (after about 30 minutes), mix the red and green popcorn together and bag it in freezer bags or in decorative bags for seasonally colored popcorn. You can store it in plastic containers for three weeks.

Per serving: Calories 601 (From Fat 257); Fat 29g (Saturated 18g); Cholesterol 30mg; Sodium 92mg; Carbohydrate 72g (Dietary Fiber 5g); Protein 10g.

Eggnog Truffles

Ah, delicious, rich eggnog in a truffle just screams holidays. This piece may be a little soft when dipping time arrives, but you can add a little more white chocolate to the center or make white shells and pipe the centers into the shells. See Chapter 18 for more delicious truffle recipes and technique tips.

Preparation time: *15 minutes*

Yield: *80 pieces*

1 cup eggnog	*1 teaspoon invertase*
1 pound white chocolate, chopped	*1 teaspoon ground nutmeg*
1 teaspoon butter-rum flavoring	*2 pounds white chocolate, melted for coating*

1 Microwave 1 pound of white chocolate in a microwaveable bowl on high for about 2 minutes and 15 seconds, stopping every 30 seconds to stir, until the chocolate reaches 95 degrees on a chocolate thermometer.

2 In a small saucepan, heat the eggnog to scalding (which is about 180 degrees; see Chapter 18 for truffle tips) and remove it from the heat. Let the eggnog cool to 160 degrees on a candy thermometer; then pour the eggnog into the white chocolate and whisk gently from the center until the mixture is smooth (about 30 to 45 seconds).

3 Pour the mixture into a 4- or 5-quart mixing bowl and allow it to cool at room temperature for 3 hours. Add the butter-rum flavoring and run the mixer for 1 minute; stop and add the invertase, and beat for 1 minute more on high speed.

4 Place the mixture in the refrigerator to chill for 30 minutes or let the mixture cool overnight at room temperature.

5 The next day, roll the mixture into 1-inch balls. Then melt 2 pounds of white chocolate in a microwave, stopping every 30 seconds to stir, until it reaches 95 degrees on a chocolate thermometer (melting takes about 2½ to 3 minutes).

6 Coat your truffles in the chocolate, and place them on a sheet of wax paper to cool at room temperature for 30 minutes. As you coat the truffles, sprinkle a little ground nutmeg on top of each piece while the chocolate coating is still wet.

7 Place the truffles in #4 or #6 brown paper cups, and store in a plastic container for two weeks.

Per serving: Calories 70 (From Fat 35); Fat 4g (Saturated 3g); Cholesterol 6mg; Sodium 14mg; Carbohydrate 7g (Dietary Fiber 0g); Protein 1g.

With the recipes in this section and the ones I provide in the rest of the book, you have a variety of candies to choose among for your Christmas boxes and parties. Some of the pieces you make may have beautiful decorations or toppings, so you won't want to cover those with anything. However, the chocolate Santas and trees in the following recipe look wonderful with a colorful foil.

Foils usually come in packs of 500 (see Chapter 24 for suppliers), and you can find foils in almost any color you can imagine plus in seasonal patterns. You can wrap most small pieces in the smallest foils, which are 3½ x 3½ inches. As the pieces get larger, use one of the larger foils to wrap them. I use green foil for trees, red foil for Santas, and whatever else strikes me as appropriate. These foil pieces add a rich appearance to your chocolate assortment, and they're easy to use (see Figure 20-4). To wrap foil around your pieces:

1. **Lay the piece on the foil face down in the center and wrap the foil around the piece to cover.**

2. **When you have the piece covered, turn it over and rub it on the counter to press the flat bottom of the foil-wrapped piece.**

WRAPPING CANDIES IN HOLIDAY FOIL.

Figure 20-4:
You can wrap molded chocolates in foil for a festive holiday treat.

If you're having a holiday party at your house, one of the foil pieces looks very nice as part of a place setting. You can even add a little mint oil (about ¼ teaspoon of mint oil) to 1 pound of dark chocolate and mold the chocolate into a Christmas piece. Then, wrap the piece in foil and use it as a homemade after-dinner mint!

Your friends will think that you're so smart! You can thank me later. (See Chapter 22 for more decorating tips.)

Christmas Molded Candies

Just as the chocolate heart is popular at Valentine's Day and the chocolate bunnies and eggs are at Easter, Christmas is the time of chocolate Santas, chocolate wreaths, trees, reindeer, and more. And you can sprinkle your pieces, such as Christmas trees, with "lights" (sprinkles and other simple-to-make molded pieces that will delight anyone at Christmas). You add an attractive foil wrap, and the simple piece takes on a look of elegance.

Tools: *2 2-cavity flat Santa Claus molds that are 4½ x 2½ inches and 2 1-cavity flat Christmas tree molds that are 4 x 3 inches, both ½ to ¾ inches deep; 6 x 6-inch red foils and 6 x 6-inch green foils (2 each)*

Preparation time: *1 hour and 15 minutes*

Yield: *4 large mold pieces*

1½ pounds milk chocolate, chopped and melted for tempering

1 2-ounce container of assorted jimmies (multicolored sprinkles)

1 Temper the milk chocolate using one of the methods I describe in Chapter 14. First, sprinkle the assorted jimmies on the tree molds, being certain that they cover all the inside of the mold.

2 Drizzle the chocolate in the tree mold to hold the jimmies in place and then fill the molds with tempered chocolate, tapping the molds as you fill them to knock out the air bubbles. Put all the molds in the refrigerator to cool for 30 minutes.

3 When the chocolate has set for 30 minutes, remove the candy from the refrigerator and tap it out of the molds.

4 Wrap each piece in a 6 x 6-inch foil, using red for Santas and green for trees. or cup them in #4 or #6 brown paper cups. You can store these candies in a plastic container for three weeks.

Per serving: Calories 908 (From Fat 458); Fat 51g (Saturated 24g); Cholesterol 0mg; Sodium 122mg; Carbohydrate 118g (Dietary Fiber 0g); Protein 12g.

Additional Christmas-theme ideas include getting Kencraft's Royal Icing decorations and placing them on top of hand-dipped chocolates. These premade decorations are small pieces that you can apply to the top of a piece of candy before it sets. The pieces add a holiday touch for whatever occasion is at hand. These decorations are made with Royal Icing, and you can buy them at specialty stores and bakery-supply shops. The Kencraft Web site is www. KencraftCandy.com.

You can also purchase transfer sheets with Christmas themes and make seasonal pieces by pouring chocolate bark onto the sheets. See "Checking out different ideas for chocolates" earlier in this chapter for more about transfer sheets. To get the complete scoop on barks, see Chapter 16.

Chapter 21

Bring In the Kids

*O*ne of the nice things about most of the recipes in this book is their simplicity, but some of the recipes are so easy that you can let the kids make them. I enjoy the items in this chapter because, as simple as they are, these are some really tasty treats. I can attest to their popularity because my store can't keep most of these delicious treats on the shelves — they're that popular.

Another nice aspect about the recipes in this chapter is that they allow your young ones to make their own snacks. They can produce the items, and you can put them aside for treats to enjoy later. Oh, they may need your guidance here and there and they may need you to oversee the tempering of some chocolate but, otherwise, they'll want you to stay out of the way!

You're a Softie: Extra-easy Marshmallow Treats

Marshmallows combined with chocolate make a surprisingly good treat; add a few nuts to that, and you really have something. In this section, I show you a few concoctions that involve those combinations and more.

Gathering your materials

Planning to make marshmallow treats begins with the marshmallows. To compute your needs, figure that a typical 1-pound bag of large marshmallows contains about 60 marshmallows. All large marshmallows are not the same size, so you may find discrepancies, but 60 marshmallows per pound is a good rule.

To complete the confections in this section, you also need a basic understanding of chocolate tempering, so check out Chapter 14 for details. When tempering chocolate for the recipes in this chapter, you want to temper at least 1 to 1½ pounds of chocolate because the kids (and maybe the adults) are going to want to apply a pretty heavy coating of chocolate.

Another item you need for these recipes are paper lollipop sticks, which serve as your skewers. Depending on which recipe you're making, you need different sizes of sticks. For a treat with two marshmallows, you need the 4½-inch stick. For items with more marshmallows, you need skewers in the 7½-inch to 8-inch range. You can find these skewers at the stores where you find baking and candy supplies. See Chapter 24 for suppliers.

I stress using only the paper sticks here because although wooden and metal sticks are available as well, they're very sharp for the youngsters to use. Besides, you can stick the paper variety into marshmallows quite easily.

Dipping with ease

When you have your ingredients and tools ready, you can start the dipping fun. When you plan to dip an item, such as a long paper skewer with marshmallows, you need enough tempered chocolate to complete the job; you also need to keep in mind the length of the pieces. You may not have enough chocolate to completely submerge the entire skewer, but you can dip the skewer as far as possible into the chocolate and use a teaspoon to spoon the chocolate over the marshmallows to completely cover them. (I cover dipping methods in more detail in Chapter 15.)

When dipping your treats, use a plastic bowl that's about 8 to 10 inches wide. With a little practice, coating your marshmallow lollipops isn't too difficult. You simply lay the skewered marshmallows into the bowl at an angle and spoon the chocolate onto it as needed. Then spin lightly to remove the excess, and decorate as desired .

When dipping, remember to scrape the chocolate off the spoon and back into the bowl because chocolate sets up pretty quickly on a spoon, and you want the chocolate on the *marshmallows*.

Ideally, you'll have plenty of chocolate to cover all the pieces. Realistically, the suggested amounts are just enough to complete the job, so feel free to temper more chocolate than the recipe calls for to make the task easier (and to account for any uh-ohs that occur, like kid spillage).

A skewer with four or five large marshmallows dipped in chocolate requires between 1½ and 2 ounces of chocolate, so you should be able to dip eight or nine large marshmallow pops using a pound of chocolate.

Decorating effortlessly

After you dip your marshmallows, you can start the really fun part: decorating. One of the especially fun things about making these pieces is the lack of rules. I make some suggestions, but you can decorate your pieces any way that you please. If what you like can stick to the chocolate, go for it. I suggest using smaller items like sprinkles (called jimmies) or adding some more chocolate. Walk on the wild side.

Whatever candies you use for the toppings, place them in small bowls, lay the dipped skewers on wax paper, and sprinkle the toppings liberally onto the wet chocolate. Be sure to keep the toppings separated on the wax paper because you don't want them mixed up when you're finished.

 To keep your toppings separated, simply place each decorated type on separate pieces of wax paper, and sprinkle away. When the chocolate is dry, you can return any unattached toppings to the original bowl to use them again.

Another method that I use extensively in my shops is *stringing,* or drizzling, chocolate onto the dipped skewers. You can string chocolate in one of several ways by using a plastic condiment-type container, a piping bag, or a salad fork. I favor the last method for its simplicity and ease of cleanup when you finish —which is always important when you have kids around.

To use the salad-fork method, simply dip a salad fork into melted white chocolate or a tempered chocolate of a different color from the dipping color. Then shake the fork back and forth across the dipped skewers. After you string a few times, you and your kids will find the method quite easy. When you finish, simply wipe off the chocolate left on the fork (or let the kids lick it), and wash the fork.

A third great topping idea is chopped nuts. Before you add the nuts, spin the excess chocolate off the marshmallows. Then roll the chocolate-coated treat in a bowl or plate of nuts and allow the loose nuts to fall off. Last, place the skewer on a piece of wax paper to set up for about 10 to 15 minutes (as if the kids would wait that long).

You can check out the complete dipping and decorating marshmallow process in Figure 21-1. And now you get to put these ideas to work!

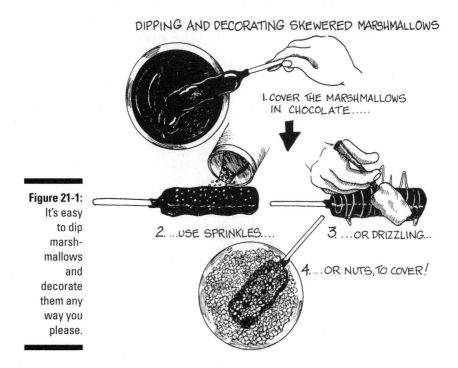

DIPPING AND DECORATING SKEWERED MARSHMALLOWS

1. COVER THE MARSHMALLOWS IN CHOCOLATE.....

2. ...USE SPRINKLES....

3. ...OR DRIZZLING...

4. ....OR NUTS, TO COVER!

Figure 21-1:
It's easy to dip marsh-mallows and decorate them any way you please.

Dipped and Decorated Individual Marshmallows

Sometimes you want the kids to have a treat, but they really don't need a whole bunch. This recipe is something they can make, put into a plastic storage container, and pull out one at a time for a treat. Okay, or Mom and Dad can pull out one treat at a time; hey, I can't guarantee that your kids won't try to grab a handful o' marshmallow and dodge just out of your grasp.

Preparation time: *1 hour and 10 minutes*

Yield: *60 pieces*

1½ pounds milk chocolate, chopped and melted for tempering

1 1-pound bag large marshmallows

Whatever small toppings or sprinkles your kids will enjoy, such as small sours, jimmies, or nuts. Have a small 2-ounce bottle of sprinkles available and 2 cups of nut pieces on hand.

1 Temper the milk chocolate using one of the methods I describe in Chapter 14. For dipping purposes, the bowl you tempered the chocolate in is fine for hand-dipping the marshmallows.

2 Hand-dip the marshmallows, one at a time, into the tempered chocolate to cover them completely. Shake off the excess, and drag the bottom of your fingers across the edge of the bowl to remove the excess. Turn the marshmallow over with your hand over a sheet of wax paper. The viscosity of the chocolate causes the marshmallow to adhere to your fingers, but when you invert the piece close to the wax paper, the dipped marshmallow releases onto the paper.

3 Sprinkle the assorted toppings onto the marshmallows and let them set for 10 to 15 minutes at room temperature. If the room isn't cool enough, you can place the pieces in the refrigerator for 5 minutes to set. When the pieces are dry, place them in a plastic container and store them for up to three weeks.

Tip: Only a certain amount of topping actually sticks to the wet chocolate. As an alternative, you can drop the chocolate-coated marshmallows into the bowl of topping to really coat it. This method is a little messier, but kids don't care about that little detail!

Per serving: Calories 57 (From Fat 17); Fat 2g (Saturated 1g); Cholesterol 0mg; Sodium 8mg; Carbohydrate 11g (Dietary Fiber 0g); Protein 1g.

Kids and sweets: A healthy combination

Using healthy foods as a component in sweet snacks is one way of getting your kids to consume treats that are, at least, partially good for them.

Given all the items available that you can combine with chocolate, you can steer your kids toward healthy items. You can provide fruits, nuts, cereal, and any food you can think of that they'll enjoy after they add a little tempered chocolate to it.

If you can get the young'uns to use dark chocolate — in moderation, of course — they'll encounter another source of goodness that's gaining momentum; dark chocolate contains high levels of antioxidants that offer healthy benefits.

When you have the kids making their own treats, you never know what they may discover next. Who knows? Your kids may discover that they like fruits and fairly healthy cereal as part of their snacks.

Skewered Marshmallows

Few items that I sell bring more smiles to the faces of young and old than chocolate-coated or decorated marshmallows on skewers (check them out in the color section). Something about that combination of a sweet chewy marshmallow covered in rich milk chocolate just brings out the kid in all of us. But if you're a kid to start with, you're ahead of the game.

Tools: *30 4½-inch paper sucker sticks or 15 7½ to 8-inch paper sucker sticks*

Preparation time: *1 hour and 20 minutes*

Yield: *15 to 30 pieces, depending on skewer size*

1 1-pound bag large marshmallows

1 ½ pounds milk chocolate, chopped and melted for tempering

Toppings as desired; you may use tiny sour pieces, jimmies, or other very small candies

1 Stick the marshmallows onto the sucker sticks. Slide the stick through the flat end of the marshmallow. Place four or five marshmallows on a long skewer and two on a shorter one. Place a 3-foot piece of wax paper on the counter for later use.

2 Temper the chocolate using one of the procedures described in Chapter 14.

3 Open several bags of small treats that the kids like, such as tiny sour pieces, and pour them into separate small bowls.

4 Dip the skewered marshmallows into the tempered chocolate, completely covering the marshmallows. Carefully and lightly twirl the skewer to spin off the excess chocolate or use a hard rubber spatula to remove any excess.

5 Lay the skewers on wax paper to dry at room temperature for about 15 minutes. If the room isn't too cool (around 70 degrees), place them in the refrigerator for 5 minutes to set.

6 You can store the skewers in a plastic container at room temperature for three weeks.

Per serving: Calories 114 (From Fat 33); Fat 4g (Saturated 2g); Cholesterol 0mg; Sodium 15mg; Carbohydrate 21g (Dietary Fiber 0g); Protein 1g.

Ski Bum Marshmallow Treats

This very popular piece is one that my mentor Randy taught me a few years ago. I gave it the name because . . . well, that's my job. This piece is really wonderful because of its combination of caramel, nuts, and chocolate. Need I say more?

Tools: *20 4½-inch paper sucker sticks*

Preparation time: *1 hour and 40 minutes*

Yield: *20 pieces*

10½-ounce bag large marshmallows (40 marshmallows)

1 pound caramel from Chapter 7 or store-bought caramel

1½ pounds milk chocolate, chopped and melted for tempering

1 8-ounce bag roasted unsalted whole almonds

4 ounces white chocolate, chopped, to melt for drizzling

1 Stick two large marshmallows on each sucker stick. Chop the almonds in a blender using the pulse setting to make fairly rough pieces. Place a 3-foot sheet of wax paper on the counter to use later for the pieces to dry.

2 Melt 1 pound of store-bought caramels in a microwave on high for about 2 to 3 minutes. Check the caramel every 30 seconds and stir as needed. You want the caramel melted enough so you can easily coat the marshmallows with a thin coat.

3 Dip each skewer into the melted caramel to coat completely and gently twirl off the excess. Roll the caramel-coated pieces in the chopped almonds and lay them on wax paper to cool. Rotate them 90 degrees every 3 minutes until they set and cool, which takes about 30 to 40 minutes.

4 While the pieces are cooling, you can temper the chocolate using one of the procedures in Chapter 14 (now that's multitasking!).

5 Then melt the white chocolate in a small bowl in the microwave for about 2 minutes, stopping and stirring every 45 seconds until it reaches 95 degrees on a chocolate thermometer.

6 When the pieces are completely cool, dip the treats in the tempered milk chocolate and coat them completely, spinning the excess into the bowl of chocolate. Lay the treats on wax paper to cool for about 15 minutes. While they're cooling, dip a fork into the white chocolate and drizzle white strings across each piece.

7 When your treats are cool, store them in a plastic container for three weeks.

Tip: *During the process, you may note some spreading around the bottom of the chocolate as it cools, but it doesn't hurt the piece.*

Per serving: *Calories 248 (From Fat 108); Fat 12g (Saturated 4g); Cholesterol 8mg; Sodium 41mg; Carbohydrate 34g (Dietary Fiber 0g); Protein 4g.*

Getting into Grains: Cereal Treats

Grains come in many forms and, fortunately for our taste buds, some people have found ways to combine grains with confections. Sure, your kids can enjoy a bowl of their favorite cereal and sweeten it with sugar, but they're still only having a bowl of sweetened cereal. To make the grain into a real treat, you need to go a bit further. In the following sections, I cover a couple of methods for taking your kids' favorite cereals to the next level.

Working with rice cereal

Many years ago, folks made a certain rice cereal treat for their families using a recipe that every mother in the United States seemed to know. I don't know anyone who didn't enjoy eating rice cereal bars at some point in his or her youth. The recipe requires only three ingredients — marshmallows, butter, and rice cereal — and isn't difficult to make. But dressing up the recipe is even easier by dipping the treats into tempered chocolate and decorating them as you please.

Preparing and cutting the rice cereal bars

Nowadays, you can purchase these treats already made. As a candy maker, I find that some things are worth making, and others are worth buying. I don't need to spend a lot of production time making rice cereal bars, but I don't believe that I can make it better than the manufacturer does, so I purchase sheets of the rice cereal treats. I recommend buying these ready-made sheets to save time, but the decision is yours. If you decide to purchase, you can buy these sheets through bakery suppliers and candy-ingredient and utensil suppliers (see Chapter 24).

Once you have your cereal bars in hand, you need to cut them. The easiest method of cutting the bars is to simply cut them into squares. Using a large knife, cut the sheet into 20 pieces, making each piece about 3 x 3 inches, although the size of the bars and how many you want really is up to you. If you purchased sheets of cereal bars, you may have received a template for cutting the sheet into squares and rectangles, ranging from 16 to 36 pieces.

If your kids want something other than squares, try cutting the bars into a variety of shapes by using a cookie cutter. If you're careful, you'll have only a little extra. You'll probably have to eat that waste: What a pity! If you purchase five rice cereal sheets (10 pounds), you may receive a cutting template but, if you purchase only one sheet, you may not receive a template. The template is useful because it shows a variety of patterns you can use to cut the sheet. To use the template, cut the size piece you want out of the template and lay it on top of the 2-pound bar. Then cut around the template.

If you purchase only one sheet, you can request a template and see whether the supplier sends you one. Otherwise, you need to estimate the size of the pieces, which you can do by measuring and cutting the size you desire. Frankly, you don't need to be exact, as long as the kids don't care (and I doubt they will). If nothing else, the supplier can give you a photocopy to allow you to see the pattern.

Skewering the bars

When I began making dipped and decorated rice cereal bars years ago, I tried to find wide, flat popsicle sticks, but this item proved difficult to find at the time. Because I was using paper sucker sticks for other items, I tried using that round stick, and now, that's all I use. If you want to use flat sticks, you can, but I prefer using the 8-inch round paper sucker sticks.

If possible, get the paper sticks with a pointed end because they make sticking the treats easier. However, a pointed end isn't a necessity.

To skewer your treats, place the pointed end of the paper stick at the center of one end of the cereal bar, and carefully skewer it, being careful to keep the stick straight. Leave about a 2½-inch handle exposed or as much as you need. Just be certain that the handle penetrates far enough into the bar that the piece is stable. After you skewer all the pieces, you're ready to dip and decorate your bars.

Dipping and decorating the bars

The next step is to dip the bars in tempered chocolate (Chapter 14 is full of easy methods you can use to temper chocolate for all sorts of treats). For large rice cereal bars, I recommend having at least 2 pounds of tempered chocolate on hand.

If you have enough chocolate in the right-size pot, you can dip the bars straight into the chocolate. But more likely, you'll need to angle the bars into the chocolate, lean the bowl over, and spoon some chocolate onto the bars to coat them. You're certainly allowed to do so because, remember, you have no rules at home! The key is to coat the bars as you desire. (Chapter 15 has more tips on dipping treats.)

When decorating your bars, you have several choices: You can use jimmies (little sprinkles), a drizzle of a contrasting color of chocolate, or a combination of the two. Try using different toppings until you see what you like; however, I don't recommend topping with large pieces, such as pieces of nuts, because you want a fairly thin coating of chocolate, which doesn't hold larger decorations well. Of course, you can use chopped nuts, such as pecans or thinly sliced almonds, and you've created something entirely different from a sprinkled cereal bar.

Dipped and Decorated Rice Cereal Bars

You can make your own rice cereal bars for this recipe if you want (which takes about 10 minutes plus 30 minutes to cool), but I recommend purchasing the 2-pound sheets from a bakery supplier or a candy-ingredient supplier. But if you want to make your own, I'll wait.

You can dip most of these bars in mild chocolate and drizzle white chocolate on top. You can also dip a few bars in white chocolate and drizzle milk chocolate on top. When I dip these bars, I leave part of the bar exposed for identification, but you don't have to do that. Check out these treats in the color section.

Tools: *20 8-inch paper sucker sticks*

Preparation time: *1 hour plus 30 minutes of cooling time*

Yield: *20 pieces*

2 pounds milk chocolate, chopped and melted for tempering

1 pound white chocolate, chopped

2-pound sheet of rice cereal bars

Toppings as desired to decorate

1 Temper the milk chocolate using one of the methods in Chapter 14.

2 In the microwave, melt the white chocolate to 94 degrees in a microwaveable bowl on high power, stopping every 30 seconds to stir and check the temperature with a chocolate thermometer; melting should take about 2 minutes, but microwaves vary.

3 Use the template that comes with the rice cereal sheets to cut the sheet into 20 pieces. If no template comes with the sheets, estimate and cut the bars as you wish. Stick a skewer into the end of each piece and insert it into each treat, leaving about a 2-inch handle exposed.

4 Dip a skewered treat into the milk chocolate, leaving about 1 inch of the bar exposed, or you can coat the entire bar. Allow the excess chocolate to drip off or scrape it lightly with the hard rubber spatula; just make sure that you leave an even coating of chocolate. Place the treat on wax paper, and sprinkle it with toppings and/or drizzle the melted white chocolate over it. Repeat with the other bars. Let the bars cool for about 15 minutes at room temperature.

5 Dip a bar in white chocolate; repeat the preceding process using a milk-chocolate drizzle and sprinkle with toppings. Continue the process until you've dipped and decorated all the cereal bars. Let the bars cool on the wax paper for about 15 minutes at room temperature. If you are concerned about the temperature in your kitchen, cool the bars in the refrigerator for 5 minutes.

6 Store these treats in a plastic container for two weeks; if you completely coated them with chocolate, you can store them for three weeks.

Per serving: Calories 332 (From Fat 112); Fat 13g (Saturated 5g); Cholesterol 1mg; Sodium 181mg; Carbohydrate 54g (Dietary Fiber 0g); Protein 4g.

Serving favorite cereals in a new way

Although most folks are familiar with rice cereal treats, most don't associate other cereals with candy. But in recent years, quite a few items that you wouldn't typically think of as desserts have become commonly used in confection products — including cereals. For example, you can take dry cereal out of the box, mix it with chocolate, and feast on a tasty confection. You may think that such a recipe seems a little strange but, after you and your kids try this combination, you'll be hooked on the taste as well as the simplicity.

Cereal Clusters

This treat is another simple, kid-friendly recipe that's at least partially good for your children, as long as you feel good about them enjoying their favorite cereals. Almost any cereal that has bite-size or smaller pieces is a good candidate for making cereal clusters. For example, you can use puffed cereals, corn flakes, and raisin bran, to name a few cereals. Now go grab your favorite cereal, and get crackin'.

Preparation time: *1½ hours*

Yield: *32 to 40 pieces*

12 ounces milk chocolate, chopped and melted for tempering

2 cups of favorite cereal

1 Temper the chocolate using one of the methods in Chapter 14.

2 Pour the cereal into the chocolate and mix.

3 Using a spoon or an ice cream scooper, scoop the mixture into chocolate cereal clusters and deposit the clusters onto wax paper to cool. Alternatively, you can scoop larger clusters into muffin cups.

4 Small clusters typically set in about 10 to 15 minutes. If you make larger clusters, as in a muffin-cup size, the pieces may require a few extra minutes to set.

5 Store your cereal clusters in a plastic container for up to two weeks. If you have more than one layer in the container, place a piece of wax paper between the layers to prevent scratching the chocolate.

Per serving: Calories 48 (From Fat 22); Fat 3g (Saturated 1g); Cholesterol 0mg; Sodium 20mg; Carbohydrate 7g (Dietary Fiber 0g); Protein 1g.

C Is for Cookies (and Chips and Chocolate)

A great medium for chocolate coating is your favorite everyday chip. More and more confectioners are combining items that aren't traditional sweets with chocolate with tremendous results. Salty chips fall into that category, and you may be amazed at the interesting flavors that confectioners create by combining some of these items.

One interesting aspect of these combinations is how the taste buds work. When you taste something, you don't taste everything at once, so you get a series of flavor notes that may include the sweetness and richness of the chocolate, the saltiness of a salty item, and the slight aftertaste of the chip itself. But a range of flavors has become the allure of so many combinations found in confections today.

The following recipe couldn't be easier for kids to make. You need only a few ingredients and a microwave, and you have a delicious treat in no time.

Dessert Nachos

For the kid in the family who really loves nachos, this recipe is a delightful variation. This dessert is a really delicious dip, and you can substitute other chips, such as corn chips or potato chips, for the nacho chips, if you want.

Preparation time: *2 to 5 minutes*

Yield: *8 servings*

3¾ ounces evaporated milk

8 1.5-ounce chocolate-covered caramel candy bars, cut into pieces

1 bag bite-size tortilla chips, about 12 to 14 ounces (you may not use the entire bag)

1 Combine the evaporated milk and caramel bars in a microwaveable bowl. Heat the mixture on high in the microwave, checking and stirring about every 45 seconds until the bars are melted.

2 When the chocolate mixture is melted, mix it well and serve it with tortilla chips. You can drizzle the chocolate mixture onto the chips or you can use the mixture as a dip. If the dip cools, reheat it for 15 seconds at a time.

Per serving: *Calories 348 (From Fat 142); Fat 16g (Saturated 8g); Cholesterol 9mg; Sodium 203mg; Carbohydrate 49g (Dietary Fiber 1g); Protein 5g.*

Another item frequently combined with chocolate is the cookie. Unlike salty chips, cookies are sweet to begin with, so adding chocolate to them isn't as surprising. Here again, you're dealing with different textures and flavors, and the result is delightful. But if you love a chocolate sandwich cookie, you will love it even more when you add a delicious, rich chocolate coating to it. Cookies like vanilla wafers are also a big hit when you add a chocolate coating. What makes the following treat especially enjoyable for kids is adding the sprinkles for decoration.

If you need more information on tempering chocolate, check out Chapter 14 and, for even more ideas on foods to dip into chocolate, see Chapter 15.

Decorated Chocolate-dipped Cookies

Kids will *love* this recipe because you have to hold the cookie in your hand and dip it into the chocolate, getting chocolate all over your fingers. They'll have to lick their fingers to clean up the mess — another dirty job that someone has to do.

I recommend using vanilla wafers for this recipe, but kids can use any cookie that they want. After all, you're mixing cookies with chocolate; how many rules can you make? If you like chocolate chip cookies, oatmeal cookies, or even those fig things, knock yourself out.

Preparation time: *1 hour and 10 minutes*

Yield: *24 pieces*

12 ounces milk chocolate, chopped and melted for tempering

24 vanilla wafers or comparable cookie

Sprinkles to decorate (2-ounce bottle)

1 Temper the milk chocolate and leave it in a bowl. Place a 3-foot piece of wax paper on the counter for later use.

2 Holding the cookie in your hand, dip it with the rounded side down or just dip one side or half of a flat cookie into the chocolate. Allow the excess to drip off, turn the cookie over, and hold with the dipped side up.

3 To decorate, drop the sprinkles onto the chocolate over the wax paper. Then place the cookie on a sheet of wax paper to cool for 10 to 15 minutes or eat them as soon as you dip 'em. Another option is to lay the cookie on the wax paper before you sprinkle it.

4 Store your treats in a plastic container for one week to keep them from getting stale. If you layer the cookies, place a sheet of wax paper between layers.

Per serving: Calories 64 (From Fat 29); Fat 3g (Saturated 1g); Cholesterol 0mg; Sodium 18mg; Carbohydrate 9g (Dietary Fiber 0g); Protein 1g.

The following recipe is great fun and quick to complete. Help the kids temper the milk chocolate, and then get out of the way unless they want you to help. Be sure to have all the toppings you want ready to go when the chocolate is ready.

The "pizza making" involves spooning a nice puddle of chocolate onto a wax paper-lined cookie sheet; spread the chocolate into a round "crust," and the rest is just pure pizza creation (see Figure 21-2). One of the really fun things about the pizza is that you have no rules when it comes to toppings: If you like it and if it fits, put it on your pizza. You can drizzle white chocolate on top or add nut pieces, mini-marshmallows, sliced cherries, and dried fruit slices. Have fun!

MAKING CHOCOLATE PIZZA

1. SHAPE TEMPERED CHOCOLATE INTO THE SHAPE OF A PIZZA. DRIZZLE WHITE CHOCOLATE ON TOP.

2. PLACE CHOCOLATE 'PEPPERONI' ON THE PIZZA, ALONG WITH OTHER TOPPINGS OF YOUR CHOICE!

Figure 21-2:
A chocolate pizza is a fun, quick treat for kids to make and eat.

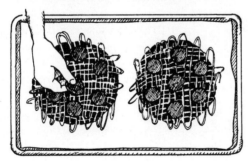

Chocolate Pizza

With just a little imagination, you can make a delicious pizza and never turn on the oven. Of course, the entire dish is chocolate, white chocolate, nuts, and fruit toppings (if desired).

Preparation time: *1 hour and 20 minutes*

Yield: *8 slices*

4 ounces white chocolate	*12 maraschino cherries, drained and halved*
¼ cup pecan pieces	*4 ounces white chocolate, chopped, to melt*
½ cup mini-marshmallows (colored, if possible)	*1 pound milk chocolate, chopped and melted for tempering*

1 Assemble the toppings (the pecans, mini-marshmallows, and cherries) in small bowls on the counter, and place a 2-foot piece of wax paper on the counter for use later.

2 Temper the milk chocolate according to the methods in Chapter 14.

3 In the microwave, melt the white chocolate in a microwaveable bowl on high, stopping every 30 seconds to stir, until it reaches 94 degrees on a chocolate thermometer. Melting takes about 1 to 1½ minutes.

4 Scrape the chocolate onto the wax paper in a puddle, and spread it using a spatula or a spoon into a circle that's about 10 to 11 inches wide. Immediately place the marshmallows and nuts evenly over the pizza, lightly pressing the toppings into the chocolate to make them stick.

5 Using a fork, drizzle the white chocolate over the pizza like cheese. Then place 24 cherry halves evenly over the pizza as "pepperoni."

6 As soon as the pizza is firm (not hard, which takes about 7 to 10 minutes), slice it into eight pieces with a pizza knife. Allow the pieces to cool for about 30 minutes at room temperature so they become hard.

7 Store the pizza in an airtight container for two weeks.

Vary It! *Sprinkle coconut, chopped pecans, natural sliced almonds, mini-marshmallows, or similar toppings, as desired, on top.*

Per serving: *Calories 405 (From Fat 207); Fat 23g (Saturated 11g); Cholesterol 3mg; Sodium 54mg; Carbohydrate 52g (Dietary Fiber 0g); Protein 5g.*

Chapter 22

Making a Stunning Presentation

*T*his book is devoted to showing you ways to make candies for you to enjoy as well as for you to give as a gift to a friend or loved one. As far as enjoying your own candy goes, you probably won't be too fussy about packaging; you simply want to partake of the fruits of your labors. But if you're making candy to give as a gift, you want to make as nice an impression with the packaging as you do with your confection.

Given the various items you find out how to make in this book, your gift-giving options are unlimited. You can combine a few of the candies in this book to create very attractive and tasty gifts for special occasions, like birthdays and holidays, or maybe you simply want to give that special someone his or her favorite treat. Whatever your reasoning, another option is to put together a *theme package,* which is specific to a sport, hobby, or other diversions that your recipient may enjoy.

In this chapter, I provide you with a number of ways to create a gift that will make an awesome impression on your friends and loved ones. Think about what the recipient may enjoy, and match his or her interests with the candies you've learned to make. When you do, you're on your way to customizing the perfect gift!

Picking the Perfect Theme for Your Gift

You need to pick a theme or motif before you select a container to fit whatever the occasion may be. The categories and choices of themes are endless, but the key is to match the theme with something that the recipient really likes in chocolates or other candies.

Some occasions for which you may consider giving a gift of candy include

- ✔ **Valentine's Day:** You can give your loved one foil-wrapped chocolates in a large mug or make molded chocolate roses and foil-wrap them. A mug of foil-wrapped truffles makes a nice gift. You can also make a lovely Valentine's Day box using a variety of your homemade candies.

- ✔ **Mother's Day:** You can give your mother a mug with molded chocolate roses wrapped in pastel foils. You should be able to find a beautiful Mother's Day mug. Another idea for the roses: You can get long plastic stems from the suppliers listed in Chapter 24 and mold the roses onto the stems like long lollipops.

- ✔ **Father's Day:** You can offer your father a mug with chocolates he enjoys. For instance, you can mold chocolate cigars, wrap them in gold foil, and put them in a mug, or you can make a molded chocolate golf set with white-chocolate balls and a milk-chocolate bag. You can also make Dad's favorite fudge and put it in a gift bag that includes a tie. When he sees the tie, he'll really love the fudge.

- ✔ **Graduation:** You can't go wrong with a graduation mug filled with cash and chocolates; the money will please the grad, and the chocolate is a tasty bonus. Or you can give the graduate divinity, pralines, and fudge in a nice basket with an envelope of cash tucked into the pile.

- ✔ **Birthdays:** Create a beautiful gift tin with truffles as the centerpiece, surrounded by caramel pecan clusters and pralines. Or make a very special assortment of chocolates for a loved one's birthday and put them in a mug. Place a chocolate candle in the top of the mug.

- ✔ **Any occasion:** A small, decorative tray with toffee, molded chocolates, and chocolate caramels would please anyone, any time. Try giving a novelty mug with chocolate pretzels; the realm of novelty mugs is vast, so you can find the appropriate mug. Fill it with chocolate caramels wrapped in foil for a nice presentation.

As you discover how to make the candies in this book, think about what a really good friend or a loved one may like. Maybe he or she would like some fine chocolate truffles, some yummy creams, or some molded chocolates. (You can find lots of different molds for your chocolates — you just have to decide which one is the right one!) Or maybe caramels, fudge, jellies, toffees, and brittles are more your recipient's style.

When putting together a gift that involves your homemade candies, you're not limited to just the candy. You can include books, toys, coffees, cheeses, and countless other items that are related in some way to the gift's theme.

Sizing Up Your Container Choices

Some of the items you may use to hold your candies (and which I cover in the following sections) are

- ✔ Mugs, cups, and glasses
- ✔ Boxes and tins
- ✔ Baskets and trays
- ✔ Gift bags

Make the gift fit the recipient(s) as well as the occasion. For example, giving an individual a really nice mug of homemade candy is great and very appropriate. But you wouldn't want to do that for a group of people like a family; sharing one mug can be difficult! When you give a gift to a couple, a family, or a larger group of people, think bigger, and think about how the recipients share (or don't share).

For two people, you can give matching or similar small items, or you can make a nice gift box, tin, basket, tray, or bag. Baskets with your candy, fresh fruit, coffee beans, a small inspirational book, and so on make lovely gifts for larger groups. Everybody will find something to enjoy, and they can share some of the items, giving the gift more appeal. Just keep in mind what the recipients like, and put in plenty of your candies.

Countless candy suppliers online provide packaging materials for your gifts. See Chapter 24 for some ideas.

Drinking up ideas for gift mugs, cups, and glasses

Mugs, cups, and glasses hold small amounts of candy, but they make a big impression on gift recipients. I provide tips on creating gifts with mugs, cups, and glasses in the following sections.

Creating marvelous candy mugs and cups

If you're concerned about the small size of a typical mug, you can select a larger mug that has room for more candy, or you can make a gift that includes more than candy.

One place to find really nice gift containers is any shop with a good variety of handcrafted items. You certainly can find mugs, but my wife and I have also found some great pottery pieces that make wonderful gifts. You may even consider going to a shop where you can paint your own pottery containers.

When you're filling a smaller container, where space is tight, consider using smaller candies, like truffles. And remember to protect the different confections by separating them with small cellophane bags. For example, you can put half a dozen pralines in a small bag and four pieces of divinity in another. Three chocolate-dipped and decorated pretzels as well as peanut brittle broken into 2-inch pieces make a lovely addition. Tie a ribbon on each bag. To cushion your goodies, fill the bottom of a mug with shredded "grass," and place the individual bags on top of the grass.

After you've found a mug or cup that you feel is appropriate to the occasion and have selected and wrapped just the right candies, the ideas for your outer wrapping are definitely endless. A simple idea is to fill a mug of whatever size you choose with foil-wrapped chocolates, pull cellophane wrapping over the mug, and tie a nice ribbon to close the top of the cellophane.

You can create an even sharper appearance with shrink-wrap, but be careful not to melt chocolates while shrinking the wrap.

Mugs and cups make an especially nice gift for coffee and tea lovers. And, as if you couldn't plan your gift any better, coffee and tea drinkers' discerning palates frequently appreciate fine chocolates, too.

Creating a presentation around coffee or tea is easy. If your recipient is a coffee-lover, include ¼ pound of a very good coffee along with the chocolates. If you know the person has a coffee grinder, add some coffee beans; if you aren't sure whether your recipient has a grinder, grind the coffee before you pack the gift. Because you probably don't know the type of coffeemaker the person has, I recommend giving beans and foil-wrapped chocolates. And as a true specialty, you can fill a mug with a variety of coffee-flavored truffles (see Chapter 18 for the recipe).

You can apply the same concept to a gift for a tea-loving friend, but include tea and a very nice teacup instead of a coffee mug. Because manufacturers package tea in many ways, you may have to shop around to find just the right kind. Select the teacup that you deem appropriate, place a small package of tea in the cup, and add a small plastic bag with beautifully decorated chocolate pretzels. Wrap the cup in cellophane, and tie the top with a ribbon.

Going for glass with class

Extend the same concept you use with the mugs to create a gift using glassware. A simple idea is to take truffles from Chapter 18 — for example, the truffles flavored with spirits — and wrap them in gold foil. Fill a snifter glass with these chocolates and wrap them with cellophane. Tie the top with a gold ribbon, and you've created one classy gift. (The snifter glass is just one suggestion, but its shape appeals to the eye and makes a nice impression.)

As far as glassware and chocolates, you can go in any direction you wish. You can try to match a flavor with a style of glass, and your friend or loved one will think you're so clever. You can thank me later. Just be sure to do a good job making the chocolates.

The glass you give doesn't have to cost very much. When you make the chocolates yourself, the effect is priceless.

To make your gift even more personal, try finding a glass engraver who can customize your gift with special engraving.

When you make a gift using a container as transparent as glassware, how you display the contents is an important consideration. You can wrap individual candies in foil to add a lot of visual appeal, or you can display unwrapped candies by arranging them with their tops against the glass. Just pack the candies tightly enough to prevent them from slipping.

Finding and packing the right box (or tin)

You can purchase very basic boxes from bakery and candy-ingredient suppliers, and you will be able to find a very good variety of decorative holiday packaging themes. Nowadays, these businesses are very good about stocking holiday boxes from major suppliers, so you won't have a difficult time finding the right box. You can also find lots of good boxes by browsing art-supply stores and good card shops. Be sure to select a sturdy box; you don't want your box to fall apart when you cram it full of your candies!

You can purchase many of the same boxes that those of us in the business use, except that the pros buy them in much larger quantities and we can have our boxes custom printed. Well, we do have a few advantages.

Just as boxes are available in a multitude of colors and themes, gift tins are available, too. You can hand-paint them or find some that depict scenes of interest to the recipient. One great bonus of a tin: A gift recipient can always find a use for a tin long after the memory of the gift has faded.

Gift tins are very popular at Christmas (they often have reprints of beautiful snow scenes and the like), but nothing says you can't give a tin for any occasion. You can find tins in sizes ranging from very small to fairly large.

To wrap your candies for a boxed or tinned gift, you have several options. You can foil-wrap your chocolates, which is always a nice touch, or you can wrap the different candies in clear plastic wrap to allow the recipient to see the contents. Of course, you can always mix and match your wrappings to create any variety you desire.

You can add decorations to any box or tin to give it a custom appearance. Select a motif and incorporate it into your box color, ribbons and bows, and even when you're filling the box. For instance, you can make a delightful gift by filling the bottom of a box or tin with your choice of colors of cellophane grass and then filling the box with an assortment of your candies. A pound of shredded cellophane goes a long way!

When you're filling a box, a tin, or a basket (see the next section) with your candies, the important parts (the candies themselves, of course) are visible. But you don't have to fill the package from top to bottom. Cellophane or other fillers take up the unseen area beneath the gift items, and you place a solid array of gifts over the filler for an overflowing appearance. (We call that merchandising.)

To make the best presentation when you pack a gift in a box, tin, or basket, layer the items with the larger items in back, and fill in the front with smaller items. This type of display allows everything to be seen from the "front" of the basket and projects an appearance of a full basket. Even a basket usually has a front and a back.

Depending on the size of the box or tin, it may have a lid on it or you may cover the box with cellophane and leave the top off. To give your box a gift appearance, add a ribbon.

To get even more ideas for packaging your candy or any other type of gift, look in stores or glance inside the countless catalogs that come in the mail. Those of us in retail are always learning new ideas from others.

Putting all your gifts in one basket (or tray)

When you plan to give a large amount of candy in a gift, you may want to try a bigger container, such as a basket or a tray. I cover the details of using both these items in the following sections.

Basket basics

Putting together a gift basket is pretty much like packing a gift box or tin (which I cover in the previous section): Select a theme, assemble and wrap the items as you like, and layer the basket with larger items in back and smaller items in front. This method allows every item to be seen.

But the lucky person who receives the basket may reuse it, unlike most boxes. So in addition to considering what you want to put inside the basket, you must also consider what to do with the *outside* of the basket. If you know someone well enough to give him or her your beautiful homemade candies, you may have some idea of what his or her house looks like and how he or she may display the basket.

Generally speaking, you would probably use a basket for a larger gift and, assuming that's the case, you need to plan how you would fill that larger space. Putting together your basket should, of course, include your candy, because that's why we're here. And I already mentioned adding coffee and tea to your gift (see "Creating marvelous candy mugs and cups" earlier in this chapter), but I've only scratched the surface on ideas. Other items you may consider including are assorted nuts, stuffed animals, canned specialties, books, jars of sauces, cheeses, meats, small gifts, bottles of adult beverages, cigars, cookies, crackers, and smoked salmon.

Obviously, you can create anything you want to put together. Let your imagination go. If you're stumped about what to include, ask yourself what you would like to receive. Once you determine what will go into the gift, the key is how to lay out the contents. If you stick with the larger-to-smaller layout, you're well on your way to making a nice basket.

You can fill the space under the gift items in your basket with padding materials, such as shredded cellophane grass, shredded paper, and even colorful, fluffed tissue paper. Having some of this colorful tissue visible around the candies adds a festive appearance.

To protect your contents and secure everything, cover the basket with shrink-wrap or use cellophane. With shrink-wrap, you create a nice tight package, and everything stays in place. Cellophane creates a loose package and is especially good for taller baskets because you can gather the cellophane at the top and tie a ribbon around the gathering for a decorative finish.

Trying trays

If you're invited to have dinner with a few friends or are planning to attend a party, a simple gift to take to the gathering is a tray of your delicious candies. Although anyone can purchase a bottle of wine to take to a function, not just anyone can make the candies you know how to make. A tray full of a variety of candies will blow your hostess away, and you will be the envy of all at the soiree. Believe me, speaking from experience, taking a tray of chocolates to a dinner is a winner, and you will be, too.

When you take such a gift to a gathering, you probably take a tray that requires returning. However, you can purchase very attractive, fairly inexpensive decorative trays and fill them with your chocolates instead. You can find these types of trays in stores that sell craft and decorating materials.

You can choose trays made of metal with painted scenes; trays with a silver finish also make a quite nice impression. The nicer the tray, the more likely the recipient is to use it again as a serving tray for a party or as a decorative piece in the house. I usually like oval and rectangular trays that are about 11 x 14 inches or even a little larger.

After you find an appropriate tray, purchase a few paper doilies to line the tray. This little decoration gives simple elegance to the gift, and you won't have to spend much to create that effect. Just remember that when your hostess tries to return the tray, it's hers (no matter how much you like it).

I recommend using shrink-wrap or cellophane to wrap your finished tray because both materials reveal the contents of the tray. The bonus of the shrink-wrap is that it creates a tight package and holds everything in place.

Bagging a gift beautifully

Another way to make a nice presentation is to use a gift bag. Gift bags have saved me many times when I didn't want to wrap something but I wanted to make a good impression.

Gift bags provide several benefits. First, you don't have to worry about finding a supplier because card shops sell all kinds of gift bags. Second, you can find a wide assortment of colored, patterned, and themed bags in a variety of sizes, ranging from a department-store–size shopping bag to tiny bags.

You can use a very small bag as the container for smaller gifts. See "Drinking up ideas for gift mugs, cups, and glasses" earlier in this chapter for more about putting together small candy gifts.

Another nice feature of gift bags is the variety of shapes and strengths they come in. You can find bags that are just sturdy enough to bags that could almost double as a basket. Like baskets (which I cover earlier in this chapter), gift bags hold an array of items, so they're ideal for larger gifts. They also create a presentation similar to that of a basket because the items are visible.

When using a gift bag, you may want to package several items to include in the bag. A couple of boxes and bags within a larger, more colorful gift bag makes a nice package. For example, you can place an assortment of creams and caramels in a small box, bag some assorted dipped pretzels, make a small clear bag of pralines, and include a large molded chocolate.

You can pad the bottom of the bag with tissue paper and give the bag a full appearance with a larger item in the top center, surrounded by smaller items.

For the finest presentation, select the bag that best suits your needs, choose a matching color of tissue paper, and fluff the tissue around the gifts inside the bag as a finishing touch. Nothing could be easier.

Part VI
The Part of Tens

The 5th Wave   By Rich Tennant

"I never cooked candy to such a high temperature, so I just wanted to take some extra precautions."

In this part...

This part is filled to the brim with even more great candy-making info. In case you don't find enough recipes in this book, I list ten Web sites where you can find more candy-making ideas. You probably also want to know where to find some of the utensils you need or some of those harder-to-find ingredients that are specific to the trade. Well, in this part, I offer ten (or so) trusted suppliers.

And how about some great places to see how professionals make candy? You may want a chance to see what you're trying to make, and this part lists many locations where you can do just that. If you have a problem with something you're making, the ten troubleshooting tips may help you out of a jam.

Enjoy your candy making!

Chapter 23

Ten Wonderful Web Sites for Candy Recipes

In This Chapter
▶ Surfing the Web for new candy recipes
▶ Finding fun candy facts online

*I*f you attempt many or even only a few of the recipes in this book, you may find yourself wanting to try something that I haven't included here. Although I give you a variety of recipes from which to choose, realize that thousands of candy recipes are available on the Internet. Many of them are similar to the ones you acquire from me. And I can't forget to mention that you can find so many items that you need in your candy production on the Internet, too (see Chapter 24 for details).

With the Web sites in this chapter, you're able to find more recipes than you could ever prepare. But with the skills you acquire from this book, you're qualified to take on almost any candy-making task. The world is your candy source. Enjoy it to the fullest!

About.com

Perhaps you're in the mood for some good Southern pecan pralines. You can make some pretty good pralines using the recipes in the book (see Chapter 11), but maybe you have a need for something else in the praline line, such as praline bars made with graham crackers. If so, go to `www.southernfood.about.com/od/pralines`. This Web site has a number of praline recipes and, of course, you can link to other sites with hundreds of recipes from there. This Web site provides a bourbon pecan praline recipe that sounds really tasty. So if you like pralines, you can find several options here.

Carrie's Chocolates

At www.carrieschocolates.com, you find an assortment of recipes. If you click on Fudge Recipes at the top of the page, you find recipes for fudge (naturally); on the same page, you find recipes for tiger butter, caramels, and rum balls, to name a few items. You'll enjoy this site because, although you may not find thousands of recipes, you'll certainly discover some that you can easily produce using the skills you've acquired in this book.

Chef 2 Chef Culinary Portal

If you go to www.chocolate-recipes.chef2chef.net, you may never leave, especially if you're a chocolate fiend. This site lists something like 280,000 recipes. I didn't count them or look them all up to verify that fact, but you can locate just about anything you need in the way of chocolate candy recipes. On this site, you also find useful conversion tables for converting measurements, such as liters to cups or cups to tablespoons, and you can ask cooking questions by clicking on the Culinary Guru.

Chocolate Cuisine

Go to www.chocolatecuisine.com and click on Delightful Desserts in the left-hand column; then click on Candy Recipes. From there, you find plenty of really good candy recipes, including almond brittles, mints, and truffles, to name a few.

If you venture into other categories of the Web site, you find recipes for making chocolate entrees, such as beef tenderloin with the addition of chocolate (who knew?) and, of course, desserts, such as brownies, cookies, and cheesecakes.

CooksRecipes.com

At www.cooksrecipes.com, click on the Candy Recipes link in the left-hand column. Several categories of candy recipes will appear on the screen. Click on whichever category you find most appealing, and a long column of choices appears. Let your tummy guide you as you make your way through the list of candy categories to find your favorite candy. Some of the recipes in these categories include Crispy Double Decker Fudge, Cinnamon Popcorn Crunch, and Licorice Caramels.

National Confectioners Association

As one of the official Web sites of the National Confectioner's Association (NCA), `www.candyusa.com` is chock full of useful and fun-to-know information.

Click on the Consumers link and go to one of the headings at the top of the page. You find historical candy data and a candy classroom. You can have a lot of fun learning all about candy and how it's made. Of course, you also find a large assortment of recipes, some as easy as microwave fudge and others as rich as fine truffles.

On this site, you find information pertaining to candy in the news and what is hot at the moment. You also find ideas about planning a party or various other occasions when giving or making candy is applicable.

The Nut Factory

On the site `www.thenutfactory.com`, click on Recipes and then on Peanut Brittle, and you find some recipes that you can make with no problem. (I cover brittles in more detail in Chapter 12.) Remember, you can substitute fresh pecan pieces for peanuts and keep the rest of the recipe the same, and you make an excellent pecan brittle.

This site has recipes for candies other than brittle, too. You can also pick up a few interesting facts about nuts, if you're so inclined.

Razzle Dazzle Recipes

When you hop onto `www.razzledazzlerecipes.com`, click on Christmas Recipes and then on Candy and Sweets. Here you're on the way to some delightful recipes — this site offers recipes for fudge, caramels, divinity, various types of hand-rolled pieces, and so much more.

If you're looking for some excellent holiday ideas, this site brims with great Christmas recipes, and they aren't particularly difficult. You find a wide variety of candies, so you're definitely able to fulfill your Christmas needs.

Recipe Goldmine

When you go to www.recipegoldmine.com, you simply enter whatever candy you desire in the search box. You can enter fudge, caramel, truffles, brittle, or whatever you wish. Pages of recipe options are instantly at your disposal, and you typically find multiple-page listings for whichever confection you want. Or, if you wish, simply click on Candy Recipes in the right-hand column, and ten general categories of candies, each one filled with recipes, appear.

Another fun category on the home page is the Candy Bar category. You find more than 100 recipes that you can make using commercial candies as ingredients.

That's My Home Recipes

If you go to www.thatsmyhome.com and type "fudge" in the search area, you find a plethora of wonderful, delicious-sounding recipes. Among these are White Christmas Cherry-Almond Fudge, Spiced Pumpkin Fudge, and Blueberry Cheesecake Euphoria Fudge. These three fudges alone should be worth checking out the site.

But the site covers much more than candy. In addition, you find charts that show you how to expand a recipe if you're interested in making a simple recipe for a larger crowd. For example, if you have a recipe that serves four and you want to make enough for 100, the chart tells you how to make the conversion. You also find a substitution chart, which is helpful for making substitutions in a candy recipe when you don't have a certain ingredient.

Chapter 24

Ten (or So) Great Places to Buy Candy-making Supplies

In This Chapter

▶ Seeking out ingredient suppliers

▶ Finding your needed utensils

*I*n this chapter, I identify many of the ingredients and utensils you use in this book for candy making. Many of these items are already in your home and, if they're not, you can find them at your local grocery store. (Check out Chapters 3 and 4 for basic info about tools and ingredients.) I also include some items that may be a little more difficult to find. You may have to contact some manufacturers online or by phone, but the resources I list here are all good sources. I've dealt with many of them in my business, and you can count on them for quality and quick responses.

I list, whenever available, Web-site information, e-mail addresses, and phone numbers (some are toll free) to give you different options of contacting these companies. If you prefer to contact a company by mail, I also provide street addresses.

Burke Candy

Burke is a candy retailer as well as a wholesaler of candy-making ingredients. Although the company may sell some items in larger amounts than you need, many items are available in smaller sizes, too. If you need less of an item, you can always ask whether the company can sell you a smaller pack of what you need.

Burke has premade cream centers available in 10-pound boxes, if you want to go that route with your dipped candies; you can also purchase fondant and commercial caramel, which you can use in your recipes. This company is a good source of invertase (an enzyme that helps keeps your candies fresh), should you choose to use that in your candies. It's available in a 1-pound bottle.

Burke Candy, 3840 N. Fratney St., Milwaukee, WI 53212; phone 888-287-5350 or 414-964-7327; fax 414-964-7644; e-mail `burkecandy@aol.com`, Web site `www.burkecandy.com`.

Butternut Mountain Farm

This company is located in maple sugar country and, although it may not have a wide variety of items you can use for candy making, it sells granulated maple sugar by the pound, and you don't have to tie up a lot of money to get what you need (between $6 and $10 per pound for this very special ingredient). This ingredient is what you need to cook an excellent maple fudge (see Chapter 9).

Butternut Mountain Farm, 37 Industrial Park, Morrisville, VT 05661; phone 800-828-2376 or 802-888-3491; fax: 802-888-5909.

Cakes 'N Things, Inc.

You can find some interesting items here that you may not find at other Web sites (the company also has a showroom you can visit). Among its mold line (which has more than 1,400 molds), the company has a fairly wide assortment of "adult molds," which allow you to make some very unusual pieces of chocolate for that special someone. Just remember that these molds aren't for the young ones. However, if you have no young ones around, you don't have to worry about such problems.

The company also stocks an assortment of items for candy-making recipes, including oil flavorings, whisks, small scoops (ideal for the truffles in Chapter 18), candy books, and so much more. You can fill a lot of your candy-making needs here.

Cakes 'N Things, Inc., 207 E Third St., Gridley, IL 61744; phone 309-747-2820; fax 309-747-2844); e-mail `customerservice@cakesnthings.com`, Web site `www.cakesnthings.com`.

Candyland Crafts

This company offers a wide variety of utensils, candy-making tools, chocolate-tempering machines, ingredients, and books. This warehouse-size business in New Jersey houses some really useful items on your list of candy-making needs. It carries more than 2,500 different molds, including some with boxes and inserts that match the molds to create really professional packaging; powdered food colorings in small containers; and oil flavorings. It also carries thermometers, priced between $14 and $24. Candyland is another of those one-stop shopping locations where you can find much of what you need to make candy and package your gifts.

Candyland Crafts, 201 W. Main St., Somerville, NJ 08876; phone 908-685-0410; fax 908-575-1640; e-mail orders@candylandcrafts.com, Web site www.candylandcrafts.com.

Chocosphere

Chocosphere features chocolates from 30 world-class chocolatiers. Its Web site offers what many people consider to be the best chocolates in the world. If you're looking for some really top-of-the-line couverture, this site is a great place to find it. It features brands such as Valhrona, Callebaut, Guittard, Scharffen Berger, and more. You can purchase products only via the company's Web site.

Chocosphere, phone 877-992-4626; fax 877-912-4626; e-mail customer-service@chocosphere.com, Web site www.chocosphere.com.

Chocovision

Chocovision offers a selection of chocolate-tempering equipment in a wide price range as well as small dipping tools and other utensils. Chocovision also features a selection of liquid food coloring and oil flavorings in 1-ounce bottles, ranging from $8.50 to $18.50. The variety of oil flavorings includes rum, amaretto, brandy, black walnut, and blueberry. If you need foils, the company sells packs of 125 for under $4.

Chocovision, P.O. Box 5201, Poughkeepsie, NY 12602; phone 800-324-6252 or 845-473-4970; fax 845-473-8004; e-mail sales@chocovision.com, Web site www.chocovision.com.

Create-a-Cake Shop

This company features a wide assortment of candy-making supplies, including molds, pans, utensils, food colorings, and more. It accepts most major credit cards and even checks. As the name indicates, the company features baking supplies but also stocks candy thermometers and parchment paper bags for piping (about $5.49 for a dozen), as well as disposable piping bags ($6.49 for 24) and tips to fit the bags.

Create-a-Cake Shop, 3944 Cobalt Ave. East, Jacksonville, FL 32210; phone/fax 904-778-1658; e-mail info@createacakeshop.com, Web site www.createacakeshop.com.

Hauser Chocolatier

Ruedi Hauser and his wife Lucille operate chocolate shops in Connecticut and Rhode Island. Ruedi has put his Swiss heritage to good use as an unparalleled manufacturer of fine European chocolates in America. You can purchase his chocolate shells online; these shells are the type you fill with ganache to make truffles (see Chapter 18). You can purchase these shells in small quantities, so Hauser provides a viable alternative to making all your own shells.

The price of shells ranges from $15 for 108 heart shells (about 1 inch in diameter) to between $15 and $22 for round shells that are about 1 inch to 1¾ inches in diameter. Chocolate cups are $15 for 126 pieces. All shells are available in white, milk, and dark chocolate. Prices are subject to change.

Hauser Chocolatier, 59 Tom Harvey Rd., Westerly, RI 02891; phone 888-599-8231 or 401-596-8866; fax 401-596-0020; e-mail info@hauserchocolates.com, Web site www.hauserchocolates.com.

Make 'n Mold Shop

This company is associated with Tomric Plastics of Buffalo, New York, a major manufacturer and supplier of molds. Make 'n Mold has a small retail operation in the same building as its mold manufacturing company. Aside from offering candy-making supplies, the company also provides molding tips and offers a few recipes for making candy. You won't find as many items for sale here as on some other sites, but you can find a storehouse of very useful information that can help you in your other recipes.

Make 'n Mold also offers wafers for melting to fill chocolate molds. The wafers come in a variety of colors for you to melt to paint details inside the molds. Make 'n Mold's Web site offers how-to information to assist you in decorating molds and planning special occasions.

Make 'n Mold Shop, 85 River Rock Dr., Buffalo, NY 14207; phone: 716-877-3146; fax 716-854-0081; e-mail `sales@makenmold.com`, Web site `www.makenmold.com`.

National Products Company

National Products Company is a specialized company that deals in flavorings for the confectionary and baking industry. I love dealing with this company because, if it doesn't have a flavor, it tries to create what I want, and it always seems to find a solution.

You can find invertase here for $13.75 a quart, and you can purchase essential oils in pints for use in truffles for between $12 and $40 per pint, with plenty of flavorings on the low end of the price range. Keep in mind that you can pay $7 or $8 for an ounce of flavorings at other places anyway, and these flavorings keep well at room temperature.

National Products Co., 1206 E. Crosstown Pkwy, P.O. Box 2153, Kalamazoo, MI 49003; phone 800-525-2431 or 269-344-3640; fax 269-344-1037; e-mail `national@nationalflavors.com`, Web site `www.nationalflavors.com`.

Williams-Sonoma

This company has stores in malls across the country that are fun to visit, even if you don't need a thing. You can find mixers, thermometers, knives, scales, measuring cups and spoons, microplanes for zesting, and a vast variety of other utensils for use in candy making. You'd have a difficult time visiting without finding something you need or at least something you want.

Williams-Sonoma, Inc., 3250 Van Ness Ave., San Francisco, CA 94109; phone 877-812-6235; fax 702-363-2541; Web site `www.williams-sonoma.com`.

Chapter 25

Ten (or So) Cool Candy Companies to Visit

. . . .

In This Chapter
▶ Visiting great candy makers
▶ Sampling some yummy treats

. . . .

Making candy or any type of recipe, for that matter, is easier when you can see what you're trying to make. Having cookbooks that show every finished recipe usually isn't practical, so sometimes you need to take other measures to see what you're trying to accomplish. When I learn new recipes, visiting a shop that makes such items and seeing the final result helps me.

Although you may not be able to go behind the scenes and see all the details of a shop, you can still visit chocolate businesses where you can see the results. Often you can even take a tour of some of these operations — especially larger factories.

The following list represents some of the locations in North America where you can see companies making some excellent chocolates; most of the locations have tours or good viewing opportunities. All these operators are people I know; I've been to most of their locations, and I can vouch for them as chocolate makers who produce excellent products. These professionals usually have a little time (within reason) to speak to visitors and to answer questions. If you see the Retail Confectioners International (RCI) emblem, the chocolate is sure to be fine chocolate.

Angell & Phelps

Dr. Alvin Smith owns Angell & Phelps, which his wife, Ann, and their son, Al, Jr. run. This Daytona-based company still makes candy the way its workers did 70 years ago — by hand and still using the original equipment, opposing any shortcuts that would affect the quality of its candy. The company still uses the original recipes as well. You can take a factory tour and see workers hand-dipping and hand-packing beautiful chocolates. While there, you can also visit the café, where you can enjoy live entertainment and delicious food. You may also take a virtual factory tour on the Web site.

Angell & Phelps, 154 South Beach St., Daytona Beach, FL 32114; phone 800-969-2634; Web site `www.angellandphelps.com`.

Boehms Candies, Inc.

My first impression of this chocolate came in 1983 when I was attending a convention. A couple of boxes of Boehms chocolates had been placed in a hospitality suite for sampling, and I had to partake. Bernard Garbusjuk, the owner of Boehms, had long been known as a great chocolatier, even among his peers. All the attendees were very good chocolate makers, but everyone wanted to sample *this* chocolate. His handmade chocolates have the look and taste of the finest pieces made in Europe. To this day, Boehms continues to manufacture these high-quality, small batches of candies and remains very high on the list of chocolates that I've tried.

Julius Boehm and a partner in Seattle started the company in 1943. Julius had learned to make candy by watching his grandfather in Austria, and he also picked up a few tips from a friend named Cecil Hall. The partners eventually moved the company to Issaquah, Washington. For years, Bernard Garbusjuk, Julius Boehm's successor (who was also his apprentice), has owned the company.

While some of the candy is made with large equipment, much of the chocolate at Boehms is hand-dipped, and the candies are hand-packed. Tours are available during the summer months by reservation only. Groups of more than 20 can tour year round if they make reservations. Even if you aren't on a tour, you can see into the production area from the retail area.

Boehms Candies Inc., 255 N.E. Gilman Blvd., Issaquah, WA 98027-2406; phone 425-392-6652; fax 425-557-0560; e-mail `info@boehmscandies.com`, Web site `www.boehmscandies.com`.

Buffett's Candies

If you happen to be in the southwestern United States— say, Albuquerque — Buffett's Candies is a nice place to check out some wonderful candy. Buffett's Candies features traditional candies, such as creams, molded chocolates, and pecan brittle, but you also find chocolate-covered pinons and pinon clusters.

(The pinon is a nut native to New Mexico.) So if you're in the area, perhaps for their huge hot-air balloon festival, check out Buffett's Candies. Look for the candy cane, which is approximately the size of a red-and-white telephone pole. Ask for Patty, and tell her you heard about her business from me.

Buffett's Candies, 7001 Lomas, N.E., Albuquerque, NM 87110-6949; phone 505-265-7731; fax 505-265-0354.

Callie's Candy Kitchen

Callie's caters to tours, and the owners love bus tours as much as individuals. Owner Harry Callie is one of the warmest, friendliest people you're likely to encounter in any business. While his wife Carol stays quietly in the background until needed, Harry is always ready with a quip or a tip. Years ago, he made a great living selling chocolate-covered Jordan crackers (small, chocolate-covered crackers about 1 inch to 1½ inches long). Although he still makes them, he expanded his business in many directions; in fact, he and his wife also operate a pretzel factory!

When a bus rolls up, Harry goes into action, entertaining the visitors. He tells stories, shows them how his candy is made, and generally amuses and amazes the crowd just by being Harry. He answers questions and makes sure that everyone gets a sample. Candies you see made at Callie's include chocolate-covered pretzels, chocolate-covered sandwich cookies, and chocolate-covered red licorice. At Callie's, everything seems to get covered in chocolate.

Callie's Candy Kitchen, Route 390, Box 126, Mountainhome, PA 8342; phone 800-252-7750 or 570-595-2280; fax 570-595-9280; e-mail `callieck@ptd.net`, Web site `www.calliescandy.com`.

Charlie's Chocolate Factory

This candy shop is one of the bright spots in the beautiful British Columbia region, and it has been a tradition for folks in the Vancouver area for many years. Charlie Sigvardsen — the "Charlie" in the name — is another of the wonderful characters in the candy business. He's often in costume — a derby hat and a colorful vest that matches his bright smile — but if he isn't in the shop, he has a life-size likeness to greet you.

The factory produces an extensive assortment of chocolates, including molded chocolates, creams, and a chocolate bear paw with cashew claws. Charlie's features beautiful assortments with chocolate caramels, creams, and solid chocolate pieces wrapped in foils. The factory also boasts a chocolate river display that you'll love! Just don't try to drink from it.

Charlie's Chocolate Factory is also a good place to purchase supplies. The store carries molds, boxes, foils, and a good assortment of other items that you need to make chocolates.

Charlie's Chocolate Factory, 3746 Canada Way, Burnaby, B.C., Canada V5G 1G4; phone 604-437-8221; fax 604-437-8222; e-mail `charlieschocolate factory@telus.net`; Web site `www.charlieschocolatefactory.com`.

The Chocolate Tree, Inc.

Located on the South Carolina coast in Beaufort, South Carolina, this delightful chocolate shop is run by one of my many friends in the chocolate business, Pat Green. This medium-size candy kitchen and retail store produces a large variety of candies, including many of the confections you encounter in this book, but the store specializes in chocolates.

Pat does a lot of chocolate molding and seasonal favorites. One of her biggest sellers is her Tiger Paw, which is Chocolate Tree's version of a turtle. At this shop, you can easily see candy production through large glass panels. Although the shop doesn't provide tours on a regular basis (tours are pretty much limited to school groups), the staff will be glad to answer your questions and explain procedures.

The Chocolate Tree, Inc., 507 Carteret Street, Beaufort, SC 29902-5001; phone 800-524-7980 or 843-524-7980; fax 843-524-6646; e-mail `choctree@islc.net`, Web site `www.islc.net/choctree`.

Hansel & Gretel Candy Kitchen

This little company, started in 1973 by Janet and David Jones (my wife and me), is a great candy company, if I do say so myself. Our business has grown from one small room to more than 8,000 square feet in two locations in the Alpine village of Helen, Georgia (`www.helenga.org`). In both locations, you can watch as our staff makes candy. Small tours are available with reservations and, during the tour, you indulge in samples and receive a special two-piece box afterward. I'm usually onsite to answer any questions (or to sign books). The business is open seven days a week, with later hours in the summertime.

Hansel & Gretel Candy Kitchen, 8651 Main St., P.O. Box 327, Helen, GA 30545; phone 800-524-3008 or 706-878-2443; fax 706-878-2176; e-mail `hanseland gretel9@aol.com`, Web site `www.hanselandgretelcandykitchen.com`.

Lammes Candies

Lammes Candies in Austin, Texas, has been around longer than most folks can remember. This business, now well over 100 years old, is in its fifth generation of operation and is still going strong.

Although something like nine Lammes stores operate in Texas, the main store produces all the candy. This store offers a wonderful selection of chocolates, but its claim to fame is its Texas Chewy Pecan Praline. You can visit the main store and ask for company President Pam Teich. If she's there and you tell her that you know me, she'll probably look at you really funny. Naw, she likes me, and Lammes is a great candy company to visit. The company doesn't conduct tours, but you can see plenty of results of this amazing company on display.

Lammes Candies, P.O. Box 1885, Austin, TX 78767-1885; phone 800-252-1885 or 512-310-1885; fax 512-310-2280; Web site `www.lammes.com`.

Nichols Candies, Inc.

Nichols Candies, Inc., is located in Gloucester, Massachusetts, the setting of *The Perfect Storm*. Bill and Barbara Nichols run this delightful chocolate operation. In their shop, you meander through an awesome collection of chocolates and fill your own box. When you're ready, someone weighs your box.

The candy production takes place behind glass on the main level as well as on a lower level. The variety of chocolates made on location is incredible, and you could spend a week without being able to count them all. This company produces meltaways, jellies, creams, chocolate caramels, and so much more in its lovely bayside kitchen.

Nichols Candies, Inc., 1 Crafts Road, Route 128, Gloucester, MA 01929; phone 978-283-9850.

Old Kentucky Candies, Inc.

Don Hurt got out of the army in the 1960s and went into the candy business. And what a business he and his wife Pam created! With the Kentucky Derby held in nearby Louisville and Kentucky bluegrass as a backdrop, Old Kentucky Candies has become a Lexington landmark in its own right. Kentucky is one of the states that allows spirits in candy and, with the assistance of Jim Beam, Don capitalizes on that opportunity, featuring bourbon truffles, bourbon chocolates, and bourbon cherries. But you don't have to have bourbon in your candy. The company is also known for its Thoroughbreds, a wonderful chocolate-caramel-pecan treat that's similar to a turtle.

If you go to Old Kentucky Candies, you want to tour the operation. Tours can accommodate anywhere from eight people to a whole busload — just make a tour reservation. On the tour, you get to see some of the finest candy made in Kentucky, and you get to sample some, too!

Old Kentucky Candies, Inc., 450 Southland Dr., Lexington, KY 40503; phone 800-786-0579 or 859-278-4444; fax 859-276-5481; e-mail oldkycandies@ worldnet.att.net, Web site www.oldkycandy.com.

Richardson's Candy House

In 1999, Terry and Pat Hicklin bought a candy business — a business that had been a Joplin, Missouri, tradition since 1970 — and they improved it by making better candy and more of it. If you visit the store today, you find a company operating four locations and making some excellent candy. With so many specialties, picking one favorite is difficult, but the English toffee made with pecans is a good starting point.

You can see plenty of good chocolate made daily in the chocolate factory, and I'm sure you will get a sample. The factory provides tours, but you have to book one in advance. If you get a chance to visit, just ask for Dexter, the owner. (If you call Terry "Dexter," he'll know I sent you.) You won't be disappointed.

Richardson's Candy House, 454 Redings Mill Road, Joplin, MO 64804; phone 800-624-1615 or 417-624-1515; fax 417-624-8385; e-mail info@candyhouse.net, Web site www.candyhouse.net.

Chapter 26

Ten Troubleshooting Tips for Candy Makers

In This Chapter

▶ Encountering little snags

▶ Resolving production problems

*N*o matter how good your recipes may be and no matter how careful you are, occasionally something may go wrong, and your candy doesn't turn out as desired. A number of factors, including the kitchen environment, simple errors in technique, or equipment malfunction may create these flops. In this chapter, I point out a few difficulties you may encounter and provide some solutions.

Your Fondant Is Too Sticky

When you make fondant, you should expect a certain amount of *tackiness,* or a slight stickiness when you handle the finished product. However, sometimes the fondant feels like a large lump of paste, and you can't do a darn thing with it.

If you have a problem with excessive stickiness, you simply need to work some confectioners' sugar into your fondant. Add 1 or 2 tablespoons at a time and knead the sugar into the mass of fondant. The stickiness will diminish, and your fondant will be fine. See Chapter 6 for more details on fondant.

Your Caramel Looks Sandy and Grainy

A couple of problems can cause your caramel to look sandy and grainy. One possibility is that your batch had an imbalance of sugar and corn syrup. Another possibility is that the grains of sugar may not have dissolved when the graining process started. If sugar grains aren't completely dissolved during the cooking process, the sugar crystals start reforming into larger crystals. What to do?

- ✔ Measure the ingredients carefully; generally, you want to have more corn syrup than sugar to create a smooth consistency.
- ✔ When the batch comes to a boil, wash the inside of the pot well with water and a pastry brush or cover the pot securely for 1 minute to allow the steam inside to dissolve the sugar crystals.

See Chapter 7 for the full scoop on making caramels.

Just like with caramel, you must watch your sugar to corn syrup ratio when making brittles (covered in Chapter 12). Corn syrup is a "stabilizer," also known as an "interfering agent." Simply put, the syrup interferes with sugar crystals attaching to one another, which keeps graining from occurring. Using too little corn syrup causes graining. Check your sugar-to-corn-syrup ratio to be sure that you haven't caused a sugar imbalance.

Your Caramel Is Too Tough

What should you do when you bite into a piece of caramel and find that it's too tough? If your caramel isn't up to your expectations, the source of your disappointment may lie in a simple error during the cooking process.

To solve the problem of tough caramel, check your final temperature and cooking time; you're aiming for a final temperature of 234 degrees, and you typically cook a batch of caramel over low heat for 45 to 50 minutes (remember that stovetops vary). If you cook a batch too fast, your temperature may exceed the ideal final temperature due to ambient heat from the pot. Slow the cooking down a little. Anticipate the final temperature and turn the heat a little lower when you're 5 degrees before your end point. And when you turn off the heat, remove the pan from the burner.

Also, make sure that your candy thermometer is working properly by checking the temperature when water comes to a boil. The temperature should be at boiling for your altitude. How do you figure out that correct temperature? Simply boil some water with your candy thermometer clipped to the side of the pan. The thermometer should read 212 degrees when the water comes to a boil. Remember to subtract 1 degree from 212 degrees for each 500 feet you are above sea level.

Your Divinity Falls Flat

Several factors may cause divinity to fall flat when you scoop it onto a cookie sheet. Part of the cooking process for divinity involves removing moisture from the batch during the boiling process. Too much moisture — even from an excessively humid day — may cause this problem. If you pour the corn syrup mixture into the beaten egg whites and invert sugar too quickly, you may have a problem with the batch retaining its aeration. Additionally, if you don't beat the batch long enough after the cooked syrup has been added to the beaten egg whites and invert sugar, the batch falls flat.

✔ If you believe that moisture is the cause of the problem, cook the granulated sugar, corn syrup, and water portion about 3 degrees higher (to 253 degrees). Cooking to a slightly higher temperature removes more water from the batch, which is especially important on a humid day.

✔ If you think that you're pouring the cooked part into the beaten part too quickly, pour in a slow, steady stream — like a water faucet running on medium speed. Good divinity involves good procedures, and this pouring method is important for you to master.

✔ If you suspect that you haven't beaten the batch long enough after the syrup mixture has been added to the egg-white mixture, be certain that the mixture has enough stability to hold its shape in the pot before you remove the batch from the mixer. You can check the stability by scooping one small kiss from the batch to see if it stands. If the kiss is going to flatten, it'll do so very quickly. If the kiss maintains its round shape, you're ready to dip.

Check out Chapter 8 for more details on making divinity.

Your Fudge Is Sticky and Syrupy

You want your fudge, when it's set, to be creamy and firm. The cooking process is designed to remove a certain amount of moisture from the fudge to give you that nice creamy richness and that desirable firmness that gives the fudge its nice bite. Occasionally, though, you end up with something that's a bit gooey and not quite what you envisioned.

If your fudge is sticky and syrupy, your batch is undercooked. Check your cooking temperature (it should be 234 degrees) and be sure that your candy thermometer is working properly (see "Your Caramel Is Too Tough" earlier in this chapter to find out how to check your thermometer). See Chapter 9 for more about fudge.

Your Chocolates Develop a Spotty Finish

When you see spots on your chocolates, you're probably experiencing sugar migration, or sugar bloom. Bloom occurs when condensation forms on the surface of the chocolate; when this moisture evaporates, it leaves a white substance behind.

Do not work with chocolate if the kitchen is really humid because chocolate needs a cool, dry room in which to properly set. Also, after you've made your chocolate, do not store it in the refrigerator or anywhere else that moisture can form.

Flip to Part IV for plenty of additional info on chocolates.

Your Chocolates Develop Gray or Light Streaks

A short list of things can cause gray or light streaks to appear on your chocolate. These streaks are the result of fat migration or fat bloom. Chocolate that hasn't been properly tempered or finished chocolate that's been stored at too warm a temperature or at an inconsistent temperature usually causes fat bloom.

To prevent fat bloom

- ✔ Make sure that you're tempering your chocolate correctly. After you've tempered your chocolate, it should set in about 5 minutes (4 to 6 minutes is good). But try to allow more time at room temperature for a nice long-term set. If you maintain the room temperature for at least a few hours, you improve the chances of having a nice finish on your chocolate.

- ✔ Store your finished chocolates in a cool, dry area with a temperature between 70 and 72 degrees.

Because fat bloom doesn't affect the taste of the chocolate — only its appearance — you may simply eat these pieces and take precautions next time.

If the pieces with fat bloom are coated centers and you plan to eat them soon, you can reapply a thin chocolate coating on top of the pieces. However, over a period of time, the bloom may penetrate the new shell.

I cover the details of chocolate tempering and storage in Chapter 14.

Your Chocolates Look Grainy

If your molded chocolate or chocolate coating looks grainy, you haven't properly tempered the chocolate. You should get an early hint that your chocolate will be grainy because it will set up very slowly. Tempered chocolate should set in 4 to 6 minutes. Chocolate that hasn't been properly tempered (or tempered at all) takes much longer.

Follow the proper tempering procedures in Chapter 14 and maintain a good working environment. Try to keep the room as free from humidity as possible, and maintain a temperature of about 70 degrees.

Your Truffles Develop Mold inside Their Shells

If you see fluffy green growth inside your truffles (either hand-rolled truffles or those filled in shells), you're looking at mold. Mold forms in truffles because of trapped moisture, which allows bacteria to form.

If you're piping the centers into chocolate shells, be sure you don't allow air pockets to form because these spaces allow for condensation, which promotes bacterial growth. To avoid air pockets in your truffles, place the tip of your piping bag in the bottom of the shell and let the bag come up as you fill the shell.

I also recommend using *invertase,* a special enzyme you add to your chocolate that prevents bacterial problems. You'll extend the life of all your truffles by weeks or even months. If you use invertase in your truffles, you can store them at room temperature for four to six weeks, frequently much longer. If you make truffle centers without invertase, you should consume them within 24 days or less or freeze them for up to two months. Check out Chapter 18 for the complete scoop on truffles.

Your Chocolates Don't Release from Their Molds

When the time comes to remove chocolates from their molds, occasionally the molds don't release, and the chocolates seem stuck, even though you've left the molds in the refrigerator for the right amount of time.

If the chocolate molds are too cool when you fill them with chocolate, they may not release the finished chocolates well. The molding process involves putting chocolate into room-temperature molds and refrigerating the molds for an appropriate period of time, during which the chocolate shrinks to release. The chocolate's release is based on the chocolate's shrinking and allowing space between the chocolate and the mold. If the mold is cold when you fill it with chocolate, however, the shrinkage of the chocolate in the refrigerator won't be significant enough to offset the cold mold, which has experienced some shrinkage itself.

Be sure that the molds are at approximately 70 to 75 degrees before you fill them with chocolate, and you should have no problem getting the molds to release the chocolates. If you need to quickly reuse molds that have already been in a refrigerator, lightly warm the mold with a hair dryer and leave the mold at room temperature for 5 minutes; then refill and start the molding process. See Chapter 19 for more details on molding.

Metric Conversion Guide

· ·

*N**ote:* The recipes in this cookbook were not developed or tested using metric measures. There may be some variation in quality when converting to metric units.

Common Abbreviations

Abbreviation(s)	What It Stands For
C, c	cup
g	gram
kg	kilogram
L, l	liter
lb	pound
mL, ml	milliliter
oz	ounce
pt	pint
t, tsp	teaspoon
T, TB, Tbl, Tbsp	tablespoon

Volume

U.S Units	Canadian Metric	Australian Metric
¼ teaspoon	1 mL	1 ml
½ teaspoon	2 mL	2 ml
1 teaspoon	5 mL	5 ml

(continued)

Volume *(continued)*

U.S Units	Canadian Metric	Australian Metric
1 tablespoon	15 mL	20 ml
¼ cup	50 mL	60 ml
⅓ cup	75 mL	80 ml
½ cup	125 mL	125 ml
⅔ cup	150 mL	170 ml
¾ cup	175 mL	190 ml
1 cup	250 mL	250 ml
1 quart	1 liter	1 liter
1½ quarts	1.5 liters	1.5 liters
2 quarts	2 liters	2 liters
2½ quarts	2.5 liters	2.5 liters
3 quarts	3 liters	3 liters
4 quarts	4 liters	4 liters

Weight

U.S Units	Canadian Metric	Australian Metric
1 ounce	30 grams	30 grams
2 ounces	55 grams	60 grams
3 ounces	85 grams	90 grams
4 ounces (¼ pound)	115 grams	125 grams
8 ounces (½ pound)	225 grams	225 grams
16 ounces (1 pound)	455 grams	500 grams
1 pound	455 grams	½ kilogram

Measurements

Inches	Centimeters
½	1.5
1	2.5
2	5.0
3	7.5
4	10.0
5	12.5
6	15.0
7	17.5
8	20.5
9	23.0
10	25.5
11	28.0
12	30.5
13	33.0

Temperature (Degrees)

Fahrenheit	Celsius
32	0
212	100
250	120
275	140
300	150
325	160
350	180

(continued)

Temperature (Degrees) *(continued)*

Fahrenheit	Celsius
375	190
400	200
425	220
450	230
475	240
500	260

Index

• D •

• **E** •

• *F* •

• *N* •

• R •

• W •

BUSINESS, CAREERS & PERSONAL FINANCE

0-7645-5307-0

0-7645-5331-3 *†

Also available:
- Accounting For Dummies †
  0-7645-5314-3
- Business Plans Kit For Dummies †
  0-7645-5365-8
- Cover Letters For Dummies
  0-7645-5224-4
- Frugal Living For Dummies
  0-7645-5403-4
- Leadership For Dummies
  0-7645-5176-0
- Managing For Dummies
  0-7645-1771-6

- Marketing For Dummies
  0-7645-5600-2
- Personal Finance For Dummies *
  0-7645-2590-5
- Project Management For Dummies
  0-7645-5283-X
- Resumes For Dummies †
  0-7645-5471-9
- Selling For Dummies
  0-7645-5363-1
- Small Business Kit For Dummies *†
  0-7645-5093-4

HOME & BUSINESS COMPUTER BASICS

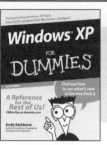

0-7645-4074-2

0-7645-3758-X

Also available:
- ACT! 6 For Dummies
  0-7645-2645-6
- iLife '04 All-in-One Desk Reference
  For Dummies
  0-7645-7347-0
- iPAQ For Dummies
  0-7645-6769-1
- Mac OS X Panther Timesaving
  Techniques For Dummies
  0-7645-5812-9
- Macs For Dummies
  0-7645-5656-8

- Microsoft Money 2004 For Dummies
  0-7645-4195-1
- Office 2003 All-in-One Desk Reference
  For Dummies
  0-7645-3883-7
- Outlook 2003 For Dummies
  0-7645-3759-8
- PCs For Dummies
  0-7645-4074-2
- TiVo For Dummies
  0-7645-6923-6
- Upgrading and Fixing PCs For Dummies
  0-7645-1665-5
- Windows XP Timesaving Techniques
  For Dummies
  0-7645-3748-2

FOOD, HOME, GARDEN, HOBBIES, MUSIC & PETS

0-7645-5295-3

0-7645-5232-5

Also available:
- Bass Guitar For Dummies
  0-7645-2487-9
- Diabetes Cookbook For Dummies
  0-7645-5230-9
- Gardening For Dummies *
  0-7645-5130-2
- Guitar For Dummies
  0-7645-5106-X
- Holiday Decorating For Dummies
  0-7645-2570-0
- Home Improvement All-in-One
  For Dummies
  0-7645-5680-0

- Knitting For Dummies
  0-7645-5395-X
- Piano For Dummies
  0-7645-5105-1
- Puppies For Dummies
  0-7645-5255-4
- Scrapbooking For Dummies
  0-7645-7208-3
- Senior Dogs For Dummies
  0-7645-5818-8
- Singing For Dummies
  0-7645-2475-5
- 30-Minute Meals For Dummies
  0-7645-2589-1

INTERNET & DIGITAL MEDIA

0-7645-1664-7

0-7645-6924-4

Also available:
- 2005 Online Shopping Directory
  For Dummies
  0-7645-7495-7
- CD & DVD Recording For Dummies
  0-7645-5956-7
- eBay For Dummies
  0-7645-5654-1
- Fighting Spam For Dummies
  0-7645-5965-6
- Genealogy Online For Dummies
  0-7645-5964-8
- Google For Dummies
  0-7645-4420-9

- Home Recording For Musicians
  For Dummies
  0-7645-1634-5
- The Internet For Dummies
  0-7645-4173-0
- iPod & iTunes For Dummies
  0-7645-7772-7
- Preventing Identity Theft For Dummies
  0-7645-7336-5
- Pro Tools All-in-One Desk Reference
  For Dummies
  0-7645-5714-9
- Roxio Easy Media Creator For Dummies
  0-7645-7131-1

* **Separate Canadian edition also available**
† **Separate U.K. edition also available**

Available wherever books are sold. For more information or to order direct: U.S. customers visit www.dummies.com or call 1-877-762-2974.
U.K. customers visit www.wileyeurope.com or call 0800 243407. Canadian customers visit www.wiley.ca or call 1-800-567-4797.

SPORTS, FITNESS, PARENTING, RELIGION & SPIRITUALITY

0-7645-5146-9

0-7645-5418-2

Also available:

- Adoption For Dummies
  0-7645-5488-3
- Basketball For Dummies
  0-7645-5248-1
- The Bible For Dummies
  0-7645-5296-1
- Buddhism For Dummies
  0-7645-5359-3
- Catholicism For Dummies
  0-7645-5391-7
- Hockey For Dummies
  0-7645-5228-7

- Judaism For Dummies
  0-7645-5299-6
- Martial Arts For Dummies
  0-7645-5358-5
- Pilates For Dummies
  0-7645-5397-6
- Religion For Dummies
  0-7645-5264-3
- Teaching Kids to Read For Dummies
  0-7645-4043-2
- Weight Training For Dummies
  0-7645-5168-X
- Yoga For Dummies
  0-7645-5117-5

TRAVEL

0-7645-5438-7

0-7645-5453-0

Also available:

- Alaska For Dummies
  0-7645-1761-9
- Arizona For Dummies
  0-7645-6938-4
- Cancún and the Yucatán For Dummies
  0-7645-2437-2
- Cruise Vacations For Dummies
  0-7645-6941-4
- Europe For Dummies
  0-7645-5456-5
- Ireland For Dummies
  0-7645-5455-7

- Las Vegas For Dummies
  0-7645-5448-4
- London For Dummies
  0-7645-4277-X
- New York City For Dummies
  0-7645-6945-7
- Paris For Dummies
  0-7645-5494-8
- RV Vacations For Dummies
  0-7645-5443-3
- Walt Disney World & Orlando For Dummies
  0-7645-6943-0

GRAPHICS, DESIGN & WEB DEVELOPMENT

0-7645-4345-8

0-7645-5589-8

Also available:

- Adobe Acrobat 6 PDF For Dummies
  0-7645-3760-1
- Building a Web Site For Dummies
  0-7645-7144-3
- Dreamweaver MX 2004 For Dummies
  0-7645-4342-3
- FrontPage 2003 For Dummies
  0-7645-3882-9
- HTML 4 For Dummies
  0-7645-1995-6
- Illustrator CS For Dummies
  0-7645-4084-X

- Macromedia Flash MX 2004 For Dummies
  0-7645-4358-X
- Photoshop 7 All-in-One Desk Reference For Dummies
  0-7645-1667-1
- Photoshop CS Timesaving Techniques For Dummies
  0-7645-6782-9
- PHP 5 For Dummies
  0-7645-4166-8
- PowerPoint 2003 For Dummies
  0-7645-3908-6
- QuarkXPress 6 For Dummies
  0-7645-2593-X

NETWORKING, SECURITY, PROGRAMMING & DATABASES

0-7645-6852-3

0-7645-5784-X

Also available:

- A+ Certification For Dummies
  0-7645-4187-0
- Access 2003 All-in-One Desk Reference For Dummies
  0-7645-3988-4
- Beginning Programming For Dummies
  0-7645-4997-9
- C For Dummies
  0-7645-7068-4
- Firewalls For Dummies
  0-7645-4048-3
- Home Networking For Dummies
  0-7645-42796

- Network Security For Dummies
  0-7645-1679-5
- Networking For Dummies
  0-7645-1677-9
- TCP/IP For Dummies
  0-7645-1760-0
- VBA For Dummies
  0-7645-3989-2
- Wireless All In-One Desk Reference For Dummies
  0-7645-7496-5
- Wireless Home Networking For Dummies
  0-7645-3910-8

HEALTH & SELF-HELP

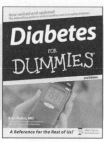

0-7645-6820-5 *†

0-7645-2566-2

Also available:

- Alzheimer's For Dummies
  0-7645-3899-3
- Asthma For Dummies
  0-7645-4233-8
- Controlling Cholesterol For Dummies
  0-7645-5440-9
- Depression For Dummies
  0-7645-3900-0
- Dieting For Dummies
  0-7645-4149-8
- Fertility For Dummies
  0-7645-2549-2

- Fibromyalgia For Dummies
  0-7645-5441-7
- Improving Your Memory For Dummies
  0-7645-5435-2
- Pregnancy For Dummies †
  0-7645-4483-7
- Quitting Smoking For Dummies
  0-7645-2629-4
- Relationships For Dummies
  0-7645-5384-4
- Thyroid For Dummies
  0-7645-5385-2

EDUCATION, HISTORY, REFERENCE & TEST PREPARATION

0-7645-5194-9

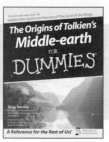

0-7645-4186-2

Also available:

- Algebra For Dummies
  0-7645-5325-9
- British History For Dummies
  0-7645-7021-8
- Calculus For Dummies
  0-7645-2498-4
- English Grammar For Dummies
  0-7645-5322-4
- Forensics For Dummies
  0-7645-5580-4
- The GMAT For Dummies
  0-7645-5251-1
- Inglés Para Dummies
  0-7645-5427-1

- Italian For Dummies
  0-7645-5196-5
- Latin For Dummies
  0-7645-5431-X
- Lewis & Clark For Dummies
  0-7645-2545-X
- Research Papers For Dummies
  0-7645-5426-3
- The SAT I For Dummies
  0-7645-7193-1
- Science Fair Projects For Dummies
  0-7645-5460-3
- U.S. History For Dummies
  0-7645-5249-X

Get smart @ dummies.com®

- **Find a full list of Dummies titles**
- **Look into loads of FREE on-site articles**
- **Sign up for FREE eTips e-mailed to you weekly**
- **See what other products carry the Dummies name**
- **Shop directly from the Dummies bookstore**
- **Enter to win new prizes every month!**

* **Separate Canadian edition also available**
~ **Separate U.K. edition also available**

Available wherever books are sold. For more information or to order direct: U.S. customers visit www.dummies.com or call 1-877-762-2974.
U.K. customers visit www.wileyeurope.com or call 0800 243407. Canadian customers visit www.wiley.ca or call 1-800-567-4797.